WOMEN IN BRITISH ROMANTIC THEATRE

DRAMA, PERFORMANCE, AND SOCIETY, *1790–1840*

This is the first collection of essays to examine the extraordinary contribution of women playwrights, actors, translators, critics and managers who worked in British theatre during the Romantic period. Focusing on women well known during their day but neglected for some one-hundred-and-fifty years, the volume provides a crucial new perspective that revises historical narratives and reflects the rapidly changing terrain of scholarship in the complex field of Romantic theatre and drama. Eleven specially commissioned essays by a distinguished team of scholars explore the role of numerous theatrical women including the eminent actress Sarah Siddons and two of the period's most prolific playwrights, Elizabeth Inchbald and Joanna Baillie. The book strikes a balance between literary and theatrical approaches, showing how the period's preoccupation with categories such as text and performance, closet drama and stage provides a key to "uncloseting" an important group of female theatre artists.

CATHERINE BURROUGHS is Associate Professor of English at Wells College. She is author of *Closet Stages: Joanna Baillie and the Theater Theory of British Romantic Women Writers* (1997) and co-editor of *Reading the Social Body* (1993).

WOMEN IN BRITISH ROMANTIC THEATRE

WOMEN IN BRITISH ROMANTIC THEATRE

Drama, Performance, and Society, 1790–1840

EDITED BY

CATHERINE BURROUGHS

CAMBRIDGE
UNIVERSITY PRESS

PUBLISHED BY THE PRESS SYNDICATE OF THE UNIVERSITY OF CAMBRIDGE
The Pitt Building, Trumpington Street, Cambridge, United Kingdom

CAMBRIDGE UNIVERSITY PRESS
The Edinburgh Building, Cambridge CB2 2RU, UK   www.cup.cam.ac.uk
40 West 20th Street, New York, NY 10011–4211, USA   www.cup.org
10 Stamford Road, Oakleigh, Melbourne 3166, Australia
Ruiz de Alarcón 13, 28014 Madrid, Spain

First published 2000

Printed in the United Kingdom at the University Press, Cambridge

Typeface Baskerville 11/12.5 pt   *System* 3b2   [CE]

A catalogue record for this book is available from the British Library

Library of Congress Cataloguing in Publication data

Women in British Romantic Theatre: drama, performance, and society, 1790–1840 /
edited by Catherine Burroughs.
p.   cm.
Includes bibliographical references and index.
USBN 0 521 66224 9
1. English drama – Women authors – History and criticism.
2. Women in the theater – Great Britain – History – 19th century.
3. Women in the theater – Great Britain – History – 18th century.
4. Women and literature – Great Britain – History – 19th century.
5. Women and literature – Great Britain – History – 18th century.
6. English drama – 19th century – History and criticism.
7. English drama – 18th century – History and criticism.
8. Theater – Great Britain – History – 19th century.
9. Theater – Great Britain – History – 18th century.
10. Romanticism – Great Britain.   I. Burroughs, Catherine
B., 1958–
PR728.W6 W665 2000 822′.7099287–dc21

ISBN 0 521 66224 9 hardback

For Rick and Nicholas

Contents

Illustrations

Contributors

SUSAN BENNETT is Professor of English at the University of Calgary. She is the author of *Theatre Audiences* (Routledge, 1990; 1997) and of *Performing Nostalgia* (Routledge, 1996), as well as editor, with David Roman, of *Theatre Journal*.

JACKY BRATTON is Professor of Theatre and Cultural History, Royal Holloway, University of London, and currently head of the Department of Drama and Theatre. Her publications include *Acts of Supremacy* (Manchester; St. Martin's, 1991); *Music Hall: Performance and Style* (Open University Press, 1996); a theatre history edition of *King Lear* (Bristol Classical Press, 1982); and monographs on several aspects of nineteenth-century culture beyond theatre.

GILLI BUSH-BAILEY is a doctoral student in the Drama Department at Royal Holloway, University of London, where she received a British Academy award for her research on female theatrical practice in the Restoration period. She has been a professional actress in television, radio, and theatre; a script reader for the Watermill at Newbury, Royal Theatre Northampton, and the Redgrave at Farnham; and a script co-ordinator for the Writers' Group at The Riverside Studios in London.

CATHERINE BURROUGHS is Associate Professor of English and co-chair of the Women's Studies Program at Wells College, and a lecturer at Cornell University. Her publications include numerous essays on Romantic theatre and drama, a co-edited volume, *Reading the Social Body* (Iowa, 1993), and a book, *Closet Stages: Joanna Baillie and the Theater Theory of British Romantic Women Writers* (Pennsylvania, 1997).

JULIE CARLSON is Associate Professor of English at University of California, Santa Barbara. She is author of *In the Theatre of*

Romanticism: Coleridge, Nationalism, Women (Cambridge, 1994) and guest editor of *Domestic/Tragedy* (*SAQ*, 98.3, 1999). She has written essays on romantic theatre, sexuality, and psychoanalysis with particular focus on Coleridge and Baillie. Currently she is working on the Godwin-Wollstonecraft-Shelley family and collaborating on a project about romantic medievalism.

MARVIN CARLSON is the Sidney E. Cohn Distinguished Professor of Theatre and Comparative Literature at the Graduate Center of the City University of New York, founding editor of *Western European Stages*, and author of numerous books and articles on theatre history and theory, the most recent of which is *Voltaire and the Theatre of the Eighteenth Century* (Greenwood, 1998).

JEFFREY N. COX is Director of the Center for Humanities and the Arts at the University of Colorado at Boulder. He is the author of *In the Shadows of Romance: Romantic Tragic Drama in Germany, England, and France* (Ohio University Press, 1987) and of *Poetry and Politics in the Cockney School: Shelley, Keats, Hunt and their Circle* (Cambridge, 1998), as well as the editor of *Seven Gothic Dramas, 1789–1825* (Ohio University Press, 1992) and the co-editor with Larry J. Reynolds of *New Historical Literary Study: Essays on Reproducing Texts, Representing History* (Princeton, 1993).

THOMAS C. CROCHUNIS is an independent scholar, currently working as a communications specialist for the US Department of Education research laboratory at Brown University. Since finishing his dissertation at Rutgers University, "Staged Reading: Theatrical Character in the Dramatic Poetry of Robert Browning," he has co-edited a volume of essays on Joanna Baillie's plays and dramaturgy (Gordon and Breach, forthcoming). In 1998, he was guest editor of a special issue of *Romanticism on the Net* on British Women Playwrights around 1800.

GREG KUCICH is Associate Professor of English at the University of Notre Dame. His publications include *Keats, Shelley, and Romantic Spenserianism* (Pennsylvania State, 1991), recent articles on romantic women writers, and a book in progress on "Romanticism and the Gendering of History." He is also co-editor of *Nineteenth-Century Contexts: An Interdisciplinary Journal*.

JANE MOODY read English at Oxford University and completed a doctorate on the politics of early nineteenth-century London theatre. After holding a Research Fellowship at Cambridge University, she is now a Lecturer at the University of York. She has published articles and essays on the relationship between Romanticism and theatre history; illegal performances of Shakespeare in early nineteenth-century London; gender, performance and theatrical authorship; and theatre and the new historicism. Her monograph, *Illegitimate Theatre in London, 1787–1843*, is forthcoming from Cambridge University Press.

JEANNE MOSKAL is Professor of English at the University of North Carolina at Chapel Hill. She is the editor of Mary Shelley's *Travel Writings*, volume eight in *The Novels and Selected Works of Mary Shelley* (Pickering and Chatto, 1996), and the author of *Blake, Ethics, and Forgiveness* (Alabama, 1994). She is currently working on a book on British women travel writers and the politics of the 1790s.

KATHERINE NEWEY is a Senior Lecturer in Theatre Studies at Lancaster University. She has published essays on nineteenth-century theatre and women's writing in *Victorian Literature and Culture*, *Journal of Dramatic Theory and Criticism*, *Bronte Society Transactions*, *Victorian Periodicals Review*, and *Literature and Aesthetics*. Her current research on nineteenth-century women playwrights has been funded by the Australian Research Council, the Society for Theatre Research, the Australian Academy of the Humanities, and the Harry Ransom Humanities Research Center.

MARJEAN PURINTON is Associate Professor of English at Texas Tech University. A member of the TTU Teach Academy, she also teaches in the Women's Studies Program. She is the author of *Romantic Ideology Unmasked: The Mentally Constructed Tyrannies in Dramas of William Wordsworth, Lord Byron, Percy Shelley, and Joanna Baillie* (Delaware, 1994). She has published articles on romantic drama, romantic women writers, and romantic theory, and she is currently working on a book entitled "British Romantic Drama and Cultural Identity."

Acknowledgments

During a period of professional uncertainty, when I left a tenured position to join my family in Ithaca, this edited volume emerged as a symbol of hope that I would once again find a productive career. For their unwavering support, I thank Rick and Nicholas, two unusually dear and loving souls who kept me cheerful and demonstrated the importance of tempering work with play. I also greatly appreciate the many ways in which Jean and Julian Burroughs and Fay Bogel provided emotional and personal assistance; each is a vital and loving grandparent to Rick's and my son. Debi Carlisle's marvelous childcare enabled me to work with concentration and a peaceful mind. Jonathan Culler, Abby Eller, J. Ellen Gainor, Katy Gottschalk, and Marianne Marsh helped me sustain this project by sharing employment information and/or work opportunities at crucial junctures. I am grateful to Anne K. Mellor, Kathryn Norberg, and William Weber for inviting me to participate in the Clark Library's conference, Women in the Theater (1700–1850) in May 1998; several essays in this volume were first formulated for that occasion. Anne Mellor merits a special acknowledgment here: she has been a source of professional inspiration and an unparalleled mentor from the time of our first meeting in the summer of 1989, and this volume owes her a great debt. I would also like to thank Tracy Davis and Ellen Donkin for inviting me to serve as a respondent at a Northwestern University gathering in August 1997, when they and their contributors put the finishing touches to *Women and Playwriting in Nineteenth-Century Britain* (Cambridge University Press 1999). Since several essays collected here were first conceived at that meeting, this volume can be viewed as a companion piece to Davis's and Donkin's excellent book. For substantial encouragement throughout this project's proposal stage, I am grateful to Tracy Davis; and I would also like to acknowledge Susan Bassnett for her keen interest in this project when it was being planned. Financial support during different phases of manuscript preparation was provided by the Center for 17th- and 18th-Century Studies at UCLA, Cornell University, and Wells College. My colleagues in the English Department at Wells College – Bruce Bennett, Alan Clugston, Cynthia Garrett, and Linda Lohn – assisted my endeavors through their example as fine writers and teachers. I very much appreciate the technological support of Dean Ellen Hall and Ken Larson. Others at Wells College who deserve my thanks for various forms of assistance include: Jen Bunyar, Candace Collmer, Erna Coon, Melanie Cullen, Frank LaCombe, Louise Rossmann, Dave Sammons, Elsie Torres, Jeri Vargo, and Karen Wikoff. In the last weeks of manuscript preparation, Angela McNally contributed her considerable editorial and technological skills, making all the difference between deadlines missed and met. Denise Huff helped the printing process go smoothly. I gratefully acknowledge my editor at Cambridge University Press – Victoria Cooper – who, from the start, expressed the kind of enthusiasm and support for this project that fueled its timely completion. And I would like to thank my copy editor, Christine Lyall Grant, for her fine work on the manuscript. For permission to cite manuscripts and images in this volume, I thank the Harvard Theatre Collection at the Huntington Library in San Marino, California, and the John Rylands University Library of Manchester, England.

Introduction: uncloseting women in British Romantic Theatre

Catherine B. Burroughs

This collection features the contributions to theatre and drama of female playwrights, actors, translators, critics, theorists, and managers who worked during the period traditionally called the "British Romantic era." By circling obsessively about some of the more prominent artists in an age of prominent theatrical women – Elizabeth Inchbald, Joanna Baillie, Sarah Siddons – this volume draws attention to a variety of other figures who participated significantly in the mainstream theatres of Great Britain.[1] Several essays focus on theatre artists who have received relatively little attention – such as Ann Yearsley, Hannah More, Mariana Starke, Anna Larpent, and Mary Russell Mitford – and some essays explore playwrights who have been more commonly associated with non-dramatic genres, such as Frances Burney and Anne Plumptre, or who were affiliated, as Jane Scott was,[2] with playhouses other than the "major" theatres of Covent Garden and Drury Lane.

By providing readers with information about women who worked in theatre during the critical transitional years between the neoclassical and Victorian eras, the essays collected here contribute to the process of revising narratives of theatre history and reinforce the idea that the dating of a theatrical period depends upon whose perspective is privileged. While this study focuses on the fifty years between 1790 and 1840, it could be said to begin with the successes of several women writers in different genres – Hannah Cowley's comedy *The Runaway* at Drury Lane in 1776, Hannah More's tragedy *Percy* at Covent Garden in 1777, and Sophia Lee's comedy at the Haymarket in 1780, *The Chapter of Accidents*, which was performed yearly until 1824.[3] And its endpoint targets the seven-year stretch that saw the publication of Joanna Baillie's last collection of plays in 1836 and the Theatres Regulation Act of 1843. The French Revolution marks a convenient starting-place for British Romantic studies, but it is not as crucial for gaining a more precise view of the situation facing late eighteenth- and early nineteenth-century female theatre artists as is – for example – the Stage Licensing Act of 1737,[4] or the changes in theatre administrations in the late eighteenth and early nineteenth centuries,[5] or the rise of female-controlled theatre spaces in the first four decades after 1800.[6] Certainly the 1770s – though not featured in this collection – are important for having spawned a generation of female playwrights (Hannah More, Hannah Cowley, Elizabeth Griffith, and Frances Brooke) whose achievements partially account for an unprecedented proliferation of dramatic writing by women between 1788 and 1800.[7] Indeed, the 1770s are particularly significant because Sarah Siddons made her second London debut in 1782, a wildly successful event that took place six years after David Garrick's retirement in 1776 and which represented not only a change in acting styles but also a shift in perceptions of female actors as less "sexually suspect."[8] That there are a number of ways to conceptualize the beginning and concluding dates of this volume requires that we rethink how periodization has sometimes worked to impede the recovery of women in British Romantic theatre.[9]

Additionally, this collection reinforces current attempts by scholars to reexamine definitions of performance, text, and theatre by balancing theatrical with literary perspectives. But it does so not to argue for infusing a largely literary tradition of scholarship with methods and approaches that attend more to performance and theatricality, though this would not be an undesirable development.[10] Rather, read collectively, the essays in this volume suggest that the Romantic period is crucial for understanding the historical roots of contemporary discussions about how reading and performing playscripts become (differently) inflected. Indeed, this collection follows the lead of late eighteenth- and early nineteenth-century British theatre theorists – many of them female – who were presciently interested in negotiating the closet/theatre division that has so problematically characterized discussions of Romantic theatre and drama in our own era and which has caused "Romantic theatricality"[11] to be misrepresented as antitheatricalism throughout the twentieth century. That is, each essay either explicitly or implicitly foregrounds the page/stage opposition to suggest how it has hindered our recovery of women in British Romantic theatre and how an investigation of this opposition can help historicize the knotty relationship between "text" and "performance," even as we theorize the relationship anew.[12]

Since the 1970s and the revival of interest in Romantic theatre and drama,[13] much of the scholarship has been produced by literary critics narrowly focused on the plays of the canonical male Romantic poets. Yet it is precisely this focus that has resulted in a relatively small but important body of critical literature[14] that seeks to explain how the genre of closet drama figures "the disjunction between text and performance,"[15] emerges as "a forerunner of the gay closet,"[16] and contributes to the growing interest in revising the concept of "public" and "private" spheres so as not to distort the ways in which late eighteenth- and early nineteenth-century women actually lived their lives.[17]

To encourage these developments, part 1 of this volume explores some of the specific features confronting female theatre artists around 1800. In their analysis of the degree to which women in Romantic theatre exercised cultural influence, Jeffrey Cox and Greg Kucich argue for the necessity of reevaluating traditional critical narratives that present nineteenth-century women theatre artists as either marginalized *or* self-empowering. Their examination of a variety of archival materials reveals how difficult and misleading it is to attach labels to the cultural performances of women who dominated their specific theatrical arena, such as Joanna Baillie in playwriting, Sarah Siddons in tragic acting, and Anna Larpent in the licensing of plays. Complicating recent claims that these women's art was politically subversive,[18] Cox observes that the dramaturgy and staging of Baillie's most pointedly Scottish play, *The Family Legend* (1810), reinforced anti-populist views.[19] Likewise, Siddons's portrayals of queens and other aristocrats as passive, sexually attractive, yet also sexually restrained paralleled Edmund Burke's anti-Jacobin representation of Marie Antoinette as a heroine in *Reflections on the Revolution in France* (1790). Anna Margaretta Larpent's diaries indicate how she exerted influence on Romantic theatre through her husband – the Lord Chamberlain's Examiner of Plays – in order to prevent the staging of dramas that featured the spectacle of the French Revolution.

Cox's argument that power in Romantic theatre was constituted variously by aesthetic, textual, social, and institutional performances sets the stage for Greg Kucich's analysis of a subject that has received little attention – the reviewing by male critics of female playwrights and actors.[20] Starting with Hannah More's *Percy* (1777) and moving forward to Harriet Lee's *The Three Strangers* (1826), Kucich traces the contradictory responses of male critics[21] to plays and stage performances by women in order to examine the cultural significance of the opposition of closet and stage between 1790 and 1840. Because the rhetoric of male reviewers often figured the female-authored text as an embodiment of the playwright's gendered position, expressing a keen desire to see her play in performance, reviews of the period underscore the intense cultural need to fetishize the female body and prescribe proper performances of feminine identity as a strategy to preclude female power. Thus, interest in (the performance of) female playscripts became a way not so much to encourage the proliferation of women writers as to submit them to yet another cultural test of whether they – as writing women – could conform to gender expectations while inhabiting a harshly scrutinizing arena.

One of the reasons that female dramaturgy from the period alternately reinforced and discouraged revolutionary tendencies is that it often identified with the politics of those in power while trying to promote the rights of the disenfranchised. Part II of this collection – "Nations, Households, Dramaturgy" – offers examples of this ideological ambivalence. Those women writers whose work was most popular in late eighteenth-century British and American repertoires – Susannah Centlivre, Hannah Parkhouse Cowley, and Elizabeth Inchbald[22] – wrote mostly variations of social comedy, which seems to have allowed female authors to participate in topical debates without alienating those audiences who would be resistant to the idea of an "unfeminine" – that is, politically serious – woman writer. Yet, as Katherine Newey describes, several British women playwrights who published between 1770 and 1830 helped to establish another pattern – one associated primarily with male Romantic poets – of writing historical tragedies[23] set in distant time periods and exotic places as a means of engaging with topical issues while still eluding the corrosive effects of the censorship institutionalized by the Licensing Act of 1737. According to Newey, playwrights like Hannah More, Ann Yearsley, Frances Burney, and Mary Russell Mitford registered their interest in the social impact of the American and French revolutions by exploring some of the ways in which women have historically challenged domestic tyranny.

Newey's essay suggests how other dramatic genres of the period managed to make political statements and still obtain licenses for performance. Certainly, the strategy of displacing controversial material to foreign locales and distant time periods appeared even in a form we might describe today as "early musical comedy." During the 1790s in America, for instance, British-born Susanna Rowson managed to intensify the pro-abolitionist and pro-feminist views of her play, *Slaves in Algiers* (1794), by setting the piece in Africa, and, simultaneously, to diffuse hostility to her work by introducing songs at potentially serious moments.[24] Indeed, a number of women playwrights – including Joanna Baillie, Hannah Cowley, Maria Edgeworth, and Elizabeth Inchbald – participated in the late eighteenth-century debates about slavery by creating plays that represented a "strange mix . . . of anti-slavery sentiments and racist attitudes."[25]

Like Cox and Kucich's essays, Jeanne Moskal's analysis of Mariana Starke's abolitionist comedy, *The Sword of Peace* (1788), manages to avoid the assumption that enlightened or progressive attitudes were (consistently) articulated by women in Romantic theatre. As Moskal explains, Starke engaged briefly but intensely with the London theatre scene in order to explore the complicated relationship between merchant imperialism, feminism, and the slave trade. Challenging cultural and legal restrictions on women's political engagement, Starke's dramaturgy shifts between conservative and liberal positions, alternately aligning her with Edmund Burke and Mary Wollstonecraft. The topical context for this shift is the 1788 impeachment trial of Warren Hastings – the former Governor-General of Bengal – and Moskal comments on some of the ways in which Starke's dramatic response to this trial drew upon theatrical convention.[26] Certainly in comparison to other genres for which Starke would become better known (such as travel writing), drama allowed this temporary playwright to explore her vision of a desirable nationalist identity as one that middle- to upper-class women could promote through their marriage choices, even though any agency they might enjoy during courtship would most likely recede after the wedding. For this reason, Starke's dramaturgy provides an opportunity to study the ideological complexities that can emerge from texts of the period, many of which aimed both to amuse their audiences and to confront controversial issues.

This double impulse structures Joanna Baillie's first comedy, *The Tryal* (1798), which also drew upon the public fascination with legal trials and contributed to the intensifying debates about women's social position during the last decade of the eighteenth century. Along with Hannah Cowley and Elizabeth Inchbald – whose play-writing careers, for the most part, ended in the 1790s – Baillie's dramatic and critical output distinguishes her as one of the more important theatre artists between 1780 and 1810. While she lacked Inchbald's experience with commercial theatre, Baillie compensated by becoming one of the era's premier theorists of theatre, attaching prefaces to her published plays that are historically significant for confronting some of the differences between reading and seeing plays (especially as these differences drastically affect reception). Furthermore, Baillie's prefaces suggest that exciting drama can be located in "closet stages" outside the bounds of "legitimate" and commercially viable playhouses.

    That these plays of the small and private space could teach audiences what Baillie described as "sympathetic curiosity"[27] is the focus of Marjean D. Purinton's analysis of *The Tryal*. By examining Baillie's dramatization of two female characters' conscious attempts to stage their resistance to marrying for money alone, Purinton underscores the degree to which the political features of marriage have historically, in courtship, been reinforced by theatrical rituals. She also highlights the potential for theatre to provide some women with strategies for exerting control over their Romantic lives, exploring how cousins Mariane and Agnes draw on their knowledge of playwriting, directing, and stage performance to create a series of "trials," or "little dramas," that flummox their male suitors. Baillie's dramaturgy permits her both to emphasize the performative aspects of women's (and men's) gendered position and to suggest that private stages are especially conducive to teaching audiences how to develop a political consciousness. For this reason, Baillie may be viewed as continuing a trend established by pre-Revolutionary women writers during the Age of Sensibility to combine sentimental comedy and the values of the Sunday School Movement with Madame de Genlis's "theatre of education."[28] But Baillie does so in order to create a new comedic form for the new century – what she calls "Characteristic Comedy" in her famous "Introductory Discourse" (1798) – a mode that "represents to us this motley world of men and women in which we live, under those circumstances of ordinary and familiar life most favourable to the discovery of the human heart . . ."[29]

Because in her day Baillie was so well received, so prolific, and so relatively unperformed (in spite of her ambition to see her plays staged), she is central to current attempts to confront the extent to which the category of "closet play" has created misperceptions about Baillie's investment in public staging and negatively affected the critical reception of her plays since the 1830s. In the book's third section – "Performance and Closet Drama" – the essays by Susan Bennett and Jacky Bratton address the way in which generic categories affect the historical evaluation of playscripts and the construction of critical narratives about theatre. As Bennett demonstrates, both Baillie's prefaces and dramaturgy convey her practical interest in, and knowledge of, early nineteenth-century London theatre, as well as her sensitivity to performance questions triggered by scenes that make use of actual closet space. Identifying Baillie as an important early advocate of "alternative theatre," Bennett looks closely at Baillie's tragedy, *Constantine Paleologus* (1804),[30] and at some of the ways that Baillie used her preface writing to intervene in the critical reception of her own work.[31] Bennett performs this analysis in order to argue that Baillie must be released from the closet of genre, periodization, and discipline so that the divide between literary critics of Romanticism and theatre historians – about which Jane Moody and Thomas Crochunis have recently written[32] – can be eroded and the historical significance of Baillie's work more widely appreciated.[33]

Perhaps the most dramatic instance of this book's aim to undermine page/stage oppositions, even as it explores their functioning, occurs in the essay on Jane Scott, the most prolific female British playwright between 1806 and 1819 (she created approximately fifty playscripts, ranging from pantomime to burletta to comic opera).[34] As Jacky Bratton tells us, the essay in this collection grew out of her desire to understand some of the ways in which gender affects the dynamics and tone of the melodramatic form produced during the period *after* the explosion of Gothic plays in the 1790s[35] and *before* the proliferation of melodrama during the Victorian period. Bratton began to explore this issue by transcribing the licenser's copy of Scott's five-act drama, *Camilla the Amazon* (1817), which was performed in Scott's own "illegitimate" playhouse, the Sans Pareil; and Bratton's search extended to the classroom where she enlisted the talents of script reader Gilli Bush-Bailey and students in the honors degree program in the Department of Drama, Theatre and Media

Arts at the University of London to perform the transcribed text. But performance was not the culmination of the course's investigation; participants were also encouraged to write about their experiences of workshopping the play. Modelling "heteroglossic critical writing," sections of the essay are interlarded with students' words about their rehearsal and performance process, the research of the tutors, quotations from *Camilla the Amazon*, reviews from Romantic periodicals, and commentary from late twentieth-century critics about Gothic melodrama. Thus, in both its origins and execution, the essay demonstrates how questions debated in scholarly research about British Romantic drama and theatre find different formulations and responses when (women's) playscripts are recovered and performed, and it argues that generalizations about genre often become productively confounded by modes of theatre research that happily insist upon placing tone, audience reception, and acting methods center-stage with the reading experience.

The extent to which studying pre-twentieth-century female dramaturgy offers new perspectives on theatre criticism and theory is central to the fourth section of this collection.[36] As Marvin Carlson notes in his essay on the critical prefaces that Elizabeth Inchbald composed for Longman's 25-volume series, *The British Theatre* (1805–08), Inchbald's distinction as one of a fairly small group of British women who wrote theatre theory becomes more impressive when one realizes that she was the first British critic of either sex to undertake a project of such prominence and scope: chosen by the series' publisher to record her critical views of 125 plays current in the early nineteenth-century British repertory, Inchbald produced a monumental record of the "legitimate" drama, those plays that had found a foothold in "major" British playhouses. Certainly Inchbald's selection as the preface-writer for Longman's series more than legitimized her as a critic; it ensured that she would be heralded in subsequent ages as a major shaper of critical taste. Yet Inchbald has not been canonized in discussions of landmark theatre theorists who wrote before Modernism, even though she was apparently, as Carlson notes, the first British critic to draw upon personal knowledge to discuss plays as both read and performed experiences. The general failure of post-Romantic scholars to appreciate that the better-known "closet critics" – like Lamb and Byron – were not so much against performance as intrigued by theatrical possibilities unavailable on commercial stages[37] has ensured that women writers from the period, even preeminent writers like Inchbald, would be disregarded.

But Inchbald deserves our attention for her remarkable achievements: one of these, as Carlson demonstrates, was the construction of a voice that would not offend readers unaccustomed to viewing a woman in the position of theatrical critic or theorist. And her published writing reveals that she could shift deftly into a more complicated voice when necessary, as when she wittingly and witheringly responds to the published complaints of playwright George Colman.[38] Additionally, Inchbald brings her performance experience to bear on the critical enterprise in ways that convey her belief in the importance of consciously addressing how different critical perspectives – whether theatrical or literary – will affect one's assessment of a dramatic work.

Because Inchbald was such a powerhouse of varied theatrical talent – creating more than 20 plays and 125 critical prefaces, and performing, less notably, as an actress – she demands more critical scrutiny than she has previously received.[39] Thomas Crochunis is interested in some of the ways that Inchbald's published work reflects a self-consciousness about "authorial performance." Thus, he compares Inchbald's critical prefaces with the prefatory writing Baillie produced in her three-volume series, *Plays on the Passions* (1798, 1802, 1812), to argue that certain female playwrights during the Romantic period often staged authorship as a complex cultural process: by publishing their plays, Baillie and Inchbald targeted their work for closet readers, even as they expressed their aim to have them performed before live audiences rather than only read. Yet, because they attached critical commentary to their work designed to shape readers' responses to (female) authorship, both Baillie and Inchbald created performances surrounding their playscripts that alternately complemented, reinforced, and competed with their dramaturgical performances. A study of the differences between these various discursive stages can cause us, Crochunis argues, to pay more attention to the ways in which the "cultural *mise en scène*" affected – and affects – any reading of a playscript or theatrical document. For if we are to receive a more culturally specific picture of a playwright's work, then we must, as Sue-Ellen Case has argued, attend to the variety of scripts contained within a dramatic text and resituate that text by exploring the many "performances" embedded in it.[40]

Among these neglected performances from the Romantic period are translations and adaptations of French and German playscripts crafted by writers such as Elizabeth Craven, Maria Geisweiler, Anne Gittins Francis, Elizabeth Gunning, Hannah Brand, Marie Thérèse DeCamp Kemble, and Mariana Starke.[41] In the volume's fifth section, Jane Moody examines the controversy surrounding Inchbald's translation of a Kotzebue play, *The Wise Man of the East* (1799) – a comedy in which a female character commits suicide. Moody suggests that the act of translation allowed women like Inchbald to transform "foreign plays" from "subversive" documents into texts that confirmed particular aspects of hegemonic ideology. And yet this conservative impulse should not overshadow what Moody characterizes as the liberatory potential of the translating and adaptive mode. Particularly for Inchbald (and for Anne Plumptre with whom Moody compares her), translation became an oblique means of raising important political questions about the construction of feminine identity. For just as suicide draws attention to the issue of agency and its restrictions, so translation enabled Inchbald to rehearse a set of potential "selves" (for herself and her characters) that freed a writing persona, even as it also closeted away the idea of one, identifiable writer to whom readers and audiences could assign responsibility and praise.

Julie Carlson, whose essay concludes this collection, has also written about adaptation in terms relevant to the topic of revision, which is the larger focus of her essay here: "[p]erformance meets sociality at adaptation, a space-time in which moving speeches can remake social relations . . ."[42] As the starting-point for Carlson's analysis of two plays on the subject of remorse – Baillie's tragedy, *Henriquez* (1836), and Inchbald's comedy, *A Case of Conscience* (1833) – Carlson revisits her earlier assertions in one of the most important books about Romantic theatre to emerge in the 1990s, *In the Theatre of Romanticism: Coleridge, Nationalism, Women* (1994). She shares her reflections on that book's arguments in order to highlight her own "remorse" at having engaged exclusively with male writers and (in her assessment) for suggesting that women writers did not undergo psychological journeys comparable to the male playwrights she features in her study. Such undefensiveness about one's own work can remind us that it is vital to encourage scholarship on women in Romantic theatre that embraces a range of practitioners and perspectives. This surprising critical strategy also allows Carlson to

demonstrate the significance of the revisionary impulses that characterize Inchbald's and Baillie's dramaturgy, which makes radical
attempts to reform love. Indeed, Inchbald's and Baillie's attempts to
offer alternative views of Romantic passion resemble the radical but
non-nostalgic aims of Mary Wollstonecraft, Mary Hays, and Amelia
Alderson (Opie), who revised both Burke and Godwin so that
"illusion" and "reason" are not opposed.

Yet Carlson's essay is less a celebration of potentially liberating
action than a pragmatic reflection on the historical limitations for
many women (whether performers or characters) created by the
theatrical apparatus. For even as Carlson praises Inchbald's and
Baillie's efforts to reform perceptions of female beauty, her essay
anticipates the melancholy that may result from expectations that
theatre can release women from concerns about body, aging, and
physical attractiveness – especially in the context of a dramaturgy
that features Romantic desire. While an actor onstage can achieve a
degree of autonomy from cultural and dramaturgical constraints –
as Ellen Donkin shows Sarah Siddons to have done[43] – when female
bodies appear in front of audiences, it is often difficult to frame them
so that viewers enculturated to objectify the female form can regard
them as subjects, especially if a play's dramaturgy seems to follow
conventional paths.[44]

With so much recovery work waiting to be done in the complex
and fascinating field of Romantic theatre and drama, the five
sections of this volume are designed to describe the rapidly changing
terrain of critical scholarship and to point to other areas of research
on women artists who worked in London theatre between 1776 and
1843.[45] Taken together, they also promote the sharing of intellectual
tools and practices from different disciplines in the project of
bringing late eighteenth- and early nineteenth-century British stages
into fuller view. And they aim to demonstrate that the uncloseting of
women in British Romantic theatre is cause for both relief and
sustained celebration.

NOTES

1 The essays in this volume collectively provide a representative list of
   female artists associated with Romantic theatre between approximately
   1790 and 1840: Mary Berry, Hannah Brand, Frances Burney, Sophia

Burrell, Georgiana Cavendish, Hannah Parkhouse Cowley, Elizabeth Craven, Mary Champion de Crespigny, Maria Edgeworth, Elizabeth Farren, Maria Geisweiler, Catherine Moody Gore, Felicia Hemans, Jessie Jackson, Dorothy Jordan, Fanny Kemble, Anna Larpent, Sophia and Harriet Lee, Harriet Litchfield, Elizabeth Macauley, Mary Russell Mitford, Hannah More, Harriet Murray (Mrs. Henry Siddons), Eliza O'Neill, Sydney Owenson (later Lady Morgan), Frances Plowden, Anne Plumptre, Mary Robinson, Jane Scott, Mary Shelley, Charlotte Smith, Mariana Starke, Madame Vestris, Sarah Ward, Jane West, Barbarina Wilmot, and Ann Yearsley.

2 Jacky Bratton's recent work is focusing attention on Jane Scott's career. See: "Miss Scott and Miss Macauley: 'Genius Comes in All Disguises'" (*Theatre Survey*, 37 [1996], pp. 59–73); "Jane Scott the Writer/Manager" in *Women and Playwriting in Nineteenth-Century Britain*, ed. Tracy C. Davis and Ellen Donkin (Cambridge University Press, 1999), pp. 77–98; Bratton's introduction to, and transcription of, Jane Scott's two-act burletta (*Broad Grins or) Whackham and Windham; or The Wrangling Lawyers* (1814) at the website, "British Women Playwrights around 1800," ed. Thomas C. Crochunis and Michael Eberle-Sinatra (http://www.sul.-stanford.edu/mirrors/romnet/wp1800); and Jacky Bratton and Gilli Bush-Bailey's transcription of Jane Scott's *Camilla the Amazon* in an Appendix to *Nineteenth Century Theatre*, 27.2, 1999.

3 This information is provided by David D. Mann and Susan Garland Mann (with Camille Garnier), *Women Playwrights in England, Ireland and Scotland, 1660–1823* (Bloomington: Indiana University Press, 1996), p. 4.

4 See Jane Moody, *Illegitimate Theatre in London, 1787–1843* (Cambridge University Press, forthcoming).

5 See Ellen Donkin, *Getting into the Act: Women Playwrights in London, 1776–1829* (New York and London: Routledge, 1995).

6 See Catherine Burroughs, *Closet Stages: Joanna Baillie and the Theater Theory of British Romantic Women Writers* (Philadelphia: University of Pennsylvania Press, 1997).

7 For more information about this flowering, see Mann, Mann, and Garnier's appendices at the end of *Women Playwrights in England, Ireland and Scotland, 1660–1823*, which helpfully document by year the names of female playwrights and their plays. The authors write: "In the last quarter of the eighteenth century . . . more women wrote, translated, published, and produced more plays than at an earlier time" (p. 20).

8 See Kristina Straub, *Sexual Suspects: Eighteenth-Century Players and Sexual Ideology* (Princeton University Press, 1992). Ellen Donkin, *Getting into the Act*, regards Garrick's death in 1779 – three years after Siddons *first* performed, disastrously, before a London audience – as a pivotal moment in late eighteenth-century British theatre, for this event consequently resulted in a dramatic decline in the quality of relationships between female playwrights and male managers, relationships that were

less paternalistic but also less hospitable to productions by women writers.

9 Many of the well-known drama anthologies currently in classroom use imply that British theatre came to a standstill in the centuries between Restoration drama and Oscar Wilde's *The Importance of Being Earnest* (1895). Representative anthologies published in the 1990s reflect priorities in theatre history that exclude Romantic theatre: Alexander W. Allison, Arthur J. Carr, and Arthur M. Eastman, ed. *Masterpieces of the Drama*. Sixth edition (New York: Macmillan Publishing Co., 1991); Jeffrey D. Hoeper, James H. Pickering, and Deborah K. Chappel, ed., *Drama* (New York: Macmillan Publishing Co., 1994); Lee A. Jacobus, ed., *The Bedford Introduction to Drama*, second edition (New York: St. Martin's Press, 1993); Carl A. Klaus, Miriam Gilbert, and Bradford S. Field, Jr., ed., *Stages of Drama*, third edition (New York: St. Martin's Press, 1995); W. B. Worthen, ed., *The Harcourt Brace Anthology of Drama*. Second edition (New York: Harcourt Brace and Co., 1996).

10 For a thoughtful discussion about the problems of trying to rehabilitate the reputation of closet drama through "reconstructing the conditions of late eighteenth- and early nineteenth-century theatre," see Michael Simpson, *Closet Performances: Political Exhibition and Prohibition in the Dramas of Byron and Shelley* (Stanford University Press, 1998), p. 6. Simpson is a fascinating theorist of closet drama, using Byron's and Percy Shelley's "Italian" closet plays to argue that the plays "recruit their readers to an agenda of polite radicalism . . . by foregrounding their status as reading minds . . . and then by representing them as consequently eligible for a civically virtuous patrician body that is poised for public actions" (4). That the genre of closet play incorporates "the critical oscillation between arguments for them as stage plays and as closet dramas" (6) liberates Simpson to "explore these texts' fantasies about how they might be something other or more than merely texts" (9) in the process of seducing readers to "fantasize . . . a civic body capable of leaving this closet" even as this body "must be confined to a decorous potentiality if it is to retain its polite profile and if the institution of censorship is to be placated" (23).

11 See Judith Pascoe, *Romantic Theatricality: Gender, Poetry, and Spectatorship* (Ithaca, NY: Cornell University Press, 1997).

12 As W. B. Worthen argues in *Shakespeare and the Authority of Performance*, the problem with the page/stage dichotomy – as conceptualized in Western thought since the early nineteenth century – stems from the fact that, even when we now "see performance as traced by a variety of gestural, figural, and ideological textualities, the notion that there *is* a text to produce onstage, and that this text is reproduced in some relatively direct manner ('page' to 'stage'),'' keeps us in thrall to the concept of an authoritative text, which we either "trangress" or "reproduce" (7). Worthen's solution is to encourage us to think of a "performance" –

whether a reading or a staging – not as "an authorized *version* . . . of the work, but as an iteration inscribed by the practice of theatre" (24). Such a conception, he argues, allows us more readily to consider the work's "emergence historically" and "not only to ask whether texts and performances are essentially related in this way, but also whether in eras prior to the institution of 'literature' the stage *could* be understood as a vehicle for the reproduction of textual, literary authority at all" (25).

13 For explanations of why Romantic scholars have themselves been slow to appreciate Romantic theatre and drama, see Jeffrey Cox's discussion of "dramatic ideology" in the introduction to *Seven Gothic Dramas, 1789–1825* (Athens: Ohio University Press, 1992); Jane Moody's "'Fine Word, Legitimate!': Toward a Theatrical History of Romanticism" (*Texas Studies in Literature and Language*, 38.3–4, 1996, pp. 223–44) and *Illegitimate Theatre in London, 1787–1843* ; and Thomas C. Crochunis, "Dramatic Closets and Literary Studies" (unpublished essay). In addition to historicizing the split between literary critics of nineteenth-century British literature and theatre historians ("'Fine Word, Legitimate!'" pp. 239–40), Moody's work interrogates "the exclusion of theatre from the discourses we call Romanticism" in order to "render problematic certain cherished dichotomies of early nineteenth-century literary history: drama/theatre, page/stage, elite/popular, reader/audience" (p. 223). In the same article, she also writes: "That dichotomy between an aesthetic, private sphere of study or closet and a 'degraded' public dramatic culture blithely ignores the embattled nature of the theatrical institution in late Georgian London and the dynamic, complex interaction between competing and overlapping theatrical spheres and publics" (240).

14 In recent years, numerous articles and conference panels have demonstrated that Romantic theatre was – rather than a "deserted stage" (Terry Otten, *The Deserted Stage: The Search for Dramatic Form in Nineteenth-Century England* [Athens: Ohio University Press, 1972]) – a place of astonishing theatricality and generic experimentation. In *Illegitimate Theatre in London,* Jane Moody demonstrates the degree to which ingenuity in "illegitimate theatres" of the period was a positive outcome of the theatrical monopoly, resulting in a wide range of theatrical activity and diversity. Throughout her volume, the endnotes provide extensive references to the bibliography on Romantic theatre and drama. See also my bibliography in *Closet Stages,* which contains a section on "closet drama revisionism" and lists other works that discuss the 1990s movement to stage closet plays, call for their performance, and reexamine the "antitheatricality" of this period (pp. 179–80). For other work that theorizes closet drama, see (on the Renaissance) Marta Straznicky's review essay, "Recent Studies in Closet Drama" (*English Literary Renaissance* 28.1, 1998, pp. 142–60). In Romantic studies, see

Michael Simpson, *Closet Performances*, especially chapter 5 – "Secrets of the Closet: The Private Mind and Public Body" – with its discussion of the trope of the closet in epistemology and architecture; and Thomas Crochunis, ed., "The Function of the Dramatic Closet at the Present Time," 'Special Issue: British Women Playwrights Around 1800: New Paradigms and Recoveries,' *Romanticism on the Net* 12 (November 1998) Online. Internet. (http://www-sul.stanford.edu/mirrors/romnet/wp1800/essays.html).

15 Michael Simpson, *Closet Performances*, p. 8.
16 Julie A. Carlson, "Forever Young: Master Betty and the Queer Stage of Youth in English Romanticism" (*South Atlantic Quarterly*, 95:3, 1996: 575–602), p. 579.
17 What Michael Simpson calls "sociality" (*Closet Performances*, p. 328), Tracy C. Davis – after Jeff Weintraub – describes as "sociability" ("The Sociable Playwright and Representative Citizen" in *Women and Playwriting*, p. 18), and Anne K. Mellor explains as "the discursive public sphere" point directions toward – in Mellor's words – "a richer, more complex and accurate understanding of the varied nature of the daily lived experiences of both men and women in England between 1780 and 1830, together with the literary culture they produced" (*Mothers of the Nation: Women's Political Writing in England, 1780–1830* [Bloomington: Indiana University Press, 2000], cited here from manuscript folio 11. I appreciate Anne Mellor's permission to quote from her ms.
18 See Catherine Burroughs, *Closet Stages*; Ellen Donkin, "Mrs. Siddons Looks Back in Anger: Feminist Historiography for Eighteenth-Century British Theater" in Janelle G. Reinelt and Joseph R. Roach, ed., *Critical Theory and Performance* (Ann Arbor: University of Michigan Press, 1992, pp. 276–90), and Claire Miller Colombo, " 'This Pen of Mine Will Say Too Much': Public Performance in the Journals of Anna Larpent" (*Texas Studies in Literature and Language*. 38.3–4 [Fall/Winter 1996], pp. 285–301).
19 For a recent analysis of the feminist overtones of *The Family Legend*, see Susan Bennett, "Genre Trouble: Joanna Baillie, Elizabeth Polack – Tragic Subjects, Melodramatic Subjects," in Davis and Donkin, ed., *Women and Playwriting*, pp. 215–32.
20 For a discussion of female reviewers in the Victorian period, see Gay Gibson Cima, " 'To Be Public as a Genius and Private as a Woman': The Critical Framing of Nineteenth-Century British Women Playwrights" in Davis and Donkin, ed., *Women and Playwriting*, pp. 35–53.
21 For a discussion of other rhetorical responses to British female theatre artists later in the nineteenth century, which simultaneously rejected and embraced them, see Kerry Powell, *Women and the Victorian Theatre* (Cambridge University Press, 1997).
22 Of the late eighteenth-century American repertory, Amelia Howe Kritzer writes: "Women playwrights of early America were helped in

the task of constructing positive images of themselves as professional dramatists by a number of models available in English theatre . . . Comedies by Susannah Centlivre (1667–1723), Hannah Parkhouse Cowley (1743–1809), and Elizabeth Inchbald (1753–1821) were among the most popular works in the early American theatrical repertoire. The comic opera *Rosina*, by Frances Moore Brooke (1724?–89), was another perennial favorite" ("Introduction" in *Plays by Early American Women, 1775–1850*, ed. Amelia Howe Kritzer [Ann Arbor: University of Michigan Press, 1995, pp. 1–28], p. 2).

23 Reflecting on the Romantics' penchant for writing history plays, Terence Alan Hoagwood writes that "[t]he central fact about Romantic drama is this suppression and consequent displacement of revolutionary sociopolitical context" ("Romantic Drama and Historical Hermeneutics" in *British Romantic Drama: Historical and Critical Essays*, ed. Terence A. Hoagwood and Daniel P. Watkins [Cranbury, NJ: Associated University Presses, 1998, pp. 22–55], p. 28). For further discussion of Romanticism, history, gender, and drama, see Greg Kucich, "Staging History: Teaching Romantic Intersections of Drama, History, and Gender" in *Approaches to Teaching British Women Poets of the Romantic Period*, ed. Stephen C. Behrendt and Harriet Kramer Linkin (New York: MLA, 1997, pp. 89–96).

24 See Susanna Rowson, *Slaves in Algiers* in *Plays by Early American Women, 1775–1850*, ed. Amelia Howe Kritzer, Ann Arbor: University of Michigan Press, pp. 55–95.

25 Jeffrey Cox, "Introduction" to vol. v of *Slavery, Abolition, and Emancipation in the British Romantic Period. The Drama*, ed. Jeffrey N. Cox (London: Chatto and Pickering, 1999), p. xviii.

26 For discussions of trials and legal proceedings in the context of Romantic theatre and drama see Julie Carlson, "Trying Sheridan's *Pizarro*" in Theresa M. Kelley, ed. (*Texas Studies in Literature and Language*, special issue, 38.3–4, 1996, pp. 359–78) and Judith Pascoe, *Romantic Theatricality*.

27 For a discussion of Baillie's concept of "sympathetic curiosity" see Anne K. Mellor, "Joanna Baillie and the Counter-Public Sphere" (*Studies in Romanticism* 33, Winter 1994, pp. 559–67).

28 See the brief discussion of moral education as one of the seven major focuses of female playwrights between 1660 and 1823 (David D. Mann, Susan Garland Mann [with Camille Garnier], *Women Playwrights in England, Ireland and Scotland, 1660–1823*, pp. 12–13) and chapter 2 of Anne K. Mellor's *Mothers of the Nation*.

29 Joanna Baillie, "Introductory Discourse" in *The Dramatic and Poetical Works of Joanna Baillie* (1851) (Hildesheim and New York: Georg Olms Verlag, 1976, pp. 1–18), p. 12.

30 See also Beth Friedman-Romell, "Staging the State: Joanna Baillie's *Constantine Paleologus*," in Davis and Donkin, ed., *Women and Playwriting*,

pp. 151–73, who observes that "managers' stagings undermined Baillie's challenging dramaturgy, while reinforcing dominant ideologies of gender and politics" (pp. 151–52).

31 For a related discussion, see Thomas Crochunis's chapter in the present volume.

32 See Jane Moody, " 'Fine Word, Legitimate!' ", pp. 223–44; Thomas C. Crochunis, "Dramatic Closets and Literary Studies" unpublished essay and *idem*, "The Function of the Dramatic Closet."

33 Bennett's discussion of Baillie's closeting points to problems that beset the recovery of Romantic women playwrights in general. For instance, Barbara Darby has remarked as recently as 1997 that the attempt to consider Fanny Burney's plays "as literary texts and as scripts for performance has been comparatively rare where late eighteenth-century drama is concerned" (*Frances Burney, Dramatist: Gender, Performance, and the Late Eighteenth Century* [Lexington: The University Press of Kentucky, 1997], p. 17).

34 David D. Mann, Susan Garland Mann (with Camille Garnier), *Women Playwrights in England, Ireland and Scotland, 1660–1823*, p. 5; see also appendices to that volume.

35 See Jeffrey Cox, ed. *Seven Gothic Dramas*.

36 For discussions of eighteenth- and nineteenth-century British women writers as critics and theorists, see The Folger Collective on Early Women Critics, ed. *Women Critics, 1660–1820* (Bloomington: Indiana University Press, 1995) and Burroughs, *Closet Stages*.

37 For a corrective to this perception, see Greg Kucich, " 'A Haunted Ruin': Romantic Drama, Renaissance Tradition, and the Critical Establishment" (*The Wordsworth Circle* 23, 1992, pp. 64–76).

38 For analyses of this same document, see essays in the present volume by Julie Carlson, Marvin Carlson, and Thomas C. Crochunis.

39 For recent provocative work on Inchbald, see Daniel O'Quinn, "Inchbald's Indies: Domestic and Dramatic Re-Orientations," *European Romantic Review*, 9.2 (1998), 217–311 and "Scissors and Needles: Inchbald's *Wives as They Were, Maids as They Are* and the Governance of Sexual Exchange" (*Theatre Journal* 51, 1999, pp. 105–25).

40 See Sue-Ellen Case, *Feminism and Theatre* (New York: Methuen, 1988).

41 Mariana Starke – the subject of an essay by Jeanne Moskal in this volume – also tried her hand at translation, purporting "to have translated Kotzebue's *Agnes Bernauer*, printed under the title of *The Tournament* (1800)" (Margarete Rubik, *Early Women Dramatists 1550–1800* [Basingstoke: Macmillan, and New York: St. Martin's Press, 1998], p. 149). For further information on women translators in the Romantic period, see David D. Mann, "Checklist of Female Dramatists, 1660–1823" (*Restoration and Eighteenth-Century Theatre Research* 5, 1990, pp. 30–62). For more information on Mariana Starke as playwright, see

Jeanne Moskal's electronic text of *The Sword of Peace* and Daniel O'Quinn's essay on the play (with a response by Donelle Ruwe) at the website, "British Women Playwrights around 1800," ed. Thomas C. Crochunis and Michael Eberle-Sinatra. (http://www-sul.stanford.edu/mirrors/romnet/wp1800).

42 Julie Carlson, "Trying Sheridan's *Pizarro*," p. 328.

43 See Ellen Donkin, "Mrs. Siddons Looks Back in Anger."

44 See Jill Dolan, *The Feminist Spectator as Critic* (Ann Arbor: UMI Research Press, 1988).

45 For recent scholarship on women in British Romantic drama and theatre, see Marjean Purinton's helpful overview, "Revising Romanticism by Inscripting Women Playwrights" in Cochunis, ed., *Romanticism on the Net* 12 (November 1998). A sampling of this bibliography includes: Julie Carlson's influential discussion of Sarah Siddons, *In the Theatre of Romanticism: Coleridge, Nationalism, Women* (Cambridge University Press, 1994); an important discussion of Joanna Baillie and Sarah Siddons in Jeffrey Cox's introduction to *Seven Gothic Dramas*; chapters on Joanna Baillie in Daniel P. Watkins's *A Materialist Critique of English Romantic Drama* (Gainesville: University Press of Florida, 1993) and Marjean Purinton's *Romantic Ideology Unmasked: The Mentally Constructed Tyrannies in Dramas of William Wordsworth, Lord Byron, Percy Shelley, and Joanna Baillie* (Newark: University of Delaware Press, 1994); Ellen Donkin, *Getting into the Act*; Catherine B. Burroughs, *Closet Stages*; *Playwriting and Women*, ed. Tracy C. Davis and Ellen Donkin, ed., *Women and Playwriting*; Anne K. Mellor, "Theatre as the School of Virtue" in *Mothers of the Nation*. Margarete Rubik includes a chapter on Hannah Cowley and Elizabeth Inchbald (along with a good overview of the notable female dramatists of the eighteenth century) in *Early Women Dramatists, 1550–1800*, and the appendices to David D. Mann, Susan Garland Mann, and Camille Garnier's *Women Playwrights* are extremely helpful for providing a picture of the the extent of female playwriting throughout the late eighteenth and early nineteenth centuries. Judith Bailey Slagle has just published two volumes of Joanna Baillie's letters (*The Collected Letters of Joanna Baillie* [Cranbury, NJ: Associated University Presses, Inc., 1999]). For discussions of the influence of theatrical culture on other aspects of late eighteenth- and early nineteenth-century society, see: Marc Baer, *Theatre and Disorder in Late Georgian London* (Oxford: Clarendon Press, 1992); Gillian Russell, *The Theatres of War: Performance, Politics, and Society 1793–1815* (Oxford: Clarendon Press, 1995); Elaine Hadley, *Melodramatic Tactics: Theatricalized Dissent in the English Marketplace 1800–1885* (Stanford University Press, 1995); Betsy Bolton, "Romancing the Stone: 'Perdita' Robinson in Wordsworth's London" (*ELH* 64, 1997, pp. 727–59); and Judith Pascoe, *Romantic Theatricality*. For anthologies of plays from the period that include, or feature, texts by women from the Romantic period, see: Jeffrey Cox, ed. with an introduction, *Seven Gothic Dramas*

and vol. v of *Slavery, Abolition, and Emancipation*; John Franceschina, ed., *Sisters of Gore: Seven Gothic Melodramas by British Women, 1790–1843* (New York and London: Garland Publishing, Inc. 1997); Amanda Gilroy and Keith Hanley, ed., *Joanna Baillie: A Selection of Poems and Plays* (London: Chatto and Pickering, 1997); Peter Sabor and Geoffrey Sill, ed., *The Witlings and The Woman Hater by Frances Burney* (London: Chatto and Pickering, 1997); Adrienne Scullion, ed., *Female Playwrights of the Nineteenth Century* (London: J. M. Dent, 1996). One of the more useful and influential factors in hastening the recovery of British Romantic women playwrights is the web project, "British Women Playwrights around 1800," ed. Thomas C. Crochunis and Michael Eberle-Sinatra, part of *Romanticism on the Net* (http://www-sul.stanford.edu/mirrors/romnet/wp1800). Since its recent inception, this site has already produced strong essays on a variety of women writers and made available bibliographies and texts by women playwrights. In addition, the site encourages readers to theorize about the project of recovering women writers from this period – as in the series of essays on electronic editing of women's theatre materials. In the early 1990s, Mary Anne Schofield and Cecilia Macheski created a timely collection of essays in *Curtain Calls: British and American Women and the Theater, 1660–1820* (Athens: Ohio University Press, 1991).

I

Historical contexts: revolution and entrenchment

CHAPTER I

Baillie, Siddons, Larpent: gender, power, and politics in the theatre of Romanticism

Jeffrey N. Cox

I

While we have come a long way from the days when the canon of Romantic writers was restricted to six male poets and when the drama of the early nineteenth century was completely ignored, we are still lacking anything like an adequate account of the place of women in the drama and theatre of what we refer to as the Romantic period. Given the work of scholars such as Anne Mellor, Stuart Curran, Marlon Ross, Nanora Sweet, Jerome McGann, Paula Feldman, and Susan Wolfson, it has become impossible to conceive of a Romanticism that does not take into account Charlotte Smith or Mary Robinson or Felicia Hemans.[1] We also now have a strong sense of the importance of the drama to the period, thanks to the efforts of scholars such as Catherine Burroughs, Julie Carlson, Joseph Donohue, Terence Alan Hoagwood, Marjean Purinton, Alan Richardson, Michael Simpson, and Daniel Watkins.[2] We still, however, have little sense of the actual power women held in the theatre and drama of the day, with the scholarly work on women writers of the period focusing on the lyric and the novel along with the production of journals and travel writing and the scholarship on the drama retaining for the most part a focus on the male canon, with only Joanna Baillie – the subject of a fine study by Burroughs, of a forthcoming volume of essays edited by Thomas Crochunis and Janice Patten, and of a number of important essays – earning a place alongside Wordsworth, Coleridge, Byron, and Shelley. Even when the presence of women in the theatre is acknowledged, their power is in some manner denied or displaced. For example, Ellen Donkin in *Getting into the Act: Women Playwrights in London 1776–1829* finally wants to argue that "playwriting was an intrinsically dangerous form for women" and that women playwrights gained power only through

23

pg 184

men with the "power to confer legitimacy . . . predicated on the power to take it away."[3] Again, Carlson's important *In the Theatre of Romanticism* explores the process whereby the theatre of the period was "feminized," but it does so in order to analyze the reaction of male writers to this process. The power to control the theatre and the discourse about the theatre remains, in these accounts, firmly in male hands.

Find X

Despite much good work, we continue, it seems to me, to be unable to conceive of women writers at this time as possessing significant aesthetic, cultural, and institutional power. As Margaret J. M. Ezell has argued in *Writing Women's Literary History*, traditional literary histories simply ignored women as insignificant, while revisionist, even feminist histories have – in creating a developmental model of women's writing that wants to celebrate women's cultural achievements in the Victorian and modern periods – also found early women writers to be either silenced or severely constrained by systems of patriarchal control.[4] Where earlier histories simply did not believe that women possessed cultural power, feminist histories have remained rather suspicious of women who acquired power in earlier historical moments that are seen as uniformly dominated by the patriarchy. Suspicions run particularly high when women wield this power for ends we find less than desirable; such women may continue to be marginalized, or they may be rediscovered as somehow contributing to a feminist tradition. To put it bluntly, powerful conservative women pose a particular problem to both traditional and revisionist literary histories, as can be seen perhaps in the cases of Hannah More and Felicia Hemans, who were largely ignored in earlier histories and who must be somehow recouped as oppositional writers – despite their strongly conservative cultural presence – by more recent accounts. We will have a full picture of the drama and theatre of the period only when we come to recognize that women did possess considerable power in the theatre of Romanticism; but, as I turn to the troubled negotiations between three women and the power of the printed page, of the theatrical stage, and of the institutions surrounding the production of the drama, I will argue that this power – while its very existence is perhaps in itself liberatory when read in relation to gender politics – was most often exercised within the theatre of Romanticism, that is on the actual stage, in support of a conservative ideology, so that finally it is possible to see men engaged with the drama and theatre of the day – Byron, Kean, Shelley, or Hunt – as offering, beyond their troubled and at times troubling views on gender issues, a more radical vision in (and of) the theatre than their female counterparts.

II

That there were many women involved in the drama and the theatre of the day is beyond doubt. If we consult David D. Mann and Susan Garland Mann's *Women Playwrights in England, Ireland, and Scotland 1660–1823*, we find more than ninety women writing dramas between 1789, one conventional starting-date for the Romantic period, and 1823.[5] These women had varying success in reaching the stage and the page, with about a third of these writers having their plays both published and performed, a third having them only published, and a third seeing them staged but not printed. In 1792, for example, six women saw plays staged (with Hannah Brand having two plays performed at Drury Lane), and another five published unacted plays (Mann and Mann, p. 411). Of course, such numbers do not include plays – such as two by Georgiana Cavendish, Duchess of Devonshire – that exist only in manuscript and which may have been circulated among friends or performed in private theatricals. With most of these women writing several plays and with Joanna Baillie writing twenty-six and Jane Scott around fifty, there is a large body of dramatic work written by women.

While we are used to recognizing that key male figures of the period tried their hands at the drama, with Wordsworth, Coleridge, Scott, Southey, Byron, Keats, Shelley, and Hunt all attempting at least one play, we are perhaps not so aware of what a distinguished list of women writers turned to the drama: Joanna Baillie, Maria Edgeworth, Felicia Hemans, Mary Shelley, Ann Yearsley, Elizabeth Inchbald, Sydney Owenson (later Lady Morgan), Charlotte Smith, Mary Robinson, Fanny Burney, Mary Russell Mitford, Hannah Cowley, Hannah More, and both Harriet and Sophia Lee. We need to remember that a woman writing plays at the dawn of the nineteenth century wrote within a long and established tradition of women's drama that went back through More – whose *Percy* (first presented at Covent Garden, 10 December 1777) was the most successful new tragedy of the later eighteenth century – and Cowley – one of the best comic writers of the 1780s – to such writers as Charlotte Lennox (1729?–1804), Frances Sheridan (1724–66), Eliza

Haywood (1693–1756), Catherine Trotter Cockburn (1679–1749), Susanna Centlivre (1669–1723), Mary Pix (1666–1709), Mary Delarivière Manley (1663–1724), and Aphra Behn (1640–89).

Women dramatists of the Romantic period wrote everything from traditional tragedies and five-act comedies to operas, interludes, farces, and melodramas. Quite a few of these plays were publishing successes, with, for example, Hannah More's *Sacred Dramas* achieving eighteen editions between 1782 and 1815. The works of women playwrights found a place on stages from Dublin, Edinburgh, Bath, and Norwich to London, including the major patent theatres of Drury Lane and Covent Garden. We find both figures such as the aristocratic Elizabeth Berkeley Craven, Margravine of Anspach, who wrote primarily for the wildly popular and apparently quite extraordinary private theatre she managed at Brandenburg House during the last two decades of the eighteenth century, and others such as Elizabeth Inchbald who made her living through the public patent theatres as an actress, author, and editor of an important drama series. While Donkin has shown how the percentage of plays by women remained at around only 10 percent of the total repertoire produced (and it had remained at that level up until the time she wrote her book),[6] it is worth noting that women such as Baillie and Inchbald, Mitford, and Hemans, had better luck in getting their plays produced than did Wordsworth, Shelley, or Keats; the women writers fare badly only when they are compared with male writers – such as the Dibdins or the two Colmans – who year-in and year-out supplied entertainments for the London theatres, often ones under their control. Of the major male writers of the period, only Coleridge had a clear success with *Remorse* (1813); even the wildly popular Byron, who had direct ties to the management of Drury Lane, saw only one of his plays, *Marino Faliero*, produced during his lifetime, and it was a failure on stage. In fact, given that few new plays, particularly new tragedies and five-act comedies, entered the repertoire in the late eighteenth and early nineteenth centuries, and given that a large amount of time in the repertoire was devoted to Christmas pantomimes, oratorios, and Shakespeare, it is quite striking how many of these women actually did manage to reach the stage.

At the center of this impressive gathering of women dramatists was Joanna Baillie; Elizabeth Inchbald may have had more success on stage, Jane Scott may have controlled a theatre, and Hannah

More may have sold more volumes, but Baillie was the most respected playwright, male or female, of the Romantic era. While Baillie has now, with Burroughs's book and other scholarly commentary, achieved something like canonical status, it is still important to stress her literary and cultural power in the face of Donkin's impressive argument that she was finally a failure and that she failed because of gender oppression.[7] The author of more than twenty-five plays, a large body of verse, and a tract on the New Testament, Baillie during her lifetime was regarded as a key figure in what we see as the age of Wordsworth and Byron. Her first volume of *A Series of Plays: in which it is attempted to delineate the stronger passions of the mind each passion being the subject of a tragedy and a comedy* (usually referred to as the *Plays on the Passions*) went through five editions in the first six years following its publication in 1798; there were more than twenty-five reviews, many more than there were of volumes by Keats or Shelley. Seven of her plays were staged during her lifetime, the most important of them – *De Monfort* – being seen in London, Bath, Birmingham, Edinburgh, Philadelphia, and New York[8] and attracting the acting skills of, first, Kemble and Siddons and later of Kean; while *De Monfort* is often seen as a failure for Kemble, it ran for eight nights during its initial run – a more than respectable run for a new tragedy at the time – and it continued in Kemble's repertoire, being offered even in his farewell tour in 1817. Her "Introductory Discourse" to the first volume of the *Plays on the Passions* has often been compared to Wordsworth's preface to *Lyrical Ballads*; as Catherine Burroughs has shown, it is perhaps the most distinguished piece of a large body of women's theatre theory penned during the period.[9] In 1851, the year of her death, Baillie issued *The Dramatic and Poetic Works of Joanna Baillie, Complete in One Volume*, her "great monster book," as she called it, running to more than 800 pages.[10]

While Donkin emphasizes the negative reviews of Baillie's work – and particularly those by the *Edinburgh Review*'s Francis Jeffrey – Baillie for the most part received favorable notices, though there were certainly questions raised about her decision to devote plays to individual passions. For example, the *Poetical Register* for 1804 offered this praise: "Among the modern writers of Tragedy the most honourable place must indubitably be awarded to Miss Baillie." The *Edinburgh Magazine and Literary Miscellany* (January 1818) argued that she ranks as a dramatist behind only Shakespeare. Scott agreed, praising her in *Marmion* as "the bold enchantress" who when (in the first volume of the *Plays on the Passions*) she chants of "Montfort's [*sic*] hate and Basil's love" convinces the swans of Avon that "their own Shakespeare lived again" ("Introduction to Canto Third," lines 103, 107–10). Byron found her to be "our only dramatist since Otway and Southerne."[11] She also received the praise of women, with Anna Laetitia Barbauld, for example, saluting her in *England in Eighteen Hundred and Eleven* (1812) as "loved Joanna" through whose power we can see "The tragic Muse resume her just controul" (lines 101, 109). Mary Russell Mitford, herself a successful dramatist, found Baillie possessing what we, adapting Keats, might see as a Shakespearean "negative capability," arguing that Baillie's tragedies "have a bold-ness and grasp of mind, a firmness of hand, and resonance of cadence, that scarcely seem within the reach of a female writer; while the tenderness and sweetness of her heroines – the grace of the love-scenes – and the trembling outgushings of sensibility, as in *Orra* (1812), for instance, in the fine tragedy on 'Fear' – would seem exclusively feminine, if we did not know that a true dramatist – as Shakespeare or Fletcher – has the wonderful power of throwing himself, mind and body, into the character that he portrays."[12] Elizabeth Inchbald, in the comments included with *De Monfort* in her series *The British Theatre* (1808), argues that "Amongst the many female writers of this and other nations, how few have arrived at the elevated character of a woman of genius! The authoress of 'De Monfort' received that rare distinction, upon this her first publi-cation" (vol. xxiv: 3). By the time Baillie's last volume of plays was published in 1836, after a long hiatus in her playwriting activity, her reputation was such that *Fraser's Magazine* (13: 236) would gush, "Had we heard that a MS. play of Shakespeare's, or an early, but missing novel of Scott's, had been discovered, and was already in the press, the information could not have been more welcome"; even her old nemesis the *Edinburgh Review* now spoke of her as a "highly gifted authoress" (119 [April 1836]: 336). *Blackwood's* (16 [1824]: 162), hardly a feminist enclave, would offer "our tribute of admiration to one, who, in point of genius, is inferior to no individual on the rolls of modern celebrity," placing Baillie beyond even Wordsworth or Byron.

Baillie, then, possessed considerable cultural power during her day. While part of this power is aesthetic or textual – people were made to think by her plays, they were moved by them, and they wondered at the beauty and simplicity of her verse – it is, of course, also social and institutional – that is, her power was dependent upon the social circulation of her texts, upon the historical contexts in which they appeared. What is interesting about Baillie is that her cultural power does not arise – as does that of the women we have found most important during the period such as Mary Wollstone-craft or even Mary Shelley – from a marginalized position.

Praised by major writers of the day, promoted in the theatre by Kemble and Siddons, Scott, Byron, and Kean, connected through family and friendships with many of the most important figures in literature, science, and politics, Baillie stood firmly within a series of cultural and social elites. Her father had risen to be Professor of Divinity at the University of Glasgow. When he died, Baillie's maternal uncle, the famous anatomist William Hunter, took care of the family, including overseeing the training of her brother Matthew, who also pursued medicine after receiving a fellowship at Balliol College, Oxford. In 1791 Matthew married Sophia Denman, sister of Lord Chief Justice Denman. Through her aunt, Mrs. Hunter, Baillie was introduced into a number of key literary and social circles in London, meeting Samuel Rogers, the Barbaulds, William Sotheby, and Henry Mackensie, among others. She came to know Words-worth, with whom she discussed politics in 1812, agreeing with him that the press should be condemned for creating dissension and lamenting the "utter extinction of all love for the royal family, and the very slight attachment remaining to the constitution itself."[13] One of her deepest friendships was with Sir Walter Scott, who admired her and supported her throughout his life. Baillie was also a key figure in a number of female circles, being close to Barbauld, Lucy Aikin, Mary Berry, Maria Edgeworth, and Harriet Martineau; she supported dramatic efforts by other women writers, including Felicia Hemans, Barbarina Wilmot, whose *Ina* was staged at Drury Lane in 1815, and the young Catherine Moody Gore, who became a key playwright in the 1830s. It comes as no surprise that when Baillie wished to put together an anthology of poetry – her *Collection of Poems, chiefly manuscript, and from living authors* (1823) published to benefit a friend – she was able to secure pieces from such friends and acquaintances as Scott, Wordsworth, Southey, Rogers, Hemans, Barbauld, Anna Maria Porter, Mrs. Grant of Langan, and Mrs. John Hunter and to acquire a long subscription list that begins with the royal family.

A small piece of textual history provides a sense of Baillie's cultural position. When Kemble came to perform Baillie's *De Monfort* (1798), he altered the text himself, changes reflected in the licensing manuscript sent to the Examiner of Plays, John Larpent.[14] This manuscript also contains the unpublished prologue and epilogue to the play: the first was written by Francis North, himself a playwright, a patron of the drama, and, as the fourth Earl of Guilford, a key contributor to the rebuilding of Covent Garden after it burned down in 1808; the epilogue came from the hand of the Duchess of Devonshire, one of the rulers of the social world who wrote some interesting verse and left two plays in manuscript. When we read contemporary accounts of the staging of Baillie's play, they describe certain scenes as being performed differently than they are recorded in either Larpent's licensing manuscript or the first edition of 1798. We find the correct passages, however, in another manuscript,[15] this one copied out by the poet Thomas Campbell – already famous for his *Pleasures of Hope* – and given to Sarah Siddons, who has inscribed it, "this manuscript is invaluable," and who has added various notes of her own; Donkin suggests Siddons used this manuscript when offering private readings of the play for both fund-raisers and social gatherings. The text of *De Monfort* fully considered, then, is not just an aesthetic object but a record of the powerful people who supported her work: the text bears the traces of the theatrical, literary, and social circles in which Baillie and her work circulated.[16]

Given that we tend to accept the Romantic ideology of the poet as outsider and then apply it with a vengeance to female authors, we have difficulty in seeing a figure such as Baillie as vital to a tradition of women's writing. Baillie can appear to have become what Mary Poovey has called the "proper lady,"[17] shaped and stunted by male authority. When Wordsworth says of her, "If I had to present any one to a foreigner as a model of an English gentlewoman, it would be Joanna Baillie,"[18] or again when we are told "her manners are those of a well-bred woman. She has none of the unpleasant airs too common to literary ladies,"[19] we wonder whether we are not dealing with a woman who has allowed herself to be co-opted by the roles provided by a patriarchal order. Such an estimate would, I feel, be unfair. Marjean Purinton and Anne Mellor,[20] among others, have shown how Baillie can be read as questioning women's roles. She certainly refused the standard role of a wife and mother, remaining single and in the company of women all of her life; as we have seen, she was very much a part of a network of women writers.

We need to be a little more careful in placing a figure such as Baillie in relation to cultural, social, and ideological debates. Baillie comes out fairly well from our point of view when we examine her representation of gender issues (or when we note that she takes up the issue of slavery in *Rayner* [1804]), but this does not by any means make her as radical as was, say, Wollstonecraft. There is finally something troubling in our insistence on reading and judging women writers primarily in relation to gender issues. Thus, we need to see that, while Baillie may not have been trapped by gendered roles, while in her works she may have queried these roles, she was certainly an ally of ugly reactionary social and political forces, and her works could be praised and used by these forces. We need to remember her ties to the arch-Tory Sir Walter Scott, with whom she seems to have shared political views, perhaps embodied in her gift to him of a gold ring containing hairs taken from the head of Charles I and inscribed "Remember": this recollection of a king beheaded by revolutionary forces is less, I think, a sign of some shared Romanticized Jacobitism than of a common anti-Jacobinism, also seen when she connected with Wordsworth by condemning the press and praising George III. When we note, as I have done, that Scott praised Baillie in one of the prologues to *Marmion*, we also have to remember that one function of these verse prefaces was to summon up and to support the world of Tory culture and power.[21] When she collected poems for her 1823 volume, she sought them from conservatives Scott, Wordsworth, and Southey, not from her one-time Hampstead neighbors Hunt and Keats, part of the circle of radical London writers; the lack of connection between Baillie and the leader of the literary left, Hunt – even though they lived quite near one another and seemed to have known everyone else, including a number of mutual friends – strikes me as particularly telling. Baillie's poem on the death of Scott includes what was seen by Lucy Aikin as a gratuitous attack on another radical poet, Byron, as Scott is found uniting the nation, both "The crowned monarch and the simple hind," while Byron is criticized for using "perverse skill" to display "Wild, maniac, selfish fiends to be admired, / As heroes with sublimest ardour fired."[22]

Of course, part of Baillie's project in this poem is to establish Scott (and perhaps indirectly herself) as the truly great writer of Scottish descent, rather than Byron. We can get a sense of how troubling the deployment of Baillie's cultural power can be if we turn briefly to her play most connected with Scotland, *The Family Legend* (1810),

which she called her "Highland Play" (*Works*, p. 480) and which
treats the struggles between the Campbells and the Macleans and
the legend of "the lady rock." The story behind the play was, Baillie
tells us, recommended to her by Mrs. Damer in 1805 (*Works*, p. 479),
but the inspiration may have come from an 1808 visit Baillie made
with her sister to Scotland, as they traveled from the Western
Highlands, to Glasgow and Edinburgh and into the northern Highlands before returning through the Lake District.[23] Shortly before
her visit, one of the worst and most brutal of the Highland
Clearances – during which the land was deliberately cleared of
people to make room for Cheviot sheep – began in Sutherland,
provoking dissent and ultimately riots (the Kildonan and Assynt riots
of 1813).[24] Baillie traveled through a countryside – her native land –
torn by conflict, but it was the scenery, not the social upheaval, that
seems to have registered with her, as the Falls of Moness, not the
collapse of Highland culture, moved her to tears.

In 1810, when economic woes – falling wages and bankruptcies
brought about by Napoleon's and England's trade policies – added
to Scotland's other problems, *The Family Legend* was staged in
Edinburgh.[25] We again see in this performance Baillie's status as a
consummate insider. The production was arranged and supervised
by Scott, who also supplied the prologue. The epilogue was written
by Scotland's "Man of Feeling," Henry Mackensie, as Scott wanted
to be sure that the evening would be "entirely of Scotch manufacture" in order to offer "every chance of succeeding before a national
audience."[26] Still, fearing that audience, Scott and Henry Siddons –
son of Sarah Siddons and recently named manager of the Edinburgh
theatre – altered the play; for example, "Knowing the strong feelings
of pride and clanship which had existed amongst Highlanders,"
Scott substituted fictitious clan names.[27] However, Scott was not
always so sensitive to the feelings of Highlanders; in order to
supplement a scene in which troops gathered, "I got," he told the
author, "my brother John's Highland recruiting party to join the
action"[28] – that is, he put on stage one of the groups of men who,
since the passage of the extremely unpopular Scottish Militia Act of
1797, had been used to coerce the Highland poor into the army, with
(as one historian puts it) "the great Highland landlords" working "to
break the monopoly of the German flesh-brokers" by raising
regiment after regiment.[29]

Whatever Baillie's intentions (though she certainly never disputed

Scott's efforts), Scott claimed that the production of the play was designed to inspire national pride. At the very least, the narrower pride of the Edinburgh establishment was aroused. As one reviewer said, "Applause was conferred almost entirely to those parts in which high compliments were paid to the Scotch; the inhabitants of Edinburgh entirely forgot that there was nothing more ludicrous than that people should applaud praise given to themselves" (*Correspondent*, 12 March 1810); looking back on the production in 1851, the *Dublin University Magazine* noted, "The Edinburgh public were pleased and flattered by a national story."[30] Perhaps the most obvious flattery came in Mackensie's epilogue, where present-day Scotland was praised in comparison not only to its "ruder" past when "Our moody lords . . . drove men's herds, and burnt their houses" but also to France with its "free code" of sexual morality and even to England which, Mackensie fears, is sometimes misled by France in matters sexual and political. Scotland, however, it is hoped "May long this current of the times withstand; / . . . here, in purity and honour bred, / Shall love and duty wreath the nuptial bed." Hearing these lines, in which Scotland is seen as the bastion of traditional social, political, and family values, one might almost forget that the play one has just watched is about a Scots husband who wrongfully accuses his wife and leaves her to perish upon an exposed rock. The audience, praising itself for leaving behind a rude past when houses were burned and herds were driven away, could forget that they lived in a time when houses were burned and *people* were driven away to make room for herds of sheep. This "Highland Play" allowed its audience to delight in a myth of the Highlands while ignoring the destruction of the actual Highlands that they and the government they supported were undertaking. Whatever the power of the play's text, in context it was put to the service of the Edinburgh Tories, and that finally means that any nationalism evoked here be directed to the United Kingdom and against England's enemy, revolutionary France:[31]

> Here, where "Rome's eagles found unvanquish'd foes,"
> The Gallic vulture fearlessly oppose,
> Chase from this favour'd isle, with baffled wing,
> Bless'd in its good old laws, old manners, and old King.[32]

Such a speech stands as the antithesis to a poem such as Shelley's "England in 1819," with its radical turn against "Golden and sanguine laws which tempt and slay" and "An old, mad, blind, despised, and dying king" (lines 10, 1).

If we are tempted to see Mackensie and Scott distorting Baillie's message, we need only turn to the final speech of *The Family Legend* where the Earl of Argyll – the head of a family that, by Baillie's day, was known for its pro-union efforts (even fighting on the side of the English at Culloden) – decries "that men / In blood so near, in country, and in valour, / Should spend in petty broils their manly strength, / That might, united for the public weal, / On foreign foes such noble service do!"; he looks forward to the time when the Highlanders will be "marshall'd forth / To meet in foreign climes their country's foes," when these often feared and even hated High-landers will march through English cities, and crowds will praise "our hardy brothers of the north" as defenders of the "rights and freedom of our native land" (v, iv; *Works*, p. 507). The struggles of Scotland's past between Highlander clans, the struggles of the preceding century between Jacobite Scotland and Hanoverian England, the current tensions between the Highlands and England with its Tory Scottish supporters must all be put aside to battle the "foreign" threat, revolutionary France. Nor were such appeals without force, since out of a population of 300,000 Highlanders it is estimated 74,000 fought in the wars against France.[33] With this and other plays serving such ideological ends, Baillie could be praised by the *Quarterly Review* (co-founded by Scott) and be used by *Blackwood's* (16 [August 1824]) as it attacked England's "internal enemies" – Baillie's radical Hampstead neighbors of the Cockney School. It is not surprising that the one dissenting note in the general praise for Baillie came from Francis Jeffrey, editor of the liberal *Edinburgh Review* and the lawyer in 1812 for Scots weavers seeking protection against massive wage reductions during the economic collapse of the day.

III

Baillie called her "our tragic queen" whose "sovereign sway was o'er the human mind; / And in the triumph of that witching hour, / Thy lofty bearing well became thy power."[34] If Baillie can represent the power of women on the page, no one better represented that power on the stage than Sarah Siddons. Siddons was the premier actress in a period of great actresses. Theatregoers could see Jane Powell, who often played in supporting roles to Mrs. Siddons but who was also compared with her as an actress of "heavy" parts; Elizabeth Farren, known for her portrayal of "fine ladies," who left the stage to become the Countess of Derby, after being the Count's mistress for many years; Dorothy Jordan, perhaps the greatest comedienne of the day and the long-time mistress of the Duke of Clarence; Eliza O'Neill, who in the second decade of the nineteenth century was seen by many as Mrs. Siddons's successor; Mary Robinson, who of course later became a major writer, but who first as Perdita bewitched the Prince of Wales, her Florizel; and many others – the great singer Angelica Catalani who figured in the "Old Price" riots, Anna Maria Crouch, Fanny Kemble, Elizabeth Inchbald, Harriett Litchfield . . .[35] Even among this illustrious company, however, Mrs. Siddons stood out. While the years during which she acted are usually named for her brother as the "Kemble Era" when people practiced the "Kemble religion," an era that is seen as giving way to the "Age of Kean," it would be more accurate to call the entire period the "Siddons Epoch," for it is she who signaled a change in acting styles while holding on to a huge audience. Leigh Hunt, in a review taking up the acting skills of Kemble, Elliston, and Young in *Macbeth*, turns from the major male actors of the day to proclaim, "There is but one great tragedian living, and that is Mrs. Siddons."[36] Hazlitt put it even more simply: "She was Tragedy personified."[37]

Siddons had enormous power on stage, as the "Siddonsmania" that raged in late eighteenth-century England attests. Hazlitt said of her, "Power was seated on her brow, passion emanated from her breast as from a shrine."[38] Her biographer, the playwright James Boaden, recalls that watching her, the audience "knew all the luxury of grief; but the nerves of many a gentle being gave way before the intensity of such appeals, and fainting fits long and frequently alarmed the decorum of the house."[39] John Waldie, who left us ninety-three journal volumes detailing his experiences in the theatre, repeatedly went to see Mrs. Siddons, always commenting that he "never was so affected" (19 January 1799), that the ways she acts "exceeds all description" (4 July 1799), that she "surpassed in acting all that I have yet seen" (6 July 1799); like Boaden, he notes that members of the audience had to be carried from the theatre after collapsing under the strain of watching Siddons act (5 July 1799).[40] Even the Examiner of Plays' wife, Anna Margaretta Larpent, who claimed in her journal that "Acting revolts in women against female Delicacy" (12 March 1790), went to see Sarah Siddons as Lady Randolph in Home's *Douglas* and was overwhelmed by her (24 April 1792).[41] Having unmatched power on stage – "No tragic actress ever had such absolute dominion over audience," as one admirer tellingly put it[42] – Sarah Siddons was the "Queen of the stage" or, as Baillie put it, the "Tragic Queen."

Julie Carlson has argued that Siddons's centrality to the theatre of the day came to suggest that the stage was a feminized realm that needed to be resisted by male writers who thus took Shakespeare and their own plays into the closet.[43] However, as the regal language surrounding Siddons suggests, there may have been other reasons for a Hazlitt in his criticism or a Shelley in his plays to resist Siddons. She could, for example, be placed in much the same political company as Baillie, with whom she was friends. We could note that, at the time of the Old Price Riots, when her brother John Philip Kemble opened the rebuilt Covent Garden to protests over higher prices and new boxes, she and her brother were attacked for their aristocratic connections.[44] A Gillray engraving, *Theatrical Mendicants, relieved*, from 15 January 1808 shows Mrs. Siddons and her brothers Charles and Philip begging at the door of the Duke of Northumberland who gives them a gift of £10,000; Siddons carries a bag overflowing with donations from various other nobles. (We might also remember in this context that Siddons had, for a long time, fought the public impression that she was personally stingy, "Lady Sarah Save-all" as she was sometimes called. She had to weather several outbreaks of popular disapproval and explain herself to her audiences.) Michael Simpson has shown how Kemble came to be seen as a "patrician" or "regal" actor as opposed to the "plebeian" and "radical" Edmund Kean, with this contrast taking on decidedly political overtones.[45] Kemble was attacked during the Old Price Riots as "King John" and the "King of the Stage" by members of the audience who would also join in political demonstrations with signs calling for "Reform" and "No King." The queenly Mrs. Siddons could be seen taking on a political valence very similar to that of her brother. The support for Kemble and Siddons by the Tory press was noted by their opponents during the Old Price Riots, and the Kemble family was seen as generally in sympathy with Pitt and the Tories despite their early and long-term theatrical ties to Sheridan (and we might note here, again, the ties between the Tory

Scott and Mrs. Siddons's son Henry in Edinburgh that not only resulted in the production of Baillie's *Family Legend* but also provided a northern outpost for the work of the Kemble clan).

It is not surprising that Siddons, as "queen" of the London stage, would have sympathies with a real queen: when Covent Garden burned down, Siddons wrote to a friend that her greatest loss was a "piece of lace which had been a toilette of the poor Queen of France."[46] Siddons might have played the part of the Marie Antoinette of conservative imaginings, had the Examiner of Plays, John Larpent, allowed any play – even a conservative one – about the French Revolution to reach the stage.[47] After all, as Christopher Reid has shown, Burke created his famous image of the French Queen with Mrs. Siddons in mind.[48] According to Burke, Marie Antoinette was to be seen as an innocent wife and mother, set upon by a raging mob, and Siddons was most renowned for her portrayals of abandoned and wronged wives, such as the long-suffering Belvidera in Otway's *Venice Preserv'd*, the unjustly accused Lady Randolph in Home's *Douglas*, Calista who is betrothed against her will in Rowe's *The Fair Penitent*, and Mrs. Beverly, the abused wife of a gambler, in Moore's *The Gamester*. As these parts suggest, Siddons's women are generally passive, offering emotional reaction rather than action. She even played Lady Macbeth not as an "unsexed" harpy but, as her notes to the play indicate, as a woman "most captivating to the other sex, – fair, feminine, nay perhaps even fragile – . . . captivating in feminine loveliness."[49] Lady Macbeth here does not control her husband through force of will, superior intellect, or sheer ruthlessness but by becoming a passive sex object, captivating but captive to the male gaze. Siddons's power on stage seems to come from embodying women whose power is passive, or, to put it another way, her power seems to arise with her ability to portray women whose sexual power is evident but contained. Where Julie Carlson sees male Romantic writers working to contain the female power of Siddons, I would argue that Siddons herself already embodied an attempt to neutralize women's sexual power. It is, perhaps, worth noting that in an era of famous theatrical mistresses – I have already mentioned Eliza Farren, Dora Jordan, and "Perdita" Robinson – *Mrs.* Siddons fought to maintain an image of strict sexual morality, even during the confused Galindo affair when she came under attack for alleged sexual impropriety. While we often assume that women who entered the theatre at the time were necessarily eroticized, Mrs. Siddons found her power in rejecting a sexualized identity. As Paula Backscheider argues, Siddons resisted "confinement in the 'symbolic space' reserved for women," that of "'love interest.'"[50] If Burke worked to convert Marie Antoinette – accused of adultery, lesbianism, and incest – into a beauty "full of life, and splendor, and joy" and embodying "lofty sentiments" and the "dignity of a Roman matron," if he wanted to depict the Queen of France accused of being a modern Lady Macbeth manipulating her husband as a dutiful wife and mother who, when Versailles is attacked, "escaped to seek refuge at the feet of a king and husband,"[51] then Siddons wanted to convert the actress as sexual suspect, to use Kristina Straub's phrase,[52] into a dauntingly moral Queen Mother, and she wanted to offer on stage women whose power came not through their own actions but through provoking action from desiring men. The only acts left to women – too virtuous to be stained by positive deeds – were suffering and dying. Of course, audiences found these images of virtue in distress powerfully affecting, as indicated again by the "many accidents of persons falling into fits" reported by the theatrical diarist John Genest about Siddons's performances.[53] Siddons's power as a woman on stage, ironically, arose from depicting women as lacking the power to act, and the sign of that power was her ability to overwhelm – to render passive, unconscious – her audience, and particularly the women in it. Whatever we finally determine about Siddons's own views on the distribution of political power, whatever we feel about the male reaction to her power on the stage, we have to see that her theatrical power was won through rendering women, on stage and off, passive.

IV

There is no doubting that women acquired power during the Romantic period as dramatists and actresses. While they would seem to have less institutional power, here too women had more of a presence than we might assume. Catherine Burroughs in *Closet Stages* has reminded us of the efforts of women as theorists of the theatre, as they took on a role often thought occupied by men. Jacky Bratton has shown how, beyond the well-known instance of Elizabeth Vestris's role as a theatrical manager, we find Jane Scott managing the Sans Pareil (later the Adelphi) and putting on many of her own plays.[54] Adrienne Scullion tells us that in the Scotland left behind by

Joanna Baillie and theatrically colonized by Sarah Siddons's son, Henry Siddons, women held important managerial roles, from Sarah Ward, manager of the first regular theatre in Edinburgh, through Jessie Jackson, "prominent in operating the Edinburgh Theatre Royal in the first decade of the nineteenth century," to Harriet Murray (Mrs. Henry Siddons), joint lessee of the theatre with her husband and then her brother, W. H. Murray.[55] In London, women may not have had comparable roles in the patent theatres, but they did have considerable control over private theatricals and even private theatres. Of the one and a half dozen or so sites for private theatricals noted by Allardyce Nicoll, about one-third seem to have been run by women.[56] For example, Elizabeth Farren conducted the amateur performances put on by the Duke of Richmond at his Whitehall residence in the 1780s. I have already mentioned Elizabeth Berkeley Craven, Margravine of Anspach, who oversaw the private performances at her Brandenburg House, where she was dramatist, composer, actress, and director. Mary Champion de Crespigny ran a theatre at Camberwell in the 1790s where Mariana Starke, for example, saw several of her plays performed. Women could, of course, also be found in the wardrobe room and in the orchestra pit, organizing dances and composing music; they were very much present in the theatre. To take one more example: Elizabeth Inchbald, as playwright and actress and as a successful negotiator for herself with several theatre managers, had enough clout to arbitrate Kemble's share in Covent Garden, and she also had considerable institutional power as the editor of Longman's important series, *The British Theatre* (1806–08).

The woman who had the most institutional power, however, was neither an actress nor a dramatist nor a member of any theatrical house. She was Anna Margaretta Larpent, the wife of John Larpent, the Lord Chamberlain's Examiner of Plays from 1778 to 1824.[57] It was to Larpent that theatres had to send their plays to be licensed before they could be performed, the stage being subject to prior censorship, unlike the press.

Anna Margaretta Porter became Larpent's second wife on 25 April 1782. She was the daughter of a diplomat, Sir James Porter, and through her family's connections came to meet such key figures as Johnson and Pitt. Larpent (1741–1824) was the son of a chief clerk of the Foreign Office, and he himself rose in the Foreign Office to become a waiter in ordinary to the Lord Chamberlain and a groom

of the privy chamber of George III. While there is little known about
the couple from external sources, sixteen volumes of Mrs. Larpent's
daily journals are held at the Huntington Library (HM 31201). They
reveal her to be very much engaged by the drama. While she often
preferred sermons, and she also made a serious study of the French
Revolution, she was an avid reader of plays, consuming seventy in
the eight years prior to her marriage;[58] she continued to read a large
number of plays, as indicated, for example, by a note for April of
1799 to acquire a copy of Baillie's *Plays on the Passions* as a book she
must read. She was a frequent theatregoer, enjoying performances
by Mrs. Siddons, as we have seen, and by other major stage figures
of the day. She attended the patent theatres – seeing Siddons at
Drury Lane (24 April 1792), for example, or viewing Inchbald's
adaptation of Kotzebue as *Lovers' Vows* (11 January 1799) and
Thomas Morton's *Speed the Plough* (3 April 1800) at Covent Garden –
and she also witnessed private theatricals such as those offered by
Mrs. Crespigny at Camberwell, where she saw Mariana Starke's
(now lost) *The British Orphan* (7 April 1790).

Anna Larpent also seems to have been directly involved in the
work of her husband as Examiner of Plays. Mr. Larpent adopted the
habit of bringing home to read the manuscripts submitted to him for
licensing; he also kept all the manuscripts at his home rather than in
his office. Many evenings, we are told, Mr. Larpent "read aloud a
MSS," with other family members taking turns at giving voice to
these new plays as well. These readings often occur on the day of or
the day before Larpent signs the license, so we can assume he
consulted his wife on his decisions.[59] She often records in her
journal her reactions to plays, as when they read "de Montfort [*sic*]
a new Tragedy being one of those written as a Series on the passions
which is altering for the Stage. The language is very poetic the
character forced. The Scene Shd. have been in Italy. The terrific is I
think too disgusting for representation" (3 April 1800). We know she
was involved in her husband's work, for she read and judged herself
all of the Italian operas submitted. There is a manuscript of a
drama, "The Virgin of the Sun,"[60] which is marked "Approved
AML," an indication that she at times acted as examiner of English
plays as well. There is evidence that as Mr. Larpent grew older, and
particularly at times when he was ill, Mrs. Larpent took over his
duties. Moreover, the comments in her journal often supply the
justification for the suppression of a play, a justification her husband

(unlike, say, his counterpart in Paris) was not required to give. For example, in her notes on Edmund John Eyre's *Death of the Queen of France; or, The Maid of Normandy* (1794), we find some explanation of why this play, which offers a sympathetic, Burkean portrait of Marie Antoinette, was twice denied a license by a government at war with France: she writes, it is as "devoid of poetry & judgment as it can be & highly improper just now were it otherwise" (14 April 1794), as she offers a political justification for the play's suppression beyond its aesthetic defects. Again, she also argues that Richard Cumberland's *Richard the Second* should be suppressed because, as she puts it, "it appears extremely unfit for representation at a time" – we are in December of 1792 – when "ye Country is full of Alarm" since the "Story [is] of Wat Tyler the killing of the Tax Gatherer & very ill judged" (8 December 1792). As was noted earlier, the office of the Examiner of Plays worked to keep off the stage any reference to the "alarms" of the day, both those in France and those closer to home. Mrs. Larpent agreed with her husband that, during the age of democratic revolutions, politics had to be kept off the stage: as one censored author said of the theatre under Larpent's control, "In that paradise . . . politics [is] the forbidden fruit, lest the people's eyes should be opened and they become as gods knowing good and evil."[61] The examiner following Larpent, the playwright George Colman the Younger, explained to the Select Committee examining the laws affecting dramatic literature in 1832 that the examiner should ban "anything that may be so allusive to the times as to be applied to the existing moment, and which is likely to be inflammatory."[62] Bulwer-Lytton describes the result of such censorship: "To see our modern plays, you would imagine there were no politicians among us."[63] Mrs. Larpent, in concert with her husband, used her power to insure that the theatre did not unleash within a crowded theatre the powerful political ideas and ideals of the French Revolution.

Claire Miller Colombo, in the first full essay on Mrs. Larpent, has argued that Mrs. Larpent's diary-writing, while in some sense informed by the institution of censorship in which her husband was so central, was still potentially subversive.[64] It seems to me, however, that Mrs. Larpent's institutional power, which might in itself be potentially subversive of a male-dominated enterprise such as the theatre, was in fact used to censor opportunities for dramatic subversion. Convinced that "Acting revolts in women against female

Delicacy" (12 March 1790) and concerned in her comments on the
French Revolution about power being granted to women, Mrs.
Larpent – like a Phyllis Schlafly of the Romantic era – wielded a
power she would have denied to other women.

It is fitting that this woman who was concerned about both the
immorality of acting and the dangers of revolutionary dramas should
hold some of the government's power over the theatre in the era of
Siddons and Baillie. Baillie, Siddons, and Larpent were all engaged
in complex, discomforting negotiations with social and cultural
power. We need to recognize the power these women won through
these negotiations – the state power exercised by Anna Larpent, the
emotional and sexual power Sarah Siddons deployed on stage, the
textual power earned by Joanna Baillie on the page. As these figures
stand for a much larger body of women engaged in the theatre, it
will not do to continue to deny the powerful place women held in
the theatre of the Romantic period. I could, of course, have selected
a different gathering of women – say, Mary Shelley, Elizabeth
Inchbald, and Jane Scott – and given a different sense of the political
valence of women's theatrical and dramatic power. However, in
identifying and even celebrating the fact of this power, we should not
forget that all power arises within particular literary, cultural,
institutional, social, and cultural contexts and that these contexts
insured that the power wielded by women – just like that wielded by
men – could be used for good or ill.

NOTES

1 The bibliography here is too long to list, but I note some highlights:
   Stuart Curran, "Romantic Poetry: The 'I' Altered," *Romanticism and
   Feminism*, ed. Anne Mellor (Bloomington: Indiana University Press,
   1988), pp. 185–207; *British Women Poets of the Romantic Era: An Anthology*,
   ed. Paula Feldman (Baltimore: Johns Hopkins University Press, 1997);
   Jerome McGann, *The Poetics of Sensibility: A Revolution in Literary Style*
   (Oxford University Press, 1996); Anne Mellor, *Romanticism and Gender*
   (London: Routledge, 1993); Marlon Ross, *The Contours of Masculine Desire:
   Romanticism and the Rise of Women's Poetry* (Oxford University Press, 1989).
2 See, for example, Catherine Burroughs, *Closet Stages: Joanna Baillie and
   the Theater Theory of British Romantic Women Writers* (Philadelphia: Uni-
   versity of Pennsylvania Press, 1997); Julie Carlson, *In the Theatre of
   Romanticism: Coleridge, Nationalism, Women* (Cambridge University Press,
   1994); Stuart Curran, *Shelley's "The Cenci": Scorpions Ringed with Fire*
   (Princeton University Press, 1970); Joseph Donohue, *Dramatic Character in*

the English Romantic Age (Princeton University Press, 1970); Terence Hoagwood and Daniel Watkins, ed., *British Romantic Drama: Historical and Critical Essays* (Cranbury, NJ: Associated University Presses, 1998); Marjean Purinton, *Romantic Ideology Unmasked: The Mentally Constructed Tyrannies in Dramas of William Wordsworth, Lord Byron, Percy Shelley, and Joanna Baillie* (Newark: University of Delaware Press, 1994); Alan Richardson, *A Mental Theater: Poetic Drama and Consciousness in the Romantic Age* (Penn State University Press, 1988); Michael Simpson, *Closet Performances: Political Exhibition and Prohibition in the Dramas of Byron and Shelley* (Stanford University Press, 1998); and Daniel P. Watkins, *A Materialist Critique of English Romantic Drama* (Gainesville: University Press of Florida, 1993).

3   Ellen Donkin, *Getting into the Act: Women Playwrights in London 1776–1829* (London: Routledge, 1995), p. 184. For a good account of the role of women in the theatre later in the century, see Tracy Davis, *Actresses as Working Women: Their Social Identity in Victorian Culture* (London: Routledge, 1991).

4   Ezell, *Writing Women's Literary History* (Baltimore: Johns Hopkins University Press, 1993).

5   David Mann and Susan Mann, with Camille Garnier, *Women Playwrights in England, Ireland, and Scotland 1660–1823* (Bloomington: Indiana University Press, 1996). This important scholarly tool allows us to see for the first time the volume of dramatic work by women of the period. We could add to it a few other women playwrights, including Mary Shelley, whose *Midas* (1820) and *Proserpine* (1820) were written during these dates but not published until later, or Georgiana Cavendish, Duchess of Devonshire, whose works remained in manuscript. See also David D. Mann, "Checklist of Female Dramatists, 1660–1823," *Restoration and Eighteenth-Century Theatre Research* 5 (1990), pp. 30–62. Allardyce Nicoll's handlists of plays included in *A History of English Drama, 1660–1900*, 3rd edn, 6 vols. (Cambridge University Press, 1952–59) are a valuable resource.

6   Donkin, *Getting into the Act*, pp. 185–89.

7   *Ibid.*, pp. 159–83. However, Donkin's argument suggests how far one can go to create a scenario in which women are oppressed and solely on gender grounds. Wondering why Sheridan, in control of Drury Lane, did not back Baillie's efforts, Donkin, in a note (219, n. 22), states, "I have weighed the possibility that Sheridan might have taken offense at Joanna Baillie's politics or even her brother's, but Baillie's brother, Dr. Matthew Baillie, was routinely in attendance on the King, so it seems unlikely, given Sheridan's long standing as a Tory, that this would have been the case." The assumption here is that Baillie's politics might trouble a conservative, but that she had enough cover through her brother to disarm the "Tory" [*sic*] Sheridan. Isn't it possible that Sheridan, given the fact of his longstanding support of Whig causes, found the conservative Baillie troubling not because she was a woman

but because she was allied with a reactionary literary culture that we might identify through Scott and *Blackwood's*, both supporters of Baillie? As the negative reaction to Baillie of the Whig *Edinburgh Review*, which has puzzled or angered commentators, suggests, she was seen as allied with the right.

8 Information on performances is gathered in Margaret S. Carhart, *The Life and Work of Joanna Baillie* (New Haven: Yale University Press, 1923), pp. 109–65.

9 Burroughs, *Closet Stages*, esp. pp. 74–109, 169–71.

10 Quoted in Martha Somerville, *Personal Recollections from Early Life to Old Age of Mary Somerville* (Boston: Roberts Brothers, 1874), p. 265.

11 Byron, letter to Annabella Milbanke, 6 September 1813, *Byron's Letters and Journals*, ed. Leslie Marchand, vol. III (London: John Murray, 1974), p. 109.

12 Mitford, *Recollections of a Literary Life* (New York: Harper, 1852), p. 152.

13 Henry Crabb Robinson's account, recorded in William Knight, *Life of Wordsworth* (1889) and quoted in Carhart, *Joanna Baillie*, p. 37.

14 Larpent Collection, Huntington Library, San Marino, California, LA 1287.

15 Huntington MS 32693, dated 29 March 1802, Huntington Library, San Marino, California.

16 See Donkin, *Getting into the Act*, p. 166. I have tried to recover some of the play's textual history in my edition of *De Monfort* included in Cox, *Seven Gothic Dramas 1789–1825* (Athens: Ohio University Press, 1992), pp. 231–314.

17 Mary Poovey, *The Proper Lady and the Woman Writer: Ideology as Style in the Works of Mary Wollstonecraft, Mary Shelley, and Jane Austen* (University of Chicago Press, 1984). For a nuanced placing of Baillie within gender and imperialist ideologies, see Amanda Gilroy, "From Here to Alterity: The Geography of Femininity in the Poetry of Joanna Baillie," in *A History of Scottish Women's Writing*, ed. Douglas Gifford and Dorothy McMillan (Edinburgh University Press, 1997), pp. 143–57.

18 Henry Crabb Robinson, *Diary, Reminiscences and Correspondence*, ed. Thomas Sadler (London: Fields, Osgood, 1869), I: 248.

19 *Ibid.* Even Mitford, in *Recollections*, says Baillie is "the very pattern of what a literary lady should be – quiet, unpretending, generous, kind, admirable in her writings, excellent in her life" (p. 152).

20 Marjean Purinton, "The Sexual Politics of *The Election*: French Feminism and the Scottish Playwright Joanna Baillie," *Intertexts* 2.2 (1998): 119–30; Anne K. Mellor, "Joanna Baillie and the Counter-Public Sphere," *Studies in Romanticism* 33 (Winter 1994): 559–67. See also Burroughs, *Closet Stages*, esp. pp. 110–17. I have argued that *De Monfort* and *Orra* can be seen as offering a critique of women's roles: *Seven Gothic Dramas*, pp. 52–57.

21 David Hewitt, "Scott's Art and Politics," in *Sir Walter Scott: The Long-*

Forgotten Melody, ed. Alan Bold (Totowa, NJ: Barnes & Noble Books, 1983), pp. 44–52.

22 Baillie, *The Dramatic and Poetical Works of Joanna Baillie* (London: Longman, Brown, Green and Longmans, 1851), p. 793. Lucy Aikin, *Memoirs, Miscellanies, and Letters of the Late Lucy Aikin*, ed. Philip Le Breton (London: Longman, Green 1864), quoted in Carhart, *Joanna Baillie*, p. 40.

23 C. J. Hamilton, *Women Writers: Their Works and Ways*, First Series (London: Ward, Lock, & Bowden, 1892), p. 124; S. Tytler and J. L. Watson, *Songstresses of Scotland* (London: Strahan , 1871), ii: 239. 2 vols.

24 See Eric Richards, *A History of the Highland Clearances: Agrarian Transformation and the Evictions 1746–1886* (London: Croom Helm, 1982), pp. 284–315.

25 The production is recounted in James C. Dibdin, *The Annals of the Edinburgh Stage* (Edinburgh: Richard Cameron, 1888), pp. 261–62, and Sir Walter Scott, letters to Joanna Baillie, 13 June 1809, 15 August 1809, 13 October 1809, 27 October 1809, 22 January 1810, 30 January 1810, 31 January 1810, 6 February 1810, 20 February 1810, *The Letters of Sir Walter Scott*, ed. H. J. C. Grierson (London: Constable & Co., 1932–36), ii:196–97, 217–21, 253–55, 257–60, 287–89, 290–92, 293–94, 295–96, 300–04. A good account of the play is found in Adrienne Scullion, "Some Women of the Nineteenth-Century Scottish Theatre: Joanna Baillie, Frances Wright, and Helen MacGregor," in *History of Scottish Women's Writing*, ed. Gifford and McMillan, pp. 161–65.

26 Scott, letter to Lady Abercorn, 21 January 1810, *Letters*, ii: 286.

27 Scott, letter to Baillie, 13 October 1809, *Letters*, ii: 253–54.

28 Scott, letter to Baillie, 30 January 1810, *Letters*, ii: 292.

29 William Ferguson, *Scotland: 1689 to the Present* (Edinburgh: Oliver and Boyd, 1968), p. 263.

30 Quoted in Carhart, *Joanna Baillie*, p. 147.

31 My argument here owes a debt to the fine account of the efforts of Scott and other Edinburgh Tories to negotiate the tensions between a Scottish national identity and membership in the United Kingdom offered by Charles Snodgrass, "Narrating Nations, Negotiating Borders: The Scottish Romantic Novel in Blackwood's Circle," Ph.D. Dissertation, Texas A&M University, Spring, 1999. See also Scullion, "Some Women," pp. 164–65.

32 Mackensie, "Epilogue," in Baillie, *Works*, p. 508.

33 John Roach Young, "Highland Regiments," in *Britain in the Hanoverian Age 1714–1837*, ed. Gerald Newman *et al.* (New York: Garland, 1997), p. 329. See also Frederick Watson, *The Story of the Highland Regiments, 1725–1925* (London: A. & C. Black, 1925).

34 Baillie, "To Mrs. Siddons," in *Works*, p. 829.

35 An interesting account of "Representing the Female Actor: Celebrity Narratives, Women's Theories of Acting, and Social Theaters" can be found in Burroughs, *Closet Stages*, pp. 27–73.

36 Hunt, "Mr. Young's Merits Considered," *Examiner*, 15 January 1809: 45.
37 Hazlitt, *Complete Works*, ed. P. P. Howe (London, Toronto: J. M. Dent and Sons, 1930–34), V: 312.
38 *Ibid.*
39 James Boaden, *Memoirs of Mrs. Siddons Interspersed with anecdotes of authors and actors* (London: Henry Colburn, 1827), p. 195.
40 John Waldie, "Journals and Letters of John Waldie of Hendersyde Park, Kelso, Scotland," Special Collections, University of California at Los Angeles, IV, 169/8.
41 Larpent, "The Diary of Anna Margaretta Larpent," 16 vols., Huntington Library, San Marino, California, HM 31201. This item is reproduced by permission of The Huntington Library, San Marino, California.
42 William Pitt, Lord Lennox, *Plays, Players, and Playhouses at Home and Abroad, with Anecdotes of the Drama and the Stage* (London: Hurst and Blackett, 1881), I: 211.
43 Carlson, *In the Theatre of Romanticism*, pp. 162–75.
44 See Marc Baer, *Theatre and Disorder in Late Georgian London* (Oxford: Clarendon Press, 1992).
45 Simpson, *Closet Performances*, pp. 63–64.
46 Roger Manvell, *Sarah Siddons: Portrait of an Actress* (London: Heinemann, 1970), p. 292.
47 Jeffrey Cox, "Ideology and Genre in the British Antirevolutionary Drama in the 1790s," *ELH* 58 (1992): 579–610.
48 Christopher Reid, "Burke's Tragic Muse: Sarah Siddons and the 'Feminization' of the *Reflections*," in *Burke and the French Revolution: Bicentennial Essays*, ed. Steven Blakemore (Athens, GA: University of Georgia Press, 1992), pp. 1–27. See also Frans De Bruyn, *The Literary Genres of Edmund Burke* (Oxford: Clarendon Press, 1996), p. 188, where he sees Burke portraying Marie Antoinette as a tragic heroine from eighteenth-century sentimental tragedy.
49 Quoted in Thomas Campbell, *Life of Mrs. Siddons* (London: Effingham Wilson, 1834), II: 11–12.
50 Paula Backscheider, *Spectacular Politics: Theatrical Power and Mass Culture in Early Modern England* (Baltimore: Johns Hopkins University Press, 1993), p. 214.
51 Burke, *Works and Correspondence of the Right Honourable Edmund Burke* (London: Francis & John Rivington, 1852), IV: 212, 209.
52 Kristina Straub, *Sexual Suspects: Eighteenth-Century Players and Sexual Ideology* (Princeton University Press, 1992).
53 John Genest, *Some Account of the English Stage: from the Restoration in 1660 to 1830* (Bath: H. E. Carrington, 1832), 10 vols. Genest was another Siddons admirer, calling her "the first actress who had ever trod the English stage – in Tragedy she may be fairly considered an equal to Garrick" (VIII: 301).

54 In addition to the essay on Jane Scott by J. S. Bratton in this volume, see Bratton's "Miss Scott and Miss Macauley: 'Genius Comes in All Disguises'," *Theatre Survey* 37 (May 1996): 59–74 and "Jane Scott the Writer/Manager" in *Women and Playwriting in Nineteenth-Century Britain*, ed. Tracy C. Davis and Ellen Donkin (Cambridge University Press, 1999), pp. 77–98.

55 Scullion, "Some Women," p. 175 n.2.

56 Nicoll, *History of English Drama*, 3: 20–21.

57 On John Larpent, see L. W. Conolly, *The Censorship of English Drama 1737–1824* (San Marino: Huntington Library, 1976), esp. pp. 34–45; Frank Power and Frank Palmer, *Censorship in England* (1913, rpt. New York: Burt Franklin, 1970), pp. 155–64; John Johnston, *The Lord Chamberlain's Blue Pencil* (London: Hodder & Stoughton, 1990), pp. 46–47.

58 Conolly, *Censorship*, p. 38.

59 The dates of the readings can be ascertained from Mrs. Larpent's diary; the dates of the licenses can be found both in the manuscripts for individual plays held in the Huntington Library's Larpent collection and in the "List of Plays Licensed by John Larpent, 1801–1824 in 2 vols" (HM 19926) where he records by date titles, actions, and fees.

60 Larpent Collection, Huntington Library, San Marino, California, LA 1868.

61 "Postscript," *Helvetic Liberty, An Opera in Three Acts by a Kentish Bowman* (London: Wayland, 1792), p. vi.

62 Colman, testimony, *Report from the Select Committee Appointed to inquire into the laws Affecting Dramatic Literature* (1832), Irish University Press Series of British Parliamentary Papers, Stage and Theatre, vol. 1 (Shannon: Irish University Press, 1968): 66.

63 Edward Bulwer-Lytton, *England and the English*, ed. Standish Meacham (University of Chicago Press, 1970), p. 306.

64 Claire Miller Colombo, "'This Pen of Mine Will Say Too Much': Public Performance in the Journals of Anna Larpent," *Texas Studies in Literature and Language* 38 (Fall/Winter 1996): 285–301.

CHAPTER 2

Reviewing women in British Romantic theatre
Greg Kucich

Most of the last decade's revisionary work on Romantic-era women authors shares a driving concern with the material impact of their writings on the gender practices and ideologies of their time. Major studies by Marlon Ross, Stuart Curran, Anne Mellor, Paula Feldman, and Theresa Kelley among others have tracked the complex dynamics of this intervention within the genres of poetry and prose writing, but analyses of similar types of social relations within the drama stand at a relatively early stage of development.[1] Ellen Donkin demonstrates the importance of extending such material inquiries to the drama in her foundational reading of eighteenth- and nineteenth-century British women playwrights, which examines the unique set of gender constraints experienced by women dramatists in the male-dominated theatrical world of managers, actors, audiences, and playwrights.[2] Catherine Burroughs shows how Romantic-era women dramatists open up "theoretical moments" that test those restrictions by utilizing performance space – textually, on the stage, and in the private closet – to critique gendered identities and power relations.[3] Julie Carlson finds such challenges provoking anxious efforts to consolidate gender boundaries and impose "masculinist visions" among the period's male dramatic writers.[4] Donkin finally stresses the overbearing effect of various forms of such masculine impositions, arguing that women writers' entry into the theatrical domain, despite various incursions, was systematically restricted by the male establishment and ultimately closed down by the early nineteenth century. According to Donkin, this increasingly negative response conditions the history of women in the Romantic theatre as a record marked by contentious interventions, pointed successes, but ultimately "struggle and defeat" (39). Much as we are beginning to learn about such a conflicted history, its dynamic of gender threats and regulation can

48

be complicated if we trace the impact of women dramatists to a material context that has not received substantial attention – the discursive field of drama-reviewing. Reactions to women dramatists in the male-controlled reviewing press remain, in fact, much more curiously divided throughout the Romantic era, split between effusive welcome and vigorous resistance, suggesting more complex patterns of accommodation, containment, and threat.

This divided attitude of drama reviewers to women writers was strong enough to make Joanna Baillie reflect on it in the 1802 preface to her second volume of experimental plays. Welcoming criticism of her first breakthrough volume of 1798 as a spur for additional creative endeavor, she characterizes the critical reaction as "praise mixed with a considerable portion of censure."[5] Such a contradictory judgment typifies the kind of reception women dramatists of the Romantic era generally receive in the reviewing press, where they are welcomed to a degree uncommon for women writers in other literary genres and simultaneously warned to curb their efforts. Baillie's "just celebrity," complains "Z" in *Blackwood's* notorious Cockney School essays, must be balanced against its "melancholy effect" of tempting so many "unmarried ladies" to assay dramatic composition.[6] The openness to Baillie here characteristically exerts at the same time a general check on perceived incursions of transgressive women dramatists. A particularly striking embodiment of this doubling form of regulation introduces Hannah More's drama *Percy* (1777), for which David Garrick wrote a prologue ventriloquizing a female actor's somewhat ambivalent case for women's dramatic abilities – "Can't we write plays, or damn 'em, if we please?"[7] – within the controlling framework of his own masculine composition. "Z"'s very apprehensiveness about a "melancholy" onslaught of females writing and damning plays, however, implies a persisting threat to any attempts at containment, a threat which Baillie actually reinforces in her claim to receive further creative incentive from critical reproofs. The split position of the reviewing industry toward women dramatists thus points toward one of Romanticism's more charged cultural sites of gender contention marked by conflicting postures of welcome, containment, and threatened resistance. To examine these unusual divisions throughout the reviewing of women's drama – mostly by men in periodicals, pamphlets, essays, and newspapers but also in some transgressive cases, like Elizabeth Inchbald's, by women writing back

– is to gain a new perspective on the unique material impact of those "theoretical moments" in women's drama, particularly on the degree to which they become partially accommodated within established gender categories put simultaneously under constant pressure.[8]

Although the prominence of Joanna Baillie's position in the field of Romantic drama has been registered by Stuart Curran and Anne K. Mellor,[9] the generally welcoming reception many other female dramatists met in the periodical press may come as a surprise to those familiar with more openly vexed responses to women poets and novelists, such as the reviews of Anna Barbauld's *Eighteen Hundred and Eleven* (1812) and Lucy Aikin's *Epistles on Women* (1810), as well as Richard Polwhele's notorious diatribe, *The Unsex'd Females* (1798). To be sure, outright repudiations of women dramatists did occur, like the *Imperial Review*'s blast against the "insult[ing] . . . effusions of female sentiment . . . and inferiority of genius" in women's drama.[10] Moreover, the amount of reviewing space devoted to women dramatists in most periodicals, according to William Ward's compilations, falls disproportionately short of the attention bestowed on male dramatists.[11] Nevertheless, the vast majority of reviews of women dramatists assume an inviting tone and express the kind of eagerness to recognize female talent indicated in the *European Magazine*'s account of popular reaction to Hannah Brand's *Huniades, a Tragedy* (1798). "The interesting novelty of a new Tragedy, with the first theatrical appearance of the Author, and that author a female, naturally attracted a very large audience to the above."[12]

This keen interest in the appearance of a female dramatist did not stem from any perceived anomaly in the situation itself, but rather partook of widespread enthusiasm for the rapidly expanding range and depth of female talent entering London's theatrical world around the turn of the nineteenth century. *The Monthly Mirror* "boldly pronounce[s]" in 1798, for instance, that Harriet Lee's *The Mysterious Marriage* (1798) is "equal to any drama that has been performed [in recent years]."[13] Just one year earlier, *The Lady's Magazine* had proclaimed Elizabeth Inchbald one of the most "eminently successful" dramatists of the age, to whom "the public" should feel deeply "obliged."[14] *The Literary Journal* echoes a broadly reiterated consensus about Joanna Baillie's stunning achievement when it ranks her with Shakespeare in 1805 and declares "her name immortal" in the annals of British dramatic history.[15] Even the reactionary *Anti-Jacobin Review*, no great friend generally to women writers, joins in this sanguine overall assessment of female dramatic talent when commending the plays of Hannah Cowley in 1814: "A collection of the writings of this lively and spirited writer was a *desideratum* in dramatic . . . literature . . . In short, she may be considered as one of the best . . . dramatic writers of the latter part of the eighteenth century."[16]

Such openness to women's dramatic writing stems in part from the diminished presence, thanks to the indefatigable rigor of the state Licenser, of overt political content in staged Romantic-era drama. It was not only the Gallican principles of all those "Unsex'd" female writers that incensed Polwhele, but the mere assumption of political polemic by the "female muse,"[17] as Anna Barbauld discovered to her mortification, could seem baneful and perverse. Reviewers of women's dramatic writing certainly recognized the textual presence of contemporary political allusions and allegories. Baillie's dramatization of Ethwald's soaring ambition, for instance, strikes *The Imperial Review* as but a slightly veiled critique of Napoleon's meteoric rise to power by 1804.[18] Yet the significance of suppressing stage politics generally for the popular reception of women's drama may be gauged by the controversy over expressions of French republican politics in Hannah Cowley's 1792 play, *A Day in Turkey; or The Russian Slaves*. Despite Cowley's popularity, *The Critical Review* thinks she should give up serious drama because she has mistakenly stumbled into the "unfeminine" domain of "democratic . . . politics."[19] Acknowledging the seriousness of this charge, *The European Magazine* defends Cowley by insisting that the politics are tangential to her play's central action and merely function as a kind of costuming for a typical Frenchman of the day: "We have heard it hinted, that this play is too deeply tainted with politics, but find nothing but those sallies in which a Frenchman of *the present day* may be allowed to indulge himself . . ."[20] In her Preface to *A Day in Turkey* Cowley herself recognizes the importance of such evasions for a female dramatist, striving somewhat coyly to establish her gender purity by asserting her ignorance of and indifference to "POLITICS": "Hints have been thrown out, and the idea industriously circulated, that the following comedy is tainted with POLITICS. I protest I know nothing about politics; – will Miss Wollstonecraft forgive me . . . if I say that politics are *unfeminine*? I never in my life could attend to their discussion."[21] Whether or not Cowley could actually bear such discussions, her professions of an appropriately feminine void of politics in *A Day in Turkey* could only gain credence from government licensing and the official practice of banishing politics from the British stage. Whatever creative and political restraints the licensing office may have imposed on Romantic-era dramatists generally, it did help create a safe haven of sorts for female writers to enter a public cultural arena without encountering the entrenched resistance they sometimes met in other genres.

Yet the robust quality of the period's openness to women dramatists suggests even more compelling motivations than a perceived absence of open political disturbances in their works. As a more positive force in contemporary drama, figures like Cowley, Baillie, Inchbald, and Harriet Lee came to be seen collectively as making a key contribution to one of Romanticism's most urgent projects of cultural renewal – the revival of Britain's national dramatic tradition. Consumed by questions about the present's relation to the rich achievements of Britain's literary past, particularly its Renaissance efflorescence of creative genius, many Romantic-era critics staked the claims of their own age to cultural greatness on the regeneration of the drama. Much has been said over the last several decades about the Romantics' gloomy assessments of cultural doom because of what Leigh Hunt characterizes as the "degraded condition of the modern drama" into gaudy spectacle, ostentatious acting, and various forms of quadruped entertainment.[22] However, cautious prognostications of hope for the renewal of the drama, and with it the general advance of culture, did emerge.[23] William Hazlitt repeatedly insists, for example, that "our times . . . [are] not unfruitful in theatrical genius,"[24] and he retaliates against "that general complaint of the degeneracy of the stage" with a progressive argument for continuous revitalization in the history of the national drama: "Within our remembrance, at least, it has not fallen off to any alarming degree, either in the written or the acted performances. It has changed its style considerably in both these respects, but it does not follow that it has altogether deteriorated: it has shifted its ground, but has found its level."[25] Even this optimism is guarded, taking into account the fact of deterioration – though not irrevocable – and a falling off from the greatness of the past – though not an "alarming" one. Few proponents of the vitality of contemporary drama were willing to go so far as the *Blackwood's* reviewer of Thomas Doubleday's *Babington*, who declared in 1825 that "dramatic genius" was "kindling over the whole land" in such creative profusion as to outstrip the achievements of "our best dramatic writers" from the golden age of the Renaissance.[26] For those who, like Hazlitt, defended the prospects of contemporary drama, a conviction of its crucial efficacy in generating Britain's cultural renewal depended on its recovery from deteriorating trends through the infusion of vibrant new talent. And one of the principal sources of that creative refreshment, many agreed, came from the influx of women dramatists and the redemptive energies they poured into the theatrical life of their time.

The European Magazine holds up the plays of Cowley, for instance, as "the Works of one highly gifted" who has reversed the flow of dramatic genius from "desert[ing] the realm."[27] *The Anti-Jacobin Review* feels the "doom" of modern "dramatic compositions" is at least partially lifted by Charlotte Smith, whose *What is She?* (1799) offers an encouraging correction to the "folly" and "bustle" of most current productions.[28] According to *The Theatrical Inquisitor*, More's "soundness of judgment" brings "pure and enlightened piety" back to the stage with the production of *Percy*.[29] Lee's *The Mysterious Marriage* and Inchbald's many "dramatic pieces" establish new models of emulation, *The Monthly Review* and *The Lady's Magazine* agree,[30] for the renewal of dramatic achievement in the modern age.

It was Joanna Baillie's accomplishment, above all, that positioned women's writing at the forefront of this rehabilitation of British drama. Although her theory and practice of dramatizing passions elicit mixed reactions, most reviewers agree that she not only ranks foremost among her female peers but unconditionally deserves the highest place among all contemporary dramatists. Beyond contemporary comparisons, many conclude that she stands alone, in all of British dramatic history, as the only genuine rival to Shakespeare himself. Thus she is variously celebrated as one of "the brightest luminaries of the present period," a "master," "a genius of native growth," an "immortal" writer who "has achieved some things which even [Shakespeare] left undone."[31] Echoing a chorus of such comparisons to Shakespeare, *The Critical Review* reveals the breathtaking heights to which an age so anxiously self-conscious about its relation to the golden days of the Renaissance, particularly in terms of dramatic achievement, could rush to elevate Baillie's genius:

"Miss Baillie's dramatic powers are of the highest order. With the miserable stage-writers of the day, it would be insult to compare her . . . Above these, above Beaumont and Fletcher we will not hesitate to rank her – above even Massinger . . . Why should praise be awarded only to the dead? She has a near approach to Shakespeare; and, if not connected with him by blood, has something superior to a mere family likeness."[32]

It is not merely this "family likeness" to Shakespeare that makes Baillie so important, but also her redemptive impact on the "miserable stage-writers of the day." For many reviewers specifically stress her leadership role in that urgent national project to rehabilitate the drama. In "the present most deplorable state of our national drama," implores *The British Critic*, a desperately needed spur to creative renewal rests with "such powers and such fascination as that of Miss Joanna Baillie."[33] A "genius like Miss Baillie's" stands out as "a matter of peculiar triumph," argues *The Annual Review*, specifically because of its power to refresh the "dispirit[ed] drama."[34] Walter Scott agrees enthusiastically, declaring that Baillie has led the way in a growing movement to "enrich" and revitalize the "national tragedy."[35] *Blackwood's* goes even further, declaring that Baillie's "strong influence" has propelled a regenerative "change" in all of "our poetic literature" that transforms the current epoch into "another Age of Genius, only second to that of Elizabeth." That spectacular "influence" clearly appears to the *Blackwood's* critic as a feminine force, acknowledged even against his own "male prejudices" and celebrated as remarkable proof of women's vital contributions to the "reformation" of Britain's national literature through dramatic achievement.[36]

Given this proliferation of enthusiasm for the age's female dramatic talent, dismissive attitudes like "Z"'s scorn for "unmarried" lady dramatists might seem anomalous. Similar expressions of disdain run throughout the period's drama criticism, however, voiced even by those champions of the drama's regeneration like Hazlitt. Thus he introduces his lecture on female writers with this condescending mockery of several who became particularly noteworthy for their dramatic achievement: "I am a great admirer of the female muses of the present day; they appear to me like so many modern Muses. I could be in love with Mrs. Inchbald, Romantic with Mrs. Radcliffe, and sarcastic with Madame D'Arblay . . . Mrs. Hannah More is another celebrated modern poetess, and I believe still living. She has written a great deal which I have never read."[37] "Z"'s reaction marks an even more striking contradiction in the reviewing of women dramatists, for it lashes out against their pretension in the same periodical that extravagantly lauds Baillie just a few years later, *Blackwood's*, and even delivers that reproof as a countermeasure to an avowed recognition of Baillie's "just celebrity." Such contradictions do not simply arise from a balanced discrimination between Baillie's unique genius and the inferiority of her female peers. Rather, they partake of that recurrently divided tendency among the period's reviewers to edge their high praise of women dramatists, as Baillie observed, with "a considerable portion of censure."

The same *Blackwood's* critic who promotes Baillie as the redeemer of British literature, for instance, also places a considerable portion of emphasis on her "defective" qualities and strenuously urges her to "cut away the weaker branches" of her art.[38] *The Monthly Review*'s final verdict on Baillie concisely summarizes what became a widely shared expression of this divided opinion. She possesses "considerable powers – injudiciously directed."[39] Such a deeply split form of judgment can be traced, in fact, as one of the most prominent features in the overall process of reviewing women dramatists. *The Monthly Censor* finds Mary Russell Mitford's *Julian* (1823) a rare dramatic success, "that most difficult production a playable tragedy," while also dismissing much of its stage business, particularly its chivalric pageantry, as the weak consequence of "the writer's sex."[40] Inchbald's dramas possess "many beauties," concludes *The Anti-Jacobin Review*, joined with "great and glaring defects."[41] Jane West's plays are invaluably "pure," according to *The Critical Review*, but marked by "the death-warrant of mediocrity, the poetical crime for which there is no redemption."[42] *The Monthly Review* finds Harriet Lee's dramatic talent bearing "testimony" to her "high rank" in the art while also emphasizing her constant lapse into a plague of "faults."[43] Not all contemporary views of women dramatists express such fundamental divisions, but the pattern recurred frequently enough to give some authors, like Baillie, pause for thought. She would have found at the core of this conflicted judgment recurring concerns with the power and the limits of "strong" female energies like her own, which implies a specific uneasiness with the gender pressures unleashed by those "theoretical moments" in women's drama. More particularly, the special preoccupation of divided reviewers with the boundaries of female talent suggests that their ambivalent evaluations function as a discursive mechanism, under certain threat, for regulating gender identities and behaviors.

The divided reactions of male critics to the material presence of female actors on stage can help explain how this dynamic of gender regulation and threat conditions the split attitude of critical responses to women dramatists. Women's emergence on the British stage provoked intensely divided responses from the seventeenth century onward, as Ellen Donkin has shown (1–39), offering the alluring spectacle of female beauty on display while also disrupting codes of proper feminine reserve. These divisions became particularly acute during the Romantic era because of the exponential influx of women actors on to a greatly expanded range of stages coupled with intensifying disputes in conduct book literature and early feminist writings about women's proper public roles.[44] As a result, male theatre enthusiasts like Hazlitt, Lamb, and Hunt grew to regard women's expanding presence on stage not simply as an object of attention for the delighted male gaze but also as an occasion for intensive debates about the propriety of female appearance and behavior, both on stage and off. Such debates reveal that, for many male theatre critics, the stage actually became, among other things, a feminized space for affirming established codes of gender appearance and behavior while simultaneously controlling strenuous, potentially uncontainable, threats to those very models of gender propriety. Hence the divided postures of welcome, regulation, and resistance that constitute the critical act of reviewing women on stage.

Hazlitt's feminized metaphor for the pleasures of the stage provocatively illustrates the various gender pressures at work in this conflicted mode of response. To emphasize his passionate delight with the visual allure of the stage, Hazlitt compares his love of watching plays to the "fond" gaze of a "fine lady" contemplating her beautiful face in a mirror.[45] This vision of the stage as a site for the display of female beauty not only welcomes women into the theatre as specular objects for the male gaze, it also imposes a standard of appearance and conduct on the female form in accord with the demeanor of a "fine lady." Such an inclination to regulate appropriate models of female identity pervades commentary by Hazlitt and other male reviewers of the period's female actors.

Hazlitt's essay on Eliza O'Neill, for instance, though deeply attentive to her acting abilities, emphasizes her "figure" and commends its conformity to "that respectable kind . . . of form."[46] He specifically endorses O'Neill's performances, moreover, in a "strictly feminine cast of heroines . . . made of softness and suffering."[47] Similar emphases condition the many notices of female actors in stage reviews like *The British Stage, and Literary Cabinet*, whose love of gazing at a "respectable kind" of feminine beauty on stage is best epitomized in the following comments on Mrs. W. S. Chatterley:

Beauty in an actress, like charity in an individual, covers a multitude of defects. There is a certain pleasure to be derived from contemplating a pretty woman, which cannot be imparted by others possessing talent without personal attractions. Such is the case with the subject of our present Sketch. She is a very pretty genteel little body, but by no means an actress of extraordinary talents.[48]

The pleasure of viewing such prettiness in theatrical women here depends significantly on the "genteel" and "respectable" form it assumes, not only in appearance but also in behavior. Hazlitt claims, for instance, that one of O'Neill's greatest professional virtues lies in the fact that she does "not once overstep the limits of propriety" in her performances of female passion.[49]

This emphasis on "propriety" extends, moreover, beyond the stage, representing its models of female decorum as regulating norms for social relations in general. *The Theatrical Inquisitor* thus praises O'Neill for her "strict observance of all the social duties" and comments generally that "females . . . upon the stage" do most "honour to [their] profession" by observing "irreproachable . . . behaviour" both on and off the stage.[50] Hunt reinforces this gendered equation between what he calls "propriety of demeanour" for women on stage and in social life, arguing that actresses should aspire to the model of those "genteel females" so celebrated in British society "for that delicate mixture of reserve and frankness which constitutes the charms of female manners."[51] The pleasurable reviewing of women's material presence on stage, then, became a substantial regulating mechanism for enforcing more far-reaching social codes of proper female appearance and behavior.

The very need to exercise such discipline, however, implies the action of pressures working against it. Indeed, Hazlitt's metaphor of gazing upon the stage as a "fine lady" also features that "lady" looking back out of the mirror at male observers who have been, within the context of the metaphor, feminized. These insinuations of uncontrollable, even threatening, female energies released on stage help to explain countering tendencies among stage reviewers to express negative assessments of theatrical women that seek to contain and resist their female improprieties. Hazlitt's reaction to O'Neill eventually becomes troubled, for instance, when he finds her moving beyond acceptable models of feminine demeanor. "She has," he complains, "of late, carried the expression of mental agony and distress to a degree of physical horror that is painful to behold, and which is particularly repulsive in a person of her delicacy of frame and truly feminine appearance."[52] Hunt feels similarly uneasy when female energies on stage broach the limits of "propriety," arguing that "actresses, like queens, lose something of the woman, in proportion as they exhibit powers of command and the more vigorous acquirements."[53] Such exhibitions of female empowerment become most disturbing when they particularly destabilize conventional gender identities. "We distinctly dislike," pronounces *The British Stage, and Literary Cabinet*, "the practice of allotting females the performance of male characters . . ."[54] Hunt adds, "It is at all times unpleasant to see a woman performing in the dress of a man . . . Let the actress who is fond of displaying her person in male attire, never forget, that the applause she gains in such a dress cannot possibly carry with it anything of *respect* . . ."[55]

Hunt finds such gender violations intrinsic to the acting profession, given its requirements for women "entirely [to] get rid of the natural timidity of [their] sex," and he warns that the corrupting effects of feminine impropriety on "disrespectful" theatre audiences can potentially carry into society at large.[56] At times Hunt tries to dismiss these larger threats of social subversion facetiously, expressing mock exasperation in a *Tatler* essay, for instance, with women's bonnets that perpetually block his view at the theatre: "If you sit right behind [the bonnet], it will swallow up the whole scene. It makes nothing of a regiment of soldiers, or a mountain, or a forest, or a rising sun; much less a hero . . ."[57] But the more disturbing implications here of devouring female energies, operating across a broad social spectrum, could also provoke intensely hostile reactions to women on stage, such as *The Universal Magazine*'s severe "repugnan[ce]" at the "prostitution" of public virtue caused by female cross-dressing in the theatres.[58] Whether ironically condescending or openly antagonistic, these defensive comments register calculated, sometimes anxious, efforts to contain significant gender threats posed by women's material presence in the theatre. Moreover, their juxtaposition with those positive endorsements of female propriety makes up a complicated mixture of affirmation, threat, and containment in reviewing gender on stage that helps to explain the basic divisions of approval and resistance in the reviewing of women who write for the stage.

For those divided views of women dramatists reveal a persisting tendency to regard their works, whether viewed in production or read in print form, as material embodiments of their gendered identity; and this incorporation of texts into bodies bears with it the kind of conflicting dynamics of accommodation, regulation, and threatened containment that conditions the reviewing of women on stage. Such a pattern of giving stage embodiment to women's dramatic texts may be partially explained by the crossover roles assumed by prominent female stage performers – like Inchbald, Robinson, Brand, and Elizabeth Macauley – who doubled as playwrights, sometimes as creators of the very stage characters they played. In their very presence on stage, they quite literally embodied female texts. Such incentives to view women's drama in this material way encouraged and gained reinforcement from a critical habit of prioritizing the issue of physically representing women's texts on stage, whether in reviews of actual performances or printed texts.

The problematic topic of stage performance surfaces throughout Romantic-era discussions of the drama, but it occupies a distinctively central role in the reviewing of women dramatists, as if their texts seem indistinguishable in the imaginations of reviewers from physical forms of realization on stage. *The Anti-Jacobin Review* commends Inchbald's *To Marry or Not to Marry* (1805), for instance, specifically because its dramatic "situations" are "highly interesting, and afford most excellent opportunities for good acting."[59] *The European Review* similarly endorses Inchbald's *Every One Has His Fault* (1793) on the basis of its performative "excellence," which rightly provoked "great and deserved applause" from an enthusiastic audience.[60] Brand's dramatic writing impresses *The British Critic* primarily because of its representational strengths, manifested to great effect in Brand's own performance of the female lead in *Huniades*.[61] Even unacted dramas published by women tend to provoke this critical attention to material effects and possibilities on stage. *The Quarterly Review,* for instance, finds Maria Edgeworth's experiment with printed comedies offering a positive contribution to modern drama in their "susceptibil[ity] of being wrought into a form proper for the stage."[62] Jane West's printed plays seem most valuable to *The Monthly Review* in their potential to give the public "much pleasure from the *representation* . . ."[63] And Baillie's published plays strike *The British Critic* as offering the "British Public" a key to the comprehensive reform of "the degraded state of our Drama" in the theatrical richness of their "scenes."[64] Negative reviews of these same works similarly give primary, though disapproving, emphasis to their representational materiality, making the physical embodiment of female creative consciousness on stage one of the dominant preoccupations of reviewers of women's dramatic writing.[65]

   This practice of textual embodiment, coupled with charged genderings of the stage – like Hazlitt's – as a site of feminine materiality in itself became so forceful as to render women's dramatic writings, at times, virtually indecipherable from their female minds and bodies. Such was particularly the case with Baillie, whose critics repeatedly view her characters as so many physical realizations of her own thoughts and, even, bodily parts. Her management of stage action, claims *The Eclectic Review*, continually draws attention from "the work to the author"; the "mouths" of her characters, moreover, seem identical to her own.[66] Her own "eager . . . talk," argues Francis Jeffrey in *The Edinburgh Review*, can be heard "obtrud[ing] itself" upon readers of her plays, just as her delicate "female . . . hand" seems manifested throughout her tragic writing, sometimes in ways that appear disturbingly masculine.[67] Hazlitt even imagines Baillie's dramatic texts as stages over which she physically presides, pulling "wires" attached to her characters.[68]

   That this equation of text and female body was not unique to reviews of Baillie, but conditioned responses to women dramatists generally, may be gauged from Cowley's irritation at her plight, as a woman writer, to have her dramatic characters constantly identified with her own sentiments, behavioral patterns, and forms of appearance. Accounting for hostile audience reactions to the perceived indecency of her play, *A School for Greybeards; or, the Mourning Bride* (1786), Cowley protests that the "public" desires only to "trace" herself in the "dramatic representation." In "my case," she complains, "it seems resolved that the point to be considered, is not whether that *dotard*, or that *pretender*, or that *coquet*, would so have given their feelings, but whether Mrs. *Cowley* ought so to have expressed herself."[69] Such embodiments of herself on stage and in her texts strike Cowley as impossibly constraining. "I feel encompassed with chains when I write," she concludes, "which check me in my happiest flights, and force me continually to reflect not whether *this is just?* but, whether *this is safe?*" (vi). That metaphor of enchainment aptly characterizes the regulatory experience Cowley and her female peers underwent in the reviewing press, as well as pointing to the causes of those fundamental divisions in reviewers' overall responses to them. For the practice of embodying female presences in both the printed texts and stage productions of women dramatists provoked imperatives to regulate those works as so many conflicting, sometimes appropriate but often threatening performances of gender identity, as was the case with female actors, to be alternately welcomed, endorsed, contained, and resisted.[70]

The centrality of this mode of regulation in the reviewing of women dramatists, as well as its intrinsic divisions, may be traced in vigilant critical concerns with forms of appropriate female behavior in women's dramatic writing, their impact on broader social codes of gender relations, and the potential danger of their subversion. Many reviewers welcome Cowley on to the boards precisely because of her readiness, in spite of her chaffing at gendered expectations, to provide numerous examples of conventional female decorum both in her works and in her own life. Her dramas please *The European Magazine*, for instance, specifically on account of their consistent delineation of models of female gentility and propriety: "Her favorite idea of female character is – a combination of the purest innocence of conduct with the greatest vivacity of manners . . . Every female performer who deems herself capable of personating a gentlewoman will at times have recourse to her works."[71] The *European* reviewer finds these staged examples of proper female behavior so valuable because they afford compelling models for women's appropriate social roles. Cowley herself made such an important link between stage and social identities, the reviewer concludes, by living out her own ideals of feminine propriety, shunning "public celebrity" in order to seek out "the shades of private life" where she assiduously devoted herself to the roles of dedicated mother, wife, and daughter.[72] *The Imperial Review* finds Baillie particularly commendable for establishing the same kind of interconnected gender models, as she demonstrates "singular felicity in portraying female excellence" based on her own "original" example.[73]

When Baillie departs from that example in her writing practices, however, she receives severe reproofs, such as Jeffrey's condemnation of barbarous "horrors" in *Ethwald* (1802) delineated perversely by "the delicate hand of a female."[74] Felicia Hemans is similarly chastised for revealing an excessive delight in bloodshed that makes *The Vespers of Palermo* (1823) "too sanguinary."[75] And Mary Berry's *Fashionable Friends* (1802) was hissed off the Drury Lane stage because of the gross impropriety of its female delineation of "loose principles."[76] Perhaps the most graphic indication of the gender threats such indiscretions could pose emerges in Byron's cynical acknowledgment of the starkly unfeminine incorporation of a masculine bodily presence in Baillie's tragic writing: "When Voltaire was asked why no woman has ever written even a tolerable tragedy? 'Ah (said the Patriarch) the composition of a tragedy requires *testicles*'. – If this be true Lord knows what Joanna Baillie does – I suppose she borrows them."[77] Such smirking asides in Byron's writing, like his scoffing at "Mrs. He-Mans," usually mask anxiousness about female strength while seeking to contain it. Given the tendency among period reviewers to locate female embodiment throughout women's dramatic writing, it should not be surprising to find extreme gender dislocations like the ones Baillie, Hemans, Berry, and other female dramatists could pose generating anxiousness on a much broader scale as well as extensive attempts at containment. It is in these various strategies of regulation that we may trace the most complicated forms of doubling responses in the reviewing of women dramatists – openness designed to enforce gender propriety coupled with resistance aimed at containing its potential subversion.

This general posture of regulation emerges most obviously in recurrent forms of semi-parodic, often condescending gallantry that welcomes women dramatists while gendering them as proper, and usually vulnerable, ladies.[78] Hunt introduces his discussion of current stage performances by acknowledging that "gallantry" obliges him to begin "with the ladies."[79] *The British Stage, and Literary Cabinet* similarly insists on its "gallantry" when judging "the female part of the theatrical community."[80] Pervading reviews of women dramatists and actors, this chivalric mode represents them as so many "fair authors," "Ladies," "Misses," and "Inventresses," whose gender identity renders them fundamentally weak and in need of deferential treatment.[81] Thus expressing a chivalric welcome that enforces both female propriety and subordination, *The British Stage, and Literary Cabinet* refuses to put its "gallantry to the test" by commenting too rigorously on the talent of female performers.[82] In order to display the same spirit of "courtesy," *The Critical Review* curtails the "freedom of our animadversions" on Baillie's plays.[83] *The Imperial Review* concludes that male critics should always exert such "cheering indulgence" to underprivileged "female writer[s]" and claims to pull its punches on Baillie because of its uneasiness "to use a strong word in speaking of a Lady's work."[84] Purportedly benevolent deference of this sort not only assumes a fundamental inferiority among women dramatists, it also positions them as submissive females in want of gentle instruction from superior male critics.

To justify the necessity of this tutorial relation to patient subjects, some reviewers emphasize women's basic lack of education and general ignorance of the rules of dramatic composition. "A female writer," explains *The Imperial Review,* has many impediments to surmount before she can rise to a given height in literature." She must "fabricate for herself" the advantages of a male education.[85] It is thus "very difficult" for a female dramatist "not educated learnedly," adds *The British Critic,* "entirely to avoid" serious "blunders."[86] By stressing the elemental character of these "blunders," which consist of basic errors in grammar, language, versification, and dramatic logic, many reviewers consign even powerful dramatists like Baillie to a kind of infantile status. She commits many mistakes "in prosody and strict construction," and she suffers from "a very vicious pronunciation" of certain words.[87] "She seems to have no ear for the melody of blank verse" and her grammatical errors "certainly would not be tolerated in a schoolboy's first copy of English verses."[88] Brand is similarly told that her "female mind" has not yet learned how to arrange syllables effectively into poetic meter.[89] Sophia Burrell has yet to master "the knowledge of dramatic contrivance, and the art of versification."[90] Such elemental flaws are repeatedly invoked to enjoin women dramatists to sit obediently at the feet of more learned, male advisors. "We earnestly exhort Miss Baillie," concludes Jeffrey, to keep her "tragedies in her portfolio; and not to give any new ones to the world, till she has submitted them to the revision of some experienced and impartial friend . . . an instructor in taste."[91] Such an "impartial" advisor, *Blackwood's* makes clear, should be a "judicious male friend . . ."[92] *A Monthly Review* critic gives the same advice to any "young lady" desirous of writing plays and offers to fulfill the role of "friendly" advisor for one such "lady," Hannah Brand, who stands in need of considerable "instruct[ion]."[93] Such "friendly" scenes of instruction, strategically peppered throughout the field of Romantic-era drama reviewing welcome women writers on to the stage precisely in order to contain female exertions within the power dynamics of established gender relations.

That process of containment becomes particularly acute, as in reviews of female actors, when women dramatists threaten to push beyond accepted models of "propriety," specifically in their attempts at tragedy. Where Hazlitt cautions Eliza O'Neill against painfully defeminizing herself in acting out "physical horrors,"[94] *The Analytical Review* warns Mary Robinson not to mix the splendid decorum of her "natural," feminine muse with an alien "vehemence of passion" required for tragedy.[95] Jane West receives similar admonitions against tragic writing, which requires levels of "energy" and "agitat[ion]" inappropriate for her "soft and gentle" female "character."[96] Even Baillie, widely recognized as the greatest writer of tragedies since Shakespeare, provokes intensely hostile reactions when she appears to breach the limits of female decorum in staging spectacles of horror. Jeffrey revolts at the "bloodiness" and "barbarity" of murder scenes in *Ethwald* specifically because they are "delineated" in a perverse fashion "by the delicate hand of a female."[97] Keeping such female hands delicate, both in and out of the theatre, may have been the central goal of these various attempts to curb women's dramatic experimentation. Yet the very necessity of throwing up such barriers implies a persisting, potentially uncontainable incursion by women dramatists across the gender limits of their time. And the palpable force of that threat within the discursive field of drama reviewing signals one of the more volatile clashes of gender ideologies in Romantic-era writing.

This apprehension of a relentless, invasive threat registers obliquely, yet with intriguing resonance, throughout reviews of women dramatists, particularly in those which labor strenuously to impose checks on female dramatic genius. In a generally positive review of Inchbald's *To Marry, or Not to Marry*, for instance, Thomas Holcroft worries that the play's representation of aggressive female matchmaking will provide a "mislead[ing]" and "dangerous" incentive for women to "throw off" indispensable models of "decency and propriety of conduct."[98] Inchbald's depiction of female gambling in

Wives as they were, and Maids as they are (1797) strikes *The British Critic* as similarly "overcharged" and subversive of proper female "charms and attractions."[99] Baillie's various types of dramatic innovations provoke the strongest examples of this anxiousness, even among reviewers generally appreciative of her talent. An *Eclectic Review* critic praises *De Monfort* (1798) as "the most original tragedy of the present age," but also expresses discomfort with "the fair author's" indecorous desire, quite opposite from Cowley's appropriate reticence, to obtrude her works on the stage in an excessive "partiality for *the boards*."[100]

That apprehension of invasive excess surfaces with revealing intensity in Jeffrey's series of *Edinburgh Review* articles on Baillie's plays on the passions. His 1803 review of Baillie's second volume repeatedly stresses her "violation" of female propriety and conventional dramatic practice. Curiously troubled, Jeffrey feels "at a loss" to account for her "strange caprice," her "vulgarity," her "voluntary perversity," and her "wanton . . . violation[s] of all our customary associations." This striking language of sexual transgression suggests deep uneasiness about bodily forms of female excess, a worry that surfaces openly in Jeffrey's complaint about Baillie's overeagerness to "obtrude" herself on the characters and actions of her stage.[101] The same apprehension persists ten years later in Jeffrey's response to Baillie's third volume, which continues the accusations of her "pervers[ity]" and "perpetual . . . sinn[ing]" in bringing herself "forward" in "a way so obtrusive."[102] Something about the experiments of Baillie and her female peers clearly resisted containment and posed graphically material, "wanton" threats to gender norms both on the stage and throughout the broader public arena it embodied.

A key to the precise nature of this violation may very well lie with the specific feature of Baillie's experimentation that provoked those vexed responses from Jeffrey – her theory of staging the passions; not simply the dramaturgical nuts and bolts of her theory, but the very act itself of theorizing dramatic writing and performance. It is the "pretensions" of the "theorist" that so bothers Jeffrey and motivates negative reactions even from generally supportive critics (263). Thus *The Critical Review* typically finds the theoretical "purpose" of her "dramatic system" fatally "injur[ing]" even the "best" of her tragedies.[103] Baillie's theorizing seemed particularly "pretentious" and injurious for a "fair author" because it transformed the stage as an embodiment of female beauty, the proper charm of Hazlitt's "fine lady," into the embodiment of strong female consciousness – what Jeffrey rebukes as the "traits" of Baillie's "own . . . character" perversely imposed upon the stage (267).

That specific "obtrusion" of female intelligence proved all the more destabilizing because of its central insistence on staging, testing, and modifying conventional gender identities as well as gendered modes of social relations. Baillie's theatre theory of "sympathetic curiosity," as Catherine Burroughs and Anne Mellor[104] have perceptively argued, calls for a theatrical revolution that will foreground the performance and examination of different gender identities within the "secret closet" in order to reconstitute and harmonize gender relations in the public sphere.[105] This theoretical focus on the sympathies of private life will transform the theatre into a national school for the domestication or feminizing of the public sphere, diffusing what Mellor calls a female "ethic of care" into the interactions of, as Baillie sees it, the "Judge . . . Magistrate . . . Advocate; and . . . ruler[s] or conductor[s] of other men . . ."[106] That such a plan to re-stage gender relations provoked some of the most hostile reactions to Baillie is evident in Hazlitt's irritable attempt to re-impose conventional gender hierarchies on her theoretical stage. To him, that stage is no more than a girlish place, reduced to "baby-house theatricals" by a theoretical system that treats "grown men and women as little girls treat their dolls . . ."[107] The hyperbole of these dismissive remarks, coupled with Baillie's undeniably high renown, suggests, in the end, just how difficult it was to contain her threat within a "baby-house" theatre.

Hazlitt's sharp interaction with Baillie may very well epitomize the interplay between Romantic-era reviewers and women drama-tists at its most contentious level. For revisionary theorizing of gender on- and offstage, like Baillie's, recurs frequently in the drama criticism of her female contemporaries, who became "reviewing women" in their own right through the publication of theoretical play prefaces.[108] In an extended preface to her plays, West proposes a major overhaul of the national drama that would transform it into a feminine school for promoting "the amiable virtues of domestic life" and suffusing them into a regenerated, and reengendered, social sphere.[109] Cowley, in a preface to her comedy, *The Town Before You* (1795), also envisions the theatre as a feminized site of social reeducation, a "great National School" where a "mother can lead her daughters."[110] Inchbald's prefaces to the twenty-five volumes of *The British Theatre* (1806–08) subtly transform the theatre from a platform for demeaning gender stereotypes – Sheridan's Mrs. Malaprop as alleged evidence against "the advance of female knowledge in Great Britain" – into a pantheon of female talent where Joanna Baillie emerges as "a woman of genius" and Sarah Siddons establishes the "charm" of "mental powers . . . in the female sex."[111] Inchbald rather sensationally pushes this sustained reengendering of theatrical life into the social sphere when she spars publicly with George Colman the Younger about the gender politics of drama reviewing. In response to her published strictures on his dramatic writing, Colman accused Inchbald of feminine incapacity and tried to dismiss her judgment as the inappropriate product of "feminine fingers" not destined for such a "rough task." Inchbald publishes these condescending insults and fires back the last, ironic words by promoting, among the many "dramatic prodigies" of the era, her own right as a "female observer" and "unlettered woman" to enter the lists of "periodical" dispute with "learned" males.[112] That such a prodigy of female intrusiveness first roused Colman's ire and then thwarted his attempt to squelch it reveals both the intensity and the potential uncontainability of those disturbances to gender norms, within and beyond the theatre, posed by women dramatists, actors, and performance theorists.

Inchbald, to be sure, felt mortified by the public scandal caused by this exchange and refused to accept any new offers to publish dramatic criticism. Such an experience only reinforced the need that she recognized, along with most of her female contemporaries in the theatre, for caution and restraint whenever pushing near the boundaries of gender propriety. But that very pressure to stay within the walls of the "baby-house" theatre also demonstrates how charged the stage, and writings related to it, had become as a cultural site of intensive gender destabilizations. And it is in the deeply divided, uneasily defensive process of reviewing women writers within such a volatile arena that we may trace some of the most striking material fault lines of their impact on the clashing gender ideologies of their time.

NOTES

1 Studies of Romantic-era drama have undergone several striking developments over the last two decades, moving from a series of excellent

works on interiorized mental drama, such as Alan Richardson's *A Mental Theater: Poetic Drama and Consciousness in the Romantic Age* (University Park: Pennsylvania State University Press, 1988), Jeffrey Cox's *In the Shadows of Romance: Romantic Tragic Drama in Germany, England, and France* (Athens: Ohio State University Press, 1987), and Janet Ruth Heller's *Coleridge, Lamb, Hazlitt, and the Reader of Drama* (Columbia: University of Missouri Press, 1990), to more recent materialist analyses of the historical and political contexts of dramatic writing in the Romantic period, such as Daniel Watkins's *A Materialist Critique of English Romantic Drama* (Gainesville: University Press of Florida, 1993) and the special issues on Romantic drama edited by Terence Hoagwood and Daniel Watkins for *The Wordsworth Circle* 23 (1992), and by Theresa Kelley for *Texas Studies in Literature and Language* 38 (1996). With few exceptions, however, these works concentrate on the period's male writers. Despite the appearance of these important studies, it has always been an uphill fight to establish the equal significance of Romantic drama in relation to the other major genres, which may explain why the major recovery work on women writers over the last decade has not considered dramatists extensively. Joanna Baillie is just beginning to attract substantial attention; see, in particular, Anne Mellor, "Joanna Baillie and the Counter-Public Sphere," *Studies in Romanticism* 33 (1994), pp. 559–67), and Catherine Burroughs, "English Romantic Women Writers and Theatre Theory: Joanna Baillie's Prefaces to the *Plays on the Passions*" in *Re-Visioning Romanticism: British Women Writers, 1776–1837*, ed. Carol Shiner Wilson and Joel Haefner (Philadelphia: University of Pennsylvania Press, 1994), 274–96; Catherine Burroughs, *Closet Stages: Joanna Baillie and the Theater Theory of British Romantic Women Writers* (Philadelphia: University of Pennsylvania Press, 1997). Burroughs, in *Closet Stages*, as well as Ellen Donkin, *Getting into the Act: Women Playwrights in London, 1776–1829* (London: Routledge, 1995) have recently initiated more comprehensive analyses of women's dramatic writing, performance theory, and theatrical activities during the Romantic era.
2 Ellen Donkin, *Getting into the Act.*
3 Burroughs, *Closet Stages*, p. 2.
4 Julie Carlson, *In the Theatre of Romanticism: Coleridge, Nationalism, Women* (Cambridge University Press, 1994), p. 150.
5 Joanna Baillie, "To the Reader" in vol. II of *A Series of Plays: In Which It Is Attempted to Delineate the Stronger Passions of the Mind*, 3 vols. (London: T. Cadell, 1802, vii–xi, p. vii).
6 "Z," "Cockney School of Poetry. No. IV," *Blackwood's Edinburgh Magazine* 3 (August, 1818), pp. 519–24, p. 519.
7 David Garrick, "Prologue" to *Percy, A Tragedy.* By Hannah More (London: T. Cadell, 1778), p. 13.
8 Periodical reviews were generally published anonymously during the Romantic era, which makes the identification of authors difficult and

frequently impossible. However, it is certain that the reviewing industry was dominated by men, despite some female incursions, throughout the period. Many periodicals grew out of men's learned societies and continued as staunchly male institutions throughout their publishing years. Compilations of periodical reviewers, such as Benjamin Nangle's *The Monthly Review, Second Series 1790–1815* (Oxford: Clarendon Press, 1955) and Elisabeth Schneider, Irwin Griggs, and John D. Kearn's "Early Edinburgh Reviewers: A New List," *Modern Philology* 43 (1946), pp. 192–210, reveal a nearly exclusive field of male reviewers. Exceptions, of course, did emerge, but mostly in relation to those forms of writing widely associated with women's investments: fiction, poetry, and educational literature. Mary Hays, Anna Barbauld, and Mary Shelley all produced literary reviews in these fields, but they commented very little on contemporary drama. Mary Wollstonecraft wrote more than two dozen drama reviews among her many contributions to *The Analytical Review*, but her entries on the drama consist of short notices, sometimes only a few sentences, rather than sustained commentary. Some women's magazines, such as *La Belle Assemblée*, featured reviews by women writers. However, the drama section of *La Belle Assemblée* offers only short notices of recent productions. Anna Larpent reviewed plays for licensing in the legitimate theatres, but her diary comments were never intended for publication. (For further discussion of Larpent, see Jeffrey Cox's essay in this volume.) For the purposes of this essay, then, I will focus primarily on the reviewing of women dramatists by men, assuming male authorship for anonymous drama reviews in periodicals not self-designated as women's magazines. Nevertheless, women did find creative ways to write back to the drama reviewing establishment, mainly in the form of prefaces to plays, and I will turn to such an alternative presence of "reviewing women" at the end of this chapter. For a fuller understanding of the deep material impact of the gender politics at work in these reviewing exchanges see the following, more general, studies of the political significance of the reviewing industry during the Romantic period: Derek Roper, *Reviewing Before the Edinburgh, 1788–1802* (London: Methuen, 1978), Joanne Shattock, *Politics and Reviewers: The Edinburgh and the Quarterly in the Early Victorian Age* (Leicester University Press, 1987), and Greg Kucich, "'A Haunted Ruin': Romantic Drama, Renaissance Tradition, and the Critical Establishment," *The Wordsworth Circle* 23 (1992), pp. 64–76. See also Gay Gibson Cima, "'To Be Public as a Genius and Private as a Woman': The Critical Framing of Nineteenth-Century British Women Playwrights" in *Women and Playwriting in Nineteenth-Century Britain*, ed. Tracy C. Davis and Ellen Donkin (Cambridge University Press, 1999), pp. 35–53.

9 See Stuart Curran, "Romantic Poetry: The 'I' Altered" in *Romanticism and Feminism*, ed. Anne K. Mellor (Bloomington: University of Indiana

Press, 1988), pp. 185–207, and Anne K. Mellor, *Romanticism and Gender* (London: Routledge, 1993), p. 7.

10   "Plays, by Joanna Baillie," *The Imperial Review; or London and Dublin Literary Journal* I, 1804, pp. 335–44; II, 1804, pp. 89–97, I.338.

11   William Ward, ed., *Literary Reviews in British Periodicals. 1798–1820* (New York: Garland, 1972); *Literary Reviews in British Periodicals. 1821–1826* (New York: Garland, 1977); *Literary Reviews in British Periodicals. 1789–1797* (New York: Garland, 1979).

12   "Rev. of *Huniades, a Tragedy*, by Hannah Brand," *The European Magazine* 21 (1792), pp. 66–67, p. 66.

13   "Rev. of *The Mysterious Marriage, or the Hermit of Roselva*, by Harriet Lee," *The Monthly Mirror* 5 (March, 1798), pp. 166–69, p. 166.

14   "Account of Mrs. Inchbald's New Comedy [*Wives as They Were*]," *The Lady's Magazine* 28 (1797), pp. 119–23, p. 120.

15   "Miss Baillie's Plays," *The Literary Journal, or Universal Review of Literature Domestic and Foreign* 5 (1805), pp. 49–64, p. 51.

16   "Mrs. Cowley's *Works*," *The Anti-Jacobin Review* (February, 1814), pp. 134–38, pp. 134; 136.

17   Richard Polwhele, *The Unsex'd Females* in *British Literature 1780–1830*, ed. Anne K. Mellor and Richard E. Matlak (New York: Harcourt, 1996), p. 49.

18   "Plays by Joanna Baillie," II: 92.

19   "Rev. of *A Day in Turkey; or The Russian Slaves*, by Hannah Cowley," *The Critical Review* 4 (1792), pp. 323–26, p. 323.

20   "Rev. of *A Day in Turkey; or The Russian Slaves*, by Hannah Cowley," *The European Magazine* 21 (1792), pp. 443–46, p. 444.

21   Hannah Cowley, "Preface" to *A Day in Turkey; or The Russian Slaves* (London: G. J. and J. Robinson, 1792), pp. i–iii, p. i.

22   Leigh Hunt, reviewing Tom Moore's *M. P.; or, The Blue Stocking*, representatively laments, "The degraded condition of the modern drama has long been a matter of ridicule, regret, or contempt . . ." (*Leigh Hunt's Dramatic Criticism*, ed. Lawrence Hustorn Houtchens and Carolyn Washburn Houtchens [New York: Columbia University Press, 1949], p. 52). Sharing that view, Thomas Beddoes labels Romantic drama "a haunted ruin" (Thomas Lovell Beddoes, *The Letters of Thomas Lovell Beddoes*, ed. Edmund Gosse [New York: Macmillan, 1894], p. 51); and Matthew Lewis, deploring a voracious public demand for sensational spectacle, doubts in the Preface to his *Alfonso, King of Castile* "whether even an *excellent* Tragedy . . . would succeed on the Stage at present" (Matthew Lewis, "Preface" to *Alfonso, King of Castile* [London: J. Bell, 1801], pp. iv–vii, p. vi). For detailed studies of Romantic-era resistance to the stage and pronouncements of the drama's collapse, see Timothy Webb's "The Romantic Poet and the Stage: A Short, Sad History," in *The Romantic Theatre: An International Symposium*, ed. Richard Allen Cave (Totowa, NJ: Barnes and Noble Books, 1986), pp. 9–46, and

Terry Otten's *The Deserted Stage: The Search for Dramatic Form in Nineteenth-Century England* (Athens: Ohio University Press, 1972).

23 For important qualifications of current critical views of Romantic "anti-theatricality" and despair about the drama, see Donkin's *Getting into the Act*, as well as the special issues on Romantic drama edited by Hoagwood and Watkins for the *Wordsworth Circle*, and Kelley, *Texas Studies in Literature and Language* 38.

24 William Hazlitt, *A View of the English Stage; or A Series of Dramatic Criticisms* (London: Robert Stoddart, 1818), p. ix.

25 William Hazlitt, "The Drama. No. I," *The London Magazine* 1 (Jan.–June, 1820), pp. 64–70, p. 64.

26 "Analytical Essays on the Modern English Drama," *Blackwood's Edinburgh Magazine* 18 (July 1825), pp. 119–30, p. 119. Elizabeth Inchbald is one who did forcefully elaborate on such counter-claims for the progress of the national drama, arguing in the Preface to her *Every One Has His Fault* (1793):

It is said, that modern dramas are the worst that ever appeared on the English stage, – yet it is well known, that the English theatres never flourished as they do at present . . . never was there such high remuneration conferred upon every person, and every work, belonging to the drama.

A new play, which, from a reputed wit of former times, would not, with success, bring him a hundred pounds, a manager now will purchase, from a reputed blockhead, at the price of near a thousand; and sustain all risk whether it be condemned or not.

Great must be the attraction of modern plays to repay such speculation. (Elizabeth Inchbald, "Preface" to *Every One Has His Fault*. By Elizabeth Inchbald in vol. XXIII of *The British Theatre* [London: Longman, 1808], pp. 3–4).

27 "Mrs. Cowley's *Works*," *The European Magazine* 66 (August–September, 1814), pp. 128–30; 232–34, p. 234.

28 "Rev. of *What is She?* by Charlotte Smith," *The Anti-Jacobin Review* 3 (June, 1799), pp. 150–55, p. 150.

29 "Dialogue on the Drama," *The Theatrical Inquisitor* (February, 1820), pp. 74–76, p. 75.

30 "Rev. of *The Mysterious Marriage*," p. 166; "Account," p. 120.

31 "Miss. J. Baillie's *Series of Plays. Vol. II*," *The British Critic* 20 (1802), pp. 184–94, p. 194; "Miss Baillie's Plays," *The Eclectic Review* 10 (1813), pp. 21–32, 167–86, p. 173; "Plays, by Joanna Baillie," p. 97; "Miss Baillie's Plays," *The Literary Journal*, pp. 51–52.

32 "Miss Baillie's *Series of Plays*," *The Critical Review* 37 (February, 1803), pp. 200–21, p. 212.

33 "Miss J. Baillie's Miscellaneous Plays," *The British Critic* 27 (January, 1806), pp. 22–28, p. 22.

34 "Baillie's *Series of Plays*," *The Annual Review; and History of Literature* 1 (1802), pp. 680–85, p. 680.

35 Walter Scott, *Essay on the Drama. Essays on Chivalry, Romance, and the Drama* (London: Frederick Warne, n.d.), p. 223.

36 "Celebrated Female Writers. No. I. Joanna Baillie," *Blackwood's Edinburgh Magazine* 16 (August, 1824), pp. 162–78, pp. 162; 165.

37 William Hazlitt, *Lectures on the English Poets*, ed. Catherine MacDonald MacLean (London: Dent, 1967), pp. 146–47.

38 "Celebrated Female Writers," p. 178.

39 "Miss Baillie's *Miscellaneous Plays*," *The Monthly Review* 49 (March, 1806), pp. 303–10, p. 303.

40 "*Julian, a Tragedy*, by Miss Mitford," *The Monthly Censor, or General Review of Domestic & Foreign Literature* 2 (April, 1823), pp. 452–60, p. 458.

41 "Rev. of *To Marry or Not to Marry*, by Elizabeth Inchbald," *The Anti-Jacobin Review* 21 (1805), p. 208.

42 "Mrs. West's *Poems and Plays*," *The Critical Review* 27 (October, 1799), pp. 131–36, p. 134.

43 "Rev. of *The Three Strangers*, by Harriet Lee," *The Monthly Review* (January, 1826), pp. 138–47, p. 147.

44 Donkin, *Getting into the Act*, treats eighteenth-century debates about female conduct as a central concern throughout her analysis of the social restraints imposed upon women actors and dramatists. See also William Galperin's "The Theatre at Mansfield Park: From Classic to Romantic Once More," *Eighteenth-Century Life* 16 (1992), pp. 247–71.

45 William Hazlitt, *A View of the English Stage; or A Series of Dramatic Criticisms*, p. vi.

46 *Ibid.*, p. 148.

47 William Hazlitt, "The Drama. No. II," *The London Magazine* 1 (Jan.–June, 1820), pp. 162–68, p. 165.

48 "Mrs. W. S. Chatterley," *The British Stage, and Literary Cabinet* 4 (1820), p. 238.

49 William Hazlitt, *A View of the English Stage; or A Series of Dramatic Criticisms*, p. 192.

50 "Memoir of Miss O'Neill," *The Theatrical Inquisitor* 8 (May, 1816), pp. 326–32, p. 329; and "Memoir of Mrs. Horn," *The Theatrical Inquisitor* 8 (May, 1816), pp. 323–26, p. 324.

51 James Henry Leigh Hunt, *Critical Essays on the Performers of the London Theatres* (London: John Hunt, 1807), p. 156.

52 William Hazlitt, "The Drama. No. I," p. 69.

53 James Henry Leigh Hunt, *Critical Essays on the Performers of the London Theatres*, p. 204.

54 "Madame Vestris," *The British Stage, and Literary Cabinet* 5 (1821), pp. 1–3, p. 1.

55 James Henry Leigh Hunt, *Critical Essays on the Performers of the London Theatres*, p. 177.

56 *Ibid.*, p. 156.

57 James Henry Leigh Hunt, *Leigh Hunt's Dramatic Criticism*, p. 264.

58 "On the Present State of the Drama," *The Universal Magazine of Knowledge and Pleasure* 92 (May, 1793), pp. 357–60, p. 360.

59 "Rev. of *To Marry or Not to Marry*, by Elizabeth Inchbald," *The Anti-Jacobin Review*, p. 208.

60 "Rev. of *Every One Has His Fault*, by Elizabeth Inchbald," *The European Magazine* 23 (1793), pp. 148–49, p. 149.

61 "Plays and Poems, by Miss H. Brand," *The British Critic* 11 (May, 1798), pp. 525–28, p. 525.

62 "Miss Edgeworth's Comic Drama," *The Quarterly Review* 17 (April, 1817), pp. 96–107, p. 104.

63 "Mrs. West's *Poems and Plays*," *The Monthly Review* 30 (November, 1799), pp. 262–64, p. 263.

64 "Rev. of *The Family Legend*, by Joanna Baillie," *The British Critic* 38 (July, 1811), pp. 53–59, p. 53. The theoretical views on stagecraft expressed by many women dramatists certainly contributed to this critical emphasis on the representational embodiment of their works. Baillie and West, for instance, explain in prefaces to their collections of printed plays (Joanna Baillie, "Preface" *Miscellaneous Plays* [London: Longman, 1804], pp. iii–xix; Jane West, "Preface to the Plays" in vol. iv, *Poems and Plays* [London: Longman, 1799], pp. iii–xv, 4 vols.) that they have decided to publish their unacted plays with the express intention of promoting experimental, stageworthy models for reforming current modes of theatrical representation. Inchbald was convinced that such investments in the life of the stage had thoroughly renewed London's theatrical life by 1808, much to the detriment of closet plays. "Plays of former times," she concludes, "were written to be read, not seen. Dramatic authors succeeded in their aim; their works were placed in libraries, and the theatres were deserted. – Now, plays are written to be seen, not read – and present authors gain their views; for they and the managers are enriched, and the theatres crowded . . ." (Elizabeth Inchbald, "Preface to *The Dramatist; or Stop Him Who Can*." By Frederick Reynolds, in vol. xx of *The British Theatre*, pp. 3–5, p. 3).

65 Edgeworth is also told by *The British Critic*, for instance, that her comic dramas should be retitled "Dramatic Narratives" because they "have very little in them adapted to the stage . . ." ("Miss Edgeworth's Comic Dramas" [*The British Critic* 7, May 1817, pp. 506–14]), p. 513. *The Annual Review*, disputing the *Anti-Jacobin*'s verdict, claims that Inchbald is ultimately "incompetent" at "satirical representation" (Rev. of *To Marry or Not to Marry*, by Elizabeth Inchbald [*The Annual Review and History of Literature* 4, 1805, p. 640]. Jane West's dramaturgy seems equally hopeless to *The Annual*: "In dramatic efforts she has failed" ("Rev. of *Poems and Plays. Vols. III–IV*, by Jane West" [*The Annual Review and History of Literature* 4, 1805, pp. 602–04], p. 602). Although some critics remain convinced that Baillie's theoretical modes of performing separate passions in each play "would have great effect upon the stage" ("Baillie's Series of Plays," p. 681), the majority react negatively to her performance theory and practice. Her theoretical "*purpose*" of analyzing

a single passion in each play strikes many reviewers as a fatal constraint on "dramatic effect" ("Joanna Baillie's *Series of Plays*" [*The Critical Review* 1, May 1812, pp. 449–62, p. 449]). To some, the intensive psychological interiority of plays like *De Monfort* render it impossible to stage her works successfully within the "present preposterous size . . . [of] our theatres . . ." ("Miss Baillie's *Series of Plays*," p. 206). Others find her alternative efforts to write for large theatres, as in *Constantine Paleologus*, encouraging impossibly large scenic effects and excessive stage "bustle" ("Miss Baillie's Miscellaneous Plays," p. 307). Still others focus on her moral intrusiveness and "laborious stage-directions" as serious draw-backs on the theatrical "interest" of her plays ("Miss Baillie's Plays" [*The Eclectic Review*, p. 31]).

66 "Miss Baillie's Plays," *The Eclectic Review*, pp. 168, 31.

67 Francis Jeffrey, "Miss Baillie's *Plays on the Passions*," *The Edinburgh Review* 2 (July, 1803), pp. 269–86, pp. 277, 280.

68 William Hazlitt, *Lectures on the English Poets*, p. 147.

69 Hannah Cowley, "Preface" to *A School for Greybeards; or, the Mourning Bride* (London: G. J. and J. Robinson, 1786, pp. iii–ix), p. v.

70 Donkin, *Getting into the Act*, elaborates on the material pressures within the theatrical world that women's playwriting exerted against estab-lished gender norms: "Playwriting, as a profession, violated all the rules of conduct. It conferred on women a public voice. It gave them some control over how women were represented on stage. It required that they mingle freely with people of both sexes in a place of work that was not the home. It made ambition a prerequisite, and, perhaps most importantly, it offered the possibility of acquiring capital. In other words, playwriting was something of a loophole; it allowed women to push the system considerably further than it was prepared to go . . . When women started writing for the theatre, no matter how innocuous the material, male critics were quick to sense that something was slipping out of their control" (18, 38).

71 "Mrs. Cowley's *Works*," p. 130.

72 *Ibid.*, pp. 129, 233.

73 "Plays, by Joanna Baillie," p. 90.

74 Francis Jeffrey, "Miss Baillie's *Plays on the Passions*," p. 280.

75 "Mrs. Hemans's *Vespers of Palermo*," *The Monthly Review, or Literary Journal* 102 (December, 1823), pp. 164–69, p. 169.

76 Cited in Donkin, *Getting into the Act*, p. 159.

77 George Gordon Byron, vol. v of *Byron's Letters and Journals*, ed. Leslie A. Marchand (Harvard University Press, 1973–81), p. 203. 12 vols.

78 Donkin, *Getting into the Act*, traces Garrick's establishment of an "ethos of gallantry" toward women playwrights earlier in the eighteenth century and finds this attitude disappearing around the turn of the nineteenth century as theatre managers grew increasingly resistant to women writers (159). The regulating form of gallantry I discuss, though,

continues to operate in the reviewing press throughout the Romantic era.

79 James Henry Leigh Hunt, *Leigh Hunt's Dramatic Criticism*, p. 87.
80 "Mrs. Gibbs," *The British Stage and Literary Cabinet* 2 (1818), pp. 217–18, p. 217.
81 "Rev. of *The Battle of Waterloo, a Tragedy*, by Mary Hornby," *The British Stage, and Literary Cabinet* 3 (May, 1819), pp. 131–33, p. 132; "Miss Baillie's Miscellaneous Plays," *The Imperial Review*, p. 262 ; Francis Jeffrey, "Miss Baillie's *Plays on the Passions*," p. 276; "Joanna Baillie's *Series of Plays*," p. 449.
82 "Miss Foote," *The British Stage, and Literary Cabinet*, 3 (1819), p. 1.
83 "Joanna Baillie's *Series of Plays*," p. 453.
84 "Plays, by Joanna Baillie" 1: 335; "Miss Baillie's *Miscellaneous Plays*," p. 262.
85 "Plays, by Joanna Baillie" 1: 335.
86 "Miss J. Baillie's *Miscellaneous Plays*," p. 28.
87 Francis Jeffrey, "Miss Baillie's *Plays on the Passions*," p. 285.
88 Francis Jeffrey, "Miss Baillie's *Plays on the Passions. Vol. III*," *The Edinburgh Review*, 19 (February, 1812), pp. 261–90, pp. 270, 272.
89 "Miss Brand's *Plays and Poems*," *The Monthly Review* 32 (August, 1800), pp. 377–81, p. 377.
90 "Rev. of *Theodora, or the Spanish Daughter; a Tragedy*, by Lady Sophia Burrell," *The British Critic* 16 (December, 1800), p. 682.
91 Francis Jeffrey, "Miss Baillie's *Miscellaneous Plays*," *The Edinburgh Review*, 5 (January, 1805), pp. 405–21, p. 421.
92 "Celebrated Female Writers," p. 178.
93 "Miss Brand's *Plays and Poems*," p. 377.
94 William Hazlitt, "The Drama. No. I," p. 69.
95 "Mrs. Robinson's *Sicilian Lover; a Tragedy*," *The Analytical Review* 23 (April, 1796), pp. 394–97, pp. 394; 396.
96 "Rev. of *Poems and Plays, Vols I–II*, by Jane West," *The Monthly Review* 30 (November, 1799), pp. 262–65, p. 263.
97 Francis Jeffrey, "Miss Baillie's *Plays on the Passions*," p. 280.
98 Thomas Holcroft, "Rev. of *To Marry, or Not to Marry*, by Elizabeth Inchbald," *The Theatrical Recorder* 1 (1805), pp. 208–13, p. 211.
99 "Rev. of *Wives as they were, and Maids as they are*, by Elizabeth Inchbald," *The British Critic* 10 (August, 1797), pp. 133–36, p. 133.
100 "Miss Baillie's Plays," p. 186.
101 Francis Jeffrey, "Miss Baillie's *Plays on the Passions*," pp. 277–78.
102 Francis Jeffrey, "Miss Baillie's *Plays on the Passions. Vol. III*," pp. 261, 267, 271.
103 "Joanna Baillie's *Series of Plays*," p. 449.
104 See Burroughs, *Closet Stages* and Anne K. Mellor, "Joanna Baillie and the Counter-Public Sphere," *Studies in Romanticism* 33 (1994), pp. 560–67.

105 Joanna Baillie, "Introductory Discourse" in vol. 1 of *A Series of Plays: In Which It Is Attempted to Delineate the Stronger Passions of the Mind* (London: T. Cadell, 1802), p. 30.

106 Mellor, "Joanna Baillie"; Baillie, "Introductory Discourse," p. 14.

107 Hazlitt, *Lectures on the English Poets*, p. 147.

108 In the opening two chapters of *Closet Stages*, Burroughs provides a particularly rich and comprehensive analysis of the various ways in which women dramatists of the Romantic era theorize social and theatrical performances of gender.

109 Jane West, "Preface to the Plays" in vol. iv *Poems and Plays* , pp. vii–x.

110 Hannah Cowley, "Preface" to *The Town Before You, A Comedy* (London: Longman, 1795), pp. ix–xi, p. xi; also published as a periodical review, "The Present State of the Stage, by Mrs. Cowley," *The Pocket Magazine; or, Elegant Repository of Useful and Polite Literature* 2 (1795), pp. 108–09, p. 109.

111 Elizabeth Inchbald, "Preface" to *De Monfort; A Tragedy*. By Joanna Baillie, vol. xxiv of *The British Theatre*, pp. 3–6; Inchbald, "Preface" to *Isabella; or The Fatal Marriage*. By Thomas Southerne, vol. vii of *The British Theatre*, pp. 3–5; Inchbald, "Preface" to *The Rivals*. By Richard Brinsley Sheridan, vol. xix of *The British Theatre*, pp. 3–5. For an illuminating discussion of Inchbald's formulation of a "distinctly feminist message" throughout her prefaces, see Anna Lott's "Sexual Politics in Elizabeth Inchbald," *Studies in English Literature* 34.3 (1994), pp. 635–48. Marvin Carlson's chapter in the present volume provides a detailed analysis of the transgressive nature of Inchbald's critical prefaces on the British drama.

112 Elizabeth Inchbald, "Preface" to *The Heir at Law*. By George Colman, the Younger, vol. xxi of *The British Theatre*, pp. i–ix.

Nations, Households, Dramaturgy

CHAPTER 3

Women and history on the Romantic stage: More, Yearsley, Burney, and Mitford

Katherine Newey

This chapter will examine the use of history in tragedy written by women playwrights in the late eighteenth and early nineteenth centuries. I am particularly interested in the ways that Hannah More, Ann Yearsley, Frances Burney, and Mary Russell Mitford (all better known for their work in other media) used public theatrical performance to participate in public discussions of the character of the English nation-state and English national identity in the shadow of the revolutions in America and France in 1776 and 1789. In a survey of a selection of tragedies that deal with episodes from English history, I argue that these Romantic women playwrights manipulated the cultural capital of historical tragedy in order to claim the citizenship largely denied them through other political and social institutions. Through their use of tragedy, More, Yearsley, Burney, and Mitford could claim both aesthetic and political serious-ness, inhabiting the apparently masculine realm of national politics on the stage when female voices were constrained or even proscribed from other arenas of public debate – most obviously that of Parliament. In using history and the high cultural form of tragedy, Romantic women playwrights were appropriating the "traditional authorit[ies] of those national objects of knowledge."[1] In this way, the authority of genre could be used to overcome the disabilities of gender.

Furthermore, I argue that a reinscription of the theatre and public stage performance – those largely forgotten endeavors of the Romantic period – into feminist literary history is important for contemporary scholarship, and might offer us a way out of the theoretical bind inherent in our focus on fiction. In her persuasive version of "the rise of the novel" as a political history, Nancy Armstrong argues that "the formation of the modern political state – in England at least – was accomplished largely through cultural

79

hegemony," and that this hegemony was achieved primarily through fiction:[2]

I regard fiction . . . both as the document and as the agency of cultural history. I believe it helped to formulate the ordered space we now recognize as the household, made that space totally functional, and used it as a context for representing normal behavior. In so doing, fiction contested and finally suppressed alternative bases for human relationships. In realizing this, one cannot . . . ignore the fact that fiction did a great deal to relegate vast areas of culture to the status of aberrance and noise. (23–24)

And the theatre is one of those "vast areas" relegated to "aberrance and noise." Armstrong's is an important argument, as it is an attempt to establish female culture and sociability as the center of a new kind of political history, but it is double-edged. The cultural hegemony that Armstrong finds is an ideological construction which rests on the relegation of women to the private, domestic sphere. Fiction, in this argument, is quite rightly seen as providing a forum for women's voices and the opportunity for exercising agency, not to mention gaining income for women writers; but it can also be an instrument in the division of experience into that series of binary oppositions with which we still struggle: masculine and feminine, public and private, history and domesticity. In writing tragedies from the source material of English history, Romantic women playwrights carefully and cautiously attempted to dissolve the limits of those binaries by forcing a confrontation between the spheres of public, masculine, political action and feminine domesticity and feeling. Through the plotlines of tragedy and its generic convention of the fall of the great man, these writers dramatized a feminist challenge to the exercise of extreme power and the actions of tyranny.

    The turn to history was not surprising, given the historical self-reflexivity of the American and French revolutions, and the speed with which the events of the French Revolution turned "from politics to history."[3] Unquestionably, the French Revolution was one of the great topics in late eighteenth- and early nineteenth-century England, becoming the paradigmatic revolution of history for succeeding generations.[4] English writers' contemplation of the events in France prompted interrogation of their own national past, as they attempted to find in history a mechanism of causality to explain and comment upon the events of the present. Julie Carlson argues that, in the context of the French Revolution, "History plays by the canonical poets dramatize contemporary reformulations of action, sovereignty, and the proper relation between the sexes."[5] Women playwrights' use of displaced history during the revolutionary period is of a piece with the broad cultural movements noted by Gary Kelly and Dror Wahrman: the "professional middle-class cultural revolution" in which language, and the rewriting of subjectivity[6] was focused through the French Revolution, literally "soaked in this one event."[7] So prevalent was this displacement of present political material into distant English history that Terence Hoagwood sees this feature of Romantic theatre writing as one of its paradigmatic strategies.[8] The use of history was prompted, as Kenneth Johnston and Joseph Nicholes argue in their discussion of Wordsworth's *The Borderers*, by the need to sublimate contemporary political concerns into historical narratives in order to pass the stringent censorship of the stage in this period.[9] But, I would argue, the desire to avoid rejection by the Examiner of Plays was only part of the reason for the widespread use of history in Romantic theatre; "historicity inhabits the Romantic works themselves"[10] and offers self-reflexive historical–political interpretations of plays, urged through their prologues and epilogues. Thinking historically, Romantic playwrights could create imagined communities in which qualities of nation and nationality could be explored, as Julie Carlson demonstrates in her lengthy discussion of Coleridge in this respect. For Romantic women playwrights, less assured of their right to pronounce as members of a Coleridgean clerisy or as Shelleyan legislators of the world, the historical consciousness of Romanticism enabled them to create imagined Englands. In these states, "Englishness" was characterized by female honor, and values of purity, piety, and filial respect, stoicism and steadiness, which were all represented as Saxon values. As well, these women playwrights created their versions of democratic rule, in which power was exercised legitimately through consensus, temperance, and moderation – not the extremism of fanaticism or tyranny.

However, this turn to history was not altogether unproblematic for women writers, as "history" was increasingly constructed as a masculine arena, connected to the role that middle- and upper-class men were destined to take as legislators and rulers of English social and political institutions. Gary Kelly notes that, in the immediate post-revolutionary period, the work of feminist historians such as Helen Maria Williams suffered from the "remasculinization of culture and literature. Williams's work, like that of other women

writers, was marginalized, trivialized, and excluded from the history
and historiography it had helped to make" (233). By 1837, when late
Romanticism had become early Victorianism, Thomas Carlyle's
history of the French Revolution was exemplary in constructing a
concept of history as encompassing all knowledge. But, as Christina
Crosby argues, such a unity of time and meaning was based on the
exclusion of women; historical truth demanded that women be
"beyond properly historical and political life."[11] In an age which
used historicity as the epistemological foundation of self and nation,
to be written out of history was to be erased as a citizen in a
fundamental way. Thus, a study of the use of history by women
playwrights in the Romantic period requires a focus on the shifting
relationship between gender and genre; I would argue that, in
Romantic women's use of historical verse tragedy, we must recognize
a dialectical movement between women's frustration at the barriers
of patriarchal theories of genre and the agency exercised by writing
tragedy.

I want to look first at the example of the politics of English
nationhood displaced as antiquarian interest, which Hannah More
creates in her play, *Percy* (1777), and the surprisingly iconoclastic view
of English history that emerges from this play. More wrote for the
theatre some ten years before the French Revolution, but just one
year *after* the American Revolution, and her view of the interaction
of public policy and private sensibility is bracingly critical of the
religious and political status quo. Her private comments at the time
suggest that More saw a connection between the theatre and the
American war, but as this letter to her sister shows, her interest was
in the way that the attractions of the theatre provided evidence of
her compatriots' frivolity:

What dreadful news from America! we are a disgraced, undone nation.
What a sad time to bring out a play in! when, if the country had the least
spark of virtue remaining, not a creature would think of going to it. But the
levity of the times will, on this occasion, be of some service to me.[12]

I do not wish to imply here that More's play anticipated the
radicalism of the French Revolution, but I do find it intriguing that
in 1777 More wrote and had produced, to great success, a play in
which the central female character protests clearly and passionately
against the linked powers of the Church and patriarchy in the figure
of her father. *Percy* is a play, furthermore, in which there is a strong

representation of the destructive actions of patriarchy on the female body, presented with all the generic codings of tragedy with its aesthetic and cultural capital.

Percy was first performed at Covent Garden early in the season for 1777–78. Genest, in his *Account of the English Stage*, judged it to be "superior to the generality of modern Tragedies," a judgment borne out by its playing nineteen times that season.[13] *Percy* remained in the repertoire for the next ten years, making it the seventeenth most popular woman's play in the period between 1660 and 1800, and, by the same calculations, the most frequently performed tragedy by a woman in this period.[14] *Percy* is set during the Crusades and concerns the feud between the Earls Douglas and Percy. Elwina, the daughter of Earl Raby, is the honorable but undefended woman caught between them. Before the play opens, Elwina, with her father's permission, has thought of Percy as her lover, until for political and dynastic reasons, Raby agreed with Douglas that Elwina should marry him (Douglas). Elwina obeyed her father and is faithful to Douglas in deed, but still loves Percy, a kind of technical infidelity, which is to cost her dearly. During the action of the play, Douglas finds out about her love for Percy and accuses her of dishonoring him (Douglas). Elwina is innocent, but, because she loves Percy still, she feels that she cannot insist on her fidelity. Douglas ambushes Percy and they fight, and Douglas slays Percy. After he has killed Percy, Douglas is forced to recognize Elwina's and Percy's honorable behavior, and his own unreasonable and dishonorable jealousy. Douglas's moment of realization comes when Elwina, no matter how she is publicly taunted by Douglas to admit her love for Percy, will not dishonor Douglas by doing so. When Elwina is reported to have poisoned herself, Douglas stabs himself, and the tragedy concludes with the usual complement of dead bodies on the stage.

The play opens at Castle Raby at the moment when the young men have just returned from the Crusades. In contrast to her father's often repeated regret at being too old to fight in Palestine, Elwina declares:

> When policy assumes religion's name,
> And wears the sanctimonious garb of faith,
> Only to colour fraud, and license murder,
> War then is tenfold guilt . . .
> 'Tis not the crosier, nor the pontiff's robe,

> The saintly look, nor elevated eye,
> Nor Palestine destroy'd, nor Jordan's banks
> Delug'd with blood of slaughtered infidels,
> No, nor th'extinction of the Eastern world,
> Nor all the mad pernicious, bigot rage
> Of your crusades, can bribe the pow'r, who see
> The motive with the act. O blind to think
> That cruel war can please the prince of peace!
> He who erects his altar in the heart,
> Abhors the sacrifice of human blood,
> And all the false devotion of that zeal,
> Which massacres the world he died to save.[15]

This is not Elwina's only outburst against the forces that shape her life, and which are controlled by the men around her. Several times Elwina refers to the use her father has made of her; for example, in telling Percy that she is now married to his enemy, Douglas, she cries:

> Oh! 'twas my father's deed! He made his child
> An instrument of vengeance on thy head.   (372)

And just before she dies of self-administered poison, she enters the stage deranged and talks to her father of the helpless lamb carelessly tended by its shepherd and left defenseless against death.

Metaphors of love and war are constantly intertwined, as if the characters can speak only of their private feelings in terms of public events. For example, Percy describes his feelings on coming home to find Elwina married to his enemy in terms of the incidents of battle:

> And have I 'scaped the Saracen's fell sword,
> Only to perish by Elwina's guilt?
> I wou'd have bar'd my bosom to the foe,
> I wou'd have died, had I but known you wish'd it.   (372)

The play is shot through with such violent imagery and infected by aggression and jealousy of personal and public honor. That such violent scenes within a family group occur just after they have been involved in a Holy War is not accidental. The return of the young men from the Crusades explicitly links state-sanctioned violence – Earl Raby's regret that he is too old to fight in Palestine is mostly his regret at being unable to serve his country – with domestic violence. More's use of Elwina as the protesting female, caught in the middle of these passions, questions the necessity for such violence, and shows us the results: the wandering and maddened Elwina, whose suicide was the tragic result of male notions of personal honor.

My analysis of More's play is inflected by surprise at its discovery of her apparent political nonconformism, given the dominant twentieth-century view of More as the "bad fairy" of feminism.[16] It is worth pausing here to consider More's participation in the public theatre in the light of current moves to complicate our understanding of her conservatism. More's politics may be more subversive than we have liked to think. Certainly More's choice of medium – the public stage – is transgressive enough of the propriety of the "proper lady" for her to feel compelled to make an extended *apologia* for her theatrical writing in the preface to her tragedies in her collected works. In this respect, any excursion into the professional theatre requires a more complex model of social engagement than the binary of conservative/subversive through which we have hitherto judged More. But More's social critique is not limited to her desire to convert "the Stage . . . into a school of virtue";[17] *Percy* is directly and rigorously critical of patriarchal political formations, an interpretation the older More herself glides over in her Preface.

The youthful More uses Elwina to make the outright criticism of war – in this case English participation in the Crusades – as "tenfold guilt" (359), a statement which condemns the use of the name of religion as justification for secular politics. Here More implies a connection between chauvinistic nationalism and violence, and self-serving deceit. Moreover, this connection is emphasized because it is not essential to the tragic plot for Elwina to feel this way – she could just as easily have expressed her horror for the Crusades because of the danger they posed to her beloved. But this specific condemnation of war as an instrument of public policy, inserted so early in the play, serves to structure and contextualize what might otherwise be a domestic family tragedy. More does not let us forget that the family tragedy is connected with the national project of the liberation of Palestine, and even though Elwina ultimately dies, her passionate voice protesting against war, and her active, physical stage presence inferred from her dialogue, provide More with a very public means of shaping discourse about national conflict. Two hundred years later, paying attention to More's use of genre and history allows us to see ways in which her writing does not need to be dismissed out of hand as patriarchal complicity.

In 1777, the American war might have provided urgent motivation
for the expression of opinions about the policy of the nation-state,
but, according to Hannah More, the apparent "levity of the times"
(cited in Roberts, 122) meant that such connections were not in the
forefront of audiences' (or censors') minds. By 1789, however, when
Ann Yearsley's play *Earl Goodwin* was first performed at the Theatre
Royal in Bristol, awareness of the volatility of political institutions
was more acute, as the revolution in France was much closer to
home, both geographically and politically. In taking up a topic from
the early history of England, Yearsley was, as Mary Waldron argues,
writing for "a contemporary audience interested in their past for
political reasons."[18] In case the audience had not realized this, a
topical interpretation of the play was pointed out to the audience in
Mr. Meyler's "Epilogue" to *Earl Goodwin*, spoken by Mrs. Smith,
which paralleled events in the reign of Edward the Confessor in the
eleventh century with the French Revolution:

> Lo! the poor Frenchman, long our nation's jest,
> Feels a new passion throbbing in his breast;
> From slavish, tyrant, priestly fetters free,
> For VIVE LE ROI, CRIES VIVE LA LIBERTÉ!
> And, daring now to ACT, as well as FEEL,
> Crushes the convent and the dread Bastile [*sic*]![19]

These lines were too directly political for the censor, however, and
the Lord Chamberlain required them to be cut from the play's
performance, although they survive in the published version,[20]
adding weight to the metatheatrical comment about the power of
action over feeling.

Mary Waldron has already discussed the political implications of
historical material of the play at some length; I want to add to this
discussion a consideration of the ways in which Yearsley deploys the
generic elements of verse tragedy to emphasize the political discourse of her play. Yearsley's use of situation and action herald the
beginning of what, just a few years later, became fully-fledged
Gothic melodrama. Paula Backscheider calls Gothic plays of this
period "fables of social identity" in which collective fears of "power
present everywhere and gone berserk" were revealed;[21] while not
mentioning the Gothic, Terence Hoagwood cites Raymond
Williams's perceptive reading of Romantic drama's "violence, fragmentation, and disorder" as figuring "the anxieties and conflicts of
the Revolutionary decades" (Hoagwood 52). Such descriptions are

apt for *Earl Goodwin*, which from its opening lines focuses attention on the legitimate and illegitimate exercise of power. As in Hannah More's *Percy*, men's political struggles are fought through the trial of female honor, allowing us see *Earl Goodwin* as a critique of a deeply embedded masculinist anxiety over female sexuality, and Yearsley's concern over the consequences of such private neuroses being made foundations for public policy.

In *Earl Goodwin*, the political battle between King Edward and Goodwin, the Earl of Kent, and his five sons is first entered into by the families' clash over the defense of "their" women's bodies. Early in the play, we witness a test of physical endurance when Queen Emma (mother of the King) is required to walk across burning ploughshares as a test of her virtue and chastity. The stage directions read like a recreation of a scene from a novel by Ann Radcliffe:

Scene draws, discovers the *King, Canterbury, Alwine, Monks, Officers,* &c. &c. Guards ranged on each side . . . From the back part of the stage, through an arch, enter *Queen Emma* veiled; a Guide attending. The *Queen* unconscious of having passed the burning ploughshares, walks solemnly on. (23)

As the stage directions indicate, the almost somnambulant Queen is not conscious of the blow she has dealt to the King and the scheming Archbishop of Canterbury, but the theatrical effect here has some potential to focus our interest on the series of conflicts Yearsley creates in the play. The lone and vulnerable figure of the woman makes physical and *dangerous* (and danger is always an important aspect of theatrical performance) the conflict between the truly "English" Anglo-Saxon heritage and the corrupting influence of the Norman aristocracy. Particularly notable in this testing of Queen Emma is the way in which Yearsley contrasts clericalism with a strong sense of female honor and heroism in a political system which does not admit the existence of women, let alone allow them a place of honor. Yearsley seems to invite an interpretation of her play which links a study of the proper exercise of power in the public realm with gender issues. To make her point about the gender politics of genre, Yearsley specifically points to her play's "unfeminine" nature in her "Exordium": "And now, Ladies, here is a play without Love. I have neglected the god, and repented of it. In my next production I will give you a heroine, who, while she yields to love, is exalted by honor" (1).

Yearsley's play offers a commentary on English national characteristics, as she presents King Edward's insistence on the trial of his mother Emma, and his wife, Editha (daughter of Earl Goodwin) as simultaneously an exercise of domestic tyranny and a symbolic act of rulership by a Norman king over the subject Saxon state. The values of familial love and respect are represented as Saxon through the characterization of the honest good-heartedness of Earl Goodwin and his sons, who react in horror to Edward's priest-ridden and unfilial actions. Goodwin's deep sense of personal injustice, stemming from the King's treatment of Editha, is not sufficient for revenge, no matter how much his hot-headed sons urge this action (3). It is only when Goodwin decides that Edward must hear "the complaint of England" and redress "the wrongs / Of this much-injur'd land" (19) that he is prepared to challenge Edward. The play's ideological argument follows its plot as a study in freedom-fighting and national liberation from tyranny. Yearsley's use of the rhetoric of national liberation is stirring and offers itself for interpretation as contemporary political commentary in the way noted by Hoagwood. In this example from the beginning of Act III, Goodwin's call to arms frames the demand for national liberation in terms which link economic exploitation with priestcraft, a combination familiar to politically aware audiences of 1791 who had heard what was happening in France:

> GOODWIN. Strike up the sounds of war, till they awake
> The drowsy spirit of the land! Arise,
> Great genius of our isle! breathe thy fierce fires
> Strongly into our bosoms! – Warm'd by thee,
> My sons and fellow-soldiers shall despise
> Each hour of vulgar circumstance, their hearts
> Pant quick for action, only dar'd by those
> Who stretch the thought thro' endless time. Despair
> Bends down our sons of industry, pale want
> Robs the young cheek of ruddy hue; while craft,
> In venerable trimming, chains our king
> To tyrant superstition. Then befriend,
> Thou great unknown, our arms, if just; if rage,
> Or private grief, malice, or cruel pride,
> Be our incentives to this war, O wrest
> Each sword from its fast hold, or turn the point
> On ev'ry guilty breast.   (35)

In fulfilling the generic imperative which has always done much to constitute tragedy as an essentially conservative form,[22] Yearsley's enactment of radical nationalism is tempered by the conclusion of the play, in which Goodwin is poisoned by the crafty priest Lodowicke. Lodowicke intends to kill himself, but at the moment of suicide, argues that

> . . . to fly,
> From man's weak wrath as an affrighted coward,
> Yet dare my God as a vindictive bravo,
> Is e'en too much for Lodowicke. How poor,
> How inconsistent, and how meanly proud,
> Is the self-murd'er! . . .
> *Harold.* In his final pray'r
> My father begg'd forgiveness for thee. Live!
> Live, and repent!   (89)

As he is forgiven by Harold, Goodwin's eldest son, the conclusion to the tragedy becomes a woman's program for nation-making, radical in its peace-making and concord, as well as in its questioning of the bravery of suicide. In a note to the published edition, Yearsley argues that

I think remorse worse than death: it is to the criminal a torture all his own, while it leaves no blemish on society. Mankind depend on mercy: – were we emulous in gaining its first gradation, would 72,000 souls have been executed in the reign of Henry VIII? or would twenty men be suspended of a morning, on a spot of some few yards wide, in London, and under the cognizance of our Most Gracious Sovereign George III? (89)

In her argument that, to escape from "man's weak wrath" by suicide is more cowardly than to face God, Yearsley opens the argument of her play to a view that secular considerations of compromise might be more important than masculinist notions of honor, and her editorial comment on the conditions in England under George III suggest that her dramatization of Saxon England ruled by the Normans is underpinned by a radical critique of England ruled by the Hanovers.

Like Yearsley's *Earl Goodwin* and More's *Percy*, Frances Burney's four verse tragedies – *Edwy and Elgiva* (1795), *Hubert de Vere* (c. 1790–91), *The Siege of Pevensey* (c. 1790) and *Elberta* (*c.* 1791) – drew on the English past. However, except for *Edwy and Elgiva*, which was produced at Drury Lane in 1795 and was not a success, Burney's tragedies remained unperformed during her lifetime.[23] Burney's laying aside of these plays may have had as much to do with her father's disapproval of her involvement in the theatre, as with her

lack of success in the theatre. This was not the only way in which
Charles Burney's social ambitions influenced his daughter's writing
career. According to recent biographers, Frances Burney's playwriting was also formed by the conditions under which she wrote:
she began writing *Edwy and Elgiva* in 1788 as an antidote to her
unhappiness as a courtier in the Queen's household. Her journals
and letters of this time indicate the anxiety and exhaustion from
which she regularly suffered, and Catherine Gallagher argues that
Burney was once again sacrificed to the ambition of her father.[24]
Kate Chisholm finds that the "sad, isolated atmosphere in which she
was living dictated her subject-matter,"[25] and Margaret Anne
Doody gives an extended reading of Burney's historical tragedies as
expressions of Burney's creative response to being "lost in a dark
world" of her "royal incarceration."[26] Doody's reading of Burney's
plays as therapy is an insightful and a rare discussion of the
seriousness of purpose of Burney's writing, yet it focuses almost
entirely on a psychoanalytical interpretation of Burney's historical
plots (178–83). A more challenging view is that Burney's intimate
view of royal power finds its expression in her writing of this period;
during the king's illness, which coincided with the early stirrings of
anti-establishment feeling in France, Burney witnessed the fragility
and contingency of power. Like More and Yearsley's plays, *Edwy and
Elgiva* concentrates on an Anglo-Saxon past, which is defined by its
religious superstition, chivalric code, and the use of women's bodies
as objects of exchange and territory in the conflicts between men.
Public debates about the powers of monarchs in England and France
in the 1780s are paralleled in *Edwy and Elgiva* by a constant discussion
of the power of the church and the Pope, in Burney's imaginative
recreation of an England potentially in thrall to a foreign power.
The audience is prepared for the importance of English independence in the play by her brother, Charles Burney, whose "Prologue"
ends on the stirring lines:

> . . . O Spirit of our Sires
> Breathe into every Soul a Britons [*sic*] fires
> Give us the value of those joys to know
> Which rights bequeath'd and holy truths bestow
> Teach us to love our Country and her Laws
> To glow united in her sacred cause
> And boast with swelling hearts and loud acclaim
> Our Faiths [*sic*] Defender and our King the same.[27]

The play opens at the delicate moment of Edwy's succession to the English throne on the death of his uncle Edred. Edwy has married his cousin, Elgiva, and it is this act which precipitates a power struggle between Edwy's faction and the remainder of his uncle's advisors and favorites. Principal among these is Dunstan, Abbot of Glastonbury, who is the play's villain, and not the least of his villainy is his representation of Rome in England. Canon law, although not common law, proscribed marriage between cousins, and Edwy and Elgiva were second or third cousins.[28] Through Burney's use of historical situation and formal verse, the private love of Edwy and Elgiva is constantly enlarged into a political and religious struggle of the state. A particularly striking example of the issues of public power that are at stake in the relationship between Edwy and Elgiva comes in Act 2, when Edwy enters Elgiva's room in his coronation robes, and their mutual declarations of love are made against the visible signs of state power. Edwy's love for Elgiva increases in this scene as he contemplates her unselfish happiness in Edwy's success:

> Thou fair assemblage of all female excellence!
> Thus canst thou greet me, with this generous warmth,
> Those open smiles, those Eyes of radiant kindness,
> When thou beholdst me powerless to sustain
> Thy rights, and issuing fresh from unshar'd honours? (29)

Burney portrays Edwy throughout the play as somewhat naive and overly confident in asserting his new power, whereas Elgiva is constantly aware of her vulnerable situation and aware also of the national interests involved in their marriage. Those interests are voiced by Dunstan, who leads the other clerics in openly condemning Elgiva and plotting rebellion against Edwy. His villainy is made very clear by his open contempt for the people when plotting to replace Edwy with Edgar:

ODO [Archbishop of Canterbury]: . . . But might the people not resist? Would the crowd comprehend our arguments?

DUNSTAN: The crowd require illusion, not conviction.
Entic'd by Terror, caught by Ambiguity,
Weakly beguil'd, and eagerly amaz'd,
To them 'twere useless to discuss opinions;
They must be led more vigourously to action
By calling forth their passions and their interests,
By raising fears unnam'd, and Hopes mysterious. (42)

This is a fascinating speech to be made on the English stage in 1795 – it escapes notice perhaps because it is spoken by the villain of the piece – but it reveals a cynical and knowledgeable view of political power and the manipulation of public opinion which perhaps changes our view of "Fanny Burney," the novelist of female comic heroism.

The play continues under the increasing threat of civil war and rebellion against the king until the plotting of Dunstan brings about the inevitable tragic denouement: Edwy and Elgiva are separated by Odo's declaration of their divorce; Elgiva is excommunicated, Edwy's noble allies, such as Redwald of Mercia, desert him, and finally Dunstan's and Edwy's forces are ranged against each other in combat, in which Dunstan is beaten, but Edwy is killed. The sense of civil unrest is a constant background to the individual struggle between Edwy and Dunstan. For example:

> SIGEBERT: Pardon, my liege, this boldness –
> But all are up in arms. The tumult spreads
> From Class to Class: the Nobles, Monks, and Rabble
> Confus'dly mixing, with one common voice
> Clamour for Dunstan, and, with ceaseless din
> Claim his recall, or . . . menace Civil War!   (67)

Burney's voice in this play indicates a knowledge and experience of the manipulations of power and politics which is not normatively feminine, but which confidently takes on the combination of passionate love with state intrigue and politics between England and Rome. Her view of nation emerging from the conflicts and battles of this play is significant in its awareness of the complexity of forces which rule England – although her representation of these conflicts always emphasizes the central integrity of the throne and the ideal of its independence from external influences.

While Burney retreated quickly from the public stage after the humiliating experience of *Edwy and Elgiva* in production,[29] and More explained away her playwriting as youthful optimism about the possibility of reforming the stage,[30] Mary Russell Mitford demonstrated a lasting determination to become a playwright. Ironically, while Mitford is now remembered principally as a prose writer of pastoral idylls, she represented herself as primarily interested in the drama, and worked very hard to establish herself as a serious dramatist. Writing to her friend William Harness in 1825, Mitford expressed her commitment to the drama: "You are the only friend whose advice agrees with my strong internal feeling respecting the drama. Everybody else says, Write novels – write prose!"[31] But Mitford's commitment to dramatic writing was a double-edged sword: it promised money and fame, but also required her to engage with a profession increasingly organized around powerful and capricious actor-managers, whose ways of doing business were increasingly at odds with notions of sociability for middle-class women.

At the end of the Romantic period, as a playwright Mitford faced a series of difficulties that had not been so pointed for women writers earlier in the period. Her playwriting career serves as an exemplum of the changed circumstances for women playwrights by the 1820s, as the ideologies of Romanticism gave way to the moral and aesthetic constraints of Victorianism.[32] In their survey of women playwrights in Britain from 1660 to 1823, David and Susan Mann show that in the last decade of the eighteenth century more women than ever before turned to playwriting, in both public and private capacities,[33] and Ellen Donkin argues that, by the mid-1790s, "women's presence in playwriting had a modest momentum and stability for the first time in over a hundred years."[34] But by the 1820s, when Mary Mitford began to write plays, both the conditions of the theatre profession and conditions for women writers had changed. The conservative reaction to the French Revolution had forced what Alison Sulloway has called the "compensatory equation" in which "women's segregated domesticity was supposed to compensate for man's expanding universes and to forestall revolution both at home and overseas."[35] After the revolutionary decades of the 1780s and 1790s, the almost-confident voice of female political subjectivity was diverted or directed against itself, in a "flood of literature whose intention was to reinforce doctrines of female subordination" from both female and male pens.[36]

By the 1820s, the theatre was no longer the relatively stable business of the late eighteenth century, as the social, political, and demographic changes in London and England of the late eighteenth and early nineteenth centuries were reflected in the volatility of audiences, and the destabilization of the duopoly of the Theatres Royal by new stages and audience demands.[37] When Mitford began to write seriously for the theatre, conditions had changed so markedly that her mentor Thomas Noon Talfourd could not guarantee Mitford access to public performance in the way that

Garrick had arranged for Hannah More's smooth introduction to the London theatre profession and her apparent overnight success. In the light of John Russell Stephens's discussion of the economics of playwriting in the 1820s, Mitford's difficulties are consistent with the "long process of economic decline in the theatre,"[38] which Stephens argues was represented by Edward Fitzball, whose career in the 1820s and 1830s was "an important watershed between an era when it was possible to sustain a career wholly dedicated to dramatic authorship and a period around mid-century when it clearly wasn't" (19). Mitford's career may have followed a pattern typical for her times, but the combination of economic decline and masculinist organization in the theatre profession meant that Mitford's sense of her agency in authorship suffered profoundly; however much Fitzball was affected by difficulties over declining payments to authors, his autobiography was still titled *Thirty-Five Years of a Dramatic Author's Life*, a claim Mitford never made in writing of her own career.[39]

Nevertheless, Mitford wrote eight full length plays – from *Julian*, first performed at Covent Garden in 1823, to her opera libretto, *Sadak and Kalasrade*, performed at the English Opera House in 1835, to *Otto of Wittlesbach*, begun in 1829, published in 1854, but never performed, in spite of Mitford's attempts to getting it produced in the early 1830s.[40] All Mitford's plays were "legitimate" dramas: historical verse tragedies representing, in solidly Aristotelian terms, the fall of great men. Her letters to her literary mentors such as Talfourd, Benjamin Haydon, and William Harness reveal Mitford's constant mining of her extensive reading for suitable stories. Her choice of topics focused on issues of personal morality combined with public power, which were conventional to the genre of tragedy. In Shakespearean style, distanced in Mediterranean settings, and framed as historical studies, plays such as *Foscari* (1826), *Rienzi* (1828), *Julian* (1823), and *Inez de Castro* (1831) impressed advisors such as Talfourd, persuaded star actors and managers such as William Macready and Charles Kemble, and entertained audiences. But when Mitford approached one of the most powerful topics of English nation-making, the battle of wills and minds between Oliver Cromwell and Charles I, even her use of history as a type of *Verfremdungseffekt* could not disguise the possibility of a contemporary and topical interpretation of her playwriting. *Charles the First* was written in the early 1820s, but refused a license in 1825 on political grounds by George Colman Jr., then Examiner of Plays for the Lord

Chamberlain. (*Charles the First* eventually received a production at the Victoria Theatre in 1834.) As late as 1825, the banning of this play demonstrates how sensitive for the English nation-state were questions of monarchical legitimacy, and, in Johnston's and Nicholes's words, "how readily and deeply the experience of the French Revolution could be encoded in England's national character" (93).

For Mitford, Colman's action was blackly ironic, as the play was resolutely Royalist, portraying Cromwell as a single-minded tyrant, and Charles as a reasonable and pious ruler. Charles is so concerned for the greater good of England over his own pride of position that he disdains the opportunity to escape to France, preferring to compromise and negotiate with Cromwell and Parliament.

> KING. Nay, we are near agreed. I have granted more
> Than they durst think for. They set forth today
> Bearing my answer to the Commons. Look
> To see a sudden peace. Many will deem
> I have yielded overmuch; but I keep quick
> The roots of kingly power, albeit the boughs
> Be shrewdly lopt. And then to see again
> My wife, my children, to reward my poor
> And faithful servants, to walk free, to reign!
> Look to see sudden peace . . .
>   I have yielded
> Power and prerogative, and state and wealth,
> For my dear country.
> All that was mine own,
> All that was mine to give, I freely gave;
> That I withhold is of the conscience.[41]

Charles's desire for peace, and his care for his country ("my poor/ And faithful servants"), together with his concern for his wife and children, is contrasted with Cromwell's determination to bring the King to account. Cromwell is characterized as an inflexible fanatic, resolved from the outset to arrest the King for treason. He represents Queen Henrietta through violent metonymy:

> But I knew her by the wanton curls,
> The mincing delicate step of pride, the gait
> Erect and lofty. 'Twas herself, I say,
> Vain Jezabel! [*sic*]   (19)

This is consistent with Cromwell's implacable political ambition, which Mitford represents as cloaked in the language of religion.

After Charles's statements about his love for his country, his arrest on grounds of treason comes as a tragic irony, and his subsequent behavior dramatizes a "high Tory" concept of the innate nobility of the monarch.[42] In comparison with the use of early English history and myth by More, Yearsley, and Burney, Mitford's play draws on verifiable and relatively recent history, but, like her colleagues, Mitford is most interested and interesting as a dramatist when she engages with the clashes and contradictions of private desire and public duty. Discussions of freedom and tyranny are never neutral in tragedy no matter how distanced in the setting of time or place – as Colman's response to this play reminds us – and are even more loaded, not to say over-determined, in work produced by a female pen. Read as dramatic interpretations of the position of women at the turn of the nineteenth century, Mitford's dramatization of regal stoicism and Yearsley's rousing cries for national liberation have much in common, although they are opposed in contemporary party political terms.

For none of these writers can I give a triumphalist feminist account of recuperation of forgotten work into the canon of Romantic writing, or "rediscover" a powerful tradition of women's writing. But neither are their histories ones in which, as Anthony Dawson puts it, subjectivity is rewritten to become subjection.[43] The public performances of their work, however limited (and of the four plays discussed here, only *Percy* was an acknowledged critical success at the time), must be recognized as the exercise of agency in a fundamentally transgressive way. Except for *Earl Goodwin*, all of the plays I discuss were publicly performed at English Theatres Royal, and the writers put great energy into seeking and achieving these performances. And without wishing to resort to a reductive Marxist explanation of these women's desires, it is important to consider that, for the women themselves, the most fundamental consideration might have been money. Playwriting offered the promise of money and instant fame; Mary Mitford explained to Benjamin Haydon that this was why she began writing *Foscari* (cited in Chorley II: 123), and both Margarete Rubik and Judith Phillips Stanton represent the lucrative nature of playwriting in the late eighteenth century as a potent reward for women writers.[44] While it is important to consider these playwrights in the light of Catherine Burroughs's discussion of women's closet drama as positive interventions into conventional dramaturgy and theatre theory, rather than as failed plays which were "antitheatrical and politically irrelevant,"[45] the ways in which these particular plays cross and recross the boundaries of the public and the closet stage, in terms of finance, reputation, visibility, and aesthetics, need also to be recognized as a significant cultural and political phenomenon.

There is a dynamic dialectic between the disabilities of what Mary Poovey calls writing as a "proper lady"[46] and women playwrights' use of the symbolic capital invested in the high cultural form of tragedy and public performance in the legitimate theatres. More, Yearsley, Burney, and Mitford, while struggling under the disabilities of gender, use the powers of tragedy and history to claim a place in the discourses of national politics and identity. This dialectic between gender and genre, in both the activity of writing and the physical habitation of space in the London theatre, is one that continues throughout the nineteenth century. For some time it has been common, in both feminist and anti-feminist criticism, to characterize the dominant mode of women's writing from the late eighteenth century as domestic and private. But by writing plays and having them performed, women necessarily participated in the public and professional spheres of English culture. To see women playwrights' work as part of a dialectical process, rather than structured in a set of oppositional binaries, is to refuse to confine them to the subordinate terms of the "violent hierarchies" (to use Derrida's term) of the separate spheres of feminine and masculine life. When women playwrights exert agency through writing history and tragedy, they inhabit that field of cultural production which resists the exclusion and abatement of female subjectivity, and they begin to make claims to the world of public policy, of history, and of power.

NOTES

Acknowledgments: Research for this essay was supported by the Australian Research Council. My thanks to Gillian Sykes for research assistance.

1 Homi K. Bhabha, ed., "Introduction: Narrating the Nation" in *Nation and Narration* (London & New York: Routledge, 1990), pp. 1–7, p. 3.
2 Nancy Armstrong, *Desire and Domestic Fiction* (Oxford University Press, 1987), p. 9.
3 Hedva Ben-Israel, *English Historians of the French Revolution* (Cambridge University Press, 1968), p. 4.

4 Ronald Paulson, *Representations of Revolution (1789–1820)* (London & New Haven: Yale University Press, 1983), p. 3.

5 Julie Carlson, *In the Theatre of Romanticism: Coleridge, Nationalism, Women* (Cambridge University Press, 1994), p. 2.

6 Gary Kelly, *Women, Writing, and Revolution, 1790–1827* (Oxford: Clarendon Press, 1993), p. 8.

7 Dror Wahrman, *Imagining the Middle Class: The Political Representation of Class in Britain, 1780–1840.* (Cambridge University Press, 1995), p. 21.

8 Terence Hoagwood, "Prolegomenon for a Theory of Romantic Drama," *The Wordsworth Circle*, 23: 2 (1992), 49–64, p. 59.

9 Kenneth Johnston and Joseph Nicholes, "Transitory Actions, Men Betrayed: The French Revolution in the English Revolution in Romantic Drama," *Wordsworth Circle*, 23: 2 (1992), 76–96, p. 76.

10 Hoagwood, "Prolegomenon," p. 57.

11 Christina Crosby, *The Ends of History* (London and New York: Routledge, 1991), pp. 144–46.

12 William Roberts, citing Hannah More, vol. 1 of *Memoirs of the Life and Correspondence of Mrs. Hannah More* (London: R. B. Seeley and W. Burnside, 1835), p. 122. 4 vols.

13 John Genest, vol. VI of *Some Account of the English Stage From the Restoration in 1660 to 1830* (Bath: H. E. Carrington, 1832), p. 16.

14 Judith Philips Stanton, " 'This New Found Path Attempting': Women Dramatists in England, 1660–1800," in *Curtain Calls: British and American Women and the Theatre, 1660–1820*, ed. Mary Anne Schofield and Cecilia Macheski (Athens: Ohio University Press, 1991, pp. 325–54), p. 333.

15 Hannah More, *Percy*, in *The Works of Miss Hannah More in Prose and Verse*, (Cork: Thomas White, 1778), pp. 249–309. 2 vols.

16 Elizabeth Kowaleski-Wallace, *Their Father's Daughters. Hannah More, Maria Edgeworth and Patriarchal Complicity* (Oxford University Press, 1991), p. 5.

17 Hannah More, vol. II of *The Works of Hannah More* (London: T. Cadell, 1830), pp. 125–26. 5 vols.

18 Mary Waldron, *Lactilla, Milkwoman of Clifton* (Athens, GA: University of Georgia Press, 1996), p. 191.

19 See Ann Yearsley, *Earl Goodwin, an Historical Play* (London: G. G. J. and J. Robinson, 1791).

20 Waldron, *Lactilla*, pp. 195–203.

21 Paula R. Backscheider, *Spectacular Politics: Theatrical Power and Mass Culture in Early Modern England* (Baltimore and London: Johns Hopkins University Press, 1993), p. 189.

22 See, for example, Augusto Boal's class-based critique of the Aristotelian view of tragedy in *Theatre of the Oppressed*, trans. Charles A. and Maria-Odilia Leal McBride (London: Pluto Press, 1979).

23 According to her most recent biographer, Burney planned to revise and

re-present her plays for public performance (Kate Chisholm, *Fanny Burney: Her Life, 1752–1840* [London: Chatto and Windus, 1998], p. 178). Burney's comedies also remained unperformed in her lifetime; indeed, the production of *A Busy Day* (1800) at the King's Head Theatre, Islington, in June 1994 claimed to be the first professional production of the play in Britain.

24 Catherine Gallagher, *Nobody's Story: The Vanishing Acts of Women Writers in the Marketplace, 1670–1820* (Berkeley and Los Angeles: University of California Press, 1994), pp. 251–52.
25 Chisholm, *Fanny Burney*, p. 144.
26 Margaret Anne Doody, *Frances Burney: The Life in the Works* (Cambridge University Press, 1989), p. 178.
27 Frances Burney, vol. 1 of *Complete Plays: Tragedies*, ed. Peter Sabor (London: William Pickering, 1995), p. 14. 2 vols.
28 Sabor, ed., in Frances Burney, *Complete Plays*, vol. 1, 16n.
29 Chisholm, *Fanny Burney*, pp. 176–77.
30 More, vol. 11, *Works*, p. 126.
31 Mary Russell Mitford cited in Henry Chorley, vol. 1 of *Letters of Mary Russell Mitford*, 2 vols, second series (London: Richard Bentley and Son, 1872), p. 213.
32 There is an extensive and important debate amongst historians of class and culture about the historical moment of the change from a liberatory Romanticism to a constraining Victorianism. As well as the critics I quote here, see, for example: Dror Wahrmann, "The New Political History: A Review Essay" (*Social History*, 21: 3 [1996], 343–54), as well as his *Imagining the Middle Class*; Linda Colley, *Britons: Forging the Nation, 1707–1837* (New Haven & London: Yale University Press, 1992); and particularly Amanda Vickery, *The Gentleman's Daughter: Women's Lives in Georgian England* (New Haven: Yale University Press, 1998), and her historiographical survey, "Golden Age to Separate Spheres? A Review of the Categories and Chronology of English Women's History" (*The Historical Journal*, 36: 2 [1993], 383–414), in which she questions the partial terms on which the debate about the position of women and the progress of liberation has taken place in feminist historiography. Without reducing or simplifying the complexities and significance of this debate, it is necessary for the purposes of this chapter to truncate the discussion, allowing the particular difficulties of Mitford's career as a playwright to stand for the more general sense that between the 1790s and the 1820s there were noticeable changes in the professional personae available to middle-class women.
33 David D. Mann and Susan Garland Mann with Camille Garnier, *Women Playwrights in England, Ireland, and Scotland, 1660–1823* (Bloomington: Indiana University Press, 1996), p. 4.
34 Ellen Donkin, *Getting into the Act: Women Playwrights in London, 1776–1829* (London: Routledge, 1995), p. 185.

35 Alison Sulloway, *Jane Austen and the Province of Womanhood* (Philadelphia: University of Pennsylvania Press, 1989), p. 4.
36 Norma Clarke, *Ambitious Heights. Writing, Friendship, Love – The Jewsbury Sisters, Felicia Hemans, and Jane Welsh Carlyle* (London and New York: Routledge, 1990), p. 21.
37 For general accounts of these changes, see the standard histories of the nineteenth-century theatre, such as that of Michael R. Booth, Richard Southern, R. Davies, and F. and L.-L. Marker, eds., *The Revels History of Drama in English, Vol. VI, 1750–1880* (London: Methuen, 1975), and also Ernest Bradlee Watson, *Sheridan to Robertson: A Study of the Nineteenth-Century London Stage* (New York: Benjamin Blom, 1926; 1963). For an explanation of the theatrical patents, see Dewey Ganzel, "Patent Wrongs and Patent Theatres: Drama and Law in the Early Nineteenth Century" (*PMLA*, 76.4 [1961]: 384). For further detailed discussion of the regulation of the theatres, if only to comment on the effects of the monopoly of the Patent theatres, see Allardyce Nicoll, "The Theatre," in *A History of English Drama, 1660–1900, vol. IV, Early Nineteenth Century Theatre*, 1930 (Cambridge, 1955); Watson Nicholson, *The Struggle for a Free Stage*, 1906 (New York: Benjamin Blom, 1966); and Gilbert Cross, *Next Week–East Lynne* (Lewisburg: Bucknell University Press, 1977). For contemporary versions of the debate, see particularly Eugene Macarthy, *A Letter to the King, on the Question Now at Issue between the "Major", and "Minor" Theatres* (London: Effingham Wilson, 1832); T. J. Thackeray, *On Theatrical Emancipation and the Rights of Dramatic Authors* (London: C. Chapple, 1832); Francis Place, *A Brief Examination of the Dramatic Patents* (London: Baylis and Leighton, 1834); Frederick G. Tomlins, *The Past and Present State of Dramatic Art* (London: C. Mitchell, 1839), *A Brief View of the English Drama* (London: C. Mitchell, 1840), and *The Nature and State of the English Drama* (London: C. Mitchell, 1841); Alfred Bunn, *The Stage: Both Before and Behind the Curtain* (London: Richard Bentley, 1840), especially his defense of the monopoly in vol. I, Chapter II; Edward Mayhew, *Stage Effect: or, The Principles which Command Dramatic Success in the Theatre* (London: C. Mitchell, London, 1840), especially the "Introduction," where the patent monopoly is blamed for the poor quality of contemporary dramatic writing. Finally, a wealth of contemporary comment on the theatre profession and politics is to be found in the British House of Commons, Sessional Papers, *Report from the Select Committee on Dramatic Literature: with the Minutes of Evidence*, vol. VII, 1831–32.
38 John Russell Stephens, *The Profession of the Playwright. British Theatre 1800–1900* (Cambridge University Press, 1992), p. 48.
39 See Edward Fitzball, *Thirty-Five Years of a Dramatic Author's Life* (London: T. C. Newby, 1859). Mitford's memoirs are titled *Recollections of a Literary Life* (London: Richard Bentley, 1853), and, while the book contains a series of her critical accounts of various authors, there is little auto-

biographical writing. Henry Chorley's and A.G. L'Estrange's collections of Mitford's letters (*The Life of Mary Russell Mitford, Related in a Selection from Her Letters to Her Friends*, ed. A. G. L'Estrange, 3 vols. [London: Richard Bentley, 1870]) are the best source of contemporary biography for Mitford.

40 Mary Russell Mitford, "Letters from Mary Russell Mitford to Sir Thomas Noon Talfourd," Eng Mss 665, John Rylands Library, University of Manchester. Cited by courtesy of the Director and Librarian, the John Rylands University Library of Manchester.

41 Mary Russell Mitford, *Charles the First, An Historical Tragedy in Five Acts*, (London: John Duncombe, 1834), pp. 11–12.

42 See Mitford, "Letters," Eng Mss 665.

43 Anthony B. Dawson, "Performance and Participation: Desdemona, Foucault, and the Actor's Body" in *Shakespeare, Theory and Performance*, ed. James C. Bulman (London: Routledge, 1996), pp. 29–45, p. 30.

44 See Margarete Rubik, *Early Women Dramatists, 1550–1800* (Basingstoke: Macmillan, 1998), p. 137; and Stanton, "'This New Found Path Attempting,'" p. 325.

45 Catherine B. Burroughs, *Closet Stages: Joanna Baillie and the Theater Theory of British Romantic Women Writers* (Philadelphia: University of Pennsylvania Press, 1997), p. 87.

46 See Mary Poovey, *The Proper Lady and the Woman Writer: The Ideology of Style in Mary Wollstonecraft, Jane Austen, and Mary Shelley* (University of Chicago Press, 1984).

CHAPTER 4

English national identity in Mariana Starke's "The Sword of Peace": India, abolition, and the rights of women

Jeanne Moskal

It is ironic that what slim reputation Mariana Starke (?1762–1838) has possessed since the nineteenth century depends on her European travels, summarized in her *Handbook and Directions for Travellers on the Continent* (1828) and later absorbed into the lucrative *Handbook* series begun by publisher John Murray in 1836. For Starke's expertise in foreign matters originated in India, where she grew up, and where her father, Richard Starke, served as governor of the British East India Company's post at Fort St. George in Madras. The Indian experiences did not go unrecorded, however. Starke began her literary career as a playwright with two plays, *The Sword of Peace* (1788) and *The Widow of Malabar* (1791), which capitalized on her experiences in India for London audiences.[1] The plays were moderately successful but have fallen into obscurity, a condition that is now being remedied by new facsimile and electronic editions of *The Sword of Peace* and by the beginnings of some critical attention to Starke's œuvre.[2]

In this chapter, I contribute to this scholarly recovery of Starke by locating her play, *The Sword of Peace*, within the discourse about English national identity of the late eighteenth century, when, as Gerald Newman has demonstrated, artists and intellectuals of the middle class, enraged over their exclusion from the privileges of the aristocracy, retaliated by accusing the aristocrats of cultural treason, and found solace in creating the myth that they, the middle class, would regenerate the nation by restoring its native English national identity. Although Starke's play addresses two of the most controversial political issues of the late 1780s, the Warren Hastings trial and the abolition of the slave trade, her mode of addressing them is not pragmatically political but mythical; nationalism, writes Newman, is "something larger than mere politics . . . it *enters* the political domain from a sphere outside it."[3] Starke accordingly implies that political problems can be solved by the nation's adoption of its "true" English national identity.[4] (My own guess is that Starke preferred to write about "English" rather than "British" in order both to disguise her own colonial origins and to disenfranchise the Scots, who were blamed in the Hastings affair.) Specifically, I argue that *The Sword of Peace*, which depicts the replacement of a corrupt British official in an unnamed Indian colony by a more just regime, obliquely but unavoidably participates in the controversies over British India, controversies centering on Warren Hastings, in part by celebrating Lord Cornwallis, who had just replaced Hastings as Governor-General of India in 1786. That year, Edmund Burke had moved for Hastings's impeachment in the House of Commons on the charges of violation of property, destruction of native customs and institutions, and the dishonoring of native women. Backed by the House of Commons, Burke, Charles James Fox, and Richard Brinsley Sheridan, the playwright and manager of Drury Lane, began the impeachment in the House of Lords in February 1788, and the trial was raging in the House of Commons at the time of the play's premiere that summer. In fact, Starke herself noted the point of contact between her myth of national identity and pragmatic politics, declaring her intention to celebrate the new regime in India (headed by Cornwallis) by saying that her colony's new governor, David Northcote, had a real-life antecedent, and that her play was "dictated by a heart glowing with gratitude and admiration of his noble and unbounded goodness!"[5] This 1789 avowal makes explicit a connection with British India that could not be missed, even when unspoken, by a 1788 audience fascinated by and saturated with the Hastings proceedings.

Even though Hastings was, to some extent, himself a reformer, he inherited and exacerbated the abuses of power which preceded him, and thus served as a lightning rod for powerful, unresolved issues in British colonial policy and the class conflict of the late eighteenth century. Britain's colonizing of India, and especially its profiteering there, had long been felt as a disturbance to English national identity. In 1773, Horace Walpole asked, "What is England now? A sink of Indian wealth, filled by nabobs . . . a gaming, robbing, wrangling, railing nation, without principles, genius, character or allies, the overgrown shadow of what it was!"[6] The

corrupt, unscrupulous men of the East India Company (hereafter
EIC) who returned, enriched, to England were also the subjects of
Samuel Foote's 1772 satire, *The Nabob*, and of Agnes Maria Bennett's
1785 novel, *Anna; or the Memoirs of a Welsh Heiress. Interspersed with
Anecdotes of a Nabob*. Corruption was indeed widespread in the EIC
and implicitly encouraged. The salaries were so low – in the mid-
1700s, £5 annually for a writer (an apprentice), £15 for a factor,
£30 for a junior merchant – that impecunity invited EIC personnel
to augment their incomes by engaging in private trade within
India.[7] The tradition of corruption can be traced to Robert Clive,
victor of the Battle of Plassey (1757), on whom the grateful Nawab
of Bengal bestowed the military rank of *jagir*, which brought with it
a stipend derived from land taxes. Clive returned to England with
£300,000 and an additional £28,000 a year. Hastings continued in
the same tradition: on his first return to England, after fourteen
years in India, he possessed a fortune of £30,000; this was well
before his service in Madras and in Bengal as Governor-General
(Spear 58). In his impeachment charges, Burke declared that
Hastings personified avarice: "In short, money is the beginning, the
middle and the end of every kind of act done by Mr. Hastings,
pretendedly for the Company, but really for himself."[8] Thus, the
Hastings trial brought to the bar the long-standing practice of
British profiteering in India.

Such corruption was given its scope by Britain's military control of
India, and Hastings had a reputation as a strongman who conducted
his campaigns ruthlessly. For example, Hastings's forces and their
allies committed atrocities against Afghans already defeated in battle
during the Rohilla War of 1774. As a result of his ruthlessness,
Hastings forced Britons to confront the anomaly that a mercantile
enterprise was functioning as a civil state, with power to wage wars,
levy taxes, and so forth, with minimal accountability to recognized
civil authorities.[9] Since the Seven Years War (1748–63), the EIC had
departed from its original charter as a purely mercantile enterprise,
taking on increasing military and political power, beginning with
Clive's subjugation of the Moguls (Muslims who had ruled much of
India) at the Battle of Plassey, and his installing a puppet ruler at
Bengal. Philip Lawson concludes that, "[in] all but name, the
Company had usurped imperial authority and sovereignty over
[Bengal]," the wealthiest kingdom under Mogul rule.[10] The question
of the political authority of the EIC remained contentious in the

1780s, since the India Bill of 1784 left open the constitutional question of whether the state or the Company owned the territory in India on which the taxes were paid. Hastings's conduct of the Rohilla War prompted the charge of genocide brought against him by Burke.[11] Even though that charge was later dropped, it reminded 1780s Londoners of the excesses of EIC power. The fact that the Rohilla War also extended the domain of the EIC 800 miles from Calcutta (Spear 64) underlined the temptation wealth provided to the abuse of power.

But who should control the piratical EIC? Parliament or the monarchy? The India Bill, passed in 1784, also tried to address this contested question, which had led to the removal of four prime ministers and their governments between April 1782 and April 1784. Burke, Fox, and Lord North favored a strong parliamentary commission, based in London, to superintend the Company, while Henry Dundas and William Pitt the Younger championed strengthening the power of crown appointees in the sub-continent itself. The Fox–North coalition fell in December 1783 over the defeat of its India Bill, brought down "on strong direction from the crown" (Musselwhite 84). The passage of Dundas's and Pitt's India Bill in August 1784, a bill supported by the king, provided that the Governor-General be a governmental, rather than an EIC, appointee. It thus marked a triumph of the crown over parliament and exacerbated tensions in the domestic balance of power.

More subtly and more pervasively, the Hastings trial evoked long-standing anxiety about "upstarts" and about the status of the middle class in an aristocratic social order. Newman has countered the traditional assumption of class mobility in eighteenth-century Britain with a demonstration of the aristocracy's dogged defense of its privileges and its cultural superiority through such practices as ostentatious gambling, dress, and travel.[12] As a result, many bourgeois artist-intellectuals (William Hogarth, Henry Fielding, Tobias Smollett, Josiah Wedgewood, Mary Wollstonecraft) chafed under the system of "privilege" that denied advancement to "merit."[13] In this class standoff, Indian nabobs in particular evoked the fear and envy of the aristocracy, emotions the artist-intellectuals echoed even while they admired the nabobs' mobility; as Siraj Ahmed observes, "the late eighteenth-century satire of the nabob as one who attempts to efface his class origins when he returns to England by ostentatious shows of imperial wealth expressed the general awareness that those who served the British empire tended to come from Britain's lower classes" (n.p.). Fear and loathing of the nabobs took its harshest form in the Hastings trial where, as Isaac Kramnick has shown, Burke demonized Hastings as the embodiment of the avaricious, ambitious bourgeois spirit Burke loathed, branding Hastings as an upstart and a leader of upstarts who interfered with the received order of power and status.[14] But since Burke was, simultaneously, deeply attracted by this bourgeois spirit, his actions arose from a matrix of

> the peculiar combination of love and hate that the bourgeoisie felt towards the aristocracy. The bourgeoisie despised the idleness and unproductivity of men of rank. They resented their unearned status and privileges; they were repulsed by their immorality and luxury. Yet the bourgeoisie also envied the wealth and power of their betters. As much as they resented their style of life they coveted it. (Kramnick 193)

Burke's ambivalence thus encapsulates the spirit of the age; he stands as typical for the man of the middle class in close contact with his "betters" in the 1780s.

The class issue of "upstarts" had ethnic overtones and gender implications. As Linda Colley notes, talented Scots had often needed to seek positions in the colonies, but Hastings, himself an Englishman, accelerated the pace of bringing Scots into positions of influence in India, a trend marked by Hastings's name for his inner circle as his "Scotch guardians."[15] Katie Trumpener notes that "Britain's national disenfranchisements and domestic penury created generations of predatory fortune hunters," many of whom settled in the colonies.[16] Burke, like many other Britons, resented this advancement of Scots, and argued that Hastings's employment of them revealed his own arbitrary, despotic politics and consequently merited impeachment (Colley 130).

Gender too played a role in Burke's critique of bourgeois upstarts, though, crucially for Burke, only men (aristocrats or middle class) are agents, while women are passive indicators of men's chivalry or lack of it. (Working from Burke, Starke granted women some agency.) The importance of gender is attested by Burke's famous passage, in *Reflections on the Revolution in France* (1790), on the lascivious Jacobins who pursued the virtuous Marie Antoinette as she fled from her bedroom, and who, in so pursuing her, killed chivalry. Burke foreshadowed this gendered line of argument in the indictment of Hastings by dramatizing the methods that the British colonial government had used to extract land taxes from peasants in the Bengali town of Rangpur:

> But, my Lords, there was more. Virgins whose fathers kept them from the sight of the sun, were dragged into the public Court. . . . There in the presence of day . . . while their shrieks were mingled with the cries and groans of an indignant people, those virgins were cruelly violated by the basest and wickedest of mankind. It did not end there. The wives of the people of the country only differed in this; that they lost their honour in the bottom of the most cruel dungeons, where all their torments were a little buried from the view of mankind . . . But they were dragged out, naked and exposed to the public view, and scourged before all the people . . . But it did not end there. . . . they put the nipples of the women into the sharp edges of split bamboos and tore them from their bodies. Grown from ferocity to ferocity, from cruelty to cruelty, they applied burning torches and cruel slow fires (My Lords, I am ashamed to go further); those infernal fiends, in defiance of every thing divine and human, planted death in the source of life . . .[17]

This harrowing passage riveted Burke's audience, overwhelming them with the horror of what he was describing.[18] It made gender an index of the central issue of the Hastings trial, by framing the question of bourgeois, mercantile government as: "in which kind of social order will women be treated civilly?" As David Musselwhite has observed, "trials often show the confrontation of systems of thought and cultural codings and expectations which are completely impenetrable to one another" (77).

Throwing the corruption of Hastings into contrast, Cornwallis established himself as a reformer immediately upon his arrival in 1786; within the first few months he had suspended most of the members of the EIC Board of Trade for financial irregularities and had uncovered fraudulent EIC payments to Britons in the forbidden private trade. Cornwallis was chosen for the post, despite his surrender in the American war at Yorktown, on the theory that "only a personality from British public life high above local jealousies and ambitions could control the Company's servants in Bengal" (Spear 104). During his tenure as Governor-General, which lasted until 1793, he raised EIC salaries to lessen the temptation to corruption; enforced the much-neglected ban on private trade; separated the commercial and revenue branches of the EIC, so that those who decided on investment strategies were removed from conflicts of interest; reorganized the collection of land taxes (a system not universally admired); and reformed the civil and criminal justice systems, stressing that all British revenue officers were subject to the rule of law.[19] Even as early as 1788 his record would deserve the tribute Starke offers:

Yet, however I may have failed in other parts of the drama, the character of David Northcote is a real one. – To Indians this is needless: the sketch, however, is not too faint, I hope, for others; it was dictated by a heart glowing with gratitude and admiration of his noble and unbounded goodness. (Preface, viii)

In the context of the Hastings trial and the India Bill of 1784, Starke's idealized new governor of India resembles Cornwallis in his unique qualification for such "gratitude and admiration."

The primacy in the minds of Starke's audience of these political and social questions – EIC military power, EIC corruption, class envy as indexed by ethnicity and gender, and the efficacy of reforms such as Cornwallis's – can be assessed by the public's simultaneous fascination by and saturation with the Hastings affair. Parliament had tired of Burke's perseveration on Hastings and India as early as 1785, when they shouted Burke down in protest, and their annoyance culminated in 1789 when he was censured by the House of Commons for his alleged excesses in handling Hastings's case (Kramnick 127). Yet Londoners were simultaneously enthralled. Burke's opening speech in February 1788, which took four days, drew standing-room only crowds; the impeachment itself has been referred to as "the greatest public sensation of the seventeen-eighties."[20]

Starke's play addresses these questions. Most importantly, she addresses the question of national degeneration, as indexed by the Hastings affair, by employing the broad mythmaking strategy of nationalist ideology, as described by Newman:

a structure consisting basically of two opposed networks of national-social-moral valuation, each identified with the various characters by a multi-plicity of family-linked cultural cues ("the dumb rhetoric of the scenery"); dual networks of value which, as activated in the evolution of the plot, involve the emotions of the English reader in the perilous vicissitudes and at last the final triumph of what is English-sincere-good over its enemy, what is frenchified-insincere-corrupting. (136)

In Starke's case, the issue of Francophobia that so concerns Newman is minimized in favor of the emphasis on insincerity and corruption.

Nonetheless, his identification of the dichotomous structure of nationalist mythmaking explains much, including the plot's lack of suspense: since each of the characters belongs to a distinct "national-social-moral" party, no one has a change of heart along the way, forcing the plot to depend on mechanical complications and unravellings instead. Within this stasis of plot, however, her conceptual achievement is to extend and amend Burke's position. Like Burke, Starke roundly criticizes the profit-driven Britons who have plundered India; she also follows Burke in attributing their greed to their bourgeois status. But Starke extends Burke by considering the implications of these value-systems for women, and she amends Burke by treating Anglo-Indian women as agents who can embrace or eschew mercantilism by their marriage choices. Paradoxically, however, Starke's utopia is a re-masculinized regime in British India, in which married women, having exercised their agency in courtship, relinquish it to their husbands, Starke thus circling back to a Burkean ideal of women's silence and passivity through a detour of advocacy for women's temporary rights.[21] These are the broad political implications of her mythic nationalist drama.

However consciously or unconsciously Starke "chose" nationalist myth over direct political commentary, this strategy enabled her to elude the censorship of the Licensing Act of 1737, which cast its long shadow over the stage well into the nineteenth century. It permitted only two "major" theatres to perform "legitimate" English drama, creating a monopoly for Covent Garden and Drury Lane, and relegating other theatres to "minor" status and to the productions of melodramas or other theatrical hybrids.[22] Moreover, the Licensing Act established the office of Lord Chamberlain, who monitored the political, sexual, and social content of the plays submitted to his examination. Particularly in the last quarter of the eighteenth century, Ellen Donkin observes, "[m]ost politically volatile plays never made it past the manager and consequently were not even submitted to the censor."[23] In the 1790s, even plays with what present-day scholars would consider conservative or reactionary content were censored by the Licenser.[24] Starke's overriding strategy, nationalist myth over direct political commentary, encompasses several other choices. Generically, she wrote a sentimental comedy with some doses of satire, leaving audiences to construe the political implications for British India and the rights of women (though the abolitionist subplot is unmistakable in its import). And her theatre

manager, George Colman the Elder, added an explicit disclaimer to
the play's Prologue:

> To India, then, our Author wafts you now,
> But not a breath of politics, I vow!
> Grave politics wou'd here appear a crime. –
> You've had enough, Heaven knows, all winter time. (lines 26–29)

Significantly, Colman's disclaimer ("Not a breath of politics, I vow!")
immediately follows the mention of India, as if to preclude the
audience's groans. At the same time, the disclaimer underlines, while
it tries to deny, the connection between the metaphorical conflict
enacted on stage and the political stakes in the Hastings trial.

Before considering in detail the political ramifications of the play,
a review of its production history may be helpful. *The Sword of Peace;
or, a Voyage of Love* is a sentimental comedy in five acts. It was
performed in the private theatre of Mary Champion Crespigny of
Camberwell, who "delight[ed] in being an encourager of talents,
and the friend of genius" in drama, a performance that probably
occurred before its public premiere, as we know was the case with
Starke's 1791 play, *The Widow of Malabar*.[25] As mentioned, *The Sword
of Peace* included a prologue by George Colman the Elder, the
proprietor of the Theatre Royal at Haymarket, and an epilogue by
George Colman the Younger. It was relatively successful, though it is
not clear whether the venture was lucrative for Starke. It premiered
on Saturday, 9 August 1788, "the last new piece brought out that
season" (Young II:45) at the Haymarket, which was licensed for
summer shows only. The play was performed six times in the 1788
season. Usually, playwrights drew their benefits on the third, sixth,
and ninth evenings; by the benefit system, once the theatre covered
its overhead expenses for the night, the playwright received the rest
of the box-office receipts. While this benefit system was not always
used with new playwrights, it is possible that Starke received two
benefit nights from her play in 1788. However, the fact that *The
Sword of Peace* premiered at the end of the season, when actors'
benefits tended to cut into those of the playwrights, suggests that
these benefit nights yielded less profit to the latter than usual. The
play's 1789 season, consisting of four performances at the
Haymarket, profited the holder of the copyright, which was probably
the theatre or the publisher, Debrett, rather than Starke.[26]

Contemporary accounts give the play some positive marks.

Memoirist Mary Julia Young records that the actors, particularly Elizabeth Farren and Elizabeth Kemble (Mrs. Stephen George Kemble, née Elizabeth Satchell) as the young women "voyag[ing] for love" to India, and John Bannister, Jr., in the comic role of Jeffreys the abolitionist, "did justice to their characters," and that "the whole [play] obtained general applause from a crowded house" (II: 44, 45). This informal review acknowledges the appeal of the young women, who sometimes ridicule their elders, as the center of the play's moral authority, and it suggests that, in Jeffreys, Starke succeeded in making an abolitionist likable, thus avoiding charges of priggishness. But the negative comments give us a clue about what issues were at the forefront of the audience's response. Starke was blasted for inaccuracy in portraying the British in India, a criticism still circulated by David Rivers in 1798[27] and by John Genest in 1832.[28] Starke defended herself by writing to *The Morning Chronicle*, "As to the characters, if I am not allowed to have drawn them from *nature*, I can assure you I have from *life*; and there are few, I fancy, acquainted with India, but would vouch this for me."[29] Starke expands on this self-defense in the 1789 preface (viii), which claims that the character of David Northcote, the (perhaps impossibly) upright leader of the new regime in Starke's play, "is a real one," whose identity as Cornwallis did not need to be explained to "Indians" (that is, Anglo-Indians, or what Starke earlier called those "acquainted with India"). Stressing the distinction between "nature" and "life," Starke claims that characters like Northcote actually exist in "life" (thus defending her verisimilitude) even though their behavior may be so morally admirable that they seem "unnatural." Since Burke had foregrounded the corruption in Hastings's regime, verisimilitude counted to this audience. Is the corrupt, lascivious Resident (who rules the colony at the opening curtain) an accurate portrayal of Hastings?[30] Will Cornwallis improve matters as much as Starke's portrayal of Northcote claims?

Another, more scurrilous criticism lays bare the class issues inherent in the 1780s, as does the playscript itself. We know it only by hearsay. Starke repeated in the 1789 preface the aspersion that she, the playwright, was a grocer's daughter in Thames Street, an "adventuress" returned from an unsuccessful trip to the Indian marriage market, who had run away with a strolling player

and as she has a Romantic turn, and a *great deal of assurance*, after having hawked this Sword about from theatre to theatre, prevailed on the manager in the Hay Market to bring it out, as the only means to prevent herself, her husband, and six children, from absolute starving. (vi; original emphasis)

This rumor attacks Starke's membership in a family associated with the EIC, which frequently welcomed ambitious members of the lower orders, by linking her to glamorless professions at the same low rank as "a grocer's daughter" loosely allied with "a strolling player." The rumor thus steals from the play its own terms of opprobrium in castigating her villainess, the wealthy Anglo-Indian widow, Mrs. Tartar, as a tallow-chandler's daughter. It registers Starke as an upstart, and thus on the wrong side of the dichotomy she, following Burke, had tried to establish. The class issues raised in this *ad hominem* argument, as well as the blame about verisimilitude, suggest that the echoes of the Hastings trial sounded in the audience's reactions.

Despite its genre as a sentimental comedy, the nationalist myth-making of *The Sword of Peace* justifies such a politicized response. Starke, like Burke, was concerned with the issue of national regeneration, with saving Britain from what Walpole called "the sink of Indian wealth." And Starke translated the Burkean charge, the uncontrolled greed of the men of the EIC, into feminine terms, as a critique of Anglo-Indian women who marry EIC men only for their money, thus plundering India at second-hand. Starke implies, however, that Englishwomen who tried their luck on the Indian marriage market did so only out of greed, that is, that they rejected domestic husbands because the EIC men were richer. But, historically, it tended to be true that they tried the EIC market when no local men made offers, for the odds were better in India: until about 1809, there were three British men to every British woman in India (Spear 129). In an era when marriage was, in Jane Austen's words, a woman's surest preservative from want, these women ventured to India motivated by pure economic necessity. Ignoring this hard reality, the playscript challenges the actions of the husband-hunters by idealizing the uncorrupted actions of two young women cousins, Louisa and Eliza Moreton. The audience's identification with them was invited by the appealing performances of Miss Farren and Mrs. Kemble, already noted; by their status as avatars of native English virtue; and by the rank and wealth that frees them from pecuniary considerations. Louisa has come to India to buy back, on behalf of Sir Thomas Clairville, the sword of his nephew, a young English solider who died in India and bequeathed it to his best friend, Lieutenant Dormer. Her cousin Eliza's trip is motivated by an odd clause in her father's will which requires her to journey to India in order to inherit her rightful wealth. And, by happy coincidence, she also seeks in India her faithful admirer George Edwards, a baronet's son, who left England for India when his family, thinking Eliza penniless, forbade the attachment. Thus Eliza comes to India only to claim the money and love that are already, "rightfully" hers, with no taint of ambition, greed, or husband-hunting; Louisa seeks the honor of an English solider. Both of them, wealthy aristocrats, are exempt from mercenary motives; as Louisa observes, "Our fortunes place us above mean obligations" (p. 9, lines 27–28).

The plot tests the cousins' resolve against that form of mercantilism manifested in the Indian marriage-market. Mrs. Tartar, the ruling dame of British society and sometime mistress of the Resident, arranges a party to advertise their eligibility; the Resident hints lewdly that he would like to marry Eliza himself and use Louisa as a reward for his sycophantic and greedy underling, Supple, enabling Supple to leave service and set up for himself. (Starke's portrayal of Supple, aspiring to leave a subordinate role and become independent, obliquely mirrors Burke's fear of Hastings promoting the "Scotch guardians.") And Louisa's purity from monetary concerns is further tested when she perseveres in making the original offer Sir Thomas proposed for the sword, rather than taking the Resident's advice to cheat Dormer. Louisa, impressed with Dormer's devotion to the late Clairville, falls in love with him. Through Dormer, the young women find Edwards, Eliza's admirer. The Resident plots to imprison Edwards on a false charge of debt and freezes Eliza's funds so she cannot post bail. The plot discovered, Eliza and Louisa take refuge in the home of Mr. and Mrs. Northcote. Their resistance to mercenary temptation is rewarded: the attachment between Dormer and Louisa is avowed and that between Eliza and Edwards restored. Their happiness is guaranteed by a new social order in the colony: a late-arriving British ship brings the news that Northcote is to succeed the current Resident, effective immediately. The entire colony, Briton, Muslim, and Hindu, rejoices.

Most powerfully, the playscript draws the audience to identify with Louisa and Eliza by positing them as avatars of unsullied English womanly virtue. This function is introduced thematically in Colman's Prologue:

To-day, two vent'rous females spread the sail,
Love points their course, and speeds the prosp'rous gale,
India they seek, but not with those enroll'd
Who barter English charms for Eastern gold;
Freighted with beauty, crossing dang'rous seas,
To trade in love, and marry for rupees.   (lines 20–25)

Eliza and Louisa, motivated by "Love" not greed, stand apart from those husband-hunters "[w]ho barter English charms for Eastern gold," "trade in love, and marry for rupees," transactions suggesting both prostitution and debasement of currency as the metaphors for the betrayal of English national identity. But the Moreton cousins' steadfastness is guaranteed from the outset:

Our heroines, tho' seeking regions new,
To English honor both hold firm and true;
Love-struck, indeed, but yet a charming pair,
Virtuous and mild like all our British fair!
Such, gentle Sirs, we trust, success shall crown,
Syrens so harmless cannot move your frown:
To such advent'rers lend a gracious hand
And bring them safely to their native land.   (lines 42–49)

Eliza and Louisa are presented as trustworthy representatives of English national identity, who will "hold firm and true" to "English honor" despite their sojourns in "regions new." Moreover, they are representative of a class of women, "[v]irtuous and mild like all our British fair." Since these women are guarantors of English national identity, they can be trusted to exercise the limited agency allowed by Starke's system in her extension of Burke's. Furthermore, Starke's heroines cast on their author the reflected nationalist glory of a "'domestic woman' as professionalized custodian of the 'national' conscience, culture, and destiny," foreshadowing the role Gary Kelly has identified among women writers of the revolutionary decade.[31]

The class conflict, drawn by Burke in the Hastings trial, between the chivalric and greedy governors of India and their benevolent replacements, is translated into a feminine key in the portrayals of the Moreton cousins. Starke emplots an Englishwoman's place in the controversies evoked by the Hastings trial in Louisa's choice between two suitors: Supple, who follows the greedy ethic articulated by the Resident, and Dormer, who embraces the code of honor given voice by Sir Thomas. Supple personifies the faults Burke found in the Hastings administration: the sycophancy and opportunism of

Hastings's "Scotch guardians," traits exemplified by Supple's equal willingness to marry wealthy Eliza, wealthy Louisa, or wealthy Mrs. Tartar. Supple's refusal to remain within British class boundaries makes him odious to the young women. Louisa comments, on hearing that he has pretensions to pay his addresses to her, "Dear me! I thought that was his situation by all his officious attentions on our first landing: 'a kind of *maitre d'hotel* to you, Sir, as Resident here'; I didn't know the man rank'd here as a gentleman" (p. 13, lines 1–4). Supple is a fairly flimsy character, his major function being to exemplify the corrupt side of the dichotomy for the plot line of Louisa's marriage choice.

But the values of that corrupt regime are most fully articulated in Supple's patron, the Resident. When Louisa presents her plan to redeem the young Clairville's sword for £5000 from Dormer, the Resident advises that she exploit Dormer's poverty to buy the sword more cheaply, exclaiming, "Five thousand pounds! Give him five thousand devils! . . . with proper management you may get this sword for five hundred rupees" (p. 14, lines 11–12). The Resident's plan thus displaces on to the figure of the sword the fear of monetary debasement in marriage raised by the Prologue's denunciation of Englishwomen "[w]ho barter English charms for Eastern gold," "trade in love, and marry for rupees." The transition from English currency to Indian is the index of devaluation and marks the loss of English identity. In fact, the Resident embodies this loss dramaturgically, for Starke clothes him in a banyan, which in India was used by the caste of Hindu merchants, a costume that shows his loss of English national identity in the sink of Indian wealth and his embrace of the role of a merchant rather than that of a civil servant. More generally, in the fashion language of 1780s London, the banyan represented a rejection of English values for "frenchified" cosmopolitanism; banyans were *de rigueur* in the metropolis as well, the obligatory morning dress for "a well-turned out London man of 1785" (Newman 40). Moreover, Starke suggests the Resident's lack of substance by giving him no proper name, just the title, a point reiterated throughout the play by his insistence on having his way, underlined with the refrain, "Ain't I Resident?" For Louisa to marry Supple would be the equivalent of buying back the sword on the Resident's mercantile, un-English terms.

But Starke presents Dormer, Louisa's other suitor, as preferring honor over money, thus exemplifying ideal British chivalry. In assessing the value of the sword, Dormer adheres to the wishes of Sir Thomas, who wants to purchase the sword for £5000 and "preserve it as trophy of honor to [his nephew's] memory" (p. 7, line 24). Eliza declares that Sir Thomas's offer is

[a]n exertion of delicate, generous sensibility towards deceased merit, that characterizes Sir Thomas *in that glorious singularity of an Englishman*, who repays with munificent gratitude, everlasting remembrance to the noble actions of their deceased heroes. (p. 7, lines 25–29; emphasis added)

Dormer conforms to the English ideal Sir Thomas exemplifies, and indeed goes one better by rejecting payment completely (favoring "honor" over "money") and chivalrously *giving* the sword in response to a lady's request. In response to Louisa's offer, he says,

No, madam, I am but a poor Lieutenant, yet such I will remain. If I can't enrich myself without mercenary views, without tarnishing the honor of a British soldier, yet think me not so selfish as to prefer my own slight satisfaction to my deceas'd friend's glory. I honor Sir Thomas's motive – *it speaks him what an Englishman should be.* – His gifts be to himself. – but – take the sword – though parting with it – leaves me wretched. (p. 26, lines 2–10; emphasis added)

Thus Dormer exemplifies chivalric values, granting a woman her desire and desiring above all things "the honor of a British soldier." Chivalry, for Burke, characterized the native aristocratic order that Hastings had violated in India (in the rapes of Rangpur), and, more famously, the *ancien régime* he later mourned in *Reflections on the Revolution in France*. Dormer's function as a linchpin in a chivalric system is underlined here: he submits to his betters by valuing the sword as Sir Thomas does, even though such valuation impoverishes him personally, but he commands his inferiors as a "Lieutenant of the Seapoys," the Indian soldiers who served the EIC with unquestioned loyalty until the Sepoy Mutiny of 1857. Starke makes clear that while on-stage Dormer exhibits only willingness to be commanded, off-stage he commands others, and, in exemplifying this chivalric code, he, not Supple and his ilk, should be in closest contact with the indigenous people.[32] Louisa's choice of Dormer over Supple ratifies the Burkean chivalric code of honor over money, of aristocratic tradition over bourgeois upstarts.

Using the same schema of greed versus honor, Starke frames Louisa's choice of suitors with the British government's choice to replace the Resident with Northcote, a member of the idealized coterie of true Britons, as the Resident's mean-spirited description to Louisa indicates:

RESIDENT: Oh, he'll just suit your ideas, I can tell you, for no one can do business but in he pops his nose to counteract every thing that don't tally with his ridiculous notions about honor, generosity, benevolence, and stuff: as if that had any thing to "do with trade." (p. 15, lines 9–13)

When pressed, the Resident is forced to concede that, in spite of his principles, Northcote is "one of the richest free merchants we have in India" (p. 15, lines 20–21). Significantly, Northcote differs from the honorable poverty of Dormer in that his honor and wealth are not mutually exclusive. (Though one is tempted to surmise that Northcote represents what the young Dormer will become in full adulthood, and hence that Dormer's poverty is temporary and his virtue will be rewarded financially as well as Romantically.) Thus, in sneering at Northcote, the Resident voices the worry that plagued reformers of the EIC: would it be possible to reconcile the phenomenal profits reaped by Hastings with the reforms – "honor, generosity, benevolence, and stuff" – instituted by Cornwallis? Northcote, "one of the richest free merchants we have in India," incarnates Starke's optimism that the answer is yes.

Northcote's rectitude – and a government that will allow profit with honor – is celebrated at the play's close. Jeffreys describes the settlement's reaction to the accession of Northcote:

JEFFREYS: [T]he whole place is run wild for joy, Sir – blacks and whites, masters and slaves, half casts and blue casts, Gentoos and Mussulmen, Hindoos and Bramins, officers and soldiers, sailors and captains – and if his honor the Resident don't stop them, they won't have an ounce of gunpowder in the whole garrison.
EDWARDS: Such an influence has goodness and benevolence over all ranks and descriptions.
JEFFREYS: They do nothing but call him father – they keep blessing him and his *children*; and King George and his children; and their great Prophet and his children. (p. 57, lines 4–15)

Here Starke echoes the hopes in Burke's call for a parliamentary commission to supervise British rule of India, rather than a crown-appointed one, in which these salutary moral outcomes are predicted:

You will teach the people that live under you, that it is their interest to be your subjects; and that, instead of courting the French, the Dutch, the Danes, or any other state, under heaven, to protect them, they ought only be anxious to preserve their connection with you; because, from you only they had to expect public proceeding, public trial, public justice. (v:137–38)

Starke's final vision of colonial acclamation adapts Burke's view that the colonies will gladly follow British rulers because "it is their interest to be your subjects," naturalizing their submission in the metaphor of the patriarchal family. When the Indians "do nothing but call [Northcote] father," imperial coercion is eclipsed, so much so that gunpowder can be expended in celebration rather than in violence. Also eclipsed is the element of rational self-interest stressed by Burke. The patriarchal metaphor implies that the Indians belong under British control as "naturally" as children belong to their fathers and that no conflict exists between Indians (the Great Prophet's children) and the EIC (Northcote's "children") or the British generally (King George's children). Starke here allocates the Indian voice solely to the Moguls – children of "the Great Prophet" who constituted the middle class of British-ruled Madras – even though she concedes the existence of the "Hindoos and Bramins." Starke does not explain the material basis of the erasure of colonial hostility she hopes for, but Cornwallis's reform of the criminal code, which brought British EIC under the same rule of law as the Indians, was particularly dear to Burke and embodies his ideal that only by "public proceeding, public trial, public justice" would Britain attract willing subjects. Though the details of judicial reform were still in the future in 1788, the need for reform was clear, and Starke celebrates it in the conceptually vague but dramaturgically powerful trope of Cornwallis as the local father blessed by all his children-subjects, whose benevolence leads them to bless the Empire, in the person of the fatherly King George, as well.

Thus far, we have seen Starke give dramatic form to Burkean themes, converting them into a marriage plot by extending their implications to women: Britain must choose between greed and honor in India just as Louisa must choose between Supple and Dormer. Generally, Starke continues in this vein by satirizing the upstart Mrs. Tartar, making her, rather than the Resident, the more sinister figure of EIC greed. But Starke undercuts this conservative line of metaphoric argument by comparing Mrs. Tartar to a despot. Here Starke sounds a note borrowed from the middle-class discontent that enraged generations of Britons, and, in France, fueled the French Revolution. And, in comparing the marriage market to slavery, Starke anticipates the argument of the radical

Wollstonecraft, sounded in *A Vindication of the Rights of Woman* in 1792. How can these progressive elements be reconciled with Burke's conservative agenda, if indeed they can be reconciled?

By calling her a greedy upstart, Starke discredits Mrs. Tartar's power. Eliza declares her intention, "Notwithstanding [Mrs. Tartar's] *hauteur*," to "teach her the difference between women who come here to make their fortunes, and those who only come to receive them" (p. 6, lines 6–8), spelling out the crucial difference between a bourgeois system of acquired wealth and an aristocratic system of inheritance. Though Starke's phrasing here seems to assume that aristocratic women will inherit wealth – which was usually but not necessarily the case – her comment applies immediately to the well-born Eliza. Mrs. Tartar, however enriched by her widowhood, is stained by her participation in the middle-class acquisition of wealth and by her working-class origins. The first epithet applied to Mrs. Tartar criticizes her "*blue*-cast, or half-cast complexion" (p. 6, lines 4–5; original emphasis), which is probably a reference to the darker skin color that resulted from her English father having married an Indian woman.[33] We find out the details of this alliance later, when the Moretons' servant Jeffreys reveals what he has learned from local gossip:

Mrs. Tartar's father was a tallow chandler, who, thinking he might retrieve a broken fortune in England, repair'd to this place, where he soon married a black merchant's daughter, "with a great deal of money," and died worth a million or two – Miss was sent over to the father's relations, in St. Mary Axe, for education and at her return, married Mr. Tartar, who originally was the son and heir of a basket-maker in St. Giles. (p. 22, lines 23–31)

Thus Mrs. Tartar herself springs from a marriage based on ambition, a tallow chandler's desire to "retrieve a broken fortune" by an Indian marriage, apparently regardless of any affection for his wife or apprehension of a mixed-race marriage. Despite Mrs. Tartar's money and education, class origins will run true, for Mrs. Tartar marries a man of her own ilk, "the son and heir of a basket-maker in St. Giles." Eliza's attack on Mrs. Tartar's *hauteur* makes it clear that her pretension to the class status of the Moretons is what constitutes the irritation, as Hastings irritated Burke for his tampering with traditional hierarchies.

Starke ridicules Mrs. Tartar's pretensions by calling her a despot, exaggerating her ambition to enter the EIC middle class as a presumption to aristocratic rank. Itself the cliché of an oriental tyrant, the name "Tartar" also alludes to a degenerating British subject in Foote's play *The Nabob*. More topically, it echoes Burke's ranking of Hastings's administration as more pernicious to India than the Tartars: "The Tartar Invasion was mischievous: but it is our protection which destroys India." What makes the Hastings administration worse than despotism, in Burke's eyes, is its usurped power as a state:

When the Tartars entered into China and Indoostan, when all the Goths and Vandals entered into Europe, when the Normans came into England, they came as a Nation. The Company in India does not exist as a Nation. (v:285)

Ignoring Burke's distinctions among degrees of ferocity, Starke exploits the metaphor's dramaturgical force of comparing the leader currently on trial with the legendary epitomes of Oriental despotism. Reinforcing the pun in her name, Starke makes this point clear when Eliza says, "I must humble this Indian Princess" (p. 8, line 32).

But the fact that Starke makes this satirical despot a woman rather than a man enables her to evoke the suspicion that Mrs. Tartar also possesses a secret cache of sinister sexual power that she exerts over the Resident, a power hidden from the Resident himself, as Louisa observes to him that she "seems to have more right over you than you chuse to avow" (p. 12, lines 10–11). Mrs. Tartar explains to the new arrivals the *modus operandi* of the place, saying "His [the Resident's] will is law here, and so you shall both find, *if I have any power with him*" (emphasis added). Louisa replies, "Oh dear Madam, I beg pardon; I did not know the Resident was under petticoat-government" (p. 12, lines 33–34). Like an absolutist king, the Resident's "will is law here," but it is an absolutism contaminated by a woman, who does indeed "have . . . power with him." Mrs. Tartar's sinister hiddenness is schematically contrasted with the invisible Mrs. Northcote, who offers refuge to Eliza and Louisa from the corruptions of Mrs. Tartar's house, and whose health is respectfully drunk by Edwards and Dormer. Other than those two mentions, however, Mrs. Northcote is absent from the text, and, more important from a theatrical point of view, she never appears on stage.

Starke here draws from a metaphoric system used by bourgeois writers to attack the aristocratic *ancien régime*. Calling Mrs. Tartar a despot employs a rhetoric that was progressive in terms of social class but conservative in terms of gender roles. As Joan Landes has observed, French middle-class men seeking to overthrow absolute monarchy attacked the few women who did participate in the public sphere of absolutism (queens, mistresses, *salonnières*) as corrupted by the world.[34] The corollary was that they presented the male monarchs as subordinate to the sexual power of women, and thus effeminate (Starke's implied charge in blaming a man for being "under petticoat-government"). The bourgeois men claimed a right to exert, in the open light of day, the political power that these few women had hitherto exerted covertly. These bourgeois men held that women of their class should be protected from the corruptions of the world by retreating to the private sphere and by participating in public life vicariously through their fathers, husbands, brothers, and sons. As Newman observes, effeminacy was a standard metaphor for the perceived cultural treason and corruption of the British aristocracy as well as the French. To take just one example, John Brown in 1757–58 attributed all his nation's ills to "the luxurious and effeminate Manners in the higher Ranks, together with a general defect of *Principle*."[35] Thus, this metaphoric system, prevalent in both Britain and France, demands that, when the public sphere is liberalized and its participants diversified by social class, it is simultaneously re-masculinized. Starke's portrayal of Mrs. Tartar as a despot, an "Indian Princess" who deviously pulls the strings of "petticoat-government" that demean the titular ruler, echoes all these gendered themes of the republican critique of absolutism, while Mrs. Northcote's invisibility prompts the audience to accept the propriety of women's retreat from view. Thus, the accession of Northcote is not only a reestablishment of English national identity, dispelling the blurred, banyan-clothed identity of the Resident, but also a re-masculinization of the public sphere. As a result, then, Starke's play enters the contradictions of its age by proclaiming the triumph of the bourgeois ideal that women should retreat to the private sphere, embodied in the visibly displayed persons of women portraying rank and wealth.

In another strain of apparent liberalism, Starke likens the marriage market in India to the slave-trade, underlining the comparison with an abolitionist subplot in which Jeffreys (spelled various ways), the head servant of the Moreton cousins, becomes intrigued by the case of Caesar, one of Mrs. Tartar's African slaves. Jeffreys, a plain-dealer figure exemplifying the nationalist value of English common sense, responds with puzzlement and irritation to Mrs. Tartar's slave-holding extravagance, and implicitly, to the economic waste of labor in the slavery system. (Young's remark that John Bannister "did justice" to the role indicates audience satisfaction and identification with this nationalist portrayal.) In one scene, the mindless specialization of labor, resulting from too many slaves, is dramatized: a slave carries Jeffreys's coat to another slave, who brushes it, and one slave may not do the other's job. In another scene, slaves play the card tricks of the Anglo-Indian women, who are too indolent to exert themselves even in pursuit of amusement. Within this wasteful system languishes Starke's character Caesar. (His is a conventional name for a black slave, used in Aphra Behn's *Oroonoko* [1688] and recycled in Maria Edgeworth's tale, *The Grateful Negro* [1804], which also names one of its slaveholders Jeffries). Caesar's previous master had promised him freedom, but died before fulfilling his promise. Jeffreys buys Caesar, and frees him. Caesar cannot imagine any freedom better than serving such a kind master, so he remains in Jeffreys's employ.

By adding this subplot, Starke caught the tide of abolitionist sentiment at the time of the play's premiere in 1788. The previous year, the Society for Effecting the Abolition of the Slave Trade had been founded in London, and in May 1788 Pitt had persuaded the House of Commons to agree that the slave-trade would be debated in the next session; abolitionists responded by waging "the largest petitioning campaign on public matters ever to have been organized in Britain up to this point."[36] In addition to the minting of Wedgewood's famous medallion of the kneeling slave ("Am I not a man and a brother?"), the anti-slavery campaign saw the outpouring of numerous abolitionist poems, such as William Cowper's "Pity for Poor Africans" (1788) and Hannah More's *Slavery, A Poem* (1788). This onslaught overwhelmed its opposition: the pro-slavery *Scriptural Researches on the Licitness of the Slave Trade* (1788) met with four refutations in the same year in Liverpool alone, a number that indicates the turning of the tide of popular opinion (Turley 23). Moreover, the anti-slavery cause had remarkably broad appeal, as women as well as men participated, and the cause's supporters were drawn from all sectors of religious life including Quakers, Unitarians, and evangelicals both within Anglicanism and outside it (Turley 17–21). As with her depiction of the changing of the guard in British India, Starke had her finger on the public pulse, deftly transplanting a controversy that had centered on the Atlantic slave-trade to an East Indian locale. Moreover, the facts as she presents them are historically accurate. A slave-trade in Africans did stretch to India (from Madagascar in English ships and from the Red Sea via Arab traders), although most slaves in India were indigenous. The EIC itself did not prohibit the export of slaves until 1789 and allowed slavery legal status until 1843.[37] Starke's Caesar is typical of the slaves coming from East Africa, most of whom labored in an urban market as domestic servants and who, as T. R. Sareen writes, were "not kept for any productive purposes, but in essence . . . serv[ed] as a badge of social honour for the masters"[38] – the very condition of excess that Starke satirizes in her play.

Among the several lines of argument an abolitionist might take – that the American Revolution demonstrated God's judgment against a slave-trading Britain, that the cruelty and inhumanity of the slave-trade degraded the slavers as well as the slaves – Starke's approach stresses the free rights of Englishmen, and the Whig heritage of the Glorious Revolution, the centenary of which, falling in 1788, gave Britons "a welcome opportunity to re-affirm their libertarian heritage" by promoting abolition (Colley 354). Following Jeffreys's purchase of Caesar, the former slave "[f]alls flat on the ground, embracing his feet," and upon Jeffreys's urging, rises (stage directions, p. 30), thus giving dramaturgical form to Wedgewood's medallion. Starke frames this act of liberation by emphasizing its affirmation of Jeffreys's national identity and his conferring it on Caesar:

JEFFREYS: . . . but you dog, I must make you a lad of spirit, like an Englishman, or else, what's your liberty good for?
CAESAR: Ah, Massa, I free! I like you! Am I Englishman? Oh teach me be Englishman.
JEFFREYS: That I will, you rogue. – An Englishman – ay, he lives as he likes – he lives *where* he likes – goes where he likes – *stays* where he likes – *works* if he likes – lets it *alone*, if he likes – starves, if he likes – abuses who he likes – boxes who he likes – thinks what he likes – speaks what he *thinks* – for, damme, he fears nothing, and will face the devil. (p. 30, lines 21–32)

Not only does abolition affirm English national identity: in the spirit of the Glorious Revolution, Starke takes the nationalistic stance that only Britons know the proper way to use their liberty, as Jeffreys implies by the offer to make Caesar "a lad of spirit, *like* an

Englishman, or else, what's your liberty good for?'' (my emphasis). In Caesar's response, the nationalist equation of liberty and English-ness is taken one step further, the similitude marker "like" disap-pears, becoming almost a copula, as he declares, "I free! I like you! *Am I Englishman.*'' (my emphasis). This dialogue seems to imply that possessing liberty is such a quintessentially English quality that those who acquire liberty become, in effect, honorary Englishmen, and it adds abolition of slavery to the correction of EIC abuses in India as the right, the English thing to do, conforming to the dichotomous schema Newman describes.

It is true that Starke mentions the apparently radical analogy between marriage and slavery. In response to Mrs. Tartar's plans for a party to welcome Eliza and Louisa and to display them for the marriage market, Eliza replies: "I look upon it with the most *sovereign contempt*; and I sincerely hope the traffic will be abolished, as still *more disgraceful* to our sex than that of poor slaves to a nation" (p. 9, lines 9–14; original emphasis). Indeed, Starke reinforces the connection between the marriage market and slavery by placing Mrs. Tartar as the head of both systems. This analogy has a radical pedigree, with one precedent in the abolitionist writings of Thomas Cooper of Manchester (Turley 160) and a descendant in Wollstonecraft's declaration: "Liberty is the mother of virtue, and if women be, by their very constitution, slaves, and not allowed to breathe the sharp invigorating air of freedom, they must ever languish like exotics, and be reckoned beautiful flaws in nature."[39] But the analogy has a less radical heritage as well, outlined in the Mansfield decision of 1772, which recognized a partial analogy between marriage and slavery, but disallowed slavery on the grounds that it was a municipal relation, while marriage was allowed to stand untouched because it was a natural relation. But the emphasis in the Mansfield decision is on England's libertarian heritage, emerging in the argument (alluded to by Wollstonecraft) that England's is "a soil whose air is deemed too pure for slaves to breathe in it; but the laws, the genius, and spirit of the constitution, forbid the approach of slavery, will not suffer it's [*sic*] existence here."[40] In light of Starke's dichotomous presentation of the bourgeoise Mrs. Tartar's marriage market on the one side and the aristocratic Eliza and Louisa's motivation solely by "Love" on the other, one must conclude that, for Starke, only mercantile marriage partakes of the evils of slavery, and that the root of evil lies in greed rather than in unequal gender relations. This conclusion squares with Starke's assessment of the evils of the EIC under Hastings and her admitted celebration of Cornwallis's reforms. However, it does not resolve Starke's paradoxical incarnation of the bourgeois value of privatized woman in the aristocratic bodies of Eliza and Louisa Moreton.

Here it is fruitful to recall Kramnick's observation of "the peculiar combination of love and hate that the bourgeoisie felt towards the aristocracy" in which the middle classes despised and resented men of rank while envying their wealth and power (193) – and to place Starke within this matrix. All of Starke's literary career bears witness to the kind of sycophancy that Kramnick has analyzed in Burke. The note is first sounded in her Preface to *The Sword of Peace*, which mentions her "unnumbered obligations" to George Colman the Elder (vii). The Preface to *The Widow of Malabar* (1791), addressed to Mrs. Crespigny, declares that "the chief part of that applause with which my Tragedy has been honored originated from your zealous friendship and powerful support" (vii). In her travel memoir, *Letters from Italy. . .* (1800), she mentions her own family's associations with the aristocracy, and in one particularly florid passage, praises "The Dutchess Dowager of A******* (whose universal benevolence adds dignity to her high rank)" for "permitting [Starke's family] to accompany her from Turin to Geneva" in order to consult her physician.[41] And her Advertisement to the hybrid volume, *The Beauties of Carlo Maria Maggi, paraphrased; to which are added Sonnets by Mariana Starke* (1811), gives all the credit for the book to the Countess Dowager Spencer, who, as Starke tells it, "discovered . . . beauties" in the poems of Maggi and gave a selection of them to Starke, saying,

the Poems it contained, tho' generally speaking unfinished, might, if abridged in some part, and considerably lengthened in others, make a better figure in English, than they had hitherto done in the Italian dress.[42]

Thus Starke gives the Countess credit for every significant step of the literary transmission: the acquisition of manuscripts, the discovery of their value, the idea of the paraphrase, and the choice of a paraphraser. Starke reduces her own creative agency to that of a pupil: "Anxious to profit by this hint, I immediately began to translate" (Advert., *Maggi*, n.p.). The merit of Starke's own creativity, like that of much of the class of artist-intellectuals, remained stultified under a system of aristocratic patronage.

Occasionally we catch a glimpse of Starke's rage smoldering. With the Preface to *The Sword of Peace*, she lashed out against a repression she saw in gendered terms:

A woman, *however possessed of genius, wit, vivacity, or knowledge of the world*, unless she continues to veil them under the modest, delicate reserve, which should ever characterise her sex, destroys their effects, and renders herself a being pitied by men of sense, envied, yet ridiculed, by every woman of her acquaintance . . . For these reasons, and these alone, *I own I have not the confidence to stand the public gaze*, nor vanity enough not to feel embarrassed as an avowed authoress. Having too often witnessed the fate of such (*however worthy, however amiable!*) I wish to conceal myself from *the censure of individuals, the flattery of sycophants, and the partiality of weak friends*. (my emphasis; vii)

Starke protests the patronage system that squelches women's merit in favor of privilege, leaving "worthy" authoresses – "however possessed of genius, wit, vivacity, or knowledge of the world" – subject to "the partiality of weak friends" and forcing them to number themselves among those "sycophants" whose flattery makes her want to hide. But the fundamental class dynamic, merit vs. privilege, remains the bedrock of the evil she protests. The mortification Starke endured was doubtless a major motive in her withdrawal from "the public gaze" of writing plays and producing them to take up the solitary pursuit of travel writing, a withdrawal obliquely chronicled in two sonnets by Starke in *The Beauties of Maggi*. One of them is addressed "To an unfortunate Friend, particularly fond of theatricals," bidding him (or her) to "view, in Fiction's varying vestments gay, / A world whose fallacies full-oft enthrall" (40); the next sonnet praises the wisdom of the traveler, "[t]he letter'd Sage, who unknown realms explores" (41). Starke's sycophancy, her frustration, and indeed her whole career trajectory, can be understood only in the light of the ambivalence endemic to her class.

This partial account of Starke's contradictions opens the further possibility that the labels "radical," "liberal," and "conservative" may themselves be instruments too blunt for continued use in our recovery of women writers of the Romantic period. Starke's "conservative" affirmation of the values of chivalry, her "liberal" critique of women's power under absolutism, and her "radical" condemnation of the slave-trade find common ground, historically, in a strongly patriotic version of religious conviction. As Newman observes, "[i]t is because the nationalist utopia lies in a realm above mere politics that nationalism often cuts across traditional party alignments" (159). The religious cast of her nationalism becomes even more evident in later works. Twelve years later, in *Letters from Italy*, having traced Napoleon's first Italian campaign, she declares, "Protestants, enlightened by a firm confidence in Holy Writ . . . saw . . . throughout the whole of this extraordinary business, the immediate hand of Heaven" (1:178). In her view, the freethinking French and the Catholic Italians are equally ignorant of the meaning of their war, which is clear to "Protestants, enlightened by a firm confidence in Holy Writ." Starke here invokes a pride in Protestant access to vernacular Scripture, which, as Colley observes, particularly characterizes English Protestants (42). And in her 1811 volume, *The Beauties of Maggi*, she adapts Maggi's *Ode on the destruction of Jerusalem* to the politics of the Napoleonic wars (Maggi having died in 1699). It is clear that for Starke, Italy should accept divine aid under the guise of British naval protection, rather than commit apostasy by trusting the Satanic French:

> – Appal'd she [Italy] stands,
> Imploring quick relief from foreign Hands:
> Nor impotent her cries – for Britain's Train,
> All-conquering Lords of Ocean's vast domain,
> With eagle-swiftness to her aid resort
> And steer her sinking vessel safe to Port.
> . . .
> Turn then to God; on his support rely;
> Upborne by Him, thou may'st this World defy:
> His power alone can vanquish Satan's plan,
> And change each Gallic Monster back to Man. (p. 17)

The import of Starke's exhortation is that British aid for Italy will be effective only if the Italians perform the kind of religious repentance and conversion she advocates – to see the military and political forces only is what she calls "a strong illusion" unless the religious– nationalist view is also accounted for. While the increase in religious language here over the 1788 *Sword of Peace* may be attributable to some private conviction on Starke's part, it can also be explained by the post-revolutionary reaction analyzed by Kelly, the reaction that made a retreat into "domesticity" and "propriety" (which includes religion) even more important for women struggling to participate in print culture. For present-day critics, a different kind of "strong illusion" may be threatening: our understandable longings to find precursors of our own feminist positions may mislead us into finding

128 JEANNE MOSKAL

proto-feminist promptings in women writers for whom advocacy for the rights of their sex was subordinated to religious commitments, to class ties, or to nationalist projects that brought an experience of provisional coherence to the contradictions of their age and culture.[43]

NOTES

1 Starke's dramatic efforts may have begun in Madras itself, for, as Allardyce Nicoll records, "[t]he fashion [for private theatricals] was carried even to India where at Madras Lady Campbell organised her private theatre for the amusement of the English residents." See *A History of Late Eighteenth Century Drama, 1750–1800* (Cambridge University Press, 1927), p. 21. Starke's second play, *The Widow of Malabar*, is an "adaptation" of Antoine Marin Le Mierre's 1780 play, *La Veuve de Malabar* (Nicoll, *A History*, pp. 308–09). See *The Widow of Malabar: A Tragedy in three Acts. As it is performed at the Theatre-Royal Covent Garden.* Third edition (London: William Lane, 1791).

2 See Jeffrey N. Cox's facsimile edition of *The Sword of Peace* in vol. v of *Slavery, Abolition, and Emancipation in the British Romantic Period. The Drama.* 8 volumes. Gen. eds. Debbie Lee and Peter Kitson (London: Pickering and Chatto, 1999). An electronic edition of the play is included at the website, *British Women Playwrights Around 1800*, ed. Thomas C. Crochunis and Michael Eberle-Sinatra (January 2000, <http://www-sul.stanford.edu/mirrors/romnet.wp1800/>). Recent critical works on Starke are: Jeanne Moskal, "Introduction to Mariana Starke's *The Sword of Peace*" in *British Women Playwrights Around 1800* (January 2000); Jeanne Moskal, "Politics and the Occupation of a Nurse in Mariana Starke's *Letters from Italy*" in *Romantic Geographies: The Discourse of Travel in the Romantic Period*, ed. Amanda Gilroy (Manchester University Press, forthcoming 2000); Jeanne Moskal, "Napoleon, Nationalism, and the Politics of Religion in Mariana Starke's *Letters from Italy*" in *Women Writers and the French Revolution*, ed. Kari Lokke and Adriana Craciun (Albany: State University of New York Press, forthcoming). Relevant forthcoming works include: Daniel O'Quinn, "The Marriage Plot in *The Sword of Peace*" in *British Women Playwrights Around 1800* (1999); and Donelle Ruwe, "Response to Daniel O'Quinn" in *British Women Playwrights Around 1800* (1999).

3 See Gerald Newman, *The Rise of English Nationalism: A Cultural History 1740–1830* (New York: St. Martin's Press, 1987), p. 159.

4 Starke thus foreshadows some of the nationalist uses of S. T. Coleridge's dramas as analyzed by Julie Carlson. See Chapter 2 of *In the Theatre of Romanticism: Coleridge, Nationalism, Women* (Cambridge University Press, 1994).

5 Mariana Starke, "Preface," *The Sword of Peace; or, A Voyage of Love: A Comedy in Five Acts* [1788] (London: J. Debrett, 1789), p. viii.

6 Cited in Newman, *Rise of English Nationalism*, p. 59.

7 Percival Spear, *The Nabobs: A Study of the Social Life of the English in Eighteenth-Century India*, second enlarged edition (London: Curzon, 1963), p. 74 and n.

8 See Edmund Burke, vol. VI of *The Writings and Speeches of Edmund Burke*, gen. ed. Paul Langford, *India: The Launching of the Hastings Impeachment, 1786–1788*, ed. Peter J. Marshall (Oxford: Clarendon, 1991), p. 377. 9 vols.

9 See chapter 4 of Siraj Ahmed, "'Where Rape and Murders are Tolerated Acts': British India in the Enlightenment," unpublished Ph.D. dissertation, Columbia University, 1999. No page numbers are available.

10 See Philip Lawson, *The East India Company: A History* (London: Longman, 1993), p. 90. Throughout this section I rely on Lawson, especially his chapters 5 and 6, and on Spear, *The Nabobs*.

11 See David Musselwhite, "The Trial of Warren Hastings" in *Literature, Politics, and Theory: Papers from the Essex Conference, 1976–84*, ed. Francis Barker *et al.* (London: Methuen, 1986), p. 80.

12 See Newman, *Rise of English Nationalism*, chapters 1 and 2.

13 *Ibid.*, chapter 5.

14 See Isaac Kramnick, *The Rage of Edmund Burke: Portrait of an Ambivalent Conservative* (New York: Basic Books, 1977), p. 130.

15 See Linda Colley, *Britons: Forging the Nation, 1707–1837* (New Haven: Yale University Press, 1992), p. 128.

16 See Katie Trumpener, *Bardic Nationalism: The Romantic Novel and the British Empire* (Princeton University Press, 1997), p. 169.

17 Edmund Burke, *Writings and Speeches*, VI, 420–21.

18 See Peter J. Marshall, ed. "Editorial Notes" to vol. VI of *The Writings and Speeches of Edmund Burke.* p. 418 n. 2.

19 Throughout this section I rely on Spear, *The Nabobs*, pp. 85–94.

20 See J. H. Plumb, *England in the Eighteenth Century* (Baltimore: Penguin Books, 1950), p. 171. In fact, trials at this time were often so theatricalized that the division between courtroom and stage had become somewhat blurred (see Judith Pascoe, *Romantic Theatricality: Gender, Poetry, and Spectatorship* [Ithaca: Cornell University Press, 1997], pp. 33–67; Julie Carlson, "Trying Sheridan's *Pizarro*" [*Texas Studies in Literature and Language* 38. 3 and 4, 1996, pp. 359–78]; and Marjean Purinton in the present volume).

21 In this I disagree with the discussion of *The Sword of Peace* in Marjean Purinton's chapter in this volume.

22 See Catherine B. Burroughs, *Closet Stages: Joanna Baillie and the Theater Theory of British Romantic Women Writers* (Philadelphia: University of Pennsylvania Press, 1997), p. 9.

23 See Ellen Donkin, *Getting into the Act: Women Playwrights in London, 1660–1800* (London and New York: Routledge, 1995), p. 5.

24 See Jeffrey N. Cox, "Ideology and Genre in the British Anti-revolutionary Drama in the 1790s" in *British Romantic Drama: Historical and Critical Essays*, ed. Terence Allan Hoagwood and Daniel P. Watkins (Teaneck, NJ: Fairleigh Dickinson University Press, 1998), pp. 84–114.

25 See Mary Julia Young, *Memoirs of Mrs. Crouch, including a retrospect of the stage during the years she performed.* 2 vols. (London: James Asperne, 1806), II:93–94.

26 For the facts of the play's run, see Charles Beecher Hogan, "Critical Introduction" and editorial notes in *The London Stage, 1660–1800*, Part Five (1776–1800), 3 vols., gen. ed. William van Lennep *et al.* (Carbondale: Southern Illinois University Press, 1968), pp. 1080–82 and 1170–76. For the attribution of the epilogue, I am following Hogan's account, though Mary Young (*Memoirs of Mrs. Crouch*) attributes both prologue and epilogue to George Colman the Younger (II:45). I rely on Donkin, *Getting into the Act*, chapter 1, throughout this paragraph.

27 [David Rivers], *Literary Memoirs of Living Authors of Great Britain* (1798). Rpt. in two vols. (New York: Garland Publishers, 1970), II:276.

28 John Genest, *Some Account of the English Stage, from the Restoration in 1660 to 1830.* [Spine title, *History of the English Stage.*] 10 vols. (Bath: H. E. Carrington, 1832), X:219–20.

29 Mariana Starke, Letter to *The Morning Chronicle.* Rpt. in vol. III, Part 2 of *Biographia Dramatica; or, a companion to the playhouse: containing historical and critical memoirs . . .*, ed. David Erskine Baker, Isaac Reed, and Stephen Jones. 3 vols. (London: Longman, Hurst, Rees, Orme, and Brown, 1812), p. 313 (original emphasis).

30 Cox's editorial notes to *The Sword of Peace*, vol. V of *Slavery, Abolition, and Emancipation*.

31 See Gary Kelly, *Women, Writing, and Revolution, 1790–1827* (Oxford: Clarendon Press, 1993), p. 21.

32 For chivalry in the period, see David Duff, *Romance and Revolution: Shelley and the Politics of a Genre* (Cambridge University Press, 1994); and Jeanne Moskal, "Cervantes and the Politics of Mary Shelley's *History of a Six Weeks' Tour*" in *Mary Shelley in Her Times*, ed. Stuart Curran and Betty T. Bennett (Baltimore: Johns Hopkins University Press, forthcoming).

33 Cox points out that the term "Resident" also designated the representative of the Governor-General at an important native court after Hastings's organization of the Civil Service. See Cox, "Introduction" to vol. V of *Slavery, Abolition, and Emancipation*, pp. vii–xxxiii.

34 Joan B. Landes, *Women and the Public Sphere in the Age of the French Revolution* (Ithaca: Cornell University Press, 1988), p. 27.

35 John Brown, cited in Newman, *Rise of English Nationalism*, p. 81; Brown's emphasis.

36 See Colley, *Britons*, p. 353, and David Turley, *The Culture of English Antislavery, 1780–1860* (New York: Routledge, 1991), p. 69.

37 See Cox, "Introduction" to vol. v of *Slavery*, and D. R. Banaji, *Slavery in British India* (Bombay: D. B. Taraporevala Sons & Co., 1933), pp. 73–79; 80–132; and 201–02.

38 See T. R. Sareen, "Slavery in India under British Rule 1772–1843," *Indian Historical Review*, 15.1–2 (1989), p. 257.

39 See Mary Wollstonecraft, *A Vindication of the Rights of Woman* (1792) in *The Vindications: The Rights of Men, The Rights of Woman*, ed. D. L. Macdonald and Kathleen Scherf (Peterborough, Ontario, Canada: Broadview Press, 1997), p. 147.

40 See *The Mansfield Judgment* (1772) in *British Literature 1780–1830*, ed. Anne K. Mellor and Richard E. Matlak (New York: Harcourt Brace College Publishers, 1996), p. 56.

41 Mariana Starke, *Travels in Italy between the years 1792 and 1798* . . . Second edition, 2 vols. (London: R. Phillips, 1802). 1:17. The first edition (1800) is entitled *Letters from Italy*. . . but has no other changes. See also Moskal, "Napoleon, Nationalism, and the Politics of Religion."

42 Mariana Starke, "Advertisement" to *The Beauties of Carlo Maria Maggi, paraphrased; to which are added Sonnets: by Mariana Starke* (Exeter: privately printed, 1811), n.p.

43 The author thanks Catherine B. Burroughs, Jeffrey N. Cox, Stuart Curran, Radhika Jones, and Larry Zelenak for their comments on previous versions of this chapter; Siraj Ahmed, Thomas Crochunis, Doucet Devin Fischer, David Savran, and James Walvin for helpful suggestions; and Tim Sadenwasser for his research assistance. Thanks are also due to the Rare Book Collections at the University of North Carolina at Chapel Hill and at Butler Library, Columbia University, New York; and to the Department of English and Comparative Literature at Columbia University for hospitality and computer support during the completion of this chapter.

CHAPTER 5

Women's sovereignty on trial: Joanna Baillie's comedy "The Tryal" as metatheatrics

Marjean D. Purinton

I

Joanna Baillie's comedy, *The Tryal*, was published in a collection of three plays entitled *Plays on the Passions* in 1798, bisecting the two tragedies in the collection, *De Monfort* and *Count Basil*. Like the tragedies, *The Tryal* challenges the prevailing ideological doctrine of separate spheres that governed gender roles and behaviors.[1] Written at a time when class and gender politics in Great Britain were responding to revolutionary events and discourses, *The Tryal* exposes the ways in which women and men resist and participate in a social system that commodifies women as objects of the marriage contract.[2] *The Tryal* cleverly dramatizes alternatives to the disguise and censorship women were compelled to endure by situating female agency within a drama about playwriting and performance. The metadramatic treatment of gendered behaviors and performative relationships is exhibited as a parody of courtroom action, the legal arena from which women were exclusively barred.[3] Agnes and Mariane Withrington stage a series of "trials" to expose, or "uncloset," the false conventions that underpin gender relations and enact revisionary treatments of female sovereignty in private and public spaces.

A "closeted drama" never publicly staged, *The Tryal* exploits theatre as a strategy for challenging culturally determined gender roles that would subsume female agency as well as male-specific institutions, like the theatre and the courtroom, which seek to contain the public performances of women. Catherine B. Burroughs, in her recent comprehensive study of Baillie's theatre theory, analyzes women's negotiations between "the closet" (domestic spaces) and the "stage" (public spaces), and she demonstrates the "psychic and social costs exacted of women who pushed their theorizing into the public arena."[4] Burroughs's work has helped us to see how Baillie might maneuver about this problem by situating public spaces within domestic spaces, pseudo-legal trials within domestic drama, so as to confuse and expose the artificiality of spaces identified as public and private. In writing a drama in which women create a series of six "little dramas," or "trials," Baillie shows how metatheatrics – drama about drama – can open new spaces for female sovereignty.

The layered dramas of *The Tryal* and the performances staged within the play create spaces for Baillie to stage the kind of revolution in women's manners excited by the prose polemics and educational tracts written by women in the late eighteenth century, many of which responded to the conduct-book tradition, a powerful conditioning vehicle of patriarchal relations that inculcated the subordination of women in the public sphere. *The Tryal* makes its own pretense as theatre ironically powerful as a teaching strategy when it places women's sovereignty on trial repeatedly in the forms of Agnes's and Mariane's playscripts. In the 1790s, sovereignty, or power, is a privilege that women do not seem to possess, especially as conventionally operative in the public spaces of the masculine sphere, but which they might exercise, at least in their own lives, by acknowledging and acting in epistemological and performative forms.[5] In putting "sovereignty" on public display as theatricalized litigation, Agnes and Mariane expose the ways in which women might exercise power that they generally accept as inappropriate, even dangerous. The metatheatrics of *The Tryal*, therefore, constitute a pedagogical strategy offering women an alternative relationship to power from that instructed in the conduct-book tradition and a theatrical foil to the cult of sentimentality so popular in the period's novels.

This chapter will demonstrate how Baillie theatricalized epistemological paradigms – appropriated and subverted from eighteenth-century women's writings – as well as incorporated the culture's fascination with theatricalized litigation and ritualized courtship/ marriage, to expose current limitations and future possibilities of women's sovereignty. If women's lives are theatrical, as the meta-theatrics of *The Tryal* suggest, then the scripts that women perform can be rewritten, as Agnes's and Mariane's playwriting, directing, and acting demonstrate. Constructing certain kinds of plays at different moments in order to achieve specific strategies, Agnes's and Mariane's "little dramas" stage pedagogical performances that sub-stitute what Judith Butler terms "excitable speech" for performative speech acts.[6] Excitable speech involves language generally not appropriate for speakers in their historical and cultural moment (for example violating utterances bound by the legal determinants of class and gender), and it frequently seeks to challenge the social patterns that would silence or limit its use. Agnes's and Mariane's uses of language as performance, as excitable speech, works to urge female emancipation by transforming the economy of courtship/ marriage to the economy of speech, a transformation in which women's words exert power. I will first consider the cultural contexts in which Baillie's emancipatory and empowering pedagogy is situated, and then I will examine how various playscripts that unfold in *The Tryal* challenge the culture's notions of women's sovereignty.

In the "Introductory Discourse" to the 1798 *Plays on the Passions*, Baillie identifies theatrics as a pedagogical strategy aimed at disrupting readers'/spectators' comfortable identifications and fostering critical considerations of cultural patterns that have come to operate performatively. In other words, *The Tryal* and the "performances" within Baillie's drama expose the normalizing effects of performative practices. The cultural pattern explicitly "uncloseted" as performative in *The Tryal* is that of the courtship/marital ritual. Baillie's preface encourages the active mind to discover concealed passions, to question "normative" patterns governing relationships, and to effect social as well as personal revolutions.

Baillie's "Introductory Discourse" recognizes the powerful role that theatre could play in the reconditioning of social relations directed by notions of gendered spaces. While the prefatory prose delineates Baillie's theory of dramaturgy, it also identifies as pedagogical strategy the human propensity of "sympathetick curiosity towards others of our own kind which is so strongly implanted within us."[7] Baillie asserts that curiosity about human passions "is our best and most powerful instructor," for in our examination of others, "we know ourselves" (12). Her dramas about passions seek to create a relationship of empathy and identification between characters and readers/spectators from which they may garner edification, but the identificatory process generated by the drama involves critical thinking and connected knowing, not a linear mimetic relationship. In other words, Baillie's "Introductory Discourse" delineates the pedagogical relationship her dramas engender theatrically: "The Drama improves us by the knowledge we acquire of our own minds, from the natural desire we have to look into the thoughts, and observe the behaviour of others" (37). Her dramaturgy invites readers/spectators to participate in the cognitive and analytical process stimulated by the drama, an exercise in problem-solving and application which invests the authority of meaning-making and knowledge construction in readers/spectators.[8]

Baillie's notion that passions constitute a point of identification and enlightenment is particularly significant in considering the challenges women raised about their miseducation at the end of the eighteenth century. She is not, however, the only writer to suggest engendering the sympathetic curiosity in a spectator as a peda-gogical strategy. In *A Vindication of the Rights of Woman* (1792), Mary Wollstonecraft emphasizes the instructional power of spectacle:

> When we hear of some daring crime – it comes full on us in the deepest shade of turpitude, and raises indignation; but the eye that gradually saw the darkness thicken, must observe it with more compassionate forbear-ance. The world cannot be seen by an unmoved spectator, we must mix in the throng, and feel as men feel before we can judge of their feelings. If we mean, in short, to live in the world to grow wiser and better, and not merely to enjoy the good things of life, we must attain a knowledge of others at the same time that we become acquainted with ourselves – knowledge acquired any other way hardens the heart and perplexes the understanding.[9]

Wollstonecraft, like Baillie, asserts that, in appealing to our sympa-thetic curiosity, spectacles teach us something about the world, about the human condition, and about ourselves. Both writers recognize how the identificatory dynamic between staged characters and spectators contributes to the process of self-actualization.[10] The pedagogical strategy emphasizes the social rather than the senti-mental potential of women's writing, indicating that Baillie's "passions," like Wollstonecraft's "manners," constitute the site of social change.[11] An enlightened female audience can, in the words of Mary Hays, "take charge of their own passions and then effect reform."[12]

Wollstonecraft and Baillie recreate courtroom scenes as private and public sites where educational reform portends legal parity for women. Wollstonecraft delineates the legal and marital "wrongs" of woman in her unfinished novel *Maria* (1798). Maria is denied a hearing before the court, and she pleads her case and that of Henry Darnford in the form of a letter, the "proper" form for female expression, which the judge magnanimously allows to be included in the public record. For Baillie, the staging of female agency and sovereignty in public spaces occurs metatheatrically in *The Tryal*, which is as much a trial about education and pedagogy as it is a trial about the respectability of would-be husbands. Agnes's and Mariane's "trials" uncloset epistemological matters as well as political and legal limitations for women. The powerful pedagogical function of drama is therefore multiplied by the metatheatrics of *The Tryal*, which invites critical readings of individual behaviors and cultural patterns, many of which were variously displayed in the period's political polemics, educational treatises, and heroine-centered sentimental novels.

II

Baillie published her dramatic *Tryal* anonymously, at a time when Britain's public attention was focused on actual trials both at home and abroad. Prior to the 1789 Revolution, the sensational trial of Cardinal Rohan, Countess Nicole LeGuay, and others created international attention. They were accused of stealing a diamond necklace commissioned by Louis XV. Cardinal Rohan purchased the jewel for Marie Antoinette in 1785, but a man masquerading as the Queen's valet, to whom Rohan gave the necklace, made off with it. Rohan's lawyer, Guy Jean Baptiste Target, became France's premier trial lawyer following his dramatic speeches and briefs during the trial.[13] The trial was conducted as a public spectacle, bringing domestic and legal matters together in theatricalized space, a courtroom drama that became the object of the British gaze.

Another trial drawing international attention involved Warren Hastings, Governor-General of India, who was tried in impeachment proceedings before the House of Lords from 1788 until 1795, even though it was clear after the first year of the trial that Hastings would be acquitted.[14] Hastings was accused of giving preferential treatment to Scottish military and civilian officers in India and of governing in an unscrupulous and despotic manner. The significance of Scottish-Jacobite sympathies in India were not lost on a British public concerned with political revolutions as well as commercial interests in the East.[15] For women especially, Hastings's colonial exploitation of the "feminized" Orient as a cultural "other" suggested analogues with patriarchal privilege of sexual assault or rape of woman's body in marital politics. Coincidentally, Mariana Starke's comedy, *The Sword of Peace; or, A Voyage of Love*, was performed at the Theatre Royal, Haymarket, in 1788, and it, like Baillie's comedy, involves two female protagonists, Eliza and Louisa Morten, who travel to India to recover a colonial soldier's sword and a banished lover.[16] *The Sword of Peace*, like *The Tryal*, challenges the valuations and spaces assigned to women, and Eliza and Louisa cleverly script their own "civilizing" mission to India, boldly asserting their sovereignty and presence in masculinized public spaces. Readers/spectators of Baillie's play might have been alerted to the intertextual possibilities of these trials, especially since one of the protagonists of *The Tryal* is named Mariane.

Mariane's name is also an important clue to French revolutionary activity, including the sensational trial of Marie Antoinette, which informs Baillie's comedy. Lynn Hunt reminds us that the name "Marianne" was a popular embodiment of the goddess Liberty in France around 1793.[17] Hunt argues that the trial of Marie Antoinette, which fascinated the British on many levels, was theatricalized, an "implicit and often unconscious gender drama."[18] Regardless of their political sympathies, British women would have recognized the importance of the former queen's trial before the Revolutionary Criminal Tribunal, for Marie Antoinette's fate was decided by a male jury and nine male judges.[19] The prevailing belief was that the Queen had used her sexual body to corrupt the body politic, and so, like Maria of Wollstonecraft's novel, the queen became a representative of all women, on trial for their sex and judged by a body of men threatened by female presence in the public sphere.[20] In naming a principal character of her comedy "Mariane," Baillie may allude to the period's conflicted French politics, its ambiguities and anxieties about the role of women in public spaces reflected by its feminized "liberty" and sexualized Marie Antoinette.

While British audiences gazed on the theatrical decapitation of the French Queen following her trial in 1793, they had also been watching the disembodiment of the English radical hero Thomas Paine, who was tried for sedition in 1792. Although Paine fled to France before the trial began, he was found guilty *in absentia* of seditious libel and exiled from Britain. In a theatricalized show of anger at Paine's absence from his trial, a mob burned an effigy of the author of *The Rights of Man*. Britain also closely followed the Treason Trials of 1794. Thomas Hardy, John Thelwall, John Horne Tooke,

and others were prosecuted for high treason at a time when
suspicions of French influences and invasions created heightened
anxiety. The accused were acquitted of the excessive charges by
male London juries, but the courtroom proceedings were, according
to Judith Pascoe, theatricalized to appeal to female spectators who
made up a substantial part of the courtroom audience (7–8). The
courtroom "theatre" of the trials took on melodramatic dimensions,
with costumes, props, and dramatic posturings used to control public
representations. Pascoe cites two crucial roles women played in the
stagings of the treason trials: (1) they constituted a significant female
presence in court, thereby influencing participants' performances –
that is, as audience; and (2) they functioned as props, used by male
principals to enhance their own self-representations – that is, as
objects (32–35). Importantly, the women in these actual courtroom
dramas remained essentially passive, commodities conveniently
transferred from their conventional objectification in the marriage
ritual to that of theatricalized justice. Like their French counterparts
during the Republic, British women were "off-stage," as Joan
Landes describes the situation, to the central drama of political life;
they were spectators, not actors, a speechless audience at the scene
of men's activities (157). In Baillie's *Tryal*, however, Agnes and
Mariane re-position themselves in relation to actual women of the
French Republic and the female spectators of Britain's 1794 Treason
Trials.

    These instances of actual, sensationalized trials illustrate that, by
1798, the performative connections between the courtroom and the
theatre were commonplace in Britain's social unconscious. The
"sympathetic curiosity" which the public expresses for courtroom
drama is unmistakably strong, and Baillie finds pedagogical potential
in the public fascination with theatricalized trials, which, in *The
Tryal*, she resituates as domestic comedy set in Bath. This domestic
framework is important, since it enables Agnes and Mariane to
perform their playscripted litigation and permits Baillie to work
against the prevailing notions of women in public politics –
especially during the post-revolutionary period – as beasts and
monsters, and women in and of the theatre as prostitutes.[21] Baillie
would have observed various women's negotiations with the public
spaces of politics and theatrics, knowing first-hand the difficulties of
having her plays staged and the consequences of her name on the
title page of her published dramas.[22] The layered performances

contained within the domestic space of *The Tryal* open up safe spaces to subvert these pejorative associations of "public" women, which denied their cognitive sovereignty.

III

The uncomplicated and domestic plot of *The Tryal* blatantly draws from the public spaces of both the courtroom and the theatre. Agnes and Mariane persuade their doting uncle, Anthony Withrington, to play along with their scheme to exchange identities so that they can test the suitability of Agnes's would-be-husbands. Agnes hopes to find a disinterested lover, a man who will marry her for herself, not for the money accompanying her social position as heiress. Thomas Harwood has designs on the independent-minded Agnes, but he is aware that class differences may impede his affections. An ambitious lawyer, Harwood is the younger son of a family of limited income, and his widowed mother hopes to see him respectably situated. Harwood represents the new bourgeois class and values, which are also on trial in a society that resists change. Mariane has no money, but she is engaged to Edward, Withrington's nephew, who may inherit a comfortable income from his uncle, especially if, as a bonus for her theatrics, Agnes can extort financial rewards from her uncle for them. Mariane happily becomes an accomplice to her cousin's deceptions because she is anxious to avenge several men who admire her beauty but disdain her poverty. These suitors include Sir Loftus Prettyman, Jack Opal, Mr. Royston, and Humphrey.

At the level of playwriting, Baillie adopts the disguise of play-acting which had become a familiar female strategy for public-space appearances. Recent studies by Catherine Burroughs, Lesley Ferris, Ellen Donkin, and Judith Pascoe have shown how stage acting and social acting were particularly connected for women of the period.[23] These studies have demonstrated the powerful connections between scripted, staged female performances and socially determined gender performatives. Replete with actual courtroom trials involving sedition and treason, with women as sexualized props and specta-tors, the turbulent historical moment at which *The Tryal* is set and published intensifies the political associations of theatrical perfor-mances and social performatives.[24] The situational context of the comedy emphasizes marriage as the social performative that had material and psychological importance for women. What better way

for Baillie to explore the performative than by resituating the court-
ship/marriage ritual as a political/legal procedure?

The courtship/marriage ritual at the core of *The Tryal* had
profound signification for women in a society in transition from
aristocratic to bourgeois class structure. Like law, marriage had
become theatricalized and politicized by 1798, for, as Christopher
Flint points out, marriage ceremonies were no longer private,
spiritual sacraments but public events, inseparable from secular
politics.[25] Lord Hardwicke's 1753 Marriage Act required marriages
to be legally contracted and performed in the presence of wit-
nesses.[26] The public display of a marriage ceremony provided
evidence that a woman had performed her duty. Consequently,
marital rituals at the end of the eighteenth century played a vital role
in the newly empowered bourgeois family paradigm, a source for
female subject-formation, one that recast women in the domestic
sphere. The performative behavior of the female role in domesticity
rendered it "natural" and desirable, despite its blatantly legal
construction, as Blackstone's *Commentaries on the Laws of England*
recognize: "Thus our own common law has declared, that the goods
of the wife do instantly upon marriage become the property and
right of the husband; . . . yet that right . . . [has] no foundation in
nature; but merely created by the law, for the purpose of civil
society."[27] Fundamentally, therefore, women existed in a problematic relation to cultural mechanisms of power. Women were treated
as commodities, with marriage functioning like a financial
contract.[28] Daughters were valued as property, and one clause of the
Marriage Act stated that no woman under the age of twenty-one
could marry without her father's consent, but nothing in the law
prevented fathers from arranging marriages without their daughters'
consent. Women were granted only a symbolic subjectivity, and they
struggled with the dilemma of how to exercise authority without
appearing "male." As political concerns entered domestic discourses, and domestic matters became performative public spectacles, women negotiated impediments to female agency in both
private and public spaces.

Agnes's and Mariane's "performances" disguise household
governance as mere playacting, and their schemes complicate the
distinctions between private and public spaces in their superimposi-
tions of the conventionally private/familial matter of marriage on
the simulated public arena of legal proceedings. By actively

participating in the courtship/marriage ritual and family governance through theatricalized courtrooms, Agnes and Mariane carve out a place for themselves (and other women) in ambiguously rendered public spaces.[29] Agnes and Mariane also alert women to the dangers and illusions of courtship/marriage. The supposed private life of women is exposed for its connection and dependence on public (masculinist, patriarchal, paternal) ideology. The law of coverture expresses marital oppression under the guise of domestic security and "natural" subservience as "legal/theatrical" typecasting: "By marriage, the husband and wife are one person in law; that is, the very being or legal existence of the woman is suspended during the marriage, or at least is incorporated and consolidated into that of the husband: under whose wing, protection, and *cover* she *performs* every thing."[30] Mariane and Agnes challenge the performative role of the married women and the relationship between private and public in "outing" a process that simultaneously sought to protect women's privacy and to restrict female subjectivity.

Throughout *The Tryal*, Agnes and Mariane are reminded of the economic terms of the courtship and marriage ritual in which they are players. Early in the play, for example, Withrington assigns economic value to Agnes's plain features: "Why there is not one feature in thy face that a man would give a farthing for."[31] Later, Opal comments to Harwood that if Agnes "could coin her words into farthings, she would be one of the best matches in the kingdom" (1.2.211). Agnes is perceived as a woman of many irritating words and little dowry, as Colonel Hardy characterizes her to Harwood as prospective wife: "An expensive and violent temper'd woman is not to be thought of" (4.1.259). Sir Loftus admonishes Mariane's imprudent behavior in monetary terms: "A large fortune may make amends for an ordinary person, madame, but not for vulgarity and impertinence" (4.2.274). Opal protests that £10,000 is an extraordinary amount for Mariane to demand for marrying her, but the presumed heiress assures him that it is "the fashion" (5.1.280). When Opal discovers that Mariane is not an heiress and that he is accountable for his written contract of marriage, he argues: "Upon honour, madame, we men of fashion don't expect to be called to an account for every foolish thing we say" (5.2.295). As we will see, however, when the men of *The Tryal* reduce women to a marketable subculture, Agnes and Mariane turn the tables on the commercial enterprise of marriage. Their performances uncover the possibilities for marital relationships based on mutual respect and gender parity by shifting the terms of the economy of marriage to the economy of speech, suggesting a revaluing of language in subject-formation and for women's sovereignty.

IV

The metatheatrical framework of *The Tryal* empowers Agnes and Mariane in ways that theatre or society could not, imbuing the cousins with a power that, as Judith Butler argues, *enacts* the subject into being[32] and that provides Agnes and Mariane with an occasion for what Elspeth Probyn describes as *enunciating* subjectivity.[33] As subjects who derive their agency from the power they oppose, Agnes and Mariane "act out" and "speak out" alternatives to the compulsory social rituals they, and other women, are expected to perform. Agnes and Mariane assume power and sociolinguistic privilege, language usually reserved for men in public spaces, unmasking their would-be-lovers' identities as genuine or fraudulent. They acquire autonomy and independence while simultaneously employing masquerade phenomenology (the mysterious nature of the "other") to test the amorous motivations and intentions of would-be-suitors. Agnes, for example, re-casts her own role as a poor cousin, then as a tempting vixen, and, in doing so, she controls her own destiny. Agnes becomes a self-made heroine, not one fashioned out of the cult of sensibility or the "happily-ever-after" fictionality of fairy-tale romance. Mariane embodies self-fashioned "liberty," a role not necessarily determined by masculinized politics that needs a feminized prop, as the fictitious Mariane of the French Revolution had been cast.

Two story-telling incidents early in the play illustrate the performative connections between speech acts and legal acts, connections that inform the various "performances" staged by Agnes and Mariane. *The Tryal* recognizes that the one who acts, acts precisely to the extent that she or he is constituted as an *actor*, and hence operates within a linguistic field of enabling constraints. The one who speaks is imagined to wield sovereign power and the authority to make words binding.[34] Sir Humphrey boasts of a lawsuit Royston has won against the widow Gibson for "letting her chickens feed amongst his corn" (2.1.219). Humphrey rails at the injustice of her being fined only a sixpence: "It was very wrong in her, you know sir, to let her hens go amongst his honour's corn, when she knew very well, she was too poor to make up the loss to his honour" (2.1.129). The judge's sentence in favor of Royston validates the sovereignty of masculinist law, its inherent double standard of justice, its legitimizing of female subordination and economic dependency.

Agnes reworks this set of operative conventions, which provide the discursive occasion for resistance to and potential subversion of the law. From the beginning of the play, she takes charge of the business of marriage by using excitable speech disguised as fantasy. Agnes captivates Uncle Withrington with her story-telling:

> You don't know perhaps, that when I went to Scotland last summer, I travelled far, and far, as the tale says, and farther than I can tell, till I came to the Isle of Sky, where every body has the second sight, and has nothing to do but tear a little hole in a tartan plaidy, and peering through it, in this manner, sees every thing past, present, and to come. (1.1.200)

Relating this improbable tale of her encounter with an old sorceress, Agnes persuades her uncle to settle a handsome provision upon Mariane's and Edward's marriage and to leave them his fortune. Agnes's sentence, no less than that of the civil court in the case of Royston *v.* Gibson, enacts sovereignty, the ability to rule, to effect economic and social consequences. Her story-telling, like the story of her experience itself, tears a little hole in the fabric of enabling constraints marked by legal language and performance speech. Just as Baillie's "Introductory Discourse" shows us how to read the pedagogical implications of *The Tryal*, so these prefatory story-telling incidents show us how to read the ideological assertions of Agnes's and Mariane's performances. For through the spaces of the plays-within-the-play, readers/spectators will see the past and present patriarchal injustices plus future possibilities for women's sovereignty.

Throughout *The Tryal*, value is bestowed on story-telling, and, as we have seen, story-telling facilitates the re-valuing of words that, in a marriage performative, render women objectified. In their play-scripts, Agnes and Mariane make words and speech-acts binding for female authority. In Act 4, for example, Mariane capitalizes on a story she gleaned from Old Mrs. Marblecake, which details how Sir Loftus ran nine times to an apothecary's to fetch green salve with which to rub her monkey's tail. The ridiculous story appreciates in its repetition, for Loftus is highly irritated that Mariane has shared it with everyone. Loftus vows that, once he has secured Mariane as wife, he will tame her tongue, or devalue her "excitable speech." Assuring Mariane that it is not in her power to make a fool of him, Loftus exclaims indignantly: "You have heard the last *words* I shall ever say to you upon the subject" (4.3.274, emphasis mine). The lesson has been staged, despite Loftus's protests, for in resignifying words with value not conventionally available to women of the late eighteenth century, Mariane has exercised sovereignty.

Agnes similarly speaks within a linguistic field of enabling constraints which she has scripted for herself and others. In Act 3, for example, Agnes's servant Betsy accidentally breaks a perfume bottle and asks Harwood: "Does she think I am going to live in her service to be call'd names so, and compared to a blackamoor too?" (3.2.248). Betsy's "cursed stories" (3.2.250) about Agnes's verbal abuse of the servant puts Harwood out of the inclination to visit her. Loaded with emotional blackmail, Agnes's speech to Harwood persuades him, half unwillingly, to join her party. He cowers at Agnes's commanding words: "You are a simpleton, or you would have half a dozen at my service" (3.2.252). Agnes's speech-acts have the power to name Harwood as "simpleton," and, at least momentarily, he comes to accept the part to which he has been named. Betsy, on the other hand, will not tolerate Agnes's "blackamoor" label, which devalues her, and she refuses to be named what she perceives herself not to be. The story-telling of *The Tryal* transfers sovereignty to women, who resignify their former value in the marriage market to speech economy, a metatheatrical and pedagogical strategy that helps readers/spectators to perceive the revolutionary potential of the excitable speech that Agnes and Mariane write into their "little plays."

Agnes and Mariane write and perform playscripts of "excitable speech" in the very context of law from which Butler asserts that it emanates,[35] giving them the appearance of sovereign power in public spaces. In their courtroom at Bath, Agnes and Mariane defuse the privilege and power Royston had come to exercise at the Inns of Court. In Act 3, for example, Agnes explains to her uncle that Royston is angered over Mariane's farcical treatment of him because "he can't take the law of her for laughing at him" (3.1.239).[36] Mariane's speech-acts in this scene are "conduct" only in a theatrical sense, having only a fictitious power to produce effects or initiate a set of consequences, or, in other words, to function as performative. The performative here, unlike that found in the sentimental novels that reify and enforce behavior delimiting for women, has the potential to excite a sympathetic curiosity, an identificatory process that moves readers/spectators to critical examination rather than blind imitation.

Critiques of conventional masculinity and femininity as performative surface from these story-telling scenes in *The Tryal*. Miss Eston's gregarious appearances on stage expose the artifice of femininity embodied as the social gossip. As the end of the first scene comes to a close, for example, Eston is heard to ramble: "Bye the bye Mrs. Mumblecake is sadly to-day; has your lady sent to enquire for her William? I wonder if her (*Exit, still talking without*) old coachman has left her; I saw a new face on the, &c.&c." (1.1.206). Eston's linguistic performances on stage differ in substance and function from those of Agnes and Mariane, whose "excitable speech" is charged with dramatic and ideological importance. In contrast to the "magpie" (1.2.211), Eston, the men of fashion are "sparing of their words," Sir Loftus tells Harwood, so that, like scholars, "they may be listened to more attentively when they do speak," and so that, Loftus elaborates, "inferior people are apt to forget themselves, and despise what is too familiar" (1.2.209). Opal mimes his principal mentor, telling Harwood that he does not study speeches for company: "I don't trouble my head to find out *bons mots* of a morning" (1.2.212). Harwood agrees that Opal would have a laborious life if he "could not speak nonsense extempore" (1.2.212). While these metatheatrical speech-acts remind readers/spectators that social positionalities, like performers' blocking on stage, are directed by culturally inculcated scripts, they also reveal the enunciatory construction of behaviors identified as masculine or feminine.

v

The story-telling vignettes that expose the artificiality of gender-based subjectivity function as a kind of prelude to the metatheatrics that follow. The remainder of *The Tryal* stages a series of playscripts, primarily written, directed, and acted by Agnes and Mariane. The pedagogical applications of excitable speech are enriched by its insertions into the cousins' theatrics, for Agnes's and Mariane's performances place female sovereignty on trial in ways that Baillie's play cannot, at least directly, thereby pointing to actual possibilities of women's sovereignty in patriarchal culture. In the first "little drama," Agnes retires into an adjoining closet to observe Mariane's performance with Sir Loftus. The ploy involves baiting Loftus's designs on Mariane as they discuss preparations for an upcoming ball. Loftus has difficulty expressing his love for Mariane: "Few words, perhaps, will better suit the energy of passion" (2.2.227). Mariane assuages his embarrassment by granting him few words: "Just as you please, Sir Loftus, if you chuse to say it in few words I am very well satisfied" (2.2.227). Loftus's timid profession of love is saved by the intrusion of Withrington and Harwood, who prevent him from additional utterances of passion. As in the story-telling vignettes of *The Tryal*, Mariane reclaims language as power for women in this theatrical with Loftus. She determines the amount and authority of spoken words. In the gender-bending of Mariane's script, Loftus is reduced to the silent and self-effacing role generally occupied by women in late eighteenth-century society.

During their second performance, Agnes and Mariane tease Jack Opal into declaring his intentions to Mariane. Their script induces Opal and Loftus to perform in affected behaviors usually associated with feminine mannerisms. Encouraged by Mariane's praise of Colonel Hardy's posture, Opal "holds his head in a constrained ridiculous posture, and then makes a conceited bow" (3.1.243). Opal's manners are uncloseted as artificially contrived as the standards that restrict women's behaviors. In a third "little drama," Agnes acts the part of a shrew, feigning anger in order to test Harwood's loyalty to her. During this trial, Harwood is conscious of his objectified position in relation to others who intensely watch his reaction to Agnes. He expresses his distress at Withrington's looking strangely at him; his anxiety about Mariane staring at him; his concern that the servants will "smile with impertinent significance"; and finally, his conviction that "Agnes herself will look so drolly at me" (3.2.247). In this playscript, Agnes subverts the masculine gaze, turning it back upon Harwood and making display into play. Agnes stages a late eigtheenth-century alternative to what Luce Irigaray calls the "specularization exchange" by casting herself as actor rather than as object of the male gaze, a position that female performers in public spaces experienced with anguish and ambiguity.[37]

The fourth performance requires Agnes and Eston to hide in the closet as Mariane stages a "second act" in the trial of Sir Loftus. Agnes congratulates her cousin on her effective acting: "You have

played your part very well hitherto; keep it up for this last time"
(4.3.265–66). On this occasion, Loftus is not of few words, and his
speech-acts threaten to take over the scene. Mariane deflects his
dominance, in presence and in speech, by staging distractions,
dropping a book and an ivory ball so that Loftus will have to retrieve
them, and chattering inconsequentially. She exclaims concern for
Eston's squirrel and wonders whether there is a mouse in the
cupboard. Unable to make his speech, Loftus turns to asides, where
he curses Mariane, promising to be revenged: "Damn her freaks! I'll
vex her! I'll drive the spirit out of her! Curse her and her nuts!"
(4.3.271). Of course, it is Mariane who tames Loftus, bringing him to
his knees, not to propose marriage, but to reclaim his composure
when he is bumped to the floor by Agnes and Eston as they burst
from the closet. In ways both humorous and instructive, Mariane's
theatrical rewrites the marriage ritual, exposing its gender bias and
its commercial basis.

The fifth "little drama" returns Agnes to center-stage. Having
tested Harwood's love for her as a shrew, Agnes devises a plan to test
whether his love for her is stronger than his love of virtue. Her ploy
involves a fictitious letter to Lady Fade in which she professes regret
for slandering a relation upon whom Fade depends. At first,
Harwood tries to devalue the words of the letter by naming it a
forgery. His own words scribbled on the back of the envelope,
however, resignify the words as true. Agnes's theatrics demonstrate
the ways in which words and naming cast human beings, usually
women in their society, in roles which they came to accept as fixed,
"natural," and performative. Her performance replays the enunciatory power that Betsy performs by resisting being likened to a
blackamoor. Agnes's theatrics suggest an alternative to the voiceless
and powerless role that women had been assigned by patriarchal
scripts.

In scripting this final test of Harwood's sincerity, Agnes promises
her uncle that she will renounce Harwood and marriage altogether
if he fails the trial: "But no other man shall ever fill his place"
(5.1.277). Agnes's proclamation seems to sentence her to female
passivity and chastity, but, in a sense, Agnes too is on trial. Her
willingness to complete her resolve and to control her own destiny is
tested. She professes here that her selfhood is not contingent upon
marriage.[38] Her rejection of marriage for marriage's sake reveals a
social fiction that defines woman in essentially sexual terms.[39]

Rather than succumbing to passivity, Agnes seeks to liberate herself by suggesting something other than the traditional pattern of male dominance and female submission inherent in the courtship/marital ritual.

The final "little drama" features Mariane's final plot against Jack Opal. Mariane pretends to control Opal through his handwritten promise of marriage to her, a promise that he wishes not to honor now that Mariane is revealed not to be an heiress. Withrington warns Opal that the note stipulates Mariane's beauty, not her money, as the basis of the marital promise, a legal contract that any court would uphold. Betrayed by a justice system that should have favored him, Opal is literally forced to eat his words. He tears the promissory note to pieces, crams them in his mouth, and vows: "I protest there is not such a word in the paper" (5.2.296). Opal argues that the promise had been given to Mariane under the false character of an heiress, a deceit that relieves him of its obligation. Ironically, the deceit of Mariane's play-acting constitutes another instance of women's sovereignty and functions pedagogically in exposing the fictitious roles that women were, in actual society, forced to perform.

Catherine Burroughs has argued that Uncle Withrington raises concerns about how Mariane's and Agnes's "acting" violates familial order and socially constructed femininity.[40] In Act 3, for example, Withrington accuses his two nieces of behaving in a way unbefitting their gender: "All this playing, and laughing, and hoydening about is not gentlewomanlike, nay, I might say, is not maidenly. A high bred elegant woman is a creature which man approaches with awe and respect" (3.1.240). Withrington tells his nieces: "I can't approve of every farce you please to play off in my family, nor to have my relations affronted, and driven from my house for your entertainment" (3.1.239). He concludes that he wishes not to have his house in a perpetual bustle with their "plots" and "pastimes" (3.1.329). Agnes and Mariane do not, however, arrest their play-acting at his insistence to behave more like conventionally "feminine" women. In fact, they employ their theatrical strategies on him to defuse his potential resistance to further playwriting. When Withrington declares that he is in bad humor, Agnes and Mariane rescript his mood, proclaiming that he is "very good humoured" (3.1.238).

Uncle Withrington's "good humor" is further tested, however, for, in response to Agnes and Mariane's final charade with Loftus, he grumbles disapproval of their script: "This is too bad, young ladies! I am ashamed to have all this rioting and absurdity going on in my house" (4.3.274). Despite his protests, Withrington none-theless follows what Agnes and Mariane tell him to do, and, as Baillie's stage directions indicate, "*shrugging up his shoulders*" (4.3.274), he resigns himself to his part. Agnes and Mariane refuse to let their uncle marginalize their theatrics as "pastimes." Agnes even chal-lenges Withrington with a bet of £200 that she can enact her role effectively; she is so confident of winning the bet that she tells her uncle that his winnings will build a couple of almshouses. Agnes's and Mariane's persistence in rescripting the courtship/marriage ritual as theatricalized litigation, even in the face of patriarchal disapproval, strengthens the pedagogical mission of *The Tryal*, encouraging women not to be subdued by resistance to their thinking and acting in new ways.

Despite Withrington's desires to put an end to the playacting, it is his suggestion to stage the final trial that Agnes has designed for Harwood, and he turns the writing and directing of this plot over to Royston, becoming himself an enthusiastic participant. Validating the theatrical enterprises in which his nieces have participated, Withrington concedes to Agnes and Mariane: "You have more sense than I thought you had 'mongst all these whimsies" (5.2.299). To illustrate support for Agnes's and Mariane's theatrics, Baillie cleverly scripts a counter-metatheatrical into the last scene, a masculinist plot as a foil to those feminist ones staged by Agnes and Mariane. Royston is coerced into his part by Withrington's promise to help him find a great lady, a prize for which Royston is willing, if necessary, to participate in election fraud. It would seem that this "little drama," now in the hands of Royston, uncloset the ways in which masculine "business" (marital, theatrical, legal) is conducted. The women are physically marginalized during this scene, as stage director/manager Royston orders a screen to obscure the ladies and Withrington "as kings and queens in a puppet show" until their time comes to appear (5.2.283).

Unlike the collaborative efforts between Agnes and Mariane during the earlier performances, Royston resists suggestions about how to explain the presence of the screen in his room. He tells the others: "I'll manage it all; I'll conduct the whole business" (5.2.285). Following the charade, Royston claims all the credit: "I thought we should amaze you. I knew I should manage it" (5.2.290). In a self-aggrandizing gesture Royston declares: "O! it was all my contrivance" (5.2.291). Royston assumes that it is his "little drama" which has unveiled the true heiress, and he asks: "Now, good folks, have not I managed it cleverly?" (5.2.294). Royston's play-acting, in fact, causes Harwood to faint, suggesting perhaps that his theatricalized trial of Harwood is as thoughtless as his earlier courtroom theatrics involving Widow Gibson had been. Ultimately, Royston's theatrics are not rewarded, as Agnes's and Mariane's are, for he loses his estate, and Baillie's comedy does not, it would seem, hold up Royston's play-acting and directing as the standard for educational or theatrical purposes.

The metatheatrical commentary of Act 5 not only juxtaposes Royston's drama-making with Agnes's and Mariane's theatrics, but it involves readers/spectators in critical re-valuations of play-acting on-stage and in society. At Withrington's insistence, the characters take leave of the story-telling from which their machinations have emanated. While his request is directed at the characters of the play, it is also an invitation for readers/spectators of Baillie's comedy to take leave of the fictions, the story-telling and play-acting, upon which social actions rest. As metatheatrics, *The Tryal* exposes the fictionality of itself, indicting multiple social systems that needed to be exposed for their shortcomings and falsity. In its theatrical courtroom, Baillie's comedy reveals and condemns ideologically charged structures that reify gender performativity designed to restrict female agency to the appearance of domestic concerns. The radical content and pedagogical function of *The Tryal* urge female emancipation from these restrictive and repressive cultural fictions. While, in putting women's sovereignty on trial, Baillie may not have accomplished either a stable, private selfhood or a secure public identity for herself, for Mariane, or for Agnes, she exposes the conditions that affected late eighteenth-century and early nineteenth-century women's negotiations of private/public spaces and identities at the very time when traditionally assigned roles were being challenged.

The metatheatrics of *The Tryal* probe behind the curtain of social conditioning to show readers/spectators how women can exercise sovereignty, and they also open up spaces for examining epistemology and for giving women, in particular, an opportunity to think differently about thinking and learning. Perhaps more than the tragedies of the 1798 *Plays on the Passions*, *The Tryal* – which Baillie terms "characteristic comedy" in her "Introductory Discourse" (49)

– gave her a site where she could test her notions about the pedagogical potential of theatre. Agnes's and Mariane's theatrics rehearse precisely the educational and identificatory processes that Baillie's prefatory discourse claims to be the function of her drama. If Agnes and Mariane's playwriting and acting can effect changes in their fictitious lives, then Baillie's drama might provoke women to think differently about their actual lives. Collective revolutionary thinking can, Baillie acknowledges in her "Introductory Discourse," disrupt cultural ideology.[41] Among the many influences and legacies that Baillie has bestowed on contemporary performance theory, on the tradition of women's writing, and on theatre history, is the idea that drama is capable of teaching and promoting individual and societal refashionings.

NOTES

1 See my analysis of *Count Basil* and *De Monfort* within the context of the feminist polemics of the 1790s in *Romantic Ideology Unmasked: The Mentally Constructed Tyrannies in Dramas of William Wordsworth, Lord Byron, Percy Shelley, and Joanna Baillie* (Newark: University of Delaware Press, 1994), pp. 125–62. Anne K. Mellor points to Baillie's recognition in *Count Basil* of an alternative "emancipatory" potential in social practices through control of what she identifies as a "counter-public sphere" ("Joanna Baillie and the Counter-Public Sphere," *Studies in Romanticism* 33 [Winter 1994]: 559–67). Marlon B. Ross situates *Basil* within the Gothic tradition and the eighteenth-century cult of sentiment (*The Contours of Masculine Desire: Romanticism and the Rise of Women's Poetry* [Oxford University Press, 1989]), pp. 285–89. Jeffrey N. Cox argues that the Gothic provided Baillie with a site for constructing women whose images challenged the period's stereotypes ("Introduction" in *Seven Gothic Dramas 1789–1825*, ed. Jeffrey N. Cox [Athens: Ohio University Press, 1992], pp. 1–77), pp. 50–57. For discussions of *De Monfort* in the contexts of German Gothic and melodrama, see Michael Gamer, "National Supernaturalism: Joanna Baillie, Germany, and the Gothic Drama" (*Theatre Survey* 38.2, 1997, 49–88) and Maureen A. Dowd, " 'By the Delicate Hand of a Female': Melo-dramatic Mania and Joanna Baillie's Spectacular Tragedies," (*European Romantic Review* 9.4 [Fall 1998]: 469–500). Catherine B. Burroughs explores the issues of homo-erotic love and performed femininity in *De Monfort* and *Count Basil*, their expression through two styles of performance (statuesque and emo-tional) that competed for audience attention in 1798 (*Closet Stages: Joanna Baillie and the Theater Theory of British Romantic Women Writers* [Philadel-phia: University of Pennsylvania Press, 1997]), pp. 110–42. See also

Catherine Burroughs, "'Out of the Pale of Social Kindred Cast': Conflicted Performances in Joanna Baillie's *De Monfort*" in *Romantic Women Writers: Voices and Countervoices*, ed. Paula R. Feldman and Teresa M. Kelley (Hanover: University Press of New England, 1995), pp. 223–35.

2 Daniel P. Watkins examines *De Monfort* in terms of class and gender anxieties, arguing that the social structures in transition, from aristocracy to bourgeois authority, undergird the tragedy's psychological conflicts (*A Materialist Critique of English Romantic Drama* [Gainesville: University Press of Florida, 1993]), pp. 39–59.

3 Ironically, Baillie's *Tryal* was never granted a hearing in the public arena of staged theatre. Only seven (including *De Monfort* and *Count Basil*) of her twenty-six plays were staged during her lifetime. See Margaret S. Carhart, *The Life and Work of Joanna Baillie* (New Haven: Yale University Press, 1923 [rpt. Archon, 1970]), p. 109. Baillie dramatizes women's efforts to enter the public arena from which they were excluded in her 1802 comedy *The Election*. Published in Baillie's second series of *Plays on the Passions*, *The Election* was to serve as the comic counterpart to *De Monfort*, about hatred, and it depicts parliamentary campaigning at a time when class and district reformations were reflected in electoral practices and "uncloseted" as fraudulent by female characters. See my discussion, "The Sexual Politics of *The Election*: French Feminism and the Scottish Playwright Joanna Baillie" (*Intertexts* 2.2, 1998, pp. 119–30).

4 Catherine Burroughs, *Closet Stages*, p. 31. Burroughs argues that Baillie's "theory of closet theatre" criticizes social demands to enact gender and sexual identity in limited ways (*Closet Stages*, 74–109). See also Catherine Burroughs, "English Romantic Women Writers and Theatre Theory: Joanna Baillie's Prefaces to the *Plays on the Passions*" in *Re-Visioning Romanticism: British Women Writers, 1776–1837*, ed. Carol Shiner Wilson and Joel Haefner (Philadelphia: University of Pennsylvania Press, 1994), pp. 274–96. For a discussion of Baillie's negotiations with theatre managers and the business of performing her plays on the public stage, see Ellen Donkin, *Getting into the Act: Women Playwrights in London 1776–1829* (London: Routledge, 1995).

5 By performative and performativity, I refer to the concept, first coined by J. L. Austin and then appropriated by feminist and cultural theorists, that recognizes how speech becomes an act in its repetitions of performance in socio-cultural contexts. Ironically, the most frequently cited example of performativity is: "I take thee to be my lawful wife," a speech act that sanctions the performance of the marriage ceremony and the "trials" motivating Agnes's and Mariane's schemes in Baillie's comedy. See J. L. Austin, *How to Do Things with Words* (Cambridge University Press, 1962), pp. 14–22; Judith Butler, "Burning Acts – Injurious Speech" in *Performativity and Performance*, ed. Andrew Parker

and Eve Kosofsky Sedgwick (New York: Routledge, 1995, pp. 197–227), p. 198; Judith Butler, *Bodies That Matter: On the Discursive Limits of "Sex"* (New York: Routledge, 1993); and Andrew Parker and Eve Kosofsky Sedgwick, "Introduction" in *Performativity and Performance*, pp. 1–18.

6 See Judith Butler, *Excitable Speech: A Politics of the Performative* (New York: Routledge, 1997), pp. 15–16 and "Burning Acts – Injurious Speech," pp. 197–206.

7 Joanna Baillie, "Introductory Discourse" in *A Series of Plays: In Which It Is Attempted to Delineate The Stronger Passions of the Mind: Each Passion Being the Subject of A Tragedy and A Comedy*, 1798 (New York: Garland, 1977, pp. 1–72), p. 9. All further citations to this work appear in the text.

8 See my forthcoming essay, "Pedagogy and Passions: Teaching Joanna Baillie's Dramas" in *Nineteenth-century Contexts*, for elaboration of the pedagogical theory expressed in her prefatory prose.

9 Mary Wollstonecraft, *A Vindication of the Rights of Woman*, 1792 in, *The Vindications: The Rights of Men, The Rights of Woman*, ed. D. L. Macdonald and Kathleen Scherf (Peterborough, Ontario: Broadview Press, 1997, pp. 99–343), pp. 239–40.

10 Jill Dolan's work has demonstrated how feminist performances have denaturalized the position of the ideal spectator as a representative of the dominant culture and invested theatre as an active, ideological force, mediating and representing social relations. See *The Feminist Spectator as Critic* (Ann Arbor: UMI Research Press, 1988), pp. 1–17 and *Presence and Desire: Essays on Gender, Sexuality, Performance* (Ann Arbor: University of Michigan Press, 1993), p. 142. As Catherine Burroughs has observed, the prefatory discourses to Baillie's dramas anticipate contemporary feminist and performance theory (*Closet Stages*, pp. 105–9).

11 According to Candace S. Ward, Wollstonecraft includes sympathetic imagination in her configuration of sensibility, which she sought to extend beyond the self and into the community ("'Active Sensibility and Positive Virtue': Wollstonecraft's 'Grand Principle of Action'," *European Romantic Review* 8.4 [Fall 1997], 409–31).

12 Mary Hays, *Appeal to the Men of Great Britain in Behalf of Women* (London: J. Johnson, 1798; New York: Garland, 1974), p. 224.

13 See Sarah Maza, "The Diamond Necklace Affair Revisited (1785–1786): The Case of the Missing Queen" in *Eroticism and the Body Politic*, ed. Lynn Hunt (Baltimore: Johns Hopkins University Press, 1991), pp. 63–89; and Lynn Hunt, "The Many Bodies of Marie Antoinette: Political Pornography and the Problem of the Feminine in the French Revolution" in *Eroticism and the Body Politic*, pp. 108–30.

14 See Jyotsna G. Singh, *Colonial Narratives/Cultural Dialogues: "Discoveries" of India in the Language of Colonialism* (London: Routledge, 1996), pp. 65–66 and David Musselwhite, "The Trial of Warren Hastings" in *Literature, Politics and Theory: Papers from the Essex Conference, 1976–84*, ed. Francis

Barker, Peter Hulme, Margaret Iversen, and Diana Loxley (London: Methuen, 1986), pp. 77–103.

15 Linda Colley, *Britons: Forging the Nation 1701–1837* (New Haven: Yale University Press, 1992), pp. 128–31.

16 See Jeanne Moskal's essay in the present volume.

17 See Lynn Hunt, *Politics, Culture, and Class in the French Revolution* (Berkeley: University of California Press, 1984), pp. 87–119 and *The Family Romance of the French Revolution* (Berkeley: University of California Press, 1992), p. 96. See also Maurice Agulhon, *Marianne into Battle: Republican Imagery and Symbolism in France, 1789–1880*, trans. Janet Lloyd (Cambridge University Press, 1981), pp. 11–37. Joan Landes points out that all women were affected by the dramatic alterations of public spaces following the French Revolution and during the years of the Republic (*Women and the Public Sphere in the Age of the French Revolution* [Ithaca: Cornell University Press, 1988]), p. 105. Bonnie S. Anderson and Judith P. Zinsser find that, by the late eighteenth century, women were excluded from the body politic in Britain (vol. II of *A History of Their Own: Women in Europe from Prehistory to the Present* [New York: Harper & Row, 1988]), p. 148. 2 vols.

18 Lynn Hunt, "The Many Bodies of Marie Antoinette," p. 126.

19 *Ibid.*, pp. 109–11.

20 Judith Pascoe has pointed out that the theatricalized Marie Antoinette served as an important model of female self-fashioning, especially as she was embodied on the British stage by Sarah Siddons and Mary Robinson (*Romantic Theatricality: Gender, Poetry and Spectatorship* [Ithaca: Cornell University Press, 1997]), pp. 95–129.

21 See Catherine Burroughs's thorough treatment of aspects of public performances negotiated by women of the late eighteenth century (*Closet Stages*, pp. 27–73). See also studies of eighteenth-century actresses by Kristina Straub (*Sexual Suspects: Eighteenth-Century Players and Sexual Ideology* [Princeton University Press, 1992]), Sandra Richards (*The Rise of the English Actress* [New York: St. Martin's, 1993]), and Joanne Lafler (*The Celebrated Mrs. Oldfield: The Life and Art of an Augustan Actress* [Carbondale: Southern Illinois University Press, 1989]). Marcia Pointon considers how audiences negotiated boundaries between portraits of society ladies and portraits of courtesans and actresses during the period (*Strategies for Showing: Women, Possession, and Representation in English Visual Culture 1665–1800* [Oxford University Press, 1997], pp. 215–16). Ellen Donkin discusses the "occupational hazards" of women playwrights in the eighteenth century (*Getting into the Act*, pp. 1–40), and Judith Phillips Stanton analyzes the challenges women encountered who pursued the "new-found path" of playwriting ("'This New-Found Path Attempting': Women Dramatists in England, 1660–1800" in *Curtain Calls: British and American Women and the Theater, 1660–1820*, ed. Mary Anne Schofield and Cecilia Macheski [Athens: Ohio University Press, pp. 325–54]).

22 At the close of the 1798 "Introductory Discourse," Joanna Baillie
    remarks that she would have preferred to see her *Plays on the Passions*
    staged, but because she lacks a channel of public introduction to the
    theatre, performances are unlikely (p. 66). Baillie's name did not appear
    on the title page of the 1798 edition, and many readers and critics
    assumed the plays had been written by Walter Scott. Ellen Donkin, in
    Getting into the Act, asserts that, when the dramatist's gender was
    revealed, it precipitated a cultural crisis over the boundaries marking
    "male" and "female" (181).

23 Lesley Ferris, for example, claims that an actress's acting on-stage is
    merely an extension and exposure of her "acting" off-stage. The
    "masquerade" gave women temporary immunity from "respectability"
    and an opportunity to play-act their fantasies and desires (*Acting Women:
    Images of Women in Theatre* [New York University Press, 1989]), pp.
    149–53. Studies by Catherine Burroughs (*Closet Stages*, pp. 51–66) and
    Judith Pascoe (*Romantic Theatricality*, pp. 68–94) demonstrate the
    problematic relationship between the private and public Sarah
    Siddons, and Pascoe reveals how Mary Robinson capitalized on her
    public acting image (163–83). Ellen Donkin outlines how Elizabeth
    Inchbald used on-stage/off-stage connections to her personal and
    professional advantages (*Getting into the Act*, pp. 110–31).

24 In *The Psychic Life of Power: Theories in Subjection* (Stanford University
    Press, 1997), Judith Butler argues that a subject derives its agency from
    precisely the power it opposes so that power is "acted on" the subject
    and "acted by" the subject (15–17). Butler reminds us that what is
    exteriorized or performed can only be understood by references to
    what is barred from performance, what cannot or will not be performed
    (144–45). The performance spaces created by the metatheatrics of *The
    Tryal* open up, in dramatic forms, the slippage between acting on and
    activating, between appearance and absence, which Butler theorizes in
    relation to psychological power-relations and subject-formation.

25 Christopher Flint, *Family Fictions: Narrative and Domestic Relations in
    Britain, 1688–1798* (Stanford University Press, 1998), p. 54. See also
    Lawrence Stone, *The Family, Sex and Marriage in England 1500–1800* (New
    York: Harper & Row, 1977), pp. 270–324, and Lenore Davidoff and
    Catherine Hall, *Family Fortunes: Men and Women of the English Middle Class,
    1780–1850* (University of Chicago Press, 1987), pp. 321–56.

26 See Julie Shaffer, "Romance, Finance, and the Marketable Woman:
    The Economics of Femininity in Late Eighteenth- and Early Nine-
    teenth-Century English Novels" in *Bodily Discursions: Genders, Representa-
    tions, Technologies*, ed. Deborah S. Wilson and Christine Moneera
    Laennec (Albany: State University of New York Press, 1997, pp. 39–56),
    pp. 41–42.

27 William Blackstone, vol. 1 of *Commentaries on the Laws of England*, 1765,
    15th edn (London, 1809), 1.55. 4 vols.

28 Marriage contracts, Bonnie Anderson and Judith Zinsser argue in *A History of Their Own*, vol. II, included provisions that subordinated the wife to the husband, granting him permission to physically punish her, and the penal code permitted husbands to kill wives whom they caught in adultery; women had no reciprocal rights (149–50). According to Catherine Hall, the bourgeoisie practiced partial inheritance rather than primogeniture, with the forms of female inheritance increasingly linked to dependence (*White, Male and Middle Class* [Oxford: Polity Press, 1992]), pp. 97–98. Lenore Davidoff and Catherine Hall (*Family Fortunes*) remind us that marriage was an "important crisis" in a man's life but the key to a woman's life (324–25).

29 According to Lenore Davidoff and Catherine Hall, *ibid.*, these dichotomous spaces were, in actuality, more ambiguous than described discursively: "public was not really public and private was not really private despite the potent imagery of 'separate spheres'" (33).

30 William Blackstone, *Commentaries*, 1.441 (emphasis mine). Lenore Davidoff and Catherine Hall, *Family Fortunes*, remind us that, under coverture, a married woman only existed under her husband's protection. She could not sign Bills of Exchange, make contracts, sue or be sued, collect debts, or stand surety. She really could not *act* as a partner, since "for all practical purposes, on marriage, a woman died a kind of civil death" (200).

31 Joanna Baillie, *The Tryal* in *A Series of Plays: In Which It Is Attempted to Delineate The Stronger Passions of the Mind: Each Passion Being the Subject of A Tragedy and A Comedy.* 1798 (New York: Garland, 1977, pp. 194–299), 1.197. All further references to the play appear in the text.

32 Judith Butler, *The Psychic Life of Power*, p. 13.

33 Elspeth Probyn, *Sexing the Self: Gendered Positions in Cultural Studies* (New York: Routledge, 1993), pp. 28–29.

34 See Judith Butler, *Excitable Speech*, pp. 15–16, and *Bodies That Matter*, pp. 107–11.

35 Judith Butler, *Excitable Speech*, p. 15.

36 In rewriting Royston's court drama, Agnes and Mariane right the "wrongs of woman" cited by Wollstonecraft in the Preface to *Maria*. Pointing to the gender inequities of the marriage ritual and British law, Wollstonecraft states: "What are termed misfortunes . . . have more of what may justly be termed *stage effect* . . ." (*The Wrongs of Woman, Or Maria*, 1798 [New York: Norton, 1994], p. 6). Agnes and Mariane reverse the "stage effect" generally associated with the female part, assigning to Royston the "hypocrisy and disguise" with which, Mary Hays argued in 1798, women were "inculcated from the cradle" (*Appeal to the Men of Great Britain in Behalf of Women*, p. 205).

37 See Luce Irigaray, *This Sex Which Is Not One*, 1977. Trans. Catherine Porter (Ithaca: Cornell University Press, 1985), pp. 170–92.

38 Katharine M. Rogers claims that radical feminism had important

indirect effects on women who might not think of asserting their right to seek a husband by themselves (*Feminism in Eighteenth-Century England* [Urbana: University of Illinois Press, 1982] p. 203). Agnes's theatricalized trials in Baillie's play contribute to the radical feminism that Rogers describes.

39 Lesley Ferris, *Acting Women*, asserts that the theme of marriage remained popular throughout the nineteenth century, with both male and female dramatists taking for granted compulsory marriage for women. Women playwrights, however, often express marital requirements from more complicated and frustrated viewpoints than men playwrights (156). The metatheatrics of *The Tryal* shows us how Baillie complicates socially scripted marriage for women.

40 See Burroughs, *Closet Stages*, pp. 156–62.

41 In the 1798 "Introductory Discourse," Baillie writes: "To change a certain disposition of mind which makes us view objects in a particular light, and thereby, oftentimes, unknown to ourselves, influences our conduct and manners, is almost impossible, but in checking and subduing those visitations of the soul, whose causes and effects we are aware of, every one may make considerable progress, if he prove not entirely successful" (11). This statement echoes the position of educational reformers at the end of the eighteenth century, who similarly argue that, in changing themselves, women could effect societal reforms. Women writers addressing female education, including Baillie, are aware that private actions have political, legal, and social consequences. *The Tryal* shows readers/spectators what the "Introductory Discourse" theorizes, the ways in which ideology and epistemology silently operating in public spaces profoundly shape private cognition and identity.

III

Performance and Closet Drama

CHAPTER 6

Outing Joanna Baillie

Susan Bennett

Joanna Baillie wrote some twenty-six plays (only part, of course, of her extensive literary output), yet she has, until very recently, been little remembered in theatre history or in studies of the Romantic period. When Baillie's career as a playwright has received critical attention, it has been chiefly to note her significance as a closet dramatist; thus, the editors of *Women Playwrights in England, Ireland, and Scotland, 1660–1823* (a volume published in 1996) quite typically comment: "Perhaps if she [Baillie] had been more familiar with stagecraft and frequented the playhouse oftener, more of her plays would have been produced."[1] In a similar vein, critic Paul Zall described Baillie's best-known play, *De Monfort*, as "less ludicrous than most" of her work, at the same time as concluding that *De Monfort*'s mixed success in the theatre proved "it would never be an acting play."[2] Even editors Robert W. Uphaus and Gretchen M. Foster in their volume entitled, *The "Other" Eighteenth Century: English Women of Letters 1660–1800* (an otherwise enormously useful collection), insist in their introduction to Baillie's "Introductory Discourse" that "[t]oday we find the plays unperformable and generally unreadable."[3] In the context of such deliberate attacks on the theatrical achievements of Baillie, the task of my chapter is two-fold. In the first place, I discuss the implications and effects of the genre category "closet drama" on the critical reception of Baillie's plays and then, more specifically, I address Baillie's dramatic œuvre (the writings about theatre as well as the plays themselves) as documents deeply invested in matters of public performance.

The category of closet drama is one with a particular history for women (although it is, of course, a category that comes into its own for both male and female writers in the Romantic period). In the bibliography of *Plays by Women to 1900*, compilers Gwenn Davis and Beverly A. Joyce classify closet drama as one of three principal types of dramatic literature by women.[4] They go on to describe the aristocratic roots of women-authored closet drama (Viscountess Falkland, Countesses of Pembroke and Winchelsea, the Duchess of Newcastle, Queen Elizabeth I)[5] and note that, while few titled women were involved in the writing of plays after 1750, "the literary aristocracy is well represented" (xii). And it is in the list which follows this statement that Baillie's name appears. Davis and Joyce understand the category "closet drama," as have most literary and dramatic critics, to mean plays "that were never acted, and were never meant to be."[6] Moreover, their naming of Baillie as literary aristocrat and closet dramatist sums up the limited attention and marginal status she has generally held as a playwright. To take another example, in an altogether more generous assessment of Baillie's career,[7] Adrienne Scullion makes much the same claim:

Although only a minority of her plays were ever performed, her position as *grande dame des lettres* during the early and middle decades of the nineteenth century was secure. The majority of these plays were written to be read, being closer to the genre of "closet" plays that the era allowed for and celebrated than to active engagements in the theatre industry. Some of her works did hold the stage, but it rested with her substantial publications to assure her a place in the public's imagination. (lix)

So what of this genre of closet drama that the Romantic period is said to have "celebrated" and which has been so integral, apparently, to women's dramatic production in general? In a survey of "Recent Studies in Closet Drama," Marta Straznicky argues that new (which is to say, for the most part, feminist) work on women writers of the early modern period has meant that "closet drama criticism has been virtually reinvented."[8] And while she is right to assert the contribution of such work to a rethinking of the category, I would suggest that reinvention is still more of a goal than a reality and perhaps especially so in Joanna Baillie's case. Closet drama still powerfully connotes writing that was emphatically not for public performance. Nonetheless, Straznicky is certainly correct to point out the normativity of stage-dominated drama criticism and history that produces such an effect as well as to indicate "[b]y the same token, a consideration of women's closet plays in the context of historical (male) precedents has led to an awareness of the political importance of this purportedly cloistered genre" (159). In other words, the strength of recent scholarship on women writers of the early modern period has led, if not to a complete reconceptualization of the category "closet drama," then to a fuller sense of the material operations of that genre as well as its cultural impacts. This gives us a fruitful place from which to move forward from the sixteenth and seventeenth centuries in order to characterize a trajectory of women's dramatic writing which is less "to be read in private, savored for the elegance of its writing" (Davis and Joyce xi) and more a dynamic imagination of "exciting theatricality in which a wide array of spaces were explored for their dramatic and theatrical potential."[9] Baillie's place in such a revisionist history is, I would suggest, of paramount importance.

The situation of women dramatists in the Romantic period is, of course, a complicated one when read against the prevailing ambivalence of male Romantic poets in their relationship to the dramatic and the theatrical. The parameters and operations of that ambivalence are finely articulated in Julie Carlson's landmark book, *In the Theatre of Romanticism* (1994), and, indeed, her observation there that "the power of poetry [asserted by poets and theorists of the period] is wishful thinking aimed to dispel emergent forms of power in London theatres" is trenchantly made.[10] Carlson specifically takes to task other critical overviews of the period's plays – notably foundational accounts such as Alan Richardson's *A Mental Theater* and Timothy Webb's "The Romantic Poet and the Stage"[11] – and argues for a richer understanding of Romantic drama and "its effective role in early consolidations of liberalism" (29). Crucially, Carlson also looks for a more attentive examination of the gendered assumptions which underpinned those poets' anxiety and ambivalence when it came to theatre, as well as how these assumptions necessarily inform any consideration of plays by women. Moreover, as Tracy C. Davis tells us, women writing plays for other than commercial theatres should not be designated as "lesser, or necessarily even different, but . . . contiguous with others who pursue the same craft."[12]

What was appropriate for the public stage and what was better suited for the private practices of reading was, in any event, a subject of much debate in late eighteenth- and early nineteenth-century England. Elizabeth Inchbald's critical prefaces (written specifically for John Bell's multi-volumed *The British Theatre*, 1808) often weighed the relative merits of individual plays in the different contexts of stage and closet,[13] while more typically in male-authored criticism "failed" attempts by women to put work on the public stage are often quickly and disparagingly consigned to closet status. The critic for *The Monthly Review*, reviewing Frances Plowden's opera *Virginia*, which was published in 1801, showed just how easily this could be done:

> The preface informs us that it was composed under the pressure of misfortune; we shall therefore be glad if it meets with more favour in the closet; and that we may throw no obstacles in the way of its success, we shall dismiss it with merely our good wishes.[14]

Rather than apply a monolithic category of closet drama to which the works of writers like Baillie might be almost automatically despatched, it is surely fairer to suggest that the territory of public and private performance spaces was contested and in flux. That Inchbald and, moreover, Baillie herself would devote so much time and effort to discussing the very categorization of plays, not to mention their own relative successes and failures in meeting the criteria of either stage or closet, conveys a sense of the category crisis which apparently troubled more than just the male Romantic poets. Ellen Donkin suggests that, within the debate, women writers were systematically denied access to professional options: "the reviewers mark their liberal position by stating their support of the *idea* of the woman as playwright. But they then simultaneously state or imply that the woman's work is not up to standard" (177).

Since then, too, such an implication has had a tenacious grip on both theatre history and criticism of the Romantic period and, in some ways, even the most recent criticism reproduces the tensions and conflicts of the original scene. Thus, Alan Richardson can write that "[p]oets working directly from such trends [Gothic emphasis on extreme mental states and eighteenth-century studies of Shakespeare], whether for the stage like Keats (in *Otho the Great*) or for the closet like Joanna Baillie, failed to move beyond the stable and static characterizations of neoclassical drama" (5).[15] Not unexpectedly, male critics have almost singlemindedly ignored the contributions of women dramatists to public stages *and*, generally, expressed little interest in the genre of the closet. Indeed, it has often seemed that Byron's claim that women, with the exception of Baillie, could not write tragedies[16] is a lone reference to the fact that women wrote plays at all in that period. Yet recent women critics have taken a much more Inchbaldian approach and looked at the particular fit of women's plays within the broad spectrum of playwriting of the time.

Catherine Burroughs's *Closet Stages* (1997) is exemplary in its careful analysis of what "closet drama" meant to Baillie and other women playwrights, and her book does much to animate new discussions of at least the potentiality of closet drama.[17]

In this regard, it is worth noting that even a recuperation of the category does not necessarily mean that representation and inclusion follow. By way of J. O. Bailey's suggestion that closet drama was in fact "the most radical experimentation with the Romantic verse plays" and "a third contender in the struggle for survival between the verse drama and the evolving melodrama,"[18] John Franceschina excludes Baillie from his 1997 collection of women melodramatists by arguing that she is too well known! He writes:

Even though Evans argues that "of her twenty-six dramatic works, ten may be classified as predominantly Gothic, and all reveal conspicuous marks of the tradition" (200), given the fact that Baillie's plays are hardly "lost" and that, as an author, she is considered more as a writer of "verse tragedies" than melodramas (Moers 118), she was omitted from this collection.[19]

I do not want to criticize Franceschina's selection of texts; in fact, it seems to me that his motivations are more than admirable in widening the scope of modern available editions of these other women's plays. But what is revealing in the justification of his choices is the repetition of those debates of category and Baillie's particularly marked location within them.

If that is the critical backdrop, both now and then, to any reception of Baillie's playwriting, it is important now to turn our attention to the work itself and to do so following Judith Pascoe's contention "that Romanticism is founded on theatrical modes of self-representation and the corollary that women played active and influential roles in public life."[20] In this latter case, particularly, we might consider how Baillie sought to intervene in the discourses and institutions of representation, even when those interventions did not immediately succeed. Since Baillie was not content to write only the plays themselves and to let those creative works fare as they might, but instead published those plays with substantial prefaces which theorize the very business of the theatre and the opportunities for her plays in that milieu, it is crucial to consider the ideas she expressed in that public format. In this regard, Mary Yudin, while joining at least partially in the critical refrain of Baillie-as-second-rate-dramatist, makes a strong case for her theatre theory: "When Baillie's dramas, in part due to forces beyond the author's control, failed to live up to these high expectations [that she might be, as the anonymous author of *Plays on the Passions*, the next Shakespeare or Southerne], Baillie's insights on aesthetics found in her prose writings were forgotten, as was her mark on nineteenth-century literary history. A rediscovery of Joanna Baillie's poetics, however, reveals the work of a formidable writer on aesthetics."[21] It is only through such processes of rediscovery that the continuities of women's challenges to dominant practices can be fully described and said, eventually, to reconstitute not only categories such as closet drama but the very narrative of theatre history.

Baillie's "Introductory Discourse," first published in 1798 as the preliminary materials to the *Plays on the Passions*, was not simply a treatise on aesthetics; it did the crucial work of introducing a readership to her playwriting even before she attempted to find a theatre that would consider producing any of them.[22] As Burroughs points out, even then, Baillie was at pains to underscore that readers should not imagine "that I have written [the plays] for the closet rather than the stage."[23] Some six years later, the first page of her preface to *Miscellaneous Plays* includes the statement: "It has been and still is, my strongest desire to add a few pieces to the stock of what may be called our national or permanent acting plays."[24] Her authorial intention is, again and again, expressed in these prefaces; that is, unequivocally, she wishes to see her works on the stage – and, crucially, a stage which suits their theatrical shape and purpose.

To examine Baillie's labor with theatrical form and to understand how she realized the limited existing market for the kinds of plays she wrote, I want to look at *Constantine Paleologus*, which was first published in *Miscellaneous Plays* (1804). This particular play serves as an instructive example in part because we know that she wrote this play with a theatre and actors in mind and because the accompanying preface deals directly with some of her desires for theatrical production.[25] *Constantine Paleologus* is, then, a tragedy that Baillie herself notes "was written in the hope of being brought out upon our largest theatre, enriched as it then was by two actors whose noble appearance and strong powers of expression seemed to me peculiarly suited to its two principal characters" (xiv). In other words, she wrote it for a Drury Lane production with Kemble and Siddons as its leading actors, though they did not choose to do the play.[26] Their rejection, however, did not mean that this was a closet play; in fact, it was produced several times – the records show that it was licensed in Liverpool on 10 October 1808 and staged as a benefit for actor Daniel Terry at the Theatre Royal.[27] The play was also revised by Thomas John Dibdin as *Constantine and Valeria* and performed at the Surrey in 1817, giving it a production life as a melodrama rather than as the tragedy Baillie had elected to name it. There was also a performance of the play in June 1820 at the Theatre Royal in Edinburgh as a benefit for John William Calcraft, who later (June/July 1825) restaged the play at the Theatre Royal, Dublin.[28] That history alone, I would think, justifies Baillie's expression of hope in her preface:

> I shall persevere in my task, circumstanced as I am, with as anxious unremitting an attention to every thing that regards the theatre as if I were there forthwith to receive the full reward of all my labours, or complete and irretrievable condemnation. So strong is my attachment to the drama of my native country. . . that a distant and uncertain hope of having even but a very few of the pieces I offer to the public represented to it with approbation, when some partiality for them as plays that have been frequently read shall have put into the power of future managers to bring them upon the stage with less risk of loss that would be at present incurred, is sufficient to animate me to every exertion that I am capable of making. (viii–ix)

What better illustration could there be of Baillie's sheer determination in getting her plays to the attention of potential producers? Especially if her expression of "distant and uncertain hope" is thought of more as typical of a discourse of gendered humility than a direct statement of her expectations. And, in the case of *Constantine*, this attempt to encourage subsequent productions did eventually pay off. While all three texts in *Miscellaneous Plays* were first available in print form, that is, as closet dramas ("I must also mention, that each of the plays contained in this volume has been, at one time or other, offered for representation to one or other of our winter theatres, and been rejected" [vii–viii]), this did not prevent the author continuing her campaign for their theatrical lives. In short, she saw the genre of closet drama as a marketing tool – one that might urge enough individual enthusiastic readers to want to be a collective theatre audience and that might persuade theatre managers of the presence of a predetermined popularity (generated by and through her readership).[29] In any case, *Constantine Paleologus* did make the leap from the closet to the stage, and Nicoll concludes in his account of the various productions and adaptations following its 1804 publication that[30] "[t]he endeavour shows that Joanna Baillie possessed more of the theatre sense, and of *the will to the theatre*, than the majority of her poetic companions" (159, my emphasis). What we must inscribe in our critical records, then, is more of Baillie's "theatre sense" and less of the history of the closet.

I have tried in another essay, on Baillie's *Witchcraft* (1836) and *The Family Legend* (1810), as well as Elizabeth Polack's *St. Clair of the Isles* (1838), to suggest some of the grounds on which women playwrights troubled genre categorizations. Their interest, I suggest, was to manipulate or rework the rules of genre to address "specific, localized concerns, those borne by a body and voice marked by ethnicity and gender."[31] In these cases, too, I would underscore Baillie's "will to the theatre" along with remarkable skill in finding theatrical form for her ideas. *Constantine* provides a further compelling example, especially because of the particularities of its theatrical history. Thus, Beth Friedman-Romell, in a key study of the same play's homoeroticism, looks at its production record to demonstrate how "middle-class managers produced a sanitized, patriotic version of *Constantine* for imagined spectators who were very much like themselves."[32] Like Friedman-Romell, I think *Constantine* can be considered a foundational text for rethinking the terms and (repressive) conditions of "closet drama."

For this reason, I want to look at *Constantine* both for the pragmatism of Baillie's theatrical script and for its enactment of the conditions of the closet by way of its women characters. In writing about the play in the preface to the published volume, Baillie describes the source material (Gibbon's account of the siege of Constantinople by the Turks) and the challenge to represent this ruler who was last of the Caesars: "to see him thus circumstanced, nobly fronting the storm, and perishing as became the last of a long line of kings, the last of the Romans; – this was a view of man – of noble and dignified exertion which it was impossible for me to resist" (xiv–xv). Yet it was precisely her own theatrical sensibility which provoked the playwright to add substantially to Gibbon's account: "But convinced that something more was requisite to interest a common audience, and give sufficient variety to the scenes, I introduced the character of Valeria, and brought forward the domestic qualities of Constantine" (xv).[33] That the audience she refers to here is one in the theatre (and thus a popular one) rather than in the closet is clear from her earlier comments on the play's suitability for Kemble and Siddons and their "noble appearance and strong powers of expression" (xiv). In other words, to get this play on the Drury Lane stage with Kemble in the role of the eponymous hero, she knew she would do well to have an equally compelling and appealing female character for Siddons to play. It had been Siddons, after all, who had commanded Baillie to craft her "some more Jane de Monforts!"[34] The emotional range of both Constantine and Valeria is perfectly in line with the kinds of roles that Kemble and Siddons might play and, more importantly, that Drury Lane audiences would expect from them.[35] In discussing this play, Nicoll refers to Baillie's ever-increasing skills with characterization and interestingly describes Constantine as a "strange mingling of heroism and effeminacy" (159); likewise Valeria moves through many different states of mind including the obligatory and spectacularly rendered mad scene.

Although later, in the third volume of *Plays on the Passions* (1812), Baillie would argue a preference for the smaller theatres (perhaps provoked by her particular experience with *Constantine*), this play is self-consciously designed for a large playing space that would rely on grand rhetoric, multiple and elaborate settings, and spectacular effects (notably the frequent and alarming sounds of artillery).[36] This is a play whose very subject and design meets the scale of Drury Lane and provides a star vehicle for the actors that Baillie believed would give it public production. Nothing about *Constantine*, with the exception of its critical history, fits in the category of closet drama – its scale and ambitions are those of London's most important theatre business.

Thus, in common with Baillie's experience of the world (both theatrical and in general), *Constantine*'s organization involves complex negotiations of public and private space. The men of the play confidently populate exterior landscapes and are the obvious agents of action and decision-making. When they are indoors, it is only because women keep them there (Valeria literally hanging on Constantine to prevent him leaving again for battle; the fact that he is even tempted to stay no doubt compels Nicoll to mark his "effeminacy"). The women, by contrast, are almost always in interior settings – even watching the action from the tower is a liminal experience that ensures they stay at a remote distance from the men's public lives. For the women to venture from domestic space is always hazardous and indicative of the very limited and largely unsuccessful opportunities they have for public roles.

Yet the very first human image in *Constantine* is of Ella, daughter of Petronius (a traitor to Constantine). She is revealed, according to the play's opening stage direction, "standing on a balcony belonging to a small tower, rising from the side of the platform."[37] She can see the ruined city and hear the sound of artillery, but is no participant in those events. The audience's perspective from the very opening moment is, then, a woman's one. And the play's first action, dialogue between Othus (a trusted member of Constantine's circle) and Marathon (another traitor to Constantine), first establishes the dynamic of active male characters watched by the passive (or, at best, reactive) female. The playwright insists that the audience takes in this doubled and gendered view of the world.

Eventually, however, Ella comes down on to the stage to comfort Othus, but is soon frightened by the noise about her and decides to go back inside to her chamber – a decision that is emphatically encouraged by her father:

> Yes, to thy chamber go: thou liv'st, methinks,
> On the house-top, or watching in the towers.
> I like it not; and maiden privacy
> Becomes thy state and years.   (288)

Petronius reminds his daughter of the appropriateness of a closeted life, one where her eye is not directed at the public world, and he turns to her again a few lines later, angrily telling her to hasten her departure inside. Valeria, like Ella, only rarely ventures outside; her one opportunity ("concealed in a long black stole" [324]) comes in a visit to a conjurer who looks into the future, sees the truth of Constantine's death, but nonetheless chooses to tell Valeria what she wants to hear (that Constantine will emerge triumphant). There is something particularly distressing about Baillie's rendition of Valeria's one public performance: not only must she wear a disguise in order to be outside at all, but her dependency on psychic prediction not just for reassurance but for "truth" underscores just how far she is kept from the reality (which is to say, the male-centered action) of the moment. More "naturally," Valeria is found either in her apartment or, again like Ella, watching from the tower.

Since the third act in *Constantine* concentrates on the soldiers on the opposing sides of the battle, there are no onstage appearances by women, and it is only in the third scene of Act 4 that Ella emerges from Valeria's chamber (only, of course, to make her return to her own chamber) – and even this is instantaneously dangerous. Petronius and his accomplice Marathon are lying in wait, ready to carry her off to be Mahomet's mistress. The capture of the white woman for the sexual pleasures of the harem is surely the most terrifying closet of all in the English colonial imagination. Ella escapes this fate only through the timely intervention of Rodrigo, who is, needless to say, a much more appropriate potential husband.

In the play's final act, the first two scenes move between the battlefield (and the onstage death of Constantine) and Valeria's apartment. When Valeria goes to the window to try and see what's happening, she immediately "shrinks back," saying "mine eyes are dark, / And I see nothing" (416). Not only does Baillie illustrate the impossibility of "doing" as a woman, she suggests the impossibility, ultimately, of "seeing." When Valeria hears the news of Constantine's death at the end of the scene, she can only scream and faint before being carried off by her attendants. The third scene of the final act is set in "A hall in the palace" and involves "a Crowd of frightened Women" who "seem hurrying on to some place of greater security" (419). Non-individualized women function as props to indicate the chaos of a society that has fallen under the control of Mahomet; presumably they are all under threat of being closeted in his harem. What is interesting, however, is how the dynamic of the play's final act is almost exclusively in the hands of women as they struggle against their predictable fate.

When Valeria enters midway through the scene, it is with "her hair dishevelled, and in all the wild disorder of violent sorrow" (422), and, confronted with an awestruck Mahomet (which, in theatre, must always be the reaction of a man of color in the presence of white female nobility, even when she is demonstrably "mad"), Valeria asks only for "A place in the quiet tomb with my fall'n lord, / Therein to rest my head" (429). She then takes her own life, an event that evokes the final – and most dramatic – tragedy in *Constantine* for both onstage and offstage audiences. As Marjean Purinton comments about two other Baillie tragedies, *Count Basil* and *De Monfort*, the plays "politicize gender not as a biological function but as a cultural practice. Unlike Victoria and Jane [in *Count Basil* and *De Monfort*], who closet themselves from social interaction, Baillie vigorously and actively participates in a political revolution that seeks to unveil the customs, habits, and prejudices that enslave women."[38] *Constantine* repeatedly enacts the literal and metaphoric

closets of women's lives – though I would suggest that Ella and
Valeria constantly strain against their confines even if they ultimately
are subsumed by them (Ella in marriage, Valeria in death). Both
women try to find avenues for social agency, but their public
performances are inevitably turned to scenes of punishment. And
irrespective of the play's title, Constantine dies in Act v scene i, and
the play's denouement is firmly shaped around the outcomes for Ella
and, especially, Valeria. In other words, Baillie privileges the characters of her dramatic invention over those of historical fact. It is
surely tempting to see Baillie as scripting into this large, spectacular
play the very social practices that are overdetermined for women
who dare to see and be seen, even peripherally, outside their
domestic context.

My argument, then, is that both in the play itself and in the
prefatory materials that accompanied its print publication, Baillie
demonstrates a deft understanding of how the theatre works – as a
craft and as an institution. Her response is not, most definitely not, a
retreat into the closet, but an imagining of what might better work
as a dynamic theatrical experience to meet the ideas and, of course,
passions that she imagined three-dimensionally. As her plays stage
the relationship of women to the possibilities of public performance,
so her prefaces continue to imagine the kinds of theatrical practice
that would serve her dramas. As Burroughs notes, Baillie continues
to imagine successful productions of her plays as late as the preface
to the three-volume *Dramas* published in 1836, where she writes of a
desire to see some of her work produced in "the smaller theatres of
the metropolis, and thereby have a chance, at least, of being
produced to the public with the advantages of action and scenic
decorations, which naturally belong to dramatic compositions"
(cited in Burroughs 89). To some extent this was what happened to
Constantine in its later manifestations, since, as Beth Friedman-
Romell notes for the 1820 Edinburgh production, "recent innovations in lighting promised greater control of mood . . . and the small
space and good acoustics ensured that Baillie's verse would be heard
and appreciated" (156).[39]

Perhaps her experiences with *Constantine* made Baillie all too
aware that the Drury Lane establishment would never do justice for
work such as her own; in any event, her continued imagination of
production, whether in second-tier theatres or under canvas or in
barns, shows her passion for performance and for alternative spaces

that would better respond to her dramaturgy. Baillie never concerns herself with the reader, except to lecture on the necessity to *see* the drama; she is far more concerned with the theatre audience and the conditions in which they might experience the emotional range and the dramatic action that her plays demand. To define Joanna Baillie, still, as closet dramatist and literary aristocrat, in that case, seems to deliberately miss the point.

Rather, I would argue, she might be seen as the champion of an alternative theatre – one who persists in the imagination of a theatre that would work for the script and one who seeks a space that would afford community with the audience. The history of western theatre has taught us that such theatrical experimentation is altogether a more recent phenomenon, born out of reactions against on stage realism or, even, that community theatre is an expression of the 1960s. But I would more provocatively suggest that this trajectory starts with Joanna Baillie, who tried again and again to describe a theatre that would realize the design and ideas in her plays and that would bring audiences into intimate connection with the drama. And let us remember, too, that she saw drama not in just a local sense but as a powerful contribution to national identity (one in which women might play a more public role). Recent scholarship concerned with the Romantic period has done a great deal to elaborate and enhance our understanding of Baillie's multifaceted contributions, but she is still, I think, too much restrained as a figure of her age. She is, if you will, in a closet of the period. The collective attention of Romanticists needs, urgently, to reach the broader audience of theatre scholars, for what has been uncovered in this work has much to say about the content and structure of both theatre history and dramatic criticism across different periods of study.

So what, in the end, does it mean to "out" Joanna Baillie? First of all, it means to disentangle her from the category of closet drama, even in its reinvented forms. Many of Baillie's plays went un-produced, but this does not mean, in any sense, that she was a closet dramatist. She was relentless in her attempts to find suitable stages for her plays. Secondly, it means to liberate her from the over-determined and deliberately limiting class of the literary aristocracy where she seems remote from the business of theatre. And thirdly, it means to consider her dramatic production as having a theatrical impact far beyond the London stage (as if somehow it was all that existed or mattered then or now). Once "outed," Joanna Baillie can participate in the public arena she sought for her plays, and there she should flourish as a foundational figure in a long, determined, and distinguished history of alternative theatre practice in Britain where many women and some men have dared to do things their way: differently.

NOTES

1 David D. Mann, Susan Garland Mann, and Camille Garnier, *Women Playwrights in England, Ireland and Scotland, 1660–1823* (Bloomington: Indiana University Press, 1996), p. 46.
2 Paul M. Zall, "The Cool World of Samuel Taylor Coleridge: The Question of Joanna Baillie" (*Wordsworth Circle* 13, 1982, 17–20), p. 17; p. 19.
3 Robert W. Uphaus and Gretchen M. Foster, ed., *The "Other" Eighteenth Century: English Women of Letters 1660–1800* (East Lansing: Colleagues Press, 1991), p. 343.
4 The other types, they argue, are professional theatre and amateur or home entertainments. See Gwenn Davis and Beverly A. Joyce, ed., *Drama by Women to 1900: A Bibliography of American and British Writers* (University of Toronto Press, 1992), especially p. xi of their introduction. These divisions are useful in downplaying the singular importance of professional theatre and instead promoting a more holistic theatre history, but none of the three types should be considered discrete and unaffected by the presence of, or interrelation with, the other two types. It is worth noting that John Franceschina in his introduction to *Sisters of Gore: Seven Gothic Melodramas by British Women, 1790–1843* (New York: Garland, 1997) quotes the Davis and Joyce delineation and uses it, among other ways, to exclude Joanna Baillie – as primarily a closet dramatist – from inclusion in his own volume.
5 See Davis and Joyce, *Drama by Women*, p. xi.
6 W. W. Greg, vol. IV of *A Bibliography of the English Printed Drama to the Restoration* (Oxford University Press, 1959), p. xii. 4 vols.
7 Scullion calls her "quite simply and irrespective of gender, the most important playwright in nineteenth-century Scotland." See Adrienne Scullion, ed. *Female Playwrights of the Nineteenth Century* (London: J. M. Dent, 1996), p. lix.
8 See Marta Straznicky, "Recent Studies in Closet Drama" (*English Literary Renaissance* 28.1, 1998, 142–60), p. 159.
9 Catherine Burroughs, *Closet Stages: Joanna Baillie and the Theater Theory of British Romantic Women Writers* (Philadelphia: University of Pennsylvania Press, 1997), p. 168.

10 Julie Carlson, *In the Theatre of Romanticism: Coleridge, Nationalism, Women* (Cambridge University Press, 1994), p. 20.

11 See Alan Richardson, *A Mental Theater: Poetic Drama and Consciousness in the Romantic Age* (University Park, PA: Pennsylvania State University Press, 1988) and Timothy Webb, "The Romantic Poet and the Stage: A Short, Sad History" in Richard Allen Cave, ed. *The Romantic Theatre: An International Symposium* (Gerrards Cross, Bucks: Colin Smythe, 1986, pp. 9–46). As Julie Carlson points out about Webb's chapter, despite the broad account of the theatrical output of the Romantic poets, his subtitle suggests the antithesis of this evidence: "A Short, Sad History." Carlson suggests that the subtitle is "startling" although typical of received characterizations of the period (*In the Theatre of Romanticism* 15).

12 See Tracy C. Davis, "The Sociable Playwright and Representative Citizen" in *Women and Playwriting in Nineteenth-Century Britain*, eds. Tracy C. Davis and Ellen Donkin (Cambridge University Press, 1999, pp. 15–34), p. 25.

13 See Burroughs, *Closet Stages*, pp. 81–86 for a useful range of Inchbald's comments. Importantly, Burroughs observes that "[i]t is the movement *between* closet and stage that Inchbald models as a critic, for the purpose, it would seem, of urging greater appreciation of two arenas often opposed and hierarchized" (84).

14 Cited in Ellen Donkin, *Getting into the Act: Women Playwrights in London, 1776–1829* (London: Routledge, 1995), p. 177. Donkin's volume is a rich resource for feminist revisionist historians. The sheer quantity and quality of primary sources consulted and described provides a ground-breaking counter to the thinly detailed, one-dimensional pictures "History" has given us of these women playwrights' contributions and of the specifics of their cultural reception in their own historical moment.

15 Alan Richardson comments in *A Mental Theater* that it "is not to say that the portrayal or revelation of character in neoclassical drama is undramatic; rather that character in itself is conceived of in static, not dynamic, terms" (192). It is precisely this kind of claim which leads Julie Carlson to point out his "antitheatrical bias" (*In the Theatre of Romanticism*, 14). It is important to observe how preliminary recuperations of the plays of this period have relied so emphatically on dismissing the theatrical environment.

16 The line is often cited – see, for example, Timothy Webb, "The Romantic Poet" in Cave, ed., *Romantic Theatre*.

17 See Burroughs, *Closet Stages*, particularly pp. 12–26.

18 J. O. Bailey, *British Plays of the Nineteenth Century: An Anthology to Illustrate the Evolution of the Drama* (New York: Odyssey Press, 1966), p. 26.

19 John Franceschina, ed. *Sisters of Gore*, p. 13, n.26.

20 See Judith Pascoe, *Romantic Theatricality: Gender, Poetry, and Spectatorship* (Ithaca: Cornell University Press, 1997), p. 7. Pascoe's book provides a

crucial linkage between gender and poetry and turns on the pivotal
figure of Sarah Siddons. Although outside the framework of this
chapter, it would be interesting to consider Pascoe's argument that
Siddons "was permitted to behave in public in a manner forbidden by
rules of female propriety" (242) in the context of Siddons's ongoing (and
often fraught) relation with Baillie and her plays.

21 Mary F. Yudin, "Joanna Baillie's 'Introductory Discourse' as a Precursor to Wordsworth's 'Preface to *Lyrical Ballads*'" (*Compar(a)ison* 1,
1994, 101–11), p. 111.

22 In his account of "The Legitimate Drama," Allardyce Nicoll gives a
surprisingly positive account of Baillie's work. See *A History of English
Drama 1660–1900: vol 4., Early Nineteenth Century Drama 1800–1850.* 2nd edn
(Cambridge University Press, 1960), 6 vols. He writes that, in "stressing
the necessity for the central emotion, therefore, Joanna Baillie was doing
something which was of the utmost importance. The very calling
attention to this fact marks out her plays as landmarks in the history of
the English theatre" (157). This is unusual praise (and more so given the
date of Nicoll's writing, 1930), and while I would differ on the particulars
for her landmark contribution, I do think this comment is useful for
pointing out how Baillie was trying something new.

23 Baillie, "Introductory Discourse," *A Series of Plays [1798–1812]*, ed. D. H.
Reiman (New York: Garland Press, 1977), p. 16. Also cited in Burroughs,
Closet Stages, p. 88.

24 Baillie, "Preface to Miscellaneous Plays," *A Series of Plays [1798–1812]*,
ed. D. H. Reiman (New York: Garland Press, 1977), p. iii.

25 It should be noted that some of the theories (and indeed, the desires)
she expresses in the "Preface to *Miscellaneous Plays*" either repeat or
develop ideas set out in the introduction to the *Series of Plays*. See
Baillie's footnote in the "Preface to Miscellaneous Plays," p. iii.
Burroughs gives a thorough and detailed account of Baillie's prefaces in
Closet Stages, especially pp. 86–91 and 162ff.

26 Donkin, *Getting into the Act*, pp. 166–70, discusses correspondence and
related events concerning Kemble's rejection of Baillie's script and
Siddons's failure, too, to support its production.

27 David Mann *et al.*, *Women Playwrights*, suggest that there were also
productions in Edinburgh and Dublin (46).

28 In a very interesting essay, Andrea Henderson argues that Baillie's
project to build a series of plays on individual passions was "shaped by
the logic of consumerism" (["Passion and Fashion in Joanna Baillie's
'Introductory Discourse'," *PMLA* 112.2, 1997, 198–213], p. 200). Henderson is not interested in theatrical history of the plays, but in their
effect as a collector's series (with, I think, both Baillie and the reader as
the exemplary eighteenth-century consumer). Notwithstanding the very
different aims of our essays, Henderson is very useful in elucidating the
acuity of Baillie's design.

29 Beth Friedman-Romell's "Staging the State: Joanna Baillie's *Constantine Paleologus*" in *Women and Playwriting in Nineteenth-Century Britain*, ed. Tracy C. Davis and Ellen Donkin (Cambridge University Press, 1999, pp. 151–73) provides descriptions of these four distinct productions; see p. 151 and pp. 154–58.

30 Nicoll suggests that it was produced in Liverpool in 1808 as *The Band of Patriots* (159).

31 See Susan Bennett, "Genre Trouble: Joanna Baillie, Elizabeth Polack – Tragic Subjects, Melodramatic Subjects" in Davis and Donkin, eds. *Women and Playwriting*, pp. 215–32), p. 230.

32 Friedman-Rommell, "Staging the State," in Davis and Donkin, eds. *Women and Playwriting*, p. 171.

33 In the following paragraph, Baillie notes that only Mahomet, Justiniiani, and Constantine are actual historical figures; in other words, it is really only the subject as such which comes from Gibbon (giving it an intellectual currency and credibility). The rest – which is to say, most – of the play is "imaginary" as she puts it [xv]).

34 Cited in Donkin, *Getting into the Act*, p. 166.

35 While Sarah Siddons did not play the role of Valeria, her daughter-in-law, Harriot Siddons, did. Beth Friedman-Romell, "Staging the State," in Davis and Donkin, ed., suggests that the casting of Harriot Siddons, as well as Miss Jarman in the Theatre Royal, Dublin, production, led to very feminine renditions of the character – effectively erasing the gender and sexual ambiguities that Baillie's script encouraged (see pp. 158–61). She concludes that the "'femme' casting of Valeria supported managers' increased emphasis on romance" (160).

36 See Burroughs (*Closet Stages*, pp. 112–15) on Baillie's theories of acting, which includes discussion of the preface to volume III of *Plays on the Passions*. Even in the preface to *Miscellaneous Plays*, Baillie expresses a preference for "canvass theatres and barns" where her plays might be produced, "preserving to my name some remembrance with those who are lovers of that species of amusement which I have above every other enjoyed" (*Series of Plays*, ed. Reiman, p. v).

37 Joanna Baillie, *Constantine Paleologus, Miscellaneous Plays* [1803] (New York: Garland, 1977, 279–438), p. 281.

38 Marjean D. Purinton, *Romantic Ideology Unmasked: The Mentally Constructed Tyrannies in Dramas of William Wordsworth, Lord Byron, Percy Shelley, and Joanna Baillie* (Newark: University of Delaware Press, 1994), p. 162.

39 Friedman-Romell's essay "Staging the State" also provides details of the various script revisions that *Constantine* underwent and how such alterations radically repositioned the politics (national as well as gender) of Baillie's play.

CHAPTER 7

The management of laughter: Jane Scott's "Camilla the Amazon" in 1998

Jacky Bratton, Gilli Bush-Bailey and DT2323A semester 97/8B

This chapter is an attempt to mirror in presentation the process and the product of the research that lies behind it. Its authors worked on the 1817 Gothic melodrama, *Camilla the Amazon*, by Jane Margaret Scott, with a group of theatre students at Royal Holloway, University of London, in the hope of reaching more understanding of the performance text than is possible in the study. The result was illuminating; but we felt that to reduce the insights of this group of people to a single authorial voice was to do violence not only to our own process but also to what that process had led us to understand about the play and its creators. The response to the play that was created during workshopping has a relation to the original experience, which could not have been arrived at without the participation of many voices; it cannot, therefore, be offered to a reader here in one voice. There is no convincing model for heteroglossic critical writing. While this experiment will demand more work from the reader, its experimental nature will, we hope, excuse its demands.

JACKY BRATTON AND GILLI BUSH-BAILEY

The Strand Theatre the Sans Pareil Monday Feb 24 1817:

an entire New and Splendid Serio-Comic heroic Melo-Dramatic Piece,
written by Miss Scott, With New Plot, Incidents & Situation, New Scenery,
Dresses, Decorations, Properties and Music, called,

CAMILLA THE AMAZON.

Or, The Mountain Robber.

FIDESCO,	*a young Nobleman, beloved by Camilla*	Mr. JAMES JONES.
EDWIN,	*Favorite Page to Fidesco,*	Mons. Le CLERQ.
ALWIN,	*Principal Page to Camilla,*	Mr. KIRBY.
ROSTOCK,	*Steward to Camilla,*	Mr. DAVIDGE.
HILLARY,	*Gardener to Camilla,*	Mr. HUCKEL.
TAPOLI,	*A Miller, Vassal to Camilla*	Mr. STEBBING

Senior and Junior Pages, attendants on the Princess, } Messrs.
J. DAVIDGE, MONTAGUE, Masters CONWAY AND ASBURY.

Guards, Messrs. BEMETZREIDER, ADDISON and WALBURN.
RUSCOLI and PETROFO, *attendants on Ferano,* Messrs. DALY
and YOUENS

FERANO,	**THE MOUNTAIN ROBBER,**	**MR. VILLIERS.**
ELLA,	*a young Tyrolean, Sister to Edwin,* *seduced & deserted by Fidesco,*	Mad. Le CLERQ.
COLINETTE,	*Daughter to Tapoli,*	Miss GARCIA.
THOMASIN,	*Wife to Tapoli,*	Mrs. DALY.
JULIAN,	*Infant Son of Ella and Fidesco,*	Miss STEBBING.

Ladies of Camilla's Court, Misses Le BRUN, YOUNG, BECK,
COX &c.

And CAMILLA, – THE AMAZON, – MISS SCOTT.

Peasants	Messrs. Turner, Brown, Terry, Gray, Bond and Smith.
Female Peasants	Misses Hart, Curtis, Bond, Davenport, Baily and Kirby.

Vassals and Attendants on the Mountain Robber.[1]

FROM ROYAL HOLLOWAY, UNIVERSITY OF LONDON, STUDENT
RECORDS SPRING 1998

Class List: DT2323A   Popular Performance IV: Melodrama
Semester: 97/8B   Convenor: Jacky Bratton
Tutors: Jacky Bratton and Gilli Bush-Bailey

Name:

Austin, Kelly	McAleese, Geraldine
Barnett, Joanne	Mercer, Sarah Ellen
Berry, Catherine Lesley	Peters, Rachel
Brett, Camilla Jane	Pudwell, Celia Louise
Buckley, Cara	Rollo, Julia Margaret
Chernoff, Lisa	Roselli, Gabriella Georgina
Clarke, Andrew Paul	Royal, Bonnie Elizabeth
Corsar, Ciaran Erin Daniel	Schlereth, Christina
Ewbank, Louise Katherine	Seymour, Mary Marcella
Gordon, Katharine Jane	Shepherd, Sarah Louise
Grant, Saul	Skegg, Susan Elizabeth
Harris, Kelly Joanne	Taylor, Katie Louise
Hills, Francesca	Todd, Amy
Hunt, Felicity Anne	Weeks, Catherine Emma
James, Rebecca Katie	Willey, Deborah
MacBride, Phoebe Catherine Janet	

Total Number of Students Enrolled: 31

STUDENT HANDBOOK ENTRY: DT2323A

Thursdays 2–5, Orchard Annexe.

The class will approach an understanding of melodrama via its special evocation of the monstrous, especially of monstrous motherhood. Practical work will centre upon workshopping the Romantic melodrama *Camilla the Amazon*, 1817, by actress/manager/writer Jane Scott; in-class presentations of rehearsed scenes in week 5. Alongside workshops we will consider the following novels, stage/screen adaptations and feature films:

The Wind (1928) Dir. Victor Seastrom. Silent film starring Lillian Gish
Shelley, Mary, *Frankenstein* (1818) revised (1831). Novel
Frankenstein (1931) Dir. James Whale. Film starring Boris Karloff

Peake, R.B. *Presumption (or The Fate of Frankenstein)* (1823)
    Adaptation for the stage

Braddon, Mary Elizabeth, *Lady Audley's Secret* (1862). Novel

Hazlewood, C. H., *Lady Audley's Secret* (1863). Adaptation for the
    stage

Wicked Lady (1945) Dir. Leslie Arliss. Film starring Margaret
    Lockwood & James Mason

Fatal Attraction (1987) Dir. Adrian Lyne. Screenplay James
    Dearden. Film starring Glenn Close & Michael Douglas

Alien (1979) Dir. Ridley Scott. Film starring Sigourney Weaver

Aliens (1986) Dir. James Cameron. Film starring Sigourney Weaver

Alien 3 (1992) Dir. David Fincher. Film starring Sigourney Weaver

Alien: The Resurrection (1997) Dir. Jean Pierre Jeunet. Film starring
    Sigourney Weaver

Single White Female (1992) Dir. Barbet Schroeder

Indiana Jones Chronicles:

Raiders of the Lost Ark (1981) Dir. Steven Spielberg

Indiana Jones and the Temple of Doom (1984) Dir. Steven Spielberg

Indiana Jones and the Last Crusade (1989) Dir. Steven Spielberg

Assessment: 40% practical work, 20% research presentation, 40% final essay

Transcription from the Larpent MS text

ACT THE 1ST SCENE THE 1ST[2]

. . . Chorus singing as they pass

Haste with roses deck the bower
While the laughing sun beams play
Joyous hail the blissfull hour
Joyous hail the nuptial day.

HILLARY: Well arrived my friends, and in good time yon distant horn – proclaims the approach of Princess Camilla and her suit.

Enter from the arch in the centre of the stage

FIDESCO: All nature smiles on this auspicious morn – let not Camilla droop.

CAMILLA: My Lord it brings to memory the day more lovely e'en than this – when with a joyous tho' beating heart I gave my love to lost, ill fated Colenburge – Whose image e'er must reign triumphant o'er my second Love.

FIDESCO: Till by ten thousand Acts of Idolatry Fidesco gains a preeminence – yet love the noble Colenburge – Love on – it is a rival I can brook yet feel no sting of jealousy.

HILLARY: (aside) Mighty generous truly – who in his senses would feel jealous of a dead man?

CAMILLA: Oh Colenburge, Colenburge, thou was't a man that nature proudly smiled upon and joyed to call thee a son.

HILLARY: (aside) And yet with all this fuss – could he pop in live and well among us now I question but he'd prove a most unwelcome guest – I warrant you the widow would start off – and should her husband follow, wish with all her heart old Nick would take the hindmost.

CAMILLA: But come my lord – the morn wears rapidly away – the panting deer now seeks the thicket whilst Phoebus soon with scorching rays will drive each eager sportsman to the forest shade. Impatient for the chase – let's hasten to the grove.

FIDESCO: Joyous I follow – when my guide is love.

Chorus

> Haste let us proclaim each valley and grove
> This day is devoted to conquering love
> All hail to Camilla the noble the great
> All hail to Fidesco the pride of the state
> Haste let us proclaim each valley and grove
> This day is devoted to conquering love.

JANE SCOTT

The theatrical flourish with which Scott announces her new melodrama is matched by her first sweeping stage entrance as Camilla, Princess of a feudal realm somewhere in an unidentified, but distinctly Romantically inspired, mid-European landscape. Both testify to Scott's experience and skill as a theatre crafts(wo)man: as a commercial theatre manager, she knows what the audience wants; as a writer and performer, she gives it to them.

My initial reading of Jane Scott's text was undertaken with some trepidation. Apart from some rather generalized preconceptions about what melodrama was, I knew very little about critical approaches to the genre and realized that the series of practical workshops we were about to embark upon would be as much of a journey of discovery for me as for the undergraduates we were working with. My approach to the text was therefore conditioned by my own experience as a theatre practitioner (first as an actress, then as a script-reader for commercial theatres).

The opening scene (that concludes with the extract above) introduces Camilla's kingdom through the comic commentary of Hillary the gardener as he prepares for the festivities celebrating Camilla's marriage. It is through his perspective, the working man who gets all the blame and none of the praise, that the audience is engaged. The Romantic theme of the play is reinforced by Hillary's love for Colinette, the simple daughter of the miller Tapoli. This young comic couple present the conventional gender constructs of the period, but the stability of this construct is undercut in the comic pairing of the miller, Tapoli, and his strident wife Thomasin; we know that the young couple will be just like the parents in years to come.

It is through the exchanges between the young couple and the comic Tapoli that Camilla's entrance is set up. In an exchange (which includes a song on the desirability of "maids" with tender hearts "who would faint at a sword"), the princess Camilla is described as a woman who "lost her senses – as some think" when she lost her husband in battle, becoming "a perfect hurricane" that "don't dress like other women but wears a kind of armour." This dispels any notions of a conventional melodramatic heroine in full bridal gown and raises the dramatic stakes (and expectations) for Camilla's potentially shocking entrance. The build-up is completed by the pastoral chorus (quoted at the beginning of the extract above), as they anticipate Camilla's traditional center-stage entrance.

Whatever the visual impact the Amazonian princess achieves, her dialogue soon gets on with the business of establishing the plot and herself as a widow still grieving for her lost husband. Again this is delightfully undercut by Hillary's comic asides that should her husband "pop in live and well amongst us now. . . he'd prove a most unwelcome guest." The high-flown language with which Camilla invites her husband-to-be to "hasten to the grove" clearly invites the audience to recognize the sexual energy (and appetite) of this unusual heroine. It is with this closely written mixture of convention and parody, traditional constructs that are acknowledged and then undercut, that Scott displays her skill in a form that both reinforces and disrupts conventions, particularly in her female characters.

GILLI BUSH-BAILEY

Through the course of the play, Camilla experiences a whole gamut of emotion from regality in the first scene to jealous rage, to repentant helplessness, to blissful happiness at the return of her lost husband. The bill reflects this as it describes the play as "A New and

Splendid Serio-Comic Heroic Melodramatic Piece" – fabulous! This means rejection of any sense of realism. There is no through line of character for Camilla.

SUE SKEGG

Very often studies of Romantic and Victorian plays by women are of writers whose relationship with theatrical production were at best problematic; in many cases the female author did not have her dramatic work staged at all, and we can only consider the literary merits and possible intentions of her closet drama. The work of Jane Margaret Scott is a very different case. She wrote more than fifty dramatic works, ranging over the whole spectrum from poems for recitation on high Romantic/heroic subjects through melodrama, burletta and farce to pantomimes specially created to showcase juvenile dancers and speciality acts. All of these were created specifically and only for production on the stage of her own theatre, the Sans Pareil, later to become the Adelphi, built for her use by her father John Scott, in the Strand, the heart of London's developing commercial theatre district. "Miss Scott's" writing was inspired by and coterminous with her practice there: after she retired from the stage in 1818, she possibly never wrote, certainly never published, another line.

This potentially very exciting example of female authorship for the stage has been occluded in subsequent theatre history for reasons having to do with the ideology of Romanticism and later of Modernism. In these discourses, open, practical outcome-and-profit-oriented composition by a woman was not eligible for serious consideration; it is disruptive, awkward to accommodate in any critical paradigm except the marginalized category of "popular performance." So Jane Scott's work is accorded a page in one of the histories of the music hall; otherwise it is conveniently forgotten. Only two of her plays are listed by Allardyce Nicoll, despite the twenty-two manuscripts clearly labeled with her name in the Larpent Collection.[3]

The Larpent plays are manuscripts submitted for licensing, and so accidentally surviving: they were never intended as satisfactory reading copies of the plays they sketchily represent. Just as the practical needs of the theatre the Scotts were running led to the creation of these texts, so it was a practical demand, the legal requirement of the license, that has preserved them. Only one of her plays was published – *The Old Oak Chest* (1816) – an interesting text which proved significantly malleable even after it was printed, being adapted for propaganda purposes by illegal radical theatres of the period and translated into a scenario for the middle-class child's toy theatre. The great majority of her work is not suited to translation into a printed text, relying as it does upon the cooperation of all the theatrical elements: the actors she wrote for, with their stage personae and their speciality acts; the visual and musical resources of her theatre; and the developed tastes of her habitual audience, as well as her own performances and the responses of her personal following.

The licensing texts are often hastily copied and defective, but they are valuable as a theatrical record in that while they are exiguous and indeed often silent on matters of staging and pictorial presentation, they are, by the same token, free of imaginative embellishment intended to evoke a finished effect for the reader. No lengthy scene-setting; often no indication how or where a scene is set; no description of characters; few prescriptive stage directions. In some ways, therefore, they can be more like a modern playtext than the well-made plays of Pinero and Shaw. They are, if you like, writerly texts that do not pre-empt the creative role of actors and audience. Equally, of course, they are difficult to use in that they offer the historian and the modern reader no conscious guidance as to how the extra-textual roles were fulfilled or could have been imagined by the writer in the early nineteenth century. But the style of these written records reflects, unwittingly but suggestively, their partial or minor witness to the text in the theatre.

They can be augmented from other records. From the cast list on the one surviving playbill, we may discover that the comic role of Hillary is played by Jane Scott's long-time employee and frequent opposite number in comic scenes, Huckel; that the villainous steward Rostock is a substantial and important part because it is assigned to Davidge, who became a manager in his own right; and that Edwin, a silent role, and Ella, a very loquacious one, are played by the Le Clerqs, the leading dancers. They appear later on the same bill in a "Scotch Ballet," with a full dance company which, on inspection, proves to be also represented, six or eight strong, in the play. And then all these written records can be both tested and augmented by the witness of our experience of the text in performance.[4]

JACKY BRATTON

With my script-reader's hat firmly in place, the textual difficulties arising from an incomplete script suggested the creative approaches employed when engaging with a text which is essentially a "work in progress." The sense of the playtext as a "blueprint," or a skeleton on which the body of the theatrical experience would grow, was reinforced by the awareness that the playwright was a woman who was skilled in the practical craft of theatre. The "gaps" in a playtext, awkward jumps from one scene to the next, can expose a writer's lack of theatre practice; it looks all right on the page, but it doesn't translate to the stage. While there are a number of problems in the text of *Camilla*, the "holes" suggested to me that Scott had a number of possibilities based not only on her own experience and ingenuity but also on that of the company she was writing for. It is in this sense that I apply the notion of a work in progress: what is on the page is everything the licenser *needed* to see; what would be on the stage is everything the audience *wanted* to see.

GILLI BUSH-BAILEY

Melodrama has a heightened awareness of its audience, and the written text is only one aspect of the performances. The melodramatic performance is not cartoonish; instead, it is a heightened version of reality.

RACHEL PETERS

There was absolutely no co-ordination between my brain and my body, and I could not get to grips with realizing the visions I had. I encountered great problems in actually freeing up my body (as did everyone else) to create an "authentic melodramatic performance" . . . What we were aiming for was a completely alien performance style – totally at odds with the naturalism we are continually fed – and I found that most of us appeared to have a built in resistance to it . . . Problems of embarrassment were rife, and what we tended to produce during the first few classes was static, insincere, and unfunny – neither naturalistic nor melodramatic but a terrible mess.

DEBORAH WILLEY

As well as finding the script itself hard to read, the students found the idea of melodrama difficult enough, with no ways in that were not barred by preconception and prejudice; and as soon as they began to see their way, they had to come to terms with its unorthodoxies even as a melodrama, which obtruded themselves undeniably as we worked. A point of access was the fact that *Camilla* is a Gothic text. Gothicism has been recognized over the last decade as a major discourse in modern art, originating alongside Romanticism and in many ways related to it, but having other meanings not coterminous with such high seriousness. One of the most interesting recent developments has been the exploration of its political dimensions, including those of sexual politics; less easily approached in critical terms are its complexities of tone, especially the balance/tension between fear and laughter. [5] It is also centrally important that the form relies as much on visual as verbal signs, and on technical innovations that do not appear on the page. These characteristics it shares with – it may be accurate to say, it imparted to – the dramatic form of melodrama, which famously interlards comic and serious or heroic scenes, and employs music, gesture, and spectacle to make good its meanings.[6]

   It is possible to invoke creatively the legacy of Gothic by reference to its modern manifestations. Gothic horror remains a living force in much modern popular entertainment, especially in film. So the possibility of approaching the understanding of the now remote form of stage melodrama through the Gothic was our starting-point. Focusing on ideas of the natural, the supernatural, and the monstrous, the course began with a showing of *The Wind* and included Mary Shelley's *Frankenstein* and its dramatizations and filmings, Braddon's *Lady Audley's Secret* and its dramatizations, and films from *The Wicked Lady* via *Fatal Attraction* and *Single White Female* to the *Aliens* series and *Indiana Jones*. (See the course outline above.) Within this setting, *Camilla the Amazon* was explored in five weeks of discussion and workshopping, leading to in-class presentation of extracts by the students.

JACKY BRATTON

It's so *big*!

FRAN HILLS

It was a great advantage to the process to be able to invoke the high production values of modern film in association with this text. Paula Backscheider says of Gothic drama that it is

almost as difficult as street pageants to reconstruct, and more difficult still for modern *readers* to integrate imaginatively... To understand this drama, its success, and how it contained the most pressing fears and hopes of its audience, modern readers must recognise the co-ordinated art forms and bring perspectives from them all to bear simultaneously upon the printed text. To a large extent, this theatre did depend upon the bombardment of the senses and the use of techniques that fixed manipulative tableaux in the audiences' memories.[7]

While nothing short of time-travel, or at least Covent Garden's stage and a budget of millions, could fully obviate this difficulty, it is possible to invoke creatively the legacy of Gothic by reference to its modern manifestations, which still deploy the rich resources required. Not that Jane Scott actually had huge resources by the standards of her time.

JACKY BRATTON

THE STRAND THEATRE – THE SANS PAREIL

This house is worthy of its name, since of all the theatres in London, it can claim to be the prettiest . . . We imagine the proprietor must be rapidly accumulating a fortune. His success is almost wholly to be attributed to the versatile talents of his daughter.

The British Stage Feb. 1817

. . . of the most elegant and commodious description. Twelve new boxes have been added, including two stage boxes, and the pit will now accommodate eight hundred persons. The gallery is so constructed that the audience have a full view of the stage even from the back seats . . . The ceiling is a finished piece of workmanship, representing Venus and her attendants . . . The house is painted on a light blue ground, with ornaments after the Grecian style. The stage is between fifty and sixty feet deep, and forty feet wide, which gives ample room for scenery . . .

Theatrical Inquisitor Dec. 14 1818, 406–07

the proscenium, twenty-eight feet in width, had stage doors either side with a box over each . . . The gallery seated about three hundred. The house would hold very nearly two hundred pounds E. L. BLANCHARD, **"History of the Adelphi Theatre" in** *Era Almanac* **(1877)**

So here was a house of about 1,500, all with a good view, but all very closely packed round a usable forestage with its own doors, allowing easy direct address to the audience, but also a deep scenic stage, for elaborate scenery and effects. The gallery was new in 1809; it contributed life and energy to the performances:

JACKY BRATTON

A gallery was added, and the merry hive,
From that bless'd moment set the house alive . . .

JANE SCOTT[8]

The text is packed with evidence that audience expectation/reception was a priority. There is "something for everyone": Gothic horror, romance, comedy, songs, villainy, heroism, tragedy, spectacle, fights, speciality acts, dance, etc. There is an exuberant energy in the playful way Scott arranges these melodramatic conventions, and indeed her central characters, which we hoped would stimulate the students' desire to "see" beyond the text and consider the creative possibilities that might have been realized in performance.

The typical representation of the heroine, the villain, and the comic couple, framed by the centrality of music and visual spectacle in *The Wind*, enabled the students to experience something of the emotional impact of gestural language that is essential to the melodramatic form. The first stage in our practical work was to explore ways of translating an understanding of gestural language into performance practice; no easy task for late-twentieth-century students wedded to the notions of naturalism. We were fortunate to have access to a variety of musical instruments, although initially the students were very tentative in their approach to creating a "melo." Building on the central deployment of music and tableaux, the students began to explore the creation of short, silent scenes, which would end in typical stage pictures. While this was nominally successful, it was clear that the deep-seated desire to rely on minimalist movement and gesture to convey meaning inhibited the students as they attempted to make some connection with the expression of gestural language they had seen.

GILLI BUSH-BAILEY

We were all thinking through the filter of Naturalism.

SUE SKEGG

Having established some basic understanding of typical characters and movement, we began to explore specific scenes in *Camilla*. Four groups looked at different scenes, each one creating a melo to accompany the dialogue and action. The presence of a script (to which the students were slavishly obedient at first) tended to undo the previous discoveries related to movement and gestural language.

In order to free the physical movement, we explored the scenes in a number of ways. Engaging with the desire to approach the text naturalistically, we discovered the limitations this imposed and soon moved on to silent, mimed versions, sometimes accompanied by a narrator, sometimes only by the melo.

GILLI BUSH-BAILEY

We found the melo doing more than merely presenting a character. What we saw happening were the two instruments not only highlighting a mood or state of mind but [also] actually voicing the feeling of the characters . . . [which] made us wonder whether the instruments could be our scene's story-teller.

CHRISTINA SCHLERETH

The music enables the characters to have a subconscious on stage without detracting from the action.

SUE SKEGG

During the discussions following this stage of the practical work, it became evident that we were moving toward an understanding of a performance approach that could be described in terms of "heightened realism." We were beginning to work toward producing the *effect* of realism, allowing for sincerity and a believability in the emotion but without obliging the performer to feel that emotion in order to reproduce it.

As students became more familiar with the text through practical work, they found *Camilla* less daunting, but they were also more keenly aware of their limited understanding of the power of gestural language. Peake's *Presumption* (1823), an adaptation of Mary Shelley's *Frankenstein* (1818), suggested an approach to the problem of the "mute" role in melodrama. Employing masks to explore the characterization of the (silent) monster in *Presumption* enabled the students to develop their physical movement and gestural expression in a quite different direction.

GILLI BUSH-BAILEY

During the mask workshop, the class seemed to approach the melodramatic text with unprecedented seriousness and respect.

LISA CHERNOFF

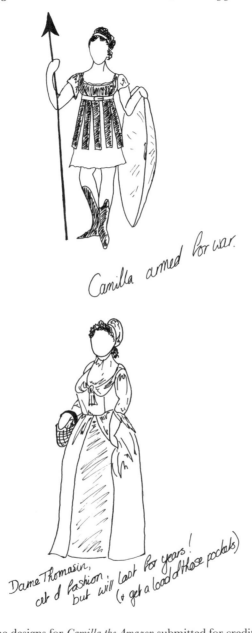

Camilla armed for war.

Dame Thomasin, cut d fashion but will last for years! (& get a load of those pockets)

7.1   Costume designs for *Camilla the Amazon* submitted for credit in course DT2323A by Sara Mercer.

Ferano/Colenburge
the robber hero

Ella in "the dress"

As part of their assessed work the students were required to perform a rehearsed scene (off script). The performance took place in the workshop environment of the preceding classes, and (apart from a further faculty member as external examiner) the audience consisted of simply the tutors and the other class members. By continuing the workshop environment for these assessed performances, we hoped to minimize the level of panic that can attend a more public display and maximize the possibility of physical expression that had been so difficult to access. As the students approached the moment of performance, the new-found confidence and respect for gestural language was (somewhat intermittently) realized. Their success was particularly evident in the presentation of an early but dramatically crucial scene in *Camilla*. The typically melodramatic heroine is introduced in the character of the deserted Ella, who, with her illegitimate son, has traveled "many a weary mile" to find Fidesco, the father of her child, before he marries Camilla. The complex revelation of her predicament is further complicated by the fact that what appears on the page as a monologue is in fact a duologue with her brother, the mute Edwin (originally created for/by the dancer Le Clerq), a character interpretation which had caused considerable difficulty in the early workshops.

GILLI BUSH-BAILEY

ACT THE 1ST, SCENE THE 1ST.

ELLA: Surely I have seen him. I could not be mistaken; this heart too faithfully retains his image. Yet at the feet of high born Camilla he proffered those vows due only to the ruin'd Ella –
(Turning sees the blooms over the arch)
Ah! Fidesco and Camilla united by love – I can no longer doubt – poor deserted infant – lost – betrayed – ill fated Ella.
(Staggers to the seat beneath the orange tree and faints. Child [Julian] runs to her)
JULIAN: Mama, Mama, don't go to sleep now, yonder comes a fine signor who will perhaps buy something *(child finds her motionless – screams) –* she's dead – she's dead signor signor signor.
ELLA: Do I still live – who has been barbarous enough to call me back to life *(turns – sees Edwin, screams)*
Heavens my brother – and is my misery complete?
I dare not name what brought me here,
I dare not name the cause of this disguise,
I dare not name the parents of that child.
The curses of the world united I could bear – but yours would kill me, brother.

JULIAN: *(kneeling at his [Edwin's] feet)* Oh do not kill my mother -
(A picture here formed)

ELLA: Oh do not call such bitter maledictions on Fidesco's head, he was no base deliberate seducer – Alas, left in infancy an orphan, no father to protect me, no tender mother to guide my erring steps – my own treacherous heart betrayed me – you Edwin loved Fidesco too – became his page and left our peaceful vale. You little dreamt of the thorn that rankled in thy wretched sister's breast – nor did Fidesco know heaven had destined him to be a father – Four years of misery slow passed away till rumour reached my ears that Lord Fidesco woo'd the proud Camilla – 'twas then I fled our lonely vale and with my own happy infant wandered many a weary mile to seek him. Yes – I will gain a restitution of my honour – a father for my child – or find a grave when every hope expires.

ELLA: Yes – I have with me the dress in which Fidesco first saw me – dancing with my young companions before our cottage door – it is concealed in my box of merchandize. Hope smiles upon the product – Yes, my dear brother, attired in the simple garb of happy innocence, I will join your festival and attempt the favourite dance of our native countries – perchance it will recall to Fidesco's mind the moment of our meeting so transporting to him, so fatal to me. $(8-9)^9$

JANE SCOTT

. . . as a mute character . . . [Edwin's] physical gesture and position on stage is his only means of communication; therefore, his only means of making himself understood is by using signs and choreographed dance gesture. Culturally, socially, and spatially, I felt inhibited using these methods as a means of expression.

FRAN HILLS

The conventional melodramatic devices are skillfully employed here, complete with tableau of innocent child, his betrayed mother, and her outraged brother; the audience is clearly set up for the inevitable confrontation between Ella and Fidesco that must, and does, take place. Ella's typical heroine construction continues to challenge Camilla's dominant position in the play as first heroine (who cedes Fidesco to Ella), then villainess (as she attempts to dispose of Ella altogether). It is here, in a scene favored by four groups for their presentation, that the most interesting aspects of the workshop experience came to fruition, and the unconventional elements of the play could be realized beyond their textual presence.

As Camilla and Fidesco prepare to defend the realm from an

impending attack from the robber band, Rostock, the villainous steward, suggests that Camilla employ the captured robber chief Ferano to dispose of Ella and her child, releasing Fidesco to marry Camilla as planned.

GILLI BUSH-BAILEY

ACT THE 1ST, SCENE THE 1ST.

CAMILLA: Come Fidesco – let us to the Castle and girding swords upon our wedding garments drive from their holds these proud disturbers of our peace.

FIDESCO: Not so sweet princess – let Fidesco's arm and sword defend thee – my Ella and her child shall be my pledge of victory.

CAMILLA: *(aside)* Oh! Say'st thou Fidesco – be it as you say. (15)

JANE SCOTT

It is clear that Ella does not feel safe in the care of "that haughty woman," and Fidesco does not entirely trust her ability to protect his wife-to-be and their child:

GILLI BUSH-BAILEY

CAMILLA: (aside) And is it come to this? – that e'en my honour doubted – Fidesco, thou hast raised a slumbering spirit of revenge that shall undo thee.

ROSTOCK: *(Coming forward)* First, let it light upon the peasant girl who came to blight thy happiness.

CAMILLA: Point out the means – thy mistress well can trust thee.

ROSTOCK: The Mountain robbers – make them your instruments of vengeance.

CAMILLA: You have said it – bring Ferano hither.
(Exit Rostock) (16–17)

JANE SCOTT

Two central issues in this scene were illuminated in performance. The first concerned the shift of power between Camilla and the men she was negotiating with. One student identified the vital presence of "dramatic choreography": the importance of the way in which the relationship between the characters was reinforced by their positions on the stage and the way that meaning(s) could be altered by changing those positions. Others became aware of the flexibility available to the performer through gestural language.

GILLI BUSH-BAILEY

Simply changing the sequence of the actions improved the clarity of the message for the audience.

RACHEL PETERS

In this scene Scott appears to tackle the problematics of patriarchal gender relations, demonstrating that however powerful a woman's position is, if she involves a man in the execution/administration of that power, he will appropriate authority for himself and use his dominant position to subjugate the woman. The fact that Ferano is actually Colenburge, Camilla's lost-presumed-dead husband, and therefore has a "right" to that authority, only works to confirm the strength of patriarchal hegemony. With both Fidesco and Ferano/Colenburge, Camilla's authority as a just and competent ruler is placed in question because she is first a woman. It seems relevant to suggest that Scott's own position as a manager/dramatist/performer – which placed her in a ruling, dictatorial position even – must have informed her approach to this issue.

The second issue in this scene concerns the approach to the highly unconventional monologue in which Camilla considers the moral implications if her plans are realized. It was in this speech (following directly after Rostock's exit) that many student-actors were tempted to return to the familiar ground of naturalism. However, those who pursued the notions of a heightened realism in their performance felt able to justify their conclusion that Scott had given her character a . . .

GILLI BUSH-BAILEY

subtle psychology which challenged [the] initial assumption that melodramatic characters contained little emotional complexity.

RACHEL PETERS

ACT THE 1ST, SCENE THE 1ST.

CAMILLA: Hold, what am I about – to blot my unstained conscience with the crime of murder and bear the penalty with guilt – no, no, it must not be – yet what have I to dread – the shafts of tyrant conscience time will quickly blunt – and reason laugh to scorn each servile fear – it shall be done.

> And yet me thinks when darksome night comes on
> Each sound will seem poor Ella's funeral song.
> And when my downy couch is pressed
> Visions of horror shall disturb my rest.

No, No, she must not die – for my repose it cannot be
But she shall live far from Fidesco – Love – and me. (17)

JANE SCOTT

Again, Scott resists the simple construction of either tyrannical villainess or meek heroic female. In a highly unconventional piece of writing, she gives Camilla a speech of internal reasoning that equivocates between her desire to destroy those who oppose her wishes and the awareness that her conscience will not allow her to commit murder.

GILLI BUSH-BAILEY

Her self-questioning revealed to the audience a softer side, occulted beneath her changeling characterization as a villainess . . . [T]hat she is in conflict with herself lent itself to a presentation which physically explored the psychological dynamics, illustrating the internal made external.

FRAN HILLS

In giving full rein to the possibilities offered by physical and gestural expression in melodramatic performance, the tense relationship between horror and laughter in melodramatic dramaturgy was revealed. The issue of laughter in *Camilla* (how to employ it and deal with it as a performer) proved most challenging to negotiate as the play draws to its dramatic close. Here the play enters the spectacular Gothic territory of mountain hideaways, ruined castles, and instruments of torture.

GILLI BUSH-BAILEY

Camilla the Amazon was written and staged in 1817. There is a fairly widely held consensus that the Gothic revival should be periodized fairly precisely, distinguishing between the first outburst of writings that culminated in the 1790s and a later period of "belated Gothic," in which the politicized and intense imagery of the nineties gave way to a self-reflexive, introspective, and ultimately playful deployment of Gothic tropes between roughly 1800 and 1820.[10] While this play is obviously self-reflexive and playful, it complicates much of the received wisdom about this periodization, especially in its gender dimensions. It corresponds very closely to the definitions of Gothic drama in the 1790s offered by Paula Backscheider, but overturns not only the periodization but also the gendering on which her descriptions are posited. She argues that "the heart of Gothic drama in the 1790s is an authority figure gone mad, or at least seriously obsessive and neurotically moody" (162) and "This man, and it always seems to be a man, is 'Gothic' because he is pushing the absolute limits of what the audience imagines to be possible in nature. He is subject to cataclysmic passions, has committed or is contemplating unspeakable crimes that reek of ancient, sacred taboos, and is engaged in a magnificent struggle with himself" (163). Jane Scott has written a role for herself, the role of a female ruler, which usurps this masculine position.

JACKY BRATTON

Having persuaded the robber chief to kidnap Ella, Camilla's plans are thwarted when Fidesco and Edwin escape from imprisonment and attempt a rescue. During the pursuit of the escaped captives, Scott introduces a high-comedy scene in which Fidesco and Edwin find refuge in the miller's cottage which is ruled by his wife, the powerful Dame Thomasin. The confrontation between Thomasin and Camilla, two strong women of different social classes, is conventionally Romantic in that the virtuous peasant opposes the corrupt power of the great. At the same time, however, the scene reverses gender expectations; and then the seriousness of this move is further complicated because it is undercut with comic byplay, including an appearance in drag by Edwin as he tries to escape. Camilla sweeps out of the humble cottage issuing threats of "future vengeance," and her obsession with Fidesco drives her to ever-more reckless acts as she attempts to persuade Ella to renounce her claim to Fidesco. The dramatic tension builds as the action moves to the mountains and the ruined castle where Ella and the child are imprisoned by Ferano and his robber band. In a final desperate move, Camilla has Ella's child, Julian, placed beneath a descending stone which will slowly crush its victim. Camilla's status as villain is at its height, and (inevitably) she becomes the victim in her own instrument of torture. Scott employs a tragic register as she moves her central character from villainess to victim and then to humble penitent.

GILLI BUSH-BAILEY

ACT THE 2ND, SCENE THE 3RD

CAMILLA: Horrible the victim of my own crimes, caught, caught in the deadly snare I plan'd for others – be firm my heart – I cannot – will not – live to be a robber's bride – ah, the impending ruin totters o'er my head – it falls – it falls to crush me – have mercy Heaven – mercy *(she kneels)* – already I feel the weight – save me – save – I fear to live – but cannot die so full of horrors *(she snatches up the bugle and sounds it – the stone reascends).*

Cowardly Camilla, thou hads't forgot the steel concealed within the foldings of thy robe *(shows a dagger)* Yet hold – some small atonement I have yet to make and then to die. (38–39)

JANE SCOTT

Paula Backscheider maintains that

Gothic plays situate the mingling and possibilities of love and violence directed at the heroine within the protagonist . . . the heroine is passive recipient, potential victim. In the fiction, women's bodies command centre stage. They are confined, badgered; pursued . . . The plays approach psychomania in which at one level a man's mind is the battle ground and at stake is what often seems the feminine, the benevolent, part of himself . . . The villain's idea of victory depends upon the sexual possession of the heroine; his final act of violence is to offer to stab her . . . The plays begin by establishing the tyrannical personality against which almost all other characters and groups are opposed. He is the problem the play must resolve, and he must be brought back within the community or expunged from the universe in order to allow the harmonious natural order that the play represents as its conclusion. (195)

Meanwhile, the females are representative of "the natural," have an innate moral sense, but are not in any way opponents of the villain:

they are only "vessels and agents." Their will is directed towards virtue, but of a rather narrowly focused kind: usually their own chastity and charity towards others. They seek relationships, especially with mothers and fathers. Most are unaware of their claims to property or positions of influence and when informed hardly notice. (Backscheider 196)

All of these prescriptions can be read off from *Camilla*, but in negative or counterpoint, recombined, reversed, or ironically cross-grained. The central woman is both villain and heroine, very much motivated by her "claims to property" and power, as well as by seeking relationship – explicitly sexual relationship; her inner struggle culminates, logically enough in Backsheider's terms, in an attempt to stab herself. The central male figure is villain and hero, whose main function is to resolve the problem she presents and bring her back within the community.

JACKY BRATTON

ACT THE 2ND, SCENE THE 3RD

[Having righted some wrongs, the penitent Camilla indicates that everyone should move back, creating an empty stage for what is effectively her last big moment in the play.]

(Ferano and Fidesco anxiously watch her – she draws a dagger)
CAMILLA: *(kneeling)* Spirit of my beloved Colenburge – look down – pity – forgive – receive me *(is going to stab herself)*
COLENBURGE: He does pity – he does forgive – he will receive thee.
    (Camilla screams and falls on the arm of Fidesco – then regarding Ferano/ Colenburge with terror exclaims)
CAMILLA: Say – does the grave give up its dead, or art thou really Colenburge?
COLENBURGE: Really, the Colenburge whom rumour had left upon the battlefield dead, but fast recovering from his wounds with some few faithful followers homeward, he returned to see with agonising grief that Camilla had changed the lovely softness of her sex – for amazonian fierceness.
CAMILLA: It was your loss, my Lord, that caused the sudden madness. (42)

JANE SCOTT

The breakneck speed with which events unfold toward this winning dramatic device suggested a comedic pace which many of the students' presentations reflected as they responded to the audiences' laughter.

GILLI BUSH-BAILEY

Melodrama, and the extent to which it is successful, is concerned with the management of laughter, owing to the variety of emotions that are shown in quick succession.

LOUISE EWBANK

The difficulty in managing the emotional turns with sincerity was clearly revealed to both performers and audience. The temptation was for the students to revert to the shallow "ham" performance style they had rejected during the previous weeks (and some clearly did).

GILLI BUSH-BAILEY

The performers noted their immediate desire to respond to the audiences' laughter by exaggerating their characters' stereotypical features. The laughter was not a mocking laughter but a laughter of delight and recognition; it indicated that they were enjoying what they were seeing.

LISA CHERNOFF

ACT THE 2ND, SCENE THE 3RD

COLENBURGE: . . . Come my beloved Camilla, forget the past where fault has brought its punishment – return to happiness and Colenburge – here take this bugle, sound it – once more breathe happiness to all around.
(She sounds the bugle)
And now let every heart give way to joy. Splendid banquet waits us at the castle. Come my own Camilla – haste – lay aside the helmet and the shield – Believe me, love, the brightest ornament to grace a woman's brow is meekness – her best defence and shield the arms of an affectionate husband –
(Curtain falls) (43)

JANE SCOTT

It is not surprising that most of the students found it hard to be satisfied with a closing scene that so firmly places Camilla back within the conventional constructs of the feminine, redeemed by a return to the role of submissive wife (although there were some expressions of pleasure at the conventional happy ending). The implicit suggestion is that Camilla's villainy is an inevitable result of female authority exercised outside the protective care of a paternalistic husband. There is no dialogue or stage direction to suggest how Camilla responds to Colenburge's request that she "lay aside the helmet and the shield" and don the "ornament" of "meekness" while allowing the "arms of an affectionate husband" to be "her best defence and shield." In a piece of theatre that has so evidently engaged with irony, it is tempting to pursue the notion that Scott may have undercut the conventional final tableau. What is not on the page might have been on the stage. However, Scott knew her audience and commercial impulses would favor "giving them what they wanted" in the form of this conventional finale.

Scott's writing continually reveals the extent of her knowledge, and manipulation, of central theatrical conventions. She paces the movement of Camilla through the play with remarkable dexterity, creating moments of high dramatic tension in which she can dominate the action and give full rein to her abilities as a performer. She doesn't exhaust herself, or her audience, by writing herself into every scene but sets up each entrance to meet the audience's expectation. (This is not only skillful in that it reinforces the centrality of her role, but also practical as she plays the lead in the burletta performed at the end of the bill.)

The sense of a shared joke, the notion of "delight and recognition" identified through the workshop experience, suggests a level of sophistication in the exchange of signs between melodramatic player and audience that is not usually assumed, particularly in relation to the generally uneducated classes supposedly frequenting the minor theatres. Through this practical work, it seemed clear that the interplay between performer and audience continues to suggest potential for further research. The familiarity with archetypes and plot conventions increases the audience's enjoyment as they anticipate the working out of those conventions. There is then also a self-reflexive humor, in both the writing and the playing, in consciously fulfilling that expectation. This, in turn, allows for a more complex appreciation of the use of irony as writer, performer, player, and audience recognize their participation in reinforcing hegemonic constructs as well as the possibility of dissent.

GILLI BUSH-BAILEY

So what are the advantages of workshopping *Camilla the Amazon* in a modern university setting? There is, of course, the extra illumination that such work throws upon any playtext, however well established or venerable: the degree and kind of attention paid to a script for presentation differs from the imaginative effort to realize the play in the study. But in this case the gain is, I would argue, much greater, and possibly of a different kind. The working environment of the rehearsal room is, in one sense, a clean slate: everyone is freshly engaged with how they might understand the text, and the operation of thirty-three minds and bodies will produce more than one person alone.

But there is more than an ordinary enrichment of textual experience by workshopping going on here. The sketchy transcription of a working script 181 years on the shelf is unapproachable without a context in which it may be understood. Critical and scholarly discourse about the writings of 1817 – Modernist disdain of melodrama, the developing discourses of British Romanticism, and new insights into the Gothic – suggest one set of contexts; in the classroom, the wisdom those contexts offered was radically challenged. The pedagogic engagement of the play with modern film (with Sigourney Weaver and James Whale's *Frankenstein*) and with techniques such as mask work offered more access than could the library to the spectacle and excitement of *Camilla*. Serious study and rehearsal of speeches that Jane Scott wrote for herself to present admitted us as performers, both student and professional, to an appreciation of the truly theatrical complexity of a forgotten dramatist. The object of this chapter is to share that access with the scholarly community.

JACKY BRATTON

NOTES

1 Transcribed from the bill held in the Theatre Museum, London, Adelphi file.

2 All transcriptions of the play are from the text submitted by John Scott for licensing, *Camilla the Amazon, or, the Mountain Robber*, Larpent Collection 1954, Huntington Library, San Marino, CA. A complete transcription was made for the use of the class, with minimal editorial intervention – only the addition of pagination and the regularization of character names and speech ascriptions. A version of Jane Scott's *Camilla the Amazon*, slightly more extensively edited for reading (by Jacky Bratton and Gilli Bush-Bailey), appears in the appendix of *Nineteenth Century Theatre*, 27. 2 (1999). Jane Scott's *The Old Oak Chest* (1816), her only printed play, is available in a modern edition, *Sisters of Gore: Seven Gothic Melodramas by British Women, 1790–1843*, ed. John Franceschina (New York and London: Garland Publishing Inc., 1997), pp. 121–72. Her most popular play *(Broad Grins, or) Whackham and Windham, or, the Wrangling Lawyers* (1814), Larpent no. 1798, is the subject of an experimental publication on the World Wide Web, accessible via http://www.lab.brown.edu/public/index.shtml.

3 For a more extensive consideration of this disappearance from history, see J. S. Bratton, "Miss Scott and Miss Macauley; 'Genius Comes in All Disguises'" (*Theatre Survey* 37, 1996, 59–73) and "Jane Scott the Writer-Manager" in *Women and Playwriting in Nineteenth-Century Britain*, ed.,

Tracy C. Davis and Ellen Donkin (Cambridge University Press, 1999), pp. 77–97. Allardyce Nicoll's omission is in vol. II of *A History of English Drama 1660–1900*, 3rd edition (Cambridge University Press, 1952); it is made good in *Women Playwrights in England, Ireland and Scotland 1660–1823*, ed. David D. and Susan Garland Mann (with Camille Garnier), (Bloomington and Indianapolis: Indiana University Press, 1996).

4 More information about the company Jane Scott hired and worked with over the years of her management of the Sans Pareil can be collected from *The Adelphi Theatre Calendar, part I, The London Stage 1880–1900: A Documentary Record and Calendar of Performances*, ed., Alfred L. Nelson and Gilbert B. Cross (New York: Greenwood Press, 1990).

5 For the political analysis, see Jeffrey N. Cox, ed., *Seven Gothic Dramas 1789–1825* (Athens: Ohio University Press, 1992). Other relevant work on the Gothic includes Eugenia C. Delamotte, *Perils of the Night* (Oxford University Press, 1990); Robert Miles, *Gothic Writing 1570–1820: A Genealogy* (London: Routledge, 1993); and Paul Ranger, *'Terror and pity reign in every breast': Gothic Drama in the London Patent Theatres, 1750–1820* (London: The Society for Theatre Research, 1991). See also J. S. Bratton, "Jane Scott the Writer-Manager."

6 Although the famous description of the form as layering comedy and tragedy like the fat and the lean in streaky bacon originates with Charles Dickens, it is of course erroneous to equate melodrama with the Victorian theatre. Peter Brooks, the theorist who has done most to rehabilitate the genre in modern criticism (in *The Melodramatic Imagination* [New Haven: Yale University Press], 1976), begins his analysis with the French Revolution and regards the "classic" period of the genre as over by 1830. During that period, most of what was new on the stages of London and Paris partook of the melodramatic temper and vision of the world, and flooded the senses of two generations shaken by previously unimaginable change and excitement with a many-facetted form of theatre commensurate with, and attempting to interpret, their intensity of experience.

7 Paula Backscheider, *Spectacular Politics: Theatrical Power and Mass Culture in Early Modern England* (Baltimore: Johns Hopkins University Press, 1993), pp. 168–69.

8 Jane Scott, "Address to the Audience, 27 December 1814"; recorded in an unidentified cutting in *The Adelphi Scrapbook* compiled by James Winston, Theatre Museum, London, Adelphi File.

9 These page numbers refer to the manuscript, though oddly they are ordinal numbers, clearly at first, but after about the sixth, they peter out into cardinal numbers plus a dot or a squiggle.

10 See Robert Miles, *Gothic Writing 1570–1820*.

IV

Criticism and theory

CHAPTER 8

Elizabeth Inchbald: a woman critic in her theatrical culture

Marvin Carlson

Elizabeth Inchbald was already a well-established figure in the British theatre world, one of its most popular living dramatists, when she was asked by the publisher Longman to provide biographical-critical prefaces for a series of 125 current acting plays that were presented in twenty-five volumes between 1805 and 1808. This project has been generally, and correctly, regarded as an important step forward for women in the British theatre culture. Women dramatists had, by the time Inchbald began writing, been important contributors to the English stage for more than a century, since the pioneering contributions of Aphra Behn and others to the Restoration theatre. During Inchbald's own career her admiring audiences also enjoyed comedies by Susannah Centlivre and Hannah Cowley, both of whom appeared in Longman's collection, and by Joanna Baillie, the most popular tragic dramatist of the era, whose importance has up until very recently been overlooked even by theatre historians, who have directed their attention to the period's male authors of the Romantic "closet" dramas.

The novelty of Inchbald's *British Drama* project requires some explanation. Since it was a common practice in British drama of the period to provide prefaces to published plays, a number of women dramatists before Inchbald had in fact provided a variety of self-criticism and commentary on their own theatrical writing. Most of this consisted of fairly standardized appeals to the goodwill of the reader, not infrequently expressing some anxiety about a woman author daring to enter a domain traditionally reserved for men. Catherine Burroughs has remarked on the commonality of this trope, citing as a typical example from the mid-eighteenth century a part of the prologue to Frances Sheridan's 1763 play, *The Discovery*:

A Female culprit at your bar appears,
Not destitute of hope, nor free of fears.
Her utmost crime she's ready to confess,
A simple trespass – neither more nor less;
For truant-like, she rambled out of bounds,
And dar'd to venture on poetic grounds.[1]

Not all prefaces consisted entirely of such self-deprecation and attempts to ingratiate oneself with a prospective reader, however. Some such prefaces, most notably those of Joanna Baillie, seriously engaged the process or theory of dramatic writing in the manner of the great Italian and French prefaces of the Renaissance and Baroque periods. Thus a certain tradition of theoretical theatrical writing by women, even if much of it was tentative and carefully self-effacing, existed before Inchbald's prefaces. Previous critical prefaces by women authors, even when these achieved the unusual sophistication of Baillie's theoretical statements, were of two types. Either they were, like Baillie's, concerned only with the author's own work, or they contributed to the by now quite substantial body of critical commentary on Shakespeare. The latter began as early as 1664, with the *Sociable Letters* of Margaret Cavendish, and included the prefaces of Charlotte Lennox in 1753–54 and the responses to the attacks of Voltaire by Elizabeth Montagu and Elizabeth Griffith.[2]

Inchbald's prefaces in *The British Theatre* represented an important, and indeed a daring, step beyond this, since she presumed to write critical commentary not only upon her own writings, but on those of other living dramatists, primarily men. This was clearly a domain even further, in Sheridan's words, "out of bounds" than presuming to "venture on poetic grounds." Even James Boaden, Inchbald's first biographer (in 1833) and a writer on the whole highly sympathetic to her work, shared the view of many of his contemporaries that women writing plays had pushed the gender boundaries quite far enough and that criticism should properly remain outside their sphere. "There is something unfeminine," Boaden concluded, "in a lady's placing herself in the seat of judgment."[3] Nevertheless, as Anne K. Mellor observed in a recent study of Inchbald and other women critics of the Romantic era, "We must recognize the significance of the fact that all these women critics set themselves up as *judges*, judges not just of aesthetic taste and literary excellence, but also of cultural morality."[4]

Inchbald's contribution to this aspect of theatre culture has been duly acknowledged by all of her subsequent biographers and critics. Early in this century S. R. Littlewood called the eighth chapter of the rather chatty 1921 *Elizabeth Inchbald and Her Circle* "The First Woman Critic,"[5] while much more recently Katharine M. Rogers contributed an essay to a 1991 collection on British and American Women and the Theatre called "Britain's First Woman Drama Critic: Elizabeth Inchbald."[6] Without denying the importance of Inchbald's contribution, or its daring, both of which I will discuss further in this chapter, I must begin by qualifying this increasingly common denomination of her as "Britain's First Woman Drama Critic." Even if we discount the already-mentioned prefaces by women dramatists that preceded *The British Stage*, there was a rich, if scattered and rather ephemeral, tradition of dramatic criticism in eighteenth-century England as a part of that century's passion for periodical literature. Naturally this field was dominated by male authors, but several women dared to place themselves publicly in the "seat of judgment" in matters theatrical. Eliza Haywood contributed dramatic criticism to *The Tea-Table* as early as 1724 and later (1744–46) to *The Female Spectator.* In the 1780s the playwright Hannah Cowley contributed regularly to *The World.*[7] And for the few women like these who had the temerity, in this male-dominated area, to sign their articles, there were doubtless many more who contributed criticism anonymously or under the guise of initials.

What then was the nature and importance of Inchbald's contribution in this area? First, and perhaps most important, the scope and visibility of her criticism far exceeded that of anything produced by any previous British woman author. A parallel might be seen in the case of Leigh Hunt, Inchbald's contemporary, who has often been referred to as "the first English dramatic critic,"[8] even though his theatrical commentaries had also been anticipated in many respects by scattered periodical contributors, from Richard Steele onward, for almost a century. The importance, visibility, and circulation of Inchbald's *The British Theatre* prefaces far surpassed the ephemeral periodical criticism of the previous century and for that matter Hunt's first contributions during these same years as a theatrical critic to *The News.* So Inchbald's claim as a pioneer woman drama critic, indeed as a drama critic *tout court*, is still substantial.

Another pioneering aspect of these prefaces was the dual nature of their orientation and their presumed readership. Despite the considerable body of eighteenth-century dramatic and theatrical criticism, there was in fact no clear model for Inchbald to follow. On the one hand there were the scattered commentaries on particular actors and productions (the critical tradition that led more directly to Leigh Hunt), and on the other hand there was the tradition of critical prefaces to plays, the prefaces of Samuel Johnson to the plays of Shakespeare being the most familiar example.

Inchbald developed a critical voice that related to both of these precedents but was different from either. She was not only the first British woman to present a series of critical prefaces for a wide range of dramatists, current and classic, but she was in fact the first British critic to do so. In the second volume of *The British Theatre*, with only six prefaces out of more than a hundred now written and while still clearly developing her approach, Inchbald made her first and only attempt to characterize these prefaces in that to *Henry IV, Part II*. They were not written, she explained, for the "classical devotee" who knows and admires every line of a dramatist like Shakespeare, but rather for those who have difficulty appreciating a play "where neither love nor murder is the subject of the scene." For such persons, the prefaces will seek to "recall to their memory some historical facts, previous to either reading or seeing the play" that "may be the means of exciting their attention" to the accomplishments of this drama.[9] These "historical facts" commonly included biographical notes and comments on the historical or literary sources of the play, although, since both "reading and seeing" were involved, stage history also was a concern, particularly recent stage history.

Inchbald seems to have been the first British critic to draw upon personal knowledge in both literary and theatrical creation to discuss plays both as read and performed experiences.[10] She was therefore obliged not only, as most of her biographers have suggested, to find a proper woman's voice in a critical establishment deeply suspicious of women "in the judgment seat," but also to find a satisfactory way of covering this disparate range of interests, for which, again, there were no direct models.

In certain ways, the prefaces that Johnson and others had written during the previous century for editions of Shakespeare were the best, or at any rate the most respected and accessible previous examples, especially for the literary side of Inchbald's concern, and there is no doubt that she perused them carefully for suggestions as to both style and standards. The opening five volumes of the collection were devoted almost entirely to Shakespeare (twenty-five plays, plus one by Ben Jonson), and in almost half of them Inchbald specifically refers to and often cites Johnson's essays, frequently supplementing these references with observations from other commentators such as Steevens. As she moves on to other dramatists, specific references to Johnson diminish, though he is still evoked in reference to Otway and Congreve.

Partly of course Inchbald is buttressing her own authority by evoking the most prominent critical names of the previous era, but although she often simply quotes Johnson without comment, allowing his voice to eclipse her own, she also makes a point from time to time to separate her voice from his. This is especially true on points of taste or gentility, a regular motif of the prefaces being the observation that material acceptable to the rather rough taste of the early eighteenth century or to the considerably rougher taste of the Restoration was often not acceptable to the more refined sensibilities of Inchbald's own time. Thus, in speaking of *Measure for Measure*, Inchbald calls Johnson's praise of the comic characters "surprising," and continues, somewhat archly: "To a delicate critic of the present day, and one thoroughly acquainted with his moral character, it must surely appear as if Johnson's pure mind had been somewhat sullied by having merely read them" (III:4,5). Inchbald in fact often suggests that Johnson was limited by the perspectives of his own time, particularly in regard to morality, but in other matters as well. "Had Johnson lived in the present time," she suggests, he would not have been so indifferent to the "historical truthfulness and political acumen" of *Julius Caesar* (IV:4,4). She also takes issue with Johnson's assertion that the passions are powerfully engaged in *The Tempest*, a play that Inchbald plainly did not care for, considering it deficient in everyday human interest and sympathy. Johnson, and others, she suggested, have in this work mistaken sensual engagement for passion, since, thanks to the scenic spectacle of theatrical production, the senses are "highly gratified" by this play in London theatres (V:3,5).

Somewhat surprisingly, Inchbald also disagrees with Johnson, but in the opposite direction and on much more interesting grounds, concerning *Cymbeline*, where she is much less troubled by a possible excess of fancy. She quotes at length Johnson's scathing conclusion to his remarks on this play, which ends:

To remark the folly of the fiction, the absurdity of the conduct, the confusion of the names, and manners of different times, and the impossibility of the events, in any system of life, were to waste criticism upon unresisting imbecility, upon faults too evident for detection, and too gross for aggravation.

"How would a modern author writhe," remarks Inchbald, "under a critique that should accuse his drama, of only one half of these failings! – Yet *Cymbeline* survives this just attack – and will live admired, and esteemed, to the end of time" (IV:2,5). Perhaps the most interesting word in Inchbald's comment is "just," showing that Inchbald recognizes a potential disparity between legitimate critical complaints and effective art.

The implications here are far greater than distinguishing her own critical voice from that of Johnson, however. From a general historical perspective we can see here a shift between enlightened rationalism in Johnson, who simply cannot accept the challenges to that system posed by a work like *Cymbeline*, and the implied Romanticism of Inchbald, who is willing to drive a wedge not only between herself and Johnson, but between "just" criticism and the unfettered achievements of genius. On a more personal level, though, Inchbald's speculations about the reactions of any "modern author" to accusations only half this serious surely suggest her anticipation of what will await her in future prefaces when she turns from Shakespeare and attempts to apply "just" criticism to the works of her own contemporaries. One might even wonder whether she is suggesting a way to make such criticism more palatable for authors who could console themselves with the thought that genius operated beyond such considerations when she turned from Shakespeare to contemporary drama.

One distinct advantage that Inchbald had over Johnson, and indeed most of the critics who had previously commented on, particularly, the plays of Shakespeare, was that she brought to her observations a solid insider's knowledge of the theatre and how audiences responded to the living experience of a play. This allowed her to create a critical voice that could claim equal experiential authority in the study and the playhouse, and one of the most common motifs in her criticism is a comparison of the very different effects the same play produces in these two very different situations. It was a voice particularly appropriate to Inchbald as a well-established and respected literary and theatrical figure, but it was also a voice particularly appropriate to this specific publication venture. Obviously prefaces to printed versions of plays are primarily directed toward a reading public, as were Johnson's prefaces to Shakespeare, but the plays selected for the *British Theatre* collection were not selected as representing some editor's idea of the great plays from the tradition of English drama. Rather, as the title page of each volume states, it is a "Collection of Plays, which are acted at The Theatre Royal, Drury Lane, Covent Garden, and Haymarket, Printed under the Authority of the Managers from the Prompt Books," and each individual play identifies the theatre where this work is being performed. Each play in the collection, then, is a work which is not only available for reading, but is also in the current repertory of one or more of London's major theatres, *in the version published in this collection.* Thus, there is clearly a theatre-going public that already has seen or can easily see these works in the theatre itself, using these printed texts as a reminder of or anticipation of that experience, and Inchbald regularly appraises plays both for theatrical and literary values.

It is worth noting also that this motif becomes increasingly dominant in the later volumes, dealing with the work of her contemporaries. In the first ten volumes, devoted to Shakespeare, Jonson, and the dramatists of the Restoration, the comparison is only occasionally made, and only discussed in some detail in relation to *The Winter's Tale*, but beginning with volume xii it is discussed in connection with at least one play in every volume. Although admitting the recent success of *The Winter's Tale* at Drury Lane, Inchbald insists that it still be considered among those works that "charm more in perusal than in representation" (iii:4,3).

Inchbald cites three different aspects of the play that lead her to this conclusion. First, comes the plot. The introduction of many new characters and situations in the middle part of the play she considers a far greater diversion in their embodiment on the stage, causing the viewer to lose the connection between the so widely separated opening and closing sequences centering on Leontes and Hermione, while the reader, book in hand, has "neither his eye nor ear distracted," and thus is able to keep constantly in mind a better vision of the whole. Second, much of the poetry of the play "is less calculated for that energetic delivery which the stage requires, than for the quiet contemplation of one who reads." Finally, the love scenes of Florizel and Perdita, though effective in their quiet intimacy, lack "the force of expression to animate a multitude," though they are "properly adapted to steal upon the heart of an individual" (III:4,3–4). Nevertheless, the scene of the statue in the final act Inchbald considers as an important exception, "being far more grand in exhibition than the reader will possibly behold in idea" (III:4,6).

The arguments set forth here distinguishing reading from performative drama form a recurring standard in the subsequent prefaces. James Thomson's *Tancred and Sigismunda* is praised as a "beautiful poem" but not for its performance values, since even more than *Winter's Tale* it relies upon quiet love scenes which "may find admirers by the fireside, on a long winter's evening; but can with difficulty obtain listeners in a brilliant theatre, where a thousand objects divert the attention which is not seized at once by some bold occurrence on the stage" (XIII:4,4). Similar is the judgment upon Hill's Voltaire adaptation, *Zara*: "It is impossible to read this play without being delighted, or to see it without being weary" (VII:3,5). On the other hand, the reader of Beaumont and Fletcher's *The Chances* "will scarcely conceive the great entertainment which it can bestow in representation" due to its reliance upon "bustle and incident" (XVI:2,3). Still other plays reveal different virtues in the study and on the stage. In Cumberland's *The Brothers*, for example, the love stories "are rather adapted to the closet," while the more boisterous and physical scenes of Sir Benjamin Dove "draw bursts of merriment and applause, from every part of a theatre" (XVIII:1,4).

Whether from a natural tolerance, a sympathy for fellow artists, a sensitivity to the resentments possibly raised by negative comments from a woman critic, or some combination of all of these, Inchbald generally attempts to find something favorable to say about each play she introduces, and being able to consider both literary and theatrical values considerably widens her possibilities for this. As she remarks in the preface to Reynolds's *The Dramatist*, "to be both seen and read, at the present day, is a degree of honour which, perhaps not one comic dramatist can wholly boast, except Shakespeare" (XX:1,3). This allows her, however, to stress the theatrical qualities of plays that she feels do not read well, such as Murphy's *The Grecian Daughter* (XV:4,3) and the literary qualities of closet dramas like *Tancred and Sigismunda*.

Only with a few dramatists, most notably Farquhar, is she consistently negative, clearly equally offended by the lack of morality in his plays and by his treatment of his wife and family in his personal life. Among the four Farquhar plays Inchbald reviews, only *The Beaux' Stratagem* is acknowledged to possess "well drawn characters, happy incidents, and excellent dialogue," but even these are dismissed as "but poor atonement for that unrestrained contempt of principle which pervades every scene." Indeed, plays with such mixtures of virtues and vices "are far more mischievous than those, which preserve less appearance of decency" (VIII:4,3).

Aside from Farquhar, the dramatist judged most severely by Inchbald is herself, although her complaints here are of course not on moral grounds. Her early play, *Such Things Are* (1787), showed, she suggests, a want of experience, though an indulgent audience kindly overlooked an "improbability in certain events, incorrectness of language, and meanness, bordering on vulgarity, in some of the characters" in view of the work's "novelty, locality, and invention" (XXIII:1,3). She says little of *Every One Has His Fault* (1793) beyond the "mere matter of fact" that it had a lengthy run and pleased its audiences, concluding "whatever critics may please to say against the production, they cannot think more humbly of its worth, than THE AUTHOR" (XXIII:2,4). For *Wives as They Were* (1797) she provides a detailed criticism of the flawed structure and tonality of the work, and for *To Marry or Not to Marry* (1800) she confesses that a desire to avoid the broad and crude farcical elements of other modern comedies has led her "from one extreme to another," producing a work insufficient in both wit and humor (XXIII:5,3).

In her remarks on Beaumont and Fletcher, Inchbald spends some time in admiration of their productive and long-lasting partnership, and makes the interesting observation that for female authors "such a conjunction of efforts had been intolerable as soon as praise became the reward: each would then have demanded the largest share, prompted by the conscientious scruples of justice" (VI:1,3). Such an opinion naturally directs attention to Inchbald's comments on women playwrights other than herself. Although direct collaboration is not a question here, clearly she recognizes that her work will be compared to theirs. Now that she is placed in the "seat of judgment," can she avoid the desire for the "largest share" that she suggests women authors by nature seek?

Her comments on Centlivre are not encouraging in this respect, although they may be excused in part by Inchbald's clear intention to justify, under certain circumstances, female playwrights in general. She begins her comments on Centlivre by the general observation that both men and women can become "unpleasing characters" when either takes on the occupation of the other. If however, women are driven, as Centlivre was, to "the masculine enterprise of an author" by necessity, not by choice, then they become "objects of compassion, and mercy should be granted to their want of skill in their irregular departments" (xi:1,3). Inchbald's strategy here is clearly to disarm critics of her own contributions, since she too was driven, as a struggling widow and actress, to gain financial security by turning to playwriting.

Having thus far defended Centlivre (and by implication herself) for undertaking a "masculine enterprise," Inchbald then makes a rather surprising turn, criticizing Centlivre for not pursuing this masculine enterprise in a more feminine manner. Because of her gender, Inchbald argued, Centlivre had certain responsibilities not placed upon male authors. Inchbald is always offended by licentiousness, as in the case of Farquhar, but finds it much more to be condemned in a play written by a woman, such as Centlivre's *The Bold Stroke for a Wife* (1718). Even financial necessity here provides no excuse: "The authoress of this comedy should have laid down her pen, and taken [in] exchange, the meanest implement of labour, rather than have imitated the licentious example given her by the renowned poets of those days" (xi:3,4).

Inchbald's striking and complex rhetorical strategy here cuts far deeper than a critique of Centlivre. Since, as we have already seen in her discussions of Shakespeare and Restoration authors, a constantly recurring theme in Inchbald is the general superiority of the modern stage, whose more refined sensitivity avoids the vulgarity and licentiousness so common in the drama of earlier and cruder periods. If, as these remarks on Centlivre imply, women can be and are expected to be more sensitive to such matters than men, then in those cases when they do take up their pens, even if compelled to by necessity, one can expect their work, whatever technical deficiencies it may have, to contribute significantly to the general advancement and civilization of the art itself. Seen in this light, even her apologies for the relative "dulness" (*sic*) of her own *To Marry or Not to Marry* take on a certain sacrificial grandeur, resulting from her desire to uplift the comic art in general.

Two other women dramatists are discussed by Inchbald, Joanna Baillie and Hannah Cowley. Baillie is celebrated as a "woman of genius," a rare, perhaps unprecedented example of achievement in both criticism and playwriting, whose *De Monfort* is strong, novel, and possessing "admirable" morality (xxiv:4,4). Cowley stimulates less enthusiastic praise, but still comes off much better than Centlivre, judged by the same standards. Although Inchbald does not feel that Cowley's *The Bold Stroke for a Husband* (1783) equals Centlivre's *The Bold Stroke for a Wife* "either in originality of design, wit, or humour," it nevertheless has "other advantages more honourable to her sex, and more conducive to the reputation of the stage, uniting "entertainment and morality" for either "a pleasant exhibition at a theatre" or "an hour's amusement in the closet" (xix:5,3). Once again the particular sensitivity of a woman author is tied to the general improvement of both literature and theatre.

Comments on particular features of each play, biographical information on its author, and sources of the play, when these are known and presumably significant, are standard features of Inchbald's prefaces, but given her theatrical background and her continuing concern with these plays both as theatrical and literary texts, it is not surprising that there is also a significant amount of production history. The distinction between the experiences of a play in the theatre and in the study was clearly a matter of considerable importance to Inchbald, but, in addition, she surely could not have been indifferent to the fact that her knowledge of and sensitivity to the specific contributions of the actors was one of her strengths as a critic, and an important way in which her critical voice could be distinguished from those of the respected Shakespearean critics of the previous century whom she so often cites.

Inchbald was well aware of and often remarks upon the importance of the work of individual actors to the success of the plays in which they appeared. In the preface to Murphy's *Know Your Own Mind*, for example, she notes that the two leading characters "are both admirable persons on the stage; although the reader, who never saw them there, may not conceive them to be so," concluding that in this play, as in many, "the actor's colouring alone, brings forth the author's true design" (xv:5,6). The continuing popularity of Congreve's *The Mourning Bride* Inchbald considers "is wholly to be ascribed to the magnificent representation of Zara by Mrs. Siddons" (xiii:2,4). Even more striking is the unique contribution Inchbald ascribes to Kemble in Colman's *The Mountaineers*:

Those persons, who have never seen Mr. Kemble in Octavian, will yet receive delight in reading this well written play: but those, who *have* seen him, will weep as they read, for it is most certain they have not forgotten him. Those, again, who have seen any other actor in the character, will peruse the play, possessed of all its claim to attention, with indifference; for this true lover requires such peculiar art, such consummate skill, in the delineation, that it is probable, his representative may have given an impression of the whole drama, unfavourable to the author. (XXI:1,3)

Similarly, the part of Donald in Holcroft's *The Deserted Daughter* Inchbald considered would be "Wholly unintelligible" to most readers, deprived of the actor Munden's "intelligent face," which she considered "requisite to every line of this part, to make it generally understood." She further praised the actor Quick in this same play since the author Holcroft had the "great merit" of creating the part with Quick in mind, even though Quick was known as a "low comedian" (XXIV:2,4).

In general Inchbald's examples of the contributions of actors are quite positive, just as are her reviews of most dramatists, especially of her contemporaries, the result perhaps of an unwillingness to offend those with whom she had worked professionally, perhaps of a cautiousness in being, as a woman, too critical, perhaps of a naturally positive disposition, or, it may be, of some combination of all three. Most commonly her comments on the physical presentation of particular dramatic texts illustrate a happy congruence between the talents of the actor, the aims of the playwright, and a commendable resulting effect upon the experience of the audience. As with the comments on playwriting, however, the exceptions to this generally positive tone provide some of Inchbald's most interesting and provocative remarks.

As has already been noted in the example of Farquhar's *Beaux' Stratagem* or Centlivre's *The Bold Stroke for a Wife*, theatrical effectiveness was not necessarily a virtue in Inchbald's eyes unless it was related to a positive morality. On the contrary, in less respectable works, it threatened to decoy susceptible members of the audience into "the snare of admiration" of morally questionable characters (VIII:4,3). In Farquhar's case the wit of the author was blamed, but the skill of the actors could have a similar result, in which case the cooler situation of reading might be morally superior. Inchbald found Moore's *The Gamester* a particularly clear example of this dynamic, a play whose effect on stage she felt was totally different from in the study:

An auditor, deluded into pity by the inimitable acting of a Mrs. Siddons and a Mr. Kemble, in Mr. and Mrs. Beverley, weeps with her; sighs with him; and conceives them to be a most amiable, though unfortunate, pair. But a reader, blessed with the common reflection which reading should give, calls the husband a very silly man, and the wife a very imprudent woman: – and as a man without sense, and a woman without prudence, degrade both the masculine and the feminine character, the punishment of the author is rather expected with impatience, than lamented as severe. (XIV:3,4)

In such cases, it is clear that Inchbald felt that actors, like authors, bore a certain responsibility for maintaining a high moral tone in the theatre. If they failed in this responsibility they not only risked corrupting the opinions of their public, as in *The Gamester*, but in more extreme cases, such as Vanbrugh's *The Provok'd Wife*, which Inchbald considered too immoral either to be seen or read, even risked corrupting themselves. Garrick might be "admired as a performer" in his interpretation of Sir John Brute in this play, but having heard him deliver its coarse wit "before a mixed audience of both sexes" and seeing him "disfigured and degraded in women's clothes," Inchbald considered that "no gentleman could feel much respect for him as a friend or acquaintance" (IX:1,5).

As I have suggested, Inchbald's most severe judgments fall on dramatists like Farquhar and Vanbrugh from an earlier era, but the moral opprobrium she brings to their works was widely shared by her public. The work of her contemporaries, naturally more in tune with her moral and aesthetic vision, was never subjected to such rough treatment at her hands, and even while she clearly considered certain plays weaker than others, she almost always expressed criticism tactfully and sought to balance it with praise, often by the strategy of separating literary from theatrical values. It is clear that she sought an authoritative, yet measured and generally supportive critical voice, particularly in dealing with her contemporaries. Her strongest negative remarks almost always have to do with moral concerns, where, as a woman, she could draw authority from traditional gender expectations even while troubling these expectations by moving into the "masculine" domain of writing, and even more particularly, of criticism.

On the whole this critical strategy was successful, and *The British*

Theatre edition was a considerable commercial and popular success, but despite Inchbald's tact and caution, her temerity in presuming to sit in judgment on male writers did not pass totally unchallenged. Near the end of the series, her really quite mild critical comments on several plays by George Colman aroused that author to such indignation that he insisted upon publishing an open letter to Inchbald along with his next play to appear in the series, *The Heir at Law.* Although he makes a number of modest "corrections" to her comments, he devotes more space to pointing out "worse faults" that she overlooked, presumably out of inadequacy as a critic. It is clear that his major irritation, however, is stimulated by the presumption of a woman to judge his work. Indeed, before proceeding to specific remarks, he speaks of his plays being "singed, in passing the fiery ordeal of feminine fingers" and suggests by classical allusions the inappropriateness of Inchbald's project, remarking on the "awkward figure" cut by Achilles "when he went into petticoats," and noting that "the delicate Deidamia never wielded a battle-axe, to slay and main the gentlemen" (xxi:3,2–3).

Inchbald's reply, printed as part of this same preface, is a model of rhetorical sophistication, and demonstrates clearly not only how aware she was of the precise tonality of the critical voice she was creating, but also how carefully she modulated and controlled it to minimize as much as possible the sort of negative response that Colman articulated. The entire reply demonstrates a delightful and carefully controlled irony, with a fascinating mixture of self-deprecation and informed, even learned, reference. Inchbald begins with an apparently abject apology, expressing regret for having undertaken this project, and blaming her own naïveté for never imagining that any dramatist "could possibly be offended, by the cursory remarks of a female observer," on plays that had already been widely praised and applauded: "Any injudicious critique of such [*sic*] female might involve her own reputation (as far as a woman's reputation depends on being a critic,) but could not depreciate the worth of the writings upon which she gave her brief intelligence" (xxi:3,5–6). Then, having used Colman's attack to give increased significance to her own work, she turns the attack back on himself, suggesting that surely "humility, and not vanity" must have inspired his concern with her "slight animad-versions," but even such humility suggests "a degree of self-contempt, which I may be pardoned for never having supposed, that any one of my manly contemporaries in the drama could have indulged" (xxi:3,7).

After similarly, and equally tellingly, turning Colman's own classical allusions against him, she concludes with perhaps her most effective rapier thrust, a reference to the Colman play here being introduced. Its central comic character was an absurd farcical pedant, Dr. Pangloss, full of learned allusions and secure in his intellectual superiority. Inchbald concludes, in mock humility: "I willingly subscribe myself an unlettered woman; and as willingly yield to you, all those scholastic honours, which you have so excellently described in the following play" (21:3,9).

This fascinating exchange strikes notes quite unlike anything else in Inchbald's prefaces, but, in doing so, it provides unexpected insight into all the rest. The devastating, though carefully modulated irony and the ability to turn her attacker's own arguments wittily back upon him illustrate the capacity Inchbald possessed as a writer to expose ruthlessly and cuttingly the flaws and follies in another writer's discourse. It is striking that this memorable critical voice, which would have fulfilled the worst fears of the male dramatists she was commenting upon, does not appear anywhere else in all of the prefaces. Instead, we encounter an equally calculated, but much more modulated, temperate, and supportive voice, without the compromise of artistic or moral standards or the loss of a specific personality. This variation provides perhaps the most impressive demonstration in this body of work of how carefully, and how successfully, Inchbald went about constructing the particular voice most appropriate for the delicate and important task of creating a significant body of critical writing as a woman author.

NOTES

1 Cited in Catherine B. Burroughs, "English Romantic Women Writers and Theatre Theory: Joanna Baillie's Prefaces to the *Plays on the Passions*," in *Re-Visioning Romanticism: British Women Writers 1776–1837*, ed. Carol Shiner Wilson and Joel Haefner (Philadelphia: University of Pennsylvania Press, 1994), p. 277.

2 See Augustus Ralli, *A History of Shakespearian Criticism*, vol. 1 (New York: The Humanities Press, 1965, 2 vols.); also *Women Reading Shakespeare, 1660–1900*, ed. Ann Thompson and Sasha Roberts (Manchester University Press, 1997).

3 James Boaden, *Memoirs of Mrs. Inchbald*, 2 vols. (London: Richard Bentley, 1833), ii:84.

4 Anne K. Mellor, "A Criticism of Their Own: Romantic Women Literary Critics," in *Questioning Romanticism*, ed. John Beer (Baltimore: Johns Hopkins University Press, 1995), pp. 29–48, p. 46.

5 S. R. Littlewood, *Elizabeth Inchbald and Her Circle: The Story of a Charming Woman*. London: Daniel O'Connor, 1921.

6 Katharine Rogers, "Britain's First Woman Drama Critic, Elizabeth Inchbald," in *Curtain Calls: British and American Women and the Theatre 1660–1820*, ed. Mary Anne Schofield and Cecilia Macheski (Athens: Ohio University Press, 1991), pp. 277–90.

7 See Charles Harold Gray, *Theatrical Criticism in London to 1795* (New York: Columbia University Press, 1931).

8 For example, in the opening sentence of William Archer's Introduction to *Dramatic Essays by Leigh Hunt*, ed. William Archer and Robert W. Lowe (London: Walter Scott, 1894), p. vii.

9 All quotes from the Inchbald prefaces are from the 25-volume edition of *The British Theatre* (London: Longman, Hurst, Rees, and Orme, 1808). Since each play is paginated separately, my citations (henceforth appearing in the body of the text) will first give the volume number, then the order of the play in the volume, then the page number. Thus the *Henry IV, Part II* quotation is III:1,4.

10 Anna Lott calls particular attention to the close relationship between critic and actress in Inchbald's fascination with the character Jane Shore. This role, argues Lott, provides a strong example of Inchbald's celebration of women who challenge the limited role their society offers them. Anna Lott, "Sexual Politics in Elizabeth Inchbald," *Studies in English Literature* 34:3 (1994), 635–48.

CHAPTER 9

Authorial performances in the criticism and theory of Romantic women playwrights

Thomas C. Crochunis

> It is difficult to write about being a writer. It's possible to write
> about being a woman, perhaps a woman writer . . . even a
> feminist writer. But in the end you're forced to the centre of it,
> which is about the writing itself – the act and nature of the
> occurrence. And here, as I say, there are problems.
> Pam Gems, "Imagination and Gender"[1]

When women wrote dramas for publication and theatrical production in the Romantic period, they sought to use their "problematic" writing to create forms of authorship that could influence the
world.[2] Because of the compelling imaginative content and dramaturgical technique of Joanna Baillie's and Elizabeth Inchbald's plays,
it is difficult to see their dramatic works simultaneously as works of
art and as authorial performances constituted of dramaturgical
gestures toward the public. In the critical writing of Baillie and
Inchbald, however, each author's positioning of herself in relation to
the theatre, to professional writing generally, and to other playwrights and women writers is enacted through her articulation of
critical positions and her discussion of her own works. Baillie's
"Introductory Discourse" to the first volume of the *Series of Plays*
(1798) and her "To the Reader," published with the third volume of
the *Series of Plays* (1812) and Inchbald's "Remarks" for *The British
Theatre* (published in serial form, beginning in 1806 and collected in
twenty-five volumes in 1808) are essential to understanding how
these women writers performed authorship within the dramaturgical
mise en scène of their time.[3]

Whatever artistic satisfactions Baillie and Inchbald might have felt
when their plays were performed, both took advantage of the
complex relationship between authorial persona and public that
their performances on page and stage produced. Although Inchbald
remained more intimately associated with the theatre throughout

her career than Baillie, both gestured significantly toward the theatre. Despite their different relationships with the theatre, they are not opposites but two women writers entering a common performance space from different directions. One important similarity between their authorial performances is that both Inchbald and Baillie wrote critical prefaces and editorial commentary that provided them with an alternative position from which to negotiate with the theatre of their day. Though Inchbald and Baillie took advantage of this alternative method of contesting theatre and dramaturgical practices, their care in performing their adversarial positions made them more difficult to attack than women whose resistance to theatre practice was more direct.[4] Women who wrote criticism and plays for theatrical production and publication, by exploiting multiple venues, added a performance of authorship to their writing of scripts for actors or readers. Their multi-faceted relationships – with the apparatus and production of theatre and with book publishing – suggest their agency apart from playwriting, creating what Sonia Hofkosh terms "the implication of individual presence in a culture of replication: the subject transacted in a world of objects."[5] Although the same might be said of any writer of dramatic texts for stage and page in the era, it is particularly salient for women writers, who both experienced distinct challenges in getting their plays staged and were understood to have experienced these challenges when finally their works were brought before the public. And so the meta-authorial figure, the woman author as agent of her own literary production in multiple media, was a subject apart from her own textual objects. She was an author of a multi-faceted authorship whose performances repeatedly demonstrated her alienation from cultural institutions.

I have chosen the term "authorial performance" to suggest a difference of approach from other theorizations of authorship. When studying women playwrights and critics like Baillie and Inchbald, Foucault's assertions that "the author does not precede the works" or "the author is an ideological product," while provocative within the terms of historiographic theory, fail to provide a theoretical tool with which to investigate how women writers sought to shape authorship for their own purposes.[6] Therefore, it might be more helpful to draw on the theories of a theatre semiotician like Patrice Pavis when studying how women performed dramatic authorship within the cultural *mise en scène* of the Romantic period.

Characterizing how dramatic texts are delivered through production, Pavis writes that "the dramatic text does not have an individual reader, but a possible collective reading, proposed by the *mise en scène*" (31). Thus, by submitting a text for performance, a playwright sets in motion a social process by which others create a *mise en scène* whose interplay with the text will stimulate the audience's observation, response, comparison of response, and recognition.[7] A published dramatic text might be presumed, then, to provide readers with a version of the play that they can encounter without the mediation and commentary produced by the theatre's complex social processes. However, for the reader of a play, theatre is a discourse and set of social practices referenced by formal or thematic gestures made by the dramatist; for the theatre audience, the potential of print publication of the playtext sets apart a kind of authorship that is distinct from that produced by the *mise en scène*. If, as Pavis suggests, "every new *mise en scène*" places the text that is spoken in a new context "which allows or facilitates a new analysis" (30), each reader of a play also provides a set of contexts in which to read the speeches written by the author for the play's characters. In response to an author's use of dramatic form, readers of the text might manufacture their own cultural *mise en scène* in which to "stage" the dramatic text; they might create some partial, psychically originated version of a *mise en scène* (a socially situated "mental theatre"), juxtapose a literary reading of the text with a projection of the kind of "reading" that the theatres of the era might produce, or interpret the author's gesture in presenting a play to the public in light of institutional discourses regarding theatre, gender, and authorship.

Reconsidered in this way, Pavis's model becomes suggestive for studying women's performances as professional playwrights, allowing us to see how any playwright who draws attention to his or her writing for both theatrical production and publication provokes a confrontation between two different interpretive relations, constituting his or her authorial performance through the harmonies and dissonances produced.[8] In particular, how did women writers like Inchbald and Baillie, who both published and staged their plays, employ the two media as offering different modes and degrees of access to the idea of theatre? While it is frequently argued that, because print publication provided a public "stage" over which a woman writer might have had more "authority" a woman writer might have published her works in order to "control" how they appeared, accepting this view demonstrates a kind of complicit commitment to what Pavis calls "faithfulness to the 'idea' of the 'author'" (27); that is, it makes women's "authorial choice" less problematic than it was in fact and fails to consider that writing that invokes theatrical production implicitly calls "authorship" into question. It seems more interesting to consider that, when writers like Inchbald and Baillie employ varying "proximities" to the stage as discursive figure and material venue of representation, they play within various sites of self-performance and use various media to multiply, rather than to delimit, their works' meanings. They activate, rather than control, meanings. Relinquishing the rhetoric of aesthetic "control" may contradict some of the authorial rhetoric of Inchbald and Baillie's critical remarks, but doing so can allow us to understand more fully the complex authorial performances they enact through both their critical commentary and their pragmatic decisions about drama and the stage.

This chapter seeks to identify the kinds of question that might be raised by considering that women playwrights and the public knew that authorial identities were influenced both by production of a woman writer's plays in theatres and by the publication of her texts for readers. While there is no question that women writers claimed authorship of both acting plays and published drama, I want to study how, in addressing themselves to both readers and theatre audiences, writers like Inchbald and Baillie created complex authorial careers that were performed in relation to the line of cultural business that we know as the "theatrical woman."[9] The skill of these two writers in managing virtuoso repertoires allowed them to denaturalize the cultural *mise en scène* by forcing it to comment on their public self-performances.[10] I look at how Inchbald's and Baillie's awareness of their era's theatrical aesthetics, its gendered parameters for authorial performance, and the responses of its readers and audiences to dramatic writing influenced the way in which these two women positioned themselves, making their authorial performances more than the sum of their theatrical and published parts.

For a woman playwright in Britain around 1800, getting plays performed was important in its own right. It provided money, an opportunity to see work presented in the theatre, and a chance to build awareness of her work. Print publication played a particularly important role in creating Baillie's authorial persona, but had important effects on the reputations of even writers like Inchbald, for whom publication of dramas might seem an almost automatic, economically driven function of professional dramatic authorship. Inchbald knew of the financial significance of the print rights to her dramatic texts, having learned from experience that without careful management of print publication, her theater works would not earn her as much as they might. In a letter to her manager, Thomas Harris, she spells out a financial arrangement that would allow her to take full advantage of her work:

This will make my demand on the theatre three hundred pounds for the first nine nights, five hundred and twenty on the twentieth night's performance, and seven hundred and twenty pounds should the play be so fortunate as to run thirty nights.

For the above proposals I reserve to myself the sale of my own altered manuscript; but which manuscript, whatever good success may attend the play, you may purchase of me, at any time previous to the third night, to two hundred pounds; which is the sum I received for "Lovers Vows," at the late date of the twenty-third night, when it was first published, and had many original manuscripts published six weeks prior to it to injure its value.[11]

In addition to showing her knowledge of business proceedings in this note, Inchbald displays awareness of how timing and public interest in a play translate into income for the author. While much of Inchbald's practical discussion in letters like this one to Thomas Harris is about money, throughout her career she demonstrated a growing awareness of herself as author, someone who had a name to trade on in her interactions with the public. By the time she was offered the opportunity to write critical and biographical introductions to the plays in *The British Theatre*, she had sufficient reputation as a professional dramatist and critical essayist to claim a kind of authority that was both lucrative and culturally influential. Skilled negotiation of the theatre and publishing benefited her financially and added to her public reputation.

A woman playwright's diversification of her dramaturgical performances in the Romantic period often emerged from her resistance to prevailing aesthetics of the era. For example, the dramaturgy of Joanna Baillie's "plays on the passions" challenged part of the tradition of acting. Playwrights typically relied on actors to adapt their texts to the discourses of the stage, but Baillie's authorial performance, especially as outlined in her "Introductory Discourse," contradicts basic tendencies in the acting of the period, insisting on character individuation (rather than generic types) and a nuanced, incremental, developmental approach to performing the passions.[12] In the prefatory essay "To the Reader" that was published with volume III of the "plays on the passions" in 1812, Baillie suggests that she welcomes but does not seek a performance style that can represent her work, commenting that her era's large theatres make it unlikely that "that which particularly regards the gradual unfolding of the passions" will be given

> that muttered, imperfect articulation, which grows by degrees into words; that heavy, suppressed voice, as of one speaking through sleep; that rapid burst of sounds which often succeeds the slow languid tones of distress; those sudden, untuned exclamations, which, as if frightened at their own discord, are struck again into silence as sudden and abrupt, with all the corresponding variety of countenance that belongs to it . . .[13]

Baillie's dramaturgy and characterization refused to accommodate to large theatres and the acting styles they produced. Though Baillie's almost clinical description implies that her conflict with theatrical practice is logistical (theatres too big, her emphasis on states of mind depending on subtleties of speech and expression), her commentary marks her refusal to compromise.[14] However, Baillie explicitly acknowledges the effect of theatrical performances on middle-class audiences, noting that the theatre's "impressions . . . are communicated, at the same instant of time, to a greater number of individuals than those made by any other species of writing; and they are strengthened in every spectator, by observing their effects upon those who surround him."[15] Given this kind of appreciation of the cultural influence that the theatre provides, it is no wonder that women writers like Baillie were unwilling simply to cede the stage, its range of audiences, and its symbolic cultural significance to those who were willing to write to its cultural specifications. Cross-performances in print and on stage allowed writers like Baillie to respond to the fragmentation of public audiences and discourses by manipulating the era's interwoven rhetorics of authorship, characterization, and institutional practices. In addition, through employing multiple forms, an author could draw attention to her agency in addressing the public.

Both Baillie and Inchbald must have known that readers understood the relationship between authors and their characters differently from theatre audiences; as writers, their dramatic characters were positioned differently when an actor presented the role than when the reader encountered the character in the author's published writing.[16] On stage a male or female actor playing in *De Monfort* (1798) – each performing in relation to perceptions of gender on the public stage – stands between Baillie as author and her audience. For readers, although a gesture toward the persona of an actor like John Phillip Kemble or Sarah Siddons can inflect Baillie's address to the audience, the actor's cultural meanings become part of the author's performance. We could perhaps test this proposition by studying how reader response to the characters of De Monfort and Jane De Monfort changed when their author's (gendered) identity was revealed or when the characters were performed onstage by Kemble and Siddons in 1800. Similarly, in a play like Inchbald's *The Widow's Vow* (prod. and publ. 1786), in which gender play and criss-crossed desires are explicit subjects, a reader of the play might be more likely than a theatre spectator to feel that the reversals of desire invite identification with the author. A published play's author might seem nearer to readers in ways that an astute playwright could use to advantage when performing authorship. The gender of characters in printed and staged dramas provides a particularly important site to observe authorial performance because members of the public often studied character as a particularly revealing aspect of the writing of women playwrights. For example, Mary Berry was fascinated by the complex authorial performance of the anonymous writer of the 1798 *A Series of Plays* : "The author . . . still refuses to come forward even to receive emolument; says the piece is before the public, that the Theatre may do what they please with it . . ." While the gender of the author had not yet been publicly acknowledged, Berry suspected that the plays were written by a woman because of their portrayal of female characters like Countess Albini in *Basil* and Jane De Monfort in *De Monfort*. Berry also notes that although the author uses her published dramas to assert her authorial "availability" and interest in the theatre, the author also indicates that she will "not interfere."[17] Not only did Baillie's writing evidence to Berry a distinctive position in relation to gendered characters and to the theatre, but these aspects of Baillie's authorial performance were noticed from the first by other women writers. In this way, character serves as a particularly important structure by which a woman positions her authorship before the public.

A playwright's gender was not only significant for characterization but also for her stance toward theatre institutions. To get their
plays performed, many women writers were coerced into giving
gender-specific authorial performances as they navigated paternal
relations with theatre managers and other male mentors. Even in
the years after Garrick's death when the paternalism of male
managers could no longer be relied on by women writers, the
oligopoly of men that "determined what the public would see in
representation" continued.[18] Some women writers repaid male
theatre managers for their "support" by giving both private and
public shows of gratitude and docility, but others, like Elizabeth
Inchbald, can be seen in the prefaces to her published plays
conspicuously to fail to thank her male mentors.[19] While print
publication also required social mobility and interaction, writing
for theatrical production required that a woman writer engage in a
complex kind of sociability in order to get her play all the way
through to production, sometimes risking transgressing the boundaries of female performance[20] or being forced into uncomfortable
and limiting public authorial performances. Furthermore, while a
playwright could expect either to have theatre personnel substantially alter her play for production or to be asked to provide
revisions on tight deadlines, a publishing author would not have
anticipated quite the same degree of "co-authorship."[21] Print
publication may have not been free of social expectations or
aesthetic interference, but the economics of print authorship and
production were different. So, women writers probably experienced
writing – or delivering already written – plays for print publication
to be less interpersonally tangled. In fact, considering that many
members of the public had some awareness of the challenges a
woman playwright might have faced in the theatre of the day, a
woman writer committed to representing women in ways contrary
to the tastes of men might have considered print publication of
dramas – especially, but not only, unstaged ones – to be an implicit
form of commentary by which a counter-theatrical sphere could be
set forth to challenge the gender aesthetics of the public stage.[22]
Even if a woman playwright had her plays staged, publication of
drama opened a significant alternative venue – both for the
dramatic texts themselves and for women playwrights as authors
and women as readers. Thus, gender influenced both the ways a
woman's dramatic characters were read and the meta-authorial

drama to which her readers and audiences may have responded when encountering her dramas or criticism.

Writing for publication had psychological as well as financial and aesthetic implications for women writers. By fashioning discursively complex authorial performances, a playwright like Baillie may have felt able to avoid difficult interpersonal negotiation. Baillie's "deep distaste for rehearsals" and preference for remaining a "quiet observer" (a stance that mirrors the central imagery of her 1798 "Introductory Discourse") may have been the source of her later "deference" to those who served as her emissaries to the public when her plays were staged. In one letter, Baillie envisions herself performing the role of author in rehearsal as a child proving to be (Baillie quotes Wordsworth) "something between a hindrance and a help." Baillie's claim that she would find it almost impossible to endure "the sight of all the actors & actresses . . . repeating what I have almost never had face enough to hear the reading of, even in the most private way by my own intimate friends" is striking.[23] Accounts of Baillie's youthful interest in theatre suggest that she had once been quite interested in acting out dramas of her own devising.[24] Perhaps observation of others performing her words would have created a dissonance with Baillie's own authorial performances that threatened to undermine her sense of her own authority. Perhaps Baillie's creation of herself as author necessitated removing herself from the scene of enactment, and keeping her performances separate from the playing of her lines by actors. It is significant, however, that when Baillie portrayed herself as retiring to her study to prepare her 1851 collected works, she suggested that private spaces could be important sites for women's public performance of dramatic authorship.[25] Baillie's sensitivity to the public and private aspects of her authorship suggests that the reading and theatre publics could also have interpreted a woman writer's social movement as significant to her performance of authorship.

If observers knew that restricted sociability (or attitudes toward sociability) provided one set of obstacles to women's authorial performances, they also knew that censorship's many layers also affected women's writing of drama. The gap between what could be staged and what published provided women like Inchbald with a complex space to navigate between the two venues of authorial performance. Acknowledging the difference between "free agent" novelists, who lived "in a land of liberty," and dramatic writers, who

exist "under a despotic government," Inchbald knew that she had
access to two forms with different limitations. But as Inchbald goes
on to note, an author's performance and its "censorship" is not just
a matter of "the subjection in which an author of plays is held by the
Lord Chamberlain's office, and the degree of dependence which he
has on his actors – he is the very slave of the audience." By
characterizing the male author who is directly judged by the
audience ("the will of such critics is the law, and execution instantly
follows judgment"),[26] Inchbald invites consideration of the state of
mind in which a female dramatic author might make decisions
about which authorial performances to give. In fact, the complexity
of a woman writer's decisions about delivering her works to the
public is illustrated by the case of Inchbald's *The Massacre* (completed
1792). Although Inchbald must have known that her play could not
be performed in the patent theatres of the day because of its
inflammatory presentation of French political unrest, she offered it
to theatre managers Thomas Harris and George Colman; they, of
course, declined to produce it.[27] However, it was Inchbald herself –
after consultation with William Godwin and Thomas Holcroft –
who withdrew the play before its impending publication. Inchbald's
retraction of the play reveals not just avoidance of public criticism; it
shows her to be engaged in complex personal and professional
negotiations with the discursive venues of print publication and
theatrical production.

Although a woman playwright's putting herself before the public
involved taking a risk with her character, writing drama for both
theatrical production and publication simultaneously allowed an
authorial performer to demonstrate her openness to judgment.[28] In
this sense, women's performances as playwrights have parallels to
the impulse of some women performers later in the nineteenth
century to live their private lives openly in an attempt to defuse any
critique of their personal conduct by the public.[29] If, as Donkin
suggests, there was "an assumption about women becoming playwrights . . . that they risked public exposure in a way that was
distinct from that of writers in other genres" (139), then we might
expect the most aware of these writers to employ public self-
exposure and openness for effect.[30] By offering her dramas as
published texts, a woman playwright like Inchbald provides the
public with textual evidence, precisely the kind of evidence that is
regularly scrutinized and judged by the licenser. When early theatri-

cal performances of Inchbald's play *Every One Has His Fault* (orig. prod. 1793, publ. 1793) were attacked by the conservative *True Briton* as seditious, one accusation made was that some dangerous passages, spoken in the first performances, had been removed subsequently.[31] Inchbald responded to the charges by asserting that no changes had been made in the play performed, thus presenting herself as an author who had been forced to defend her honesty and implicitly claiming the privilege of addressing social issues forthrightly. By publishing the play she further enacted her willingness to put herself before the eye of the public, performing a kind of forthright openness to public judgment that contributed to her reputation as author. Boaden notes that the play's "sale was immense, for the *True Briton* had been idle enough to make a political attack upon the doctrines it espoused."[32] Inchbald's canny response to the criticism paid off with the public.

At the same time, both stage performances and publication positioned a woman's dramatic writing in relation to particular kinds of institutional commentary. The range of tones adopted by male critics – favorably surprised, gallantly condescending, and morally offended – shows how provocative women's writing for the theatre was. By writing for the stage, a woman placed herself as author in the public eye – as in the case of Baillie's ongoing commentary on the period's theatre practices in relation to her published plays. Similarly, comments on published drama that reference theatrical production represent institutional commentary upon which a writer's subsequent authorial performances can be based – as in the responses Inchbald made to accusations that politically incendiary passages had been removed from *Every One Has His Fault*. Apart from what she might have been paid, and apart from the questions her work with a theatre might have raised about her reputation, theatrical production influenced how a woman writer's works were perceived and interpreted by members of the diverse publics she addressed. A woman's writing for the theatre was not merely an opportunistic professional action but also an act of public self-assertion.

Because the public knew something of the challenges that women faced in negotiating professional roles in the theatre, a woman writer might have sought to "take the stage" not just for money, not just for aesthetic or political reasons, but because having her play staged reframed her authorial persona. There may be something particularly potent about a woman taking "control of the authorship of human action,"[33] particularly when an audience understands on some level the challenges she might have faced in order to perform this type of authorship. In a sense, the woman playwright provides a crucially important public spectacle for she both "authors human action" and can be presumed to have acted herself in bringing that authorship forward. Therefore, when women's published plays are often pointedly prefaced with comments about potential or past theatrical performances, these comments invoke the spectacle of women performing the role of dramatic author in the public theatre, importing to a literary venue the aura of public assertion that her plays' production provided. Since even published deference and disclaimers can be read by the public as canny authorial gestures required of women playwrights by theatrical institutions and the men who controlled them, women's prefaces and critical comments about dramatic writing are important sites at which a playwright can remind the public of the institutional *mise en scène* within which she performed her authorship. In fact, the public may have played the "significant role in voicing support for the idea of women play-wrights"[34] that it did in the era after Garrick, because women playwrights were identified with a kind of performance of authorship that was resistant to institutional tyrannies and adroit in claiming its rights opportunistically. Women playwrights, regardless of their politics, tapped into revolutionary energies.

As Donkin notes (101–02), the presence in the late eighteenth century of a publicly recognized group of women playwrights might have invited younger women writers to consider writing for stage production.[35] The presence of these public authorial performances by a previous generation may have registered with younger women writers who, upon later encountering impediments to the same mode of authorial performance, remembered the kinds of personal aspiration knowledge of their predecessors had stimulated in them, not simply in terms of writing for the stage but in terms of performing authorship in a particular way before the public. Audiences could also have tracked the influence of this earlier generation of women playwrights, not simply valuing their play-writing, but appreciating how the mixed media employed by the younger generation of women playwrights constituted in retrospect a legacy of public performances of authorship. The possibility that both women writers and the general public were sensitive to these elements of meta-authorial performance must be weighed carefully when we consider the ways in which women playwrights were discussed, read, and critiqued.

The cultural *mise en scène* within which the authorial performances of women playwrights took place allowed audiences who were sensitive to the gender dynamics of authorship to perceive the meaning of public responses to theatrical production and publication. Hester Piozzi, writing in 1819, recalled what she understood from observing the spectacle of Baillie's first dramatic publication:

> No sooner, however, did an unknown girl own the work, than the value so fell, her booksellers complained they could not get themselves paid for what they did, nor did their merits ever again swell the throat of public applause. So fares it with *nous autres*, who expose ourselves to the shifts of malice or the breath of caprice.[36]

Baillie's performance made quite clear to those who were paying attention to the discussion of the plays that the gender of the author, who (according to Piozzi) many had initially assumed was a man, would affect how the plays were discussed in public. While commentary about the *Series of Plays* may have seemed to go from interest (when anonymous) to disregard (when their author was identified) without any public justification, the demonstration was not lost on women like Piozzi, nor, one must suspect, on many other men and women. Although such audiences were likely not surprised by critical reversals based on gender, the intellectual excitement that the anonymous *Series of Plays* had stirred could not be retracted, nor could its implications for publication as a significant alternative to the patent theatres be ignored. Regardless of her intentions or intuitions, Baillie's authorial performance redirected the subtle currents of discourse about dramatic authorship.

Writing boldly into a discursive space where political scrutiny and censorship were known to be practiced provided women playwrights with a highly charged *mise en scène* amidst which to enact their authorial performances. Even in the case of dramatists like Joanna Baillie, whose works rarely addressed inflammatory political issues, the boldness of the analytic commentary on stage practice and expression of aspirations toward theatrical production contained in the 1798 edition of the *Series of Plays* was startling as much for the cultural backdrop against which it was presented as for its content. For women writers, the cultural scene of the theatre was sexually, politically, and socially charged because it often required playwrights to take "adversarial postures."[37] There are, however, two elements of women's entry into this professional role: their personal experience of navigating these roles and the public's perception of women in these roles. Whatever personal reluctance women playwrights (like Baillie) might have felt, their assertions of their professional identities were noteworthy and publicly visible.[38] These assertions may have been particularly significant when they were critical rather than artistic. As Gay Gibson Cima notes "[The woman critic] was not toiling behind the scenes, submitting copy, but rather was visibly public . . . actually engaged in a process of 'manly' judgment and even caricature" (42). What particularly interests me, then, is how, in writing about their own plays or those of other women, women who were both critics and playwrights positioned themselves in relation to the idea of women's dramatic authorship.

Joanna Baillie made her first appearance as dramatic author and critic with her 1798 *A Series of Plays: in which it is attempted to delineate the stronger passions of the mind – each passion being the subject of a tragedy and a comedy.* The first volume of the "plays on the passions" included Baillie's "Introductory Discourse," a piece of dramatic criticism that, as much as the plays themselves, defined their author even before her identity – or gender – was known to the public. Baillie's authorial persona was (from its first appearance) constituted by an interplay between critical discourse and dramaturgy. Though it is hard to look past the numerous plays that Baillie published as part of the series, I want to put my attention on the "Introductory Discourse" of 1798 and the introductory "To the Reader" that was first published in 1812 with the third volume of the series. Rather than studying these texts as dramatic criticism, I want to consider how they helped to constitute Baillie's persona as author.[39]

It does not seem surprising that the 1798 publication of Baillie's first plays in the series commanded public attention, for even if we put aside the ambitious dramaturgy of individual plays or the boldness of Baillie's "conception" for the series, the author's critical voice in the "Introductory Discourse" is immediately compelling and direct:

It is natural for a writer, who is about to submit his works to the Public, to feel a strong inclination, by some Preliminary Address, to conciliate the favour of his reader, and dispose him, if possible, to peruse them with a favourable eye. I am well aware, however, that his endeavors are generally fruitless . . . (1)

From the author's first address to readers, he or she claims the privilege of speaking directly, performing a kind of frank directness that is startling in its effect – a confidence without boastfulness, a practicality without cynicism. Although the anonymous author at times articulates theories of human nature and of literary genre, in other passages he or she notes the limits of dramatic critics as compared to dramatists (7n) and disarmingly acknowledges to the reader that the theory of the introductory discourse may not always match the dramaturgy of the plays (15). By demonstrating honesty at his or her own expense, the author invites a reader to trust that the theories offered are more observations than self-justifying arguments.

Part of the persuasiveness of the authorial voice comes from how Baillie situates her critical comments in relation to several social contexts. Her discussion on history and human interest in character and its interpretation (1–6) positions the dramas that follow in a humanist context. Comments on the demographics of theatre's moral influence (14) and on the genres of contemporary writing for the stage (11–14) suggest that the author has knowledge of the theatre of the day. When, near the end of the introductory discourse, Baillie refers to stepping "beyond the circle of my own immediate friends" (17), she further invites readers to think of the author not as a solitary genius, but rather as someone who is part of a network of literary and social peers. Combined with the frankness of the critical voice, these references to being "of the world" allow the introductory discourse to claim quiet authority in addressing the public.

The authority of the introductory discourse is also enhanced by the centrality given to the structural and psychological importance of dramatic character. Baillie asserts that humans are generally interested in "tracing . . . the varieties of understanding and temper which constitute the characters of men" (1) and that drama is the form of art that most relies on its ability to mobilize audience interest in interpreting character. Though people may discuss superficial matters like dress and manners, they also observe nuances of words and actions and "conceive certain impressions of . . . character" based on them (2). Because of these interests in interpreting character, Baillie proposes that it is the private thoughts and feelings of historical figures that people are most interested in learning about (5). In addition to explaining public interest in character, Baillie also notes that dramatists rely on characterization, because doing so is both powerfully appealing to the theatrical audience and structurally necessary: "[T]he characters of the drama just speak directly for themselves" (7). By demonstrating that her plays focus on something that is both generally interesting to humankind and subject to observation, Baillie de-emphasizes the author's persona while adding to her discourse's apparent objectivity.

Baillie's assertion of a fundamental principle of dramaturgy – that playwrights write character speeches that actors must speak in playing the characters – opens up several important issues. The statement is presented to readers of the volume through the words of the author, whose appealing voice and character have drawn us into an intimate, imaginative "closet." Drama may be based on the structural necessity of authors allowing characters (and thus actors) to speak, but the voices of dramatic authors clearly have importance as well. How do they get heard? In a momentary double-take, a reader might notice that it is precisely our interest in reading characters that has been activated by the voice of the author. Not surprisingly, it is also the author's gendered character that helped to stimulate much of the curiosity about Baillie's anonymous first volume of plays (as both Berry and Piozzi understood). Furthermore, Baillie's emphasis on the structural necessity of the author–character relationship (that a drama must consist of "speeches") raises questions about how character "speech" functions in her plays. Taken at face value, dramatic speech would seem in Baillie to be contained within the conceit of representation – that is, the author declines to "speak" and instead lets her characters (and the actors who play them) have the stage. Speech in dramatic writing may serve characterization, but writing for the theatre is also an author's form of public utterance. Baillie's introductory discourse diverts attention from authorial performance by emphasizing dramatic speech – and gesture and facial expression – but uses the anonymous yet compelling public voice of the author-as-critic to do so. The introductory discourse's complex rhetoric establishes the volume's interplay between authorial voice and dramatic character as more than a matter of one or the other having precedence.

In the prefatory "To the Reader" of the 1812 third volume of the "Plays on the Passions," Baillie further complicates the relationship between character and voice by noting how theatrical conditions often make it difficult to hear the speeches of characters and see their expressions in the theatre (231–32), suggesting that because authorial address is at odds with the pragmatics of public theatres it is difficult for authors to be heard (through the "speaking" of actors) in contemporary theatres.[40] Baillie registers some of the ways that the size of theatres, the lighting, and other technical characteristics of production could affect what productions can convey to audiences and indicates that the size of the theatres of her time tends particularly to affect women performers, for "the features and voice of a woman, being naturally more delicate than those of a man . . . must suffer in proportion from the defects of a large theatre" (233). Baillie's point can lead her reader to a chain of realizations. If the institutional *mise en scène* of the theatre (literalized here as "size") affects actresses differently from actors because of differences in gendered codes of expression, then it must also function differently in presenting male and female characters, preventing women's roles from communicating in the same ways as men's roles. Following this train of thought one step further, if a playwright's gender has some relationship to the characters he or she creates (as Berry clearly thought it did), then Baillie's comment subtly reminds readers that theatre size influences the writing of gendered characters for the stage. Baillie's indirect argument about stage space and actor/ actress performance invites her readers to apply their own assumptions about gender, playwriting, and performance to tease out how contemporary theatres materially oppose a woman playwright's performance as author. Baillie's indirectness is strategic, for she teaches her readers to complete the institutional critique that she merely begins. Her method encourages readers to turn their own cultural observations into critical analysis.

Though what I have just outlined does not describe the terms in which Baillie explicitly described her dramaturgy's relationship to the stage, it suggests a sharp contrast between the compelling voice Baillie adopts in her critical introductions to her published volumes and the potential frustrations contemporary theatrical institutions might have created for her as author. In light of the conflicted authorial position that Baillie's critical commentary invites readers to consider, her publication of her plays appears to lay claim to a kind of critical and dramaturgical authority (as Inchbald recognized in her remarks on *De Monfort* for *The British Theatre* volumes, discussed later in this chapter), which went beyond attempting to write effective stage drama. The scale of Baillie's "conception" as enacted through her setting out to write a collection of "plays on the passions" not only placed a frame around individual plays, but also contextualized her authorial performances as part of an ambitious conceptual undertaking and not just important individual plays because of their subjects or techniques. Baillie seems to have understood that a theatre context whose social and production practices blocked the advancement of women writers would likely reject experimental plays as deliberately alienating and experimental theories of theatre as unrealizable and impractical. For an author like Baillie, who was as interested in revising theatrical practices as in using theatrical institutions to address the public, employing authorial performance to influence the public's assumptions about the stage was an essential step.

Elizabeth Inchbald's "Remarks" for *The British Theatre* provided her with ample opportunity to influence public interpretation of her era's dramatic canon by writing prefaces for a selection of plays that were chosen by the publisher for their popularity in the British theatre in the years around 1800, for their association with some star performance, or for their sales when initially published. Since Inchbald seemingly had no influence on which plays were included in the collection, and since the conditions of Inchbald's contract required that she prepare her remarks as called upon without knowing in advance when or in what order the plays would be published, her comments tend to deal with each work individually.[41] Though undoubtedly critics today are correct to note the constraints Inchbald's assignment placed on the range and depth of her critical response,[42] it seems equally important that we attend to the particular ways that she used the opportunity to position plays in the dramatic repertoire of her period for a wide readership. Inchbald's remarks are especially noteworthy I think for their ability to resituate – in only a few pages – each of a series of plays whose performances in her time were a key part of the theatre's cultural work. Despite the constraints that defined her task, Inchbald's remarks exploit the opportunity of addressing the reader before each play, going beyond simply providing biographical and historical prefaces (as was her charge) and instead slyly showing readers how to read the plays with an awareness of their cultural contexts.[43] I will focus in particular on her prefaces to plays written by women.

Inchbald's remarks on Susanna Centlivre's *A Bold Stroke for a Wife* (1718) make use of familiar moral rhetoric but enact ways of reading the works of women playwrights that allow for more than conventional moralism:

Mrs. Centlivre, as a woman, falls more particularly under censure than her contemporary writers: though her temptations to please the degraded taste of the public were certainly more vehement than those of the authors who wrote at that time, for they were men whose fortunes were not wholly dependent on their mental exertions; yet the virtue of fortitude is expected from a female, when delicacy is the object which tries it; and the authoress of this comedy should have laid down her pen, and taken, in exchange, the meanest implement of labour, rather than have imitated the licentious example given her by the renowned poets of those days . . . [T]he difficulties under which she had to struggle for subsistence . . . may plead some excuse . . . for having . . . applied to that disgraceful support of her muse, to which her own sex of those times did not blush to attend as auditors.[44]

Inchbald's approach to Centlivre's "indelicacy" is far more complex than it might at first appear.[45] Her criticism, which could certainly be less morally conditional than it is, blends the rhetoric of moral critique with contextualization. Even while presenting her comments on Centlivre's play as negative judgments on its content, Inchbald provides both plausible reasons for a woman writer's slide into the errors of her male peers and references to how women writers are judged differently from men. Despite her rhetoric of moral critique, Inchbald demonstrates how to read a woman author's writing in relation to the prevailing dramatic marketplace of her time – as an employment option to be contrasted with employment of "the meanest implements of labour" – and in the context of expectations for women's conduct. Centlivre, by having a play published in this volume, is given some form of provisional status in the canon of reading drama; Inchbald's remarks ease the play's positioning within that canon by proactively offering a kind of critique to which the play and its author might be vulnerable, even as she turns moralism toward the socio-historical. Claiming for herself the position of literary historian and marking off a contextualized space for the dramatic text of another woman playwright, Inchbald gives a sophisticated authorial performance that serves to multiply the roles that women might play in theatrical culture.

In remarks on two of her own plays included in *The British Theatre* series, Inchbald engages in adroit self-fragmentation, allowing herself as critic to comment disingenuously on the peculiar drama-turgy her works employ. In her comments on *Such Things Are* (orig. prod. 1787, publ. 1788), she writes of herself in the third person and comments that "the writer's" youthful "ignorance" led her to attempt what she likely would have avoided if she had had more "judgment." Inchbald's rhetorical approach makes a functional distinction between the critic and the young dramatist she once was, a distinction that casts the play in a personally nostalgic and generally sociological light for readers. Thus, the preface invites readers to read the play while aware of the perspectives of both the wiser critic and the distant youthful author, perhaps sensing the complicated dialogue between Inchbald's two voices. Inchbald's remarks on the play also place its political content at some distance. The play itself uses a mixture of genres and varied devices for manipulating audience perspective to temper the bald assertion of its title's address, an assertion mirrored by the play's gesture of showing its audience harsh colonial prison conditions. Throughout the play, Inchbald foregrounds her uses of rhetorical devices. For example, the cynical manipulator Twineall explains the social uses of affecting a stutter:

TWI. ... [W]hen a gentleman is asked a question which is either troublesome or improper to answer, he does not say he *won't* answer it, even though he speaks to an inferior; but he says, "Really it appears to me e-e-e-e – [*Mutters and shrugs.*] – that is – mo-mo-mo-mo-mo – [*Mutters.*] – if you see the thing – for my part – te-te-te-te – and that's all I can tell about it at present."
SIR LUKE. And you have told nothing.
TWI. Nothing upon earth.
LADY [TREMOR]. But mayn't one guess what you mean?
TWI. Oh, yes – perfectly at liberty to guess.[46]

In the context of Inchbald's own reputation for stuttering, Twineall's explanation serves both to reference the presence of the play's author, simultaneously suggesting her vulnerability (as stutterer) and her potential skill in performing strategically. Such self-referential acknowledgments of the author's rhetoric complement Inchbald's suggestion in her remarks that "the writer" chose her subject due to "ignorance" (which in this case seems to be mainly a matter of too great an ambition, not wrong political beliefs). Inchbald's performances as critic and dramatist demonstrate her rhetorical skill; by characterizing the play's naiveté, she highlights its brash rhetoric for readers of *The British Theatre* series.

Inchbald's discussion of character speech in the play supports this rhetorical performance by suggesting that the play's setting in the East Indies serves fortuitously (as if a happy accident) to justify the "incorrectness of language, and meanness, bordering on vulgarity, in some of the characters." Here, playing a clever game of bait and switch, Inchbald uses representational politics (characters speak as befits their setting) to invite assent on whether a play should represent prison conditions in colonial settings at all. At the same time, Inchbald makes sure that her reader observes where the play is set and how the characters behave, just in case the play's original political context – it was first performed at the height of the Hastings affair – has escaped notice.[47] When later in her remarks Inchbald refers to the real-life model for the play's socially committed Mr. Haswell, she provides a documentary referent, calling into question the play's aesthetic and fictional purposes and all but inviting the reader to locate the author's sympathies in what she has chosen to represent. By referencing real life, Inchbald alerts her readers to her role not just as writer of dialogue and constructor of plots, but also as manager of what values and subject-matter were offered for the audience's consideration. At the same time, her stance as commentator counterpoints the perspective of the "youthful" playwright's; by emphasizing authorial naiveté, Inchbald – from a removed and disinterested position – pointedly reminds readers of her boldness as a playwright.

When remarking on *To Marry or Not to Marry* (produced and published 1805), Inchbald again applies a third-person view of herself as writer:

It appears as if the writer of this play had said, previous to the commencement of the task, "I will shun the faults imputed by the critics to modern dramatists" . . . [W]hat is the event of her cautious plan? – Has she produced a good comedy? – No. She has passed from one extreme to another; and attempting to soar above others, has fallen even beneath herself. (*To Marry or Not to Marry* 3)

In this case, since the "writer" was Inchbald herself just a year or two before, the rhetorical stance taken in the remarks has the feeling of droll tongue-in-cheek play, dryly assessing the dramaturgy of "the author" as though Inchbald could not fathom her own motives. As a result, by hinting that the author in question exhibits unusual dramaturgical behavior, Inchbald invites the inquiring reader to speculate about the reasons for the dramaturgy that follows, creating conditions for the reading of her play calculated to sharpen a reader's interest. For those readers who had some experience with Inchbald's playfully disruptive strategies of comic writing for the stage and who had some awareness of her political reputation, an introductory remark this disingenuous seems designed to pique a reader's interest in Mrs. Inchbald the playwright and in the possible motives behind her dramaturgy. Inchbald's remarks on *To Marry or Not to Marry* illustrate how, by saying little but saying it strategically, a woman writer could position readers in ways favorable to her work. Without settling definitively the question of what Inchbald's dramaturgy might have revealed to an inquiring reader, we should consider that her use of a kind of intellectual flirtation provokes readers to interpret her plays and their strategies.

Some of Inchbald's remarks speak directly to the differences between closet and stage dramaturgy.[48] Her comments on her adaptation of Kotzebue's *Lovers' Vows* (produced and published 1798) provocatively suggest that she has attempted not a translation of the play's language but an adaptation of the German play to a British context. Tellingly, she contrasts her focus on addressing the British audience to an alternative perspective emphasizing the "rigid criticism of the closet," which for Inchbald signifies a concern for the linguistic accuracy of a translation. Of course, her remarks are in fact addressed to the closet reader of these published dramas, but her rhetorical maneuver draws on the stage as an important trope in these volumes (the series volumes also remind readers on each title page that the texts are taken "from the prompt book"). She describes that her play attempts to present "the same woman, I conceive, whom the author drew, with the self-same sentiments, but with manners adapted to the English rather than the German taste . . ." (*Lovers' Vows* 6). Her motive, it seems, was an attempt to present Kotzebue's play to a British audience, suggesting a transitive dramaturgy on her part that she distinguishes from "mere verbal translation."[49] In addition to making a case for the particular approach she has taken in adapting the play and for the significance of her labor as author, her remarks encourage consideration of playwriting's performative and transitive qualities in addressing the public.

Inchbald further draws on the stage/closet distinction in her remarks on Baillie's *De Monfort*. Noting that Baillie has achieved the rare status of "woman of genius," Inchbald examines how the "novelty of [Baillie's] conception" and the "strength of her execution" compensate for her play "fall[ing] short of dramatic excellence" (*De Monfort* 3). By distinguishing two aspects of playwriting ("conception" and "execution"), Inchbald makes an important argument for how the component parts of dramatic writing might be understood, noting of Baillie that "no one critic so good as herself has ever written a play half so good as the following tragedy"(3). Inchbald's point seems to be that Baillie is an astute dramatic theorist; therefore, if her actual dramatic achievement with *De Monfort* is not quite as noteworthy as her critical acumen, we should remain impressed by the potential her drama exhibits. By crediting Baillie's criticism, Inchbald allows readers to see Baillie's writing as illuminating the limits of theatre practice. We might see Inchbald's remarks on Baillie's *De Monfort* as an attempt, through deploying conventional critiques that point to stage practice as the final arbiter of dramatic effectiveness, to further Baillie's own project of opening a space for a kind of experimental dramaturgy. When Inchbald concludes that "the authoress has studied theatrical productions as a reader more than as a spectator" (5), her critique invites the reader of the remarks to consider whether alternative, impractical perspectives on dramatic writing might offer "conceptions" of ingenious dramaturgies beyond the limits of stage conventions. As I have noted in my previous discussion of Baillie's 1812 "To the Reader" (a title chosen by Baillie which, in the context of Inchbald's remarks on the closet/stage distinction, seems quite pointed), Baillie herself drew her reader's attention to the implications of theatrical practice for the gendering of dramatic performance, character, and authorship. I do not mean to suggest that Inchbald was in fact concealing advocacy on Baillie's behalf within the guise of critique, but instead that the particular terms of her comments, again in the context of the canon-making collection of plays for which she is writing, opens, rather than closes, options for dramatic authorship, particularly women's.[50]

This chapter has examined one way that Elizabeth Inchbald and Joanna Baillie created their authorial identities. For a fuller understanding of the authorial performance of a woman playwright in this era, we would need to study both the practical and ideological obstacles each faced over time as she navigated a number of cultural systems.[51] For example, one would need to study changes in the cultural marketplace, in perceptions about women's public self-performance, and in the reception of gendered bodies and identities. It would be particularly fruitful to consider how women's varied performances of dramatic authorship contrasted with and commented upon other familiar roles – for women, for writers, and for women writers – because Inchbald and Baillie make their authorial gestures in relation to the roles available in this era, like those of male Romantic poet, woman poet, or novelist. Consequently, there are many ways to look at how and why women writers might have written dramas for both theatrical production and print publication in the years around 1800 in Britain. The economics of the theatre in London and the publishing industry in Britain would alone provide the subject for a substantial study of how specific women writers made choices about these two media/markets/cultural venues in the context of their own personal financial situations over time. Other inquiries might ask in what ways particular women writers might be said to have "authored" the versions of their texts that were printed and read, especially in cases when the printed version may have been influenced by the theatrical system that treated women's and men's dramatic authorship differently. Even a study of textual variations in plays written by women would have to consider a variety of influences on the decision to publish, on the opportunities provided to authors to revise their plays for print, and even on the ideological pressures that might have operated on women play-wrights in particular when they made decisions about delivering their plays in print. The always-complex relationship between texts and authorship would need to be thoroughly investigated to under-stand the social context of women's dramatic writing just as, in an economic study, the shifting marketplace in "dramatic authorship" would need to be painstakingly documented and theorized. There-fore, to ground my preliminary discussion here within more fully detailed historical analysis, I propose that three broad areas for further inquiry should be investigated:

> the economics of women's dramatic authorship and publication
> the relationship of textual and performance details to women's
>   roles as dramatic "authors"
> the dialogue between women's authorial performances and public
>   reception and response

Although study of the playwriting and dramatic critical writing of this period is essential, equally important is analysis of the social systems in which this writing was produced, the discourses in relation to which it gestured, and the consequences of revisionary studies for both our assumptions about dramaturgical and literary history and our practices as scholars and teachers.[52] Women writers like Baillie and Inchbald have lacked visibility in our literary histories in part because their contextual "authorial performances" are incompatible with the imagination- and genius-based paradigms of authorship that, though frequently questioned in our historical scholarship, often still govern our styles of reading, evaluating, and teaching texts from the late eighteenth and early nineteenth centuries. To understand the contexts that construct the meanings of Baillie's and Inchbald's authorial gestures, we must allow for the possibility that women writers were particularly aware of the cultural acoustics and optics of the venues available to them. By basing historical analyses on the careers of women playwrights – those authorial performers whose position as dramatic authors was often remarked upon – we can continue to press for paradigm shifts that complicate Romantic-era authorship generally through detailed analysis of the cultural *mise en scène* against which it was performed. By studying women playwrights as authorial performers, we make it easier to see dramatic authorship – either by men or women, for stage or page – as the complex discursive act it was in the era of Romanticism.

NOTES

1 Pam Gems, "Imagination and Gender," *On Gender and Writing*, ed. Michelene Wandor (London: Pandora, 1983) p. 148.

2 Marlon Ross has written that "Romantic poeticizing is . . . what some men do in order to reconfirm their capacity to influence the world in ways sociohistorically determined as masculine" (*The Contours of Masculine Desire: Romanticism and the Rise of Women's Poetry* [Oxford University Press, 1989], p. 3); Ross further advocates that scholars "begin to flesh out the other crucial literary strains that were competing with and joining with 'Romanticism' during the period" (5). Interestingly, William Jewett suggests that it is precisely in order to examine the problematics of language's relationship with agency that Romantic poets like William Wordsworth, Samuel Taylor Coleridge, Percy Shelley, and Lord Byron wrote dramatic poems (*Fatal Autonomy: Romantic Drama and the Rhetoric of Agency* [Ithaca: Cornell University Press, 1997]). However, Jewett does not consider that the case of women playwrights, for whom the relationship between writing and agency had different valences, provides a more intriguing case from the perspective of cultural materialism. That is, while men could perhaps assume that the forms in which they addressed the public were of minor importance, the forms of women's authorial performances were frequently subject to vehement commentary.

3 Susan Bennett explores theatre reception in relation to a number of

contemporary interpretive and cultural theories (*Theatre Audiences: A Theory of Production and Reception* 2nd edn [London: Routledge, 1997]). Though the particular authorial performances of women writers that I discuss here are not literally theatrical, Bennett's discussion of the relevance of reception theory for analysis of theatrical performance has influenced my chapter.

4 The challenging social position of women involved in theatre is detailed in both Ellen Donkin, *Getting into the Act: Women Playwrights in London 1776–1829* (London: Routledge, 1995) and Catherine Burroughs, *Closet Stages: Joanna Baillie and the Theater Theory of British Romantic Women Writers* (Philadelphia: University of Pennsylvania Press, 1997). For a case study of how a woman theatre artist's dissidence in person and in print was received, see the discussion of Elizabeth Macauley's career in J. S. Bratton, "Miss Scott and Miss Macauley: 'Genius Comes in All Disguises,'" *Theatre Survey* 37.1 (May 1996): 59–73.

5 Sonia Hofkosh, *Sexual Politics and the Romantic Author* (Cambridge University Press, 1998), p. 6. Here, I resist thinking of the public self-presentations of Inchbald and Baillie as in any narrow sense "intentional," but instead see these women's authorship as performed on a discursive stage whose parameters established how readers and audiences interpreted authorial gestures, from prefatory critical remarks to the details of a play's subject and the nuances of its dramaturgy.

6 Michel Foucault looks at authorship as an effect created by interpretive and historiographic procedures. See "What is an Author?" trans. Josué Harari, *The Foucault Reader*, ed. Paul Rabinow (New York: Pantheon, 1984), pp. 101–20. Michael Gamer's study of Matthew Lewis's and Walter Scott's strategies of authorship provides an example of how studying the creation of authorial personae illuminates nuances of Romantic-period literary history ("Authors in Effect: Lewis, Scott, and the Gothic Drama" [*ELH* 66.4, 1999: 831–61]). Judith Pascoe *Romantic Theatricality: Gender, Poetry, and Spectatorship* (Ithaca: Cornell University Press, 1997), which in part examines the performativity of William Wordsworth's and Mary Robinson's authorial personae, provides a model for investigating authorship as performance. Jane Moody, "Illusions of Authorship" in *Women and Playwriting in Nineteenth-Century Britain*, ed. Tracy C. Davis and Ellen Donkin (Cambridge University Press, 1999), pp. 99–124, examines the complex questions that the particular forms of women's theatrical authorship in the mid-nineteenth century raise for theatre history. Claire Miller Colombo's essay, " 'This Pen of Mine Will Say Too Much': Public Performance in the Journals of Anna Larpent" (*Texas Studies in Literature and Language* 38.3/4 [Fall/Winter 1996], pp. 285–301), explores how Larpent's "evolving consciousness of the public sphere not as a spatial designation but as a discursive field" (p. 286) interacted with Larpent's assistance of her husband in his role as licenser of plays for the patent theatres. Colombo's essay provides me

with a different kind of example of how theatre as a public venue might have influenced a woman's textual self-performance. Coming at authorial performance from a different perspective, Richard Dyer, in "Believing in Fairies: The Author and the Homosexual" in *Inside/Out: Lesbian Theories, Gay Theories*, ed. Diana Fuss (New York: Routledge, 1991, pp. 185–201), notes that "All authorship and all sexual identities are performances . . . always problematic in relation to any self separable from the realization of self in the discursive modes available" (188). His point reminds us not to expect women dramatists' authorial performances to be seamless or absolutely confident stagings without interpersonal costs.

7 Patrice Pavis, "From Page to Stage: A Difficult Birth," trans. Jilly Daugherty, *Theatre at the Crossroads of Culture* (London: Routledge, 1992), pp. 24–47, writes, "[The] relationship between text and performance . . . does not take the form of a translation or a reduplication of the former by the latter, but rather of a transfer or a confrontation of the fictional universe structured by the text and the fictional universe produced by the stage" (p. 28).

8 Pavis *ibid.*, suggests that the "non-verbal . . . makes the verbal text speak, reduplicating its utterance, as if the dramatic text, by being uttered on stage, were able to comment on itself, without the help of another text" (p. 31).

9 Recent research has delineated the situations and perceptions of women in relation to eighteenth- and nineteenth-century British theatrical professions. See for example Julie Carlson, *In the Theatre of Romanticism: Coleridge, Nationalism, Women* (Cambridge University Press, 1994); Kristina Straub, *Sexual Suspects: Eighteenth-Century Players and Sexual Ideology* (Princeton University Press, 1992); Tracy C. Davis, *Actresses as Working Women: Their Social Identity in Victorian Culture* (London: Routledge, 1991); Burroughs, *Closet Stages*; Donkin, *Getting into the Act*; and Pascoe, *Romantic Theatricality*. Although Straub's study provides important background on the politics of gender, sexuality, and difference for performers on the eighteenth-century British stage, the relevance of the figure of the performer to authorial performance generally is suggested only by Straub's discussion of celebrity memoirs. More relevant to the period I discuss, Burroughs's second chapter in *Closet Stages* discusses ways in which women theatre artists were represented in the years around 1800. One particular theatrical woman of the period whose career has produced much recent commentary is Sarah Siddons. Her career and role as public figure have been discussed as an important theoretical and historical site by Burroughs (*Closet Stages* 51–8), Carlson (*Theatre of Romanticism* 162–75), and Pascoe (*Romantic Theatricality* 12–32); see also Ellen Donkin, "Mrs. Siddons Looks Back in Anger: Feminist Historiography for Eighteenth-Century British Theater," *Critical Theory and Performance*, ed.

Janelle G. Reinelt and Joseph R. Roach (Ann Arbor: University of Michigan Press, 1992), pp. 276–90.

10 Moody, "Illusions of Authorship," asks provocative questions about how women who were actors and managers "authored" the work in which they performed. I see a relationship between Baillie's and Inchbald's "management" of their varied authorial performances and the later examples of authorship through theatre management that Moody explores.

11 Inchbald, quoted in Roger Manvell, *Elizabeth Inchbald: England's Principal Woman Dramatist and Independent Woman of Letters in 18th Century London. A Biographical Study* (Lanham, MD: University Press of America, 1987), p. 40.

12 See Joanna Baillie, "Introductory Discourse" to the first volume of *A Series of Plays* (1798); republished in *The Dramatic and Poetical Works of Joanna Baillie* (London: Longman, Brown, Green, and Longmans, 1851), pp. 1–18. Joseph Donohue describes the aesthetics of character performance that Baillie's plays violate as "the fundamental tendency of all acting, up through the age of Kean, towards consistent objectification" (*Theatre in the Age of Kean* [Totowa, NJ: Rowman and Littlefield, 1975], p. 68).

13 See Joanna Baillie, "To the Reader," originally published in the third volume of *A Series of Plays* (1812); republished in *The Dramatic and Poetical Works of Joanna Baillie* (London: Longman, Brown, Green, and Longmans, 1851, pp. 228–35), pp. 232–33.

14 Donohue (*Theatre in the Age of Kean*, 164–67) sees playwrights' interest in character psychology as emerging in spite of the period's theatre sizes and acting styles and resulting in dramas like Baillie's that were unsuited for the stage. He does not, however, entertain the possibility that the oppositional dramaturgy of a playwright like Baillie might have been to some extent deliberate.

15 Joanna Baillie, "Introductory Discourse," p. 14.

16 Nora Nachumi shows how, even in her novels, Inchbald employs theatrical gesture as part of the rhetoric of characterization and narrative ("'Those Simple Signs': The Performance of Emotion in Elizabeth Inchbald's *A Simple Story*," (*Eighteenth-Century Fiction* 11.3 [April 1999], pp. 317–38). Inchbald's remarks for *The British Theatre* also frequently discuss the difference between a play's effectiveness in the closet and on the stage, again marking her awareness of the distinct techniques and authorial performances called for in published texts and performance.

17 Mary Berry, Letter to Mrs. Cholmley, March 1799, quoted in Donkin, *Getting into the Act*, p. 163.

18 Donkin, *Getting into the Act*, p. 97.

19 *Ibid.*, pp. 26–29.

20 *Ibid.*, pp. 11–12.

21 Stephens (*passim*) provides detailed information on the amount and kinds of revisions dramatic authors typically made, but he provides little information about women playwrights or how their experiences might have differed from those of the men on whom his book centers (*The Profession of the Playwright: British Theatre 1800–1900* [Cambridge: Cambridge University Press, 1992]).

22 I use the term "counter-theatrical sphere" as a variation on Anne K. Mellor's terminology ("Joanna Baillie and the Counter-Public Sphere," *Studies in Romanticism* 33 [Winter 1994], pp. 559–67) and to develop further some of the ideas advanced by Burroughs in *Closet Stages* concerning women's alternatives to participation in the mainstream "theatrical sphere" of the time.

23 Joanna Baillie, letter dated 12 February 1810, cited in Donkin, *Getting into the Act*, pp. 170–71.

24 See Margaret S. Carhart, *The Life and Work of Joanna Baillie*, Yale Studies in English 64 (New Haven: Yale University Press, 1923), p. 8 and Judith Bailey Slagle, "Evolution of a Writer: Joanna Baillie's Life in Letters," *Joanna Baillie, Romantic Dramatist: Critical Essays*, eds. Janice Patten and Thomas C. Crochunis (The Netherlands: Gordon and Breach, forthcoming) ms. pp. 6–8.

25 In a letter to Anna Carr of 12 December 1835, Baillie writes about preparing her 1836 *Dramas* for publication: "I have been much occupied since last June in correcting the proof sheets of my new publication. I thought I had done with all this business, but circumstances arose to make me desirous of leaving all my Dramas in print corrected under my own eye, so I was obliged to throw aside the indolence & desire of quiet & privicy [*sic*] so natural to old age"; from *The Collected Letters of Joanna Baillie*, Vol. 2., Ed. Judith Bailey Slagle (Madison, NJ: Fairleigh Dickinson University Press, 1999), p. 1198. Thanks to Tracy C. Davis for drawing my attention to this letter.

26 See Inchbald, "To the Artist," *The Artist* 1.14 (13 June 1807), p. 16. Both L.W. Conolly and Donkin quote the first part of this passage; the further portions of the same article by Inchbald on the psychological effects of censorship are cited only in Donkin. See L.W. Conolly, *The Censorship of English Drama 1737–1824* (San Marino, CA: The Huntington Library, 1976), p. 11; and Donkin, *Getting into the Act*, p. 5.

27 See Gary Kelly, *The English Jacobin Novel 1780–1805* (Oxford University Press, 1976), p. 97; and Daniel O'Quinn, "Elizabeth Inchbald's *The Massacre*: Tragedy, Violence and the Networks of Political Fantasy," *British Women Playwrights around 1800*. Website. http//www-sul.stanford.edu/mirrors/romnet/wp1800/massacreintro.html

28 Gay Gibson Cima ("To Be Public as a Genius and Private as a Woman: The Critical Framing of Nineteenth-Century British Women Playwrights" in *Women and Playwriting in Nineteenth-Century Britain*, eds. Tracy C. Davis and Ellen Donkin [Cambridge University Press, 1999,

pp. 35–53]) cites the anonymous author of *Public Characters of 1800–1*, who wrote of gentlewomen writers like Charlotte Smith that they were "arraigned, not merely as writers, but as *women*, their characters, their conduct, even their personal endowments become the subjects of severe inquisition". Cima writes: "Because women playwrights and critics were at least potentially more publicly exhibited and more closely associated with actresses than their literary counterparts in the novelistic trade, they faced unique challenges" (p. 42).

29 Tracy C. Davis, *Actresses as Working Women*, p. 69.

30 Tracy C. Davis, in discussing late-nineteenth-century scrutiny of the interaction of theatre prostitution and onstage performance, shows that many moralists understood the larger scene of the theatre to be sexualized (*Actresses as Working Women*, 151–63). In light of Kristina Straub's analysis (*Sexual Suspects*) of how actor sexualization operated in the eighteenth-century theatre, both reception and, in anticipation, composition of the plays of women playwrights were undoubtedly influenced by the sexualization of the playhouse. It is worth asking how women playwrights used or resisted the highly charged context the theatre provided even for their published dramas.

31 See Manvell, *Elizabeth Inchbald*, pp. 38–39 and Conolly, *Censorship*, pp. 84, 196n3.

32 James Boaden, *Memoirs of Mrs. Inchbald*, 2 vols. (London: Richard Bentley, 1833), I:310.

33 Donkin, *Getting into the Act*, p. 38.

34 *Ibid.*, p. 67.

35 Stuart Curran's watershed essay, "The 'I' Altered" in *Romanticism and Feminism*, ed. Anne K. Mellor (Bloomington: Indiana University Press, 1988), pp. 185–207, suggests that just such a lineage of women's poetry should inform our historiography of women's poetic writing in the late eighteenth and early nineteenth centuries. Of course, because dramatic writing was associated with the challenging social processes of theatre, it had a different – perhaps a greater – significance for women writers than had poetic writing.

36 Hester Piozzi in a letter to Sir James Fellowes dated 28 March 1819, cited in Donkin, *Getting into the Act*, p. 165.

37 Donkin, *Getting into the Act*, p. 91.

38 *Ibid.*, p. 185.

39 For a discussion of Baillie as dramatic critic, see Burroughs, *Closet Stages*, especially pp. 12–17, 86–91.

40 See also Burroughs's discussion of Baillie's response to theatre size, (*Closet Stages*, pp. 91–94).

41 Roger Manvell, *Elizabeth Inchbald*, pp. 127–28.

42 Macheski, ed. "Introduction" to *Remarks for the British Theatre, 1806–1809, By Elizabeth Inchbald* (Delmar, NY: Scholars' Facsimiles and Reprints, 1990), pp. 10–11.

43 See Marvin Carlson's chapter in this volume for a fuller discussion of the significance of Inchbald's position as dramatic critic and a consideration of the models of dramatic criticism that influenced Inchbald's critical approach. For the broader context surrounding women critics in the Romantic period, see Burroughs, *Closet Stages* and Anne K. Mellor, "A Criticism of Their Own: Romantic Women Literary Critics," *Questioning Romanticism*, ed. John Beer (Baltimore: The Johns Hopkins University Press, 1995), pp. 29–48. Burroughs sees Inchbald's critical remarks as both substantive dramatic criticism and a demonstration of the possibilities of a criticism sensitive to both page and stage (*Closet Stages* 81–86).

44 Elizabeth Inchbald, Remarks to *A Bold Stroke for a Wife*, p. 4. Inchbald's remarks in Macheski's edition (see note 42) are alphabetized by play with page numbers repeated from the original series (in which each play within a volume was numbered separately). Within my text I will indicate the play name (to locate the comments within the Macheski edition) and give page numbers for any specific reference so that it can be located within Inchbald's prefatory remarks on that particular play.

45 Within the present volume, Marvin Carlson's reading of the comments on Centlivre's play accepts Inchbald's judgment as "characteristic" of her critical views. Carlson also suggests that Inchbald might have adopted moral rhetoric as an important part of her critical performance. However, as his discussion of her adroit response to George Colman's critique of her remarks suggests, Inchbald certainly displayed elsewhere a knack for strategic use of skilled rhetoric.

46 See Elizabeth Inchbald, *Such Things Are* in *Selected Comedies*, ed. Roger Manvell (Lanham, MD: University Press of America, 1987), p. 17.

47 The Hastings affair reached its emotional peak with Richard Brinsley Sheridan's speech before the House of Commons on 7 February 1787; Inchbald's play was first staged at Covent Garden a few days later. For further discussion of the Hastings affair, see Jeanne Moskal's chapter in the present volume.

48 For a discussion of the Romantic debate about closet and stage dramaturgy, see Burroughs (*Closet Stages* 8–12). In addition to Burroughs (as noted above, *Closet Stages* 81–86), see also Marvin Carlson's chapter in the present volume for a discussion of Inchbald's comments on plays in relation to page and stage. Jane Moody (" 'Fine Word, Legitimate!': Toward a Theatrical History of Romanticism" [*Texas Studies in Literature and Language* 38.3/4, 1996, pp. 223–44]) provides a sharp account of the ideological dimensions of ongoing critical discussion of the opposition between closet and stage dramas (p. 34).

49 See Jane Moody's chapter in the present volume on translation, Inchbald, and Anne Plumptre.

50 For a discussion of Inchbald's interest in alternatives to women's roles, see Anna Lott, "Sexual Politics in Elizabeth Inchbald," *Studies in English Literature* 34.3 (1994): 635–48.

51 In *Getting into the Act*, Ellen Donkin notes that, as early as the mid- to late
    eighteenth century, playwright Frances Brooke recognized that the
    patent theatre system and the "interlocking fiefdoms" it had created,
    not individual managers, was her opponent as a writer (51). Donkin's
    book provides a thorough description of the logistical, social, and
    thereby psychological impediments that women playwrights en-
    countered in the years around 1800 in Britain.

52 See *Romanticism on the Net* 12 (November 1998), a special issue on "British
    Women Playwrights around 1800," which includes essays as well as a
    response to the special issue by Margaret J. M. Ezell; each of these
    pieces attempts to shift the terms of scholarship. See Tracy C. Davis,
    "The Sociable Playwright and Representative Citizen"; David
    Chandler, "'The Conflict': Hannah Brand and Theatre Politics in the
    1790s"; Nora Nachumi, "Acting Like a 'Lady': British Women Novelists
    and the Eighteenth-Century Stage"; Marjean D. Purinton, "Revising
    Romanticism by Inscripting Women Playwrights"; Catherine B. Bur-
    roughs, "Teaching the Theory and Practice of Women's Dramaturgy";
    Thomas C. Crochunis, "The Function of the Dramatic Closet at the
    Present Time"; Ken A. Bugajski, "Joanna Baillie: An Annotated
    Bibliography"; and Margaret J. M. Ezell, "Revisioning Responding: A
    Second Look at Women Playwrights Around 1800." In my introduction
    to that issue, "British Women Playwrights around 1800: New Paradigms
    and Recoveries," I argue that plays and theatre/dramatic criticism do
    more than expand the canon when they are given due attention. When
    we study women's dramatic writing in the years around 1800, we must
    be prepared to exchange old scholarly paradigms for new ones and to
    reconsider those texts and writers upon which Romantic studies is
    founded.

Translation, Adaptation, Revision

Suicide and translation in the dramaturgy of Elizabeth Inchbald and Anne Plumptre

Jane Moody

I

At the center of this chapter is a scene from a comedy performed at Covent Garden in November 1799. The comedy would soon be published by G. and J. Robinson; two further editions followed in quick succession before the end of 1799. None of these printed texts, however, records the scene I shall be exploring here. For that had been buried deep within the printed text: silenced, censored, sent out of theatrical and textual sight. The scene is one of female suicide. For late eighteenth-century audiences at Covent Garden, the dramatic representation of female suicide would of course have been familiar enough – Gloriana, Athenais, and Sophonisba in Nathaniel Lee's tragedies all end their own lives (as if suicide were the only decisive action available to female passivity), as does Calista, in Rowe's stock play, *The Fair Penitent* (1703).[1] In comedy, however, suicide had been taboo, unrepresentable. Yet suicide, I shall be arguing, underpins both my playwrights' generic iconoclasm as well as offers a theatrical paradigm for the ghostly presence of dead bodies and stolen property within the theatrical translations of the 1790s. For this death seems dramatically to figure the disintegration of certain moral assumptions at the heart of sentimental comedy; at the same time, the character's futile attempt at self-slaughter offers a dramatic model through which to explore the constraints and liberties of female authorship in translation. So, abandoning for the moment all printed texts, let us turn to the Larpent manuscript where this suicide narrative survives, and in particular to the bleak, austere stage direction, "Ellen discovered laying on a plank by the side of the Canal lifeless."[2]

The Hyde Park suicide scene, as it appears in the Larpent manuscript, is swiftly redeemed. The mysterious Wise Man from the

East, watched by a group of spectators, pulls Ellen from the water, and the body is carried mournfully away to his house, where Ellen will be brought slowly back to life. There, the play's other characters congregate, including Claransforth, the now-repentant rake whose abduction, and subsequent attempted seduction, of Ellen prompted her self-retributive despair. By now, Claransforth has also learned that the mysterious Eastern man (who has seemed to know his life's whole plot, his acts of dissipation as well as his deeds of generosity) is, in fact, his own father. The Wise Man then stage manages the sentimental reunion of Claransforth and Ellen (Act v scene ii). As she lies on a couch, surrounded by her family, the Wise Man asks her a series of questions, in response to which Ellen is invited to reply not by language, but by silent gesture. "And first, can you forgive this man?" the Wise Man inquires, and, without speaking, Ellen "lifts up her head." "Can you be thoroughly reconcil'd to him?" Ellen remains silent, but "raises on her elbow." Finally, he asks, "Can you venture to take him for a husband?" Ellen "rises wholly on the sopha," as if, through the words of her rescuer, she is now coming back to life. Claransforth moves toward her, and kneels. Momentarily escaping from her dumbshow afterlife, Ellen speaks for the first time since she plunged into the canal and for the last time in the play. "While heaven remits its punishment on my offence, can I be rigorous to others?" Her question – addressed not to the Wise Man nor to Claransforth but as if to some arbiter or judge – echoes, entirely unresolved, through the last few speeches of the play. Though the denouement of this comedy apparently defers to that sentimental trope of moral conversion (through which the peccadilloes and wrongdoings of its Romantic hero are subsumed into the ideology of benevolence), the union of Ellen and Claransforth seems radically tarnished, painfully compromised.

Covent Garden audiences greeted the first performance of Elizabeth Inchbald's play, *The Wise Man of the East* (1799), with confusion and unease.[3] Such was the disapprobation which accompanied Ellen's attempt at suicide, as well as various other scenes, that the playwright immediately sat down to cut, revise, and expurgate her manuscript (one on which, she told her friend Mrs. Phillips, she had already exerted "all my strength, both of body and mind").[4] Critics drew attention to what they saw as the "morally defective" character of the play.[5] "The body of Ellen was on the first night exhibited, newly taken out of the river, on a shutter," declared one writer, "but the disgustfulness of the scene . . . [was] too glaring to

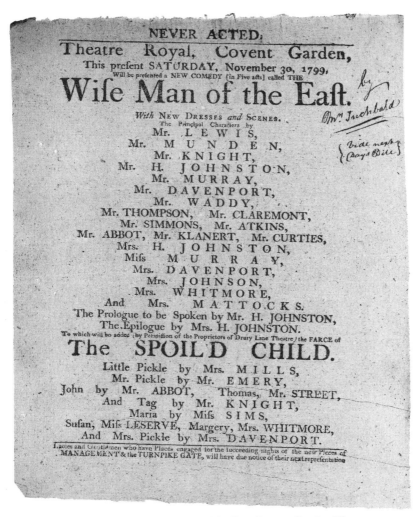

NEVER ACTED,
_____

Theatre Royal, Covent Garden,

This prefent SATURDAY, November 30, 1799,

Will be prefented a NEW COMEDY [in Five acts] called THE

Wife Man of the Eaſt.

With NEW DRESSES *and* SCENES.

The Principal Characters by

Mr. L E W I S,

Mr. M U N D E N,

Mr. K N I G H T,

Mr. H. J O H N S T O N,

Mr. M U R R A Y,

Mr. D A V E N P O R T,

Mr. W A D D Y,

Mr. THOMPSON, Mr. CLAREMONT,

Mr. SIMMONS, Mr. ATKINS,

Mr. ABBOT, Mr. KLANERT, Mr. CURTIES,

Mrs. H. J O H N S T O N,

Mifs M U R R A Y,

Mrs. D A V E N P O R T,

Mrs. J O H N S O N,

Mrs. W H I T M O R E,

And Mrs. M A T T O C K S.

The Prologue to be Spoken by Mr. H. JOHNSTON,

The Epilogue by Mrs. H. JOHNSTON.

To which will be added (by Permiffion of the Proprietors of Drury Lane Theatre) the FARCE of

The SPOIL'D CHILD.

Little Pickle by Mrs. M I L L S,

Mr. Pickle by Mr. E M E R Y,

John by Mr. ABBOT, Thomas, Mr. STREET,

And Tag by Mr. K N I G H T,

Maria by Mifs S I M S,

Sufan, Mifs LESERVE, Margery, Mrs. WHITMORE,

And Mrs. Pickle by Mrs. D A V E N P O R T.

Ladies and Gentlemen who have Places engaged for the fucceeding nights of the new Pieces of
MANAGEMENT & the TURNPIKE GATE, will have due notice of their next reprefentation

10.1 Playbill for *The Wise Man of the East*, Covent Garden Theatre,
20 November 1799

pass, even in a play manufactured from Kotzebue."[6] Elsewhere the
True Briton (2 December 1799) remarked, "The appearance of *Ellen*'s
body on the plank after her desperate immersion, must also be
omitted." Mrs. Mattocks, who played the mercurial Quaker Ruth
Starch, intent on entrapping Claransforth into marriage with her
daughter, Rachel, even began to censor some of the cynical speeches

allotted to her own character, improvising in their place comments in praise of English merchants. "The latter received much applause," reported the *Morning Post* (2 December 1799), "and the discontent abated." These critics also expressed strong disapproval about the character of Claransforth. "The *depravity* of the hero," reported James Boaden in his *Memoirs of Mrs. Inchbald*, "ought to have destroyed it outright."[7] "Instead of being marked with weaknesses as the author no doubt intended", remarked the *Morning Chronicle* reviewer, Claransforth "is tinctured with guilt, and that too of the deepest dye" (2 December 1799). But after the suppression of Ellen's attempted self-slaughter, the expurgation of the Starch family (perceived by audiences as an unjustified caricature of Quaker morality), and especially the tempering of the coercive Ruth Starch, *The Wise Man* had a successful run at Covent Garden, whilst the printed text soon ran to three editions.[8] But the controversy over *The Wise Man*, and Inchbald's hurried revisions of her play, also became the subject of a satirical text. In 1800, the editor, translator, and critic Thomas Dutton published a poem, complete with an intricate editorial commentary, wittily entitled *The Wise Man of the East, or, The Apparition of Zoroaster, the Son of Oromases, to the Theatrical Midwife of Leicester Fields* (hereafter, *The Apparition*). Dutton's text cleverly exploits public anxiety in Anti-Jacobin circles about the morality of German drama (an "actual conspiracy" against the survival of native English theatre, the Preface declares), whilst discreetly satirizing the "mercantile negotiation" conducted by the London theatre managers at Drury Lane and Covent Garden for a regular "supply" of Kotzebue's plays.

Dutton's poem – a miniature nineteenth-century *Dunciad* – mocks the improbability of Inchbald's plot, the play's lack of humor ("Your *Quaker-Scenes* a barren wit betray, / And *Rachel Starch* had nearly damned your play," 46), its unnatural characterization, especially the whimsical, capricious character of the Wise Man and, in particular, the unredeemable baseness of Claransforth ("Think'st thou, I'd give thee *Ellen* for a wife? / No! – let me see thee first reform thy life!," 56). Throughout, Dutton's editorial commentary laughs at Inchbald's own hurried and contingent expurgation of her own play ("It having been found inconvenient in the representation, for Ellen to throw herself into the water; recourse is had to a milder substitute; and she now goes mad, instead of drowning herself," 54).

"Ellen discovered laying on a plank by the side of the Canal lifeless." The sheer audacity of Inchbald's stage picture, together with the disturbingly quiescent, almost ghostly character of the play's Romantic denouement, mark Inchbald's ideological dissolution of her source text, Kotzebue's play, *Das Schreibepult* (*The Writing Desk*). For the purposes of this chapter, I set aside various important aspects of this transformation – the Romantic subplot featuring Ensign Metland, Ellen's brother, and Ruth Starch (a subplot which Inchbald deploys not only to satirize marriages entered into as commercial transactions, but also to highlight the tensions between the competing imperatives of filial obedience and Romantic autonomy). I shall also pass over Inchbald's metamorphosis of the mysterious Hadebrath – a tradesman whose misfortunes have led him into debt, poverty and finally to plunder – into Ava Thoanoa, the Cambodian sage, who will eventually be revealed as Claransforth's disguised father. What I want to explore here is rather the way in which Inchbald transforms Kotzebue's dramaturgy, notably by compounding the misdeeds of Claransforth, so as utterly to endanger the Romantic integrity of her sentimental denouement.

The ideological fracture at the heart of Inchbald's play arises out of Ellen discovering to Claransforth her mistress's plans to ruin him. When Lady Mary Diamond, who runs an aristocratic gambling establishment for which Ellen is the unwitting Romantic pawn, learns of Claransforth's knowledge, she instantly dismisses Ellen. In Kotzebue's play, the heroine then returns home to her parents, relieved that she will no longer be forced to serve beings she despises (Act v scene i). Inchbald's adaptation, however, then swerves away from Kotzebue's text. In a moment of passion, and on the pretense of escorting her to her parents' home, Claransforth abducts Ellen, and takes her to a corner house intending to seduce her. Having escaped, but too ashamed to endure the public shame of a "hooting" rabble which she imagines will now be her lot (iv.ii), Ellen casts herself despairingly into the canal.[9] Whereas Kotzebue's play asks its audience to accept the prospect of a marriage of mutual love, tarnished only by a verbal breach of confidence (Ditthelm tells the Countess about Sophia's anonymous letter to him revealing the former's plans for his ruin), Inchbald's original scheme for *The Wise Man of the East* daringly stages a sentimental reunion jeopardized by evidence of uncontrollable sexual passion and, on the part of Ellen, tragic, uncontrollable despair.

Many of Inchbald's plays, like those of her contemporaries, are derived from the French, a language she knew well. Her adaptations include: *Animal Magnetism* (1788) from Le Texier; *The Widow's Vow* (1786) from Patrat's *L'Heureuse Erreur; The Midnight Hour* (1787) from Dumaniant's *La Guerre Ouverte; The Child of Nature* (1788) from *Zélie*, by the Marchioness of Sillery; and *Young Men and Old Women* (1792) from Gresset's *Le Méchant.* An uncharitable commentator – and Inchbald's financial success as a playwright would ensure a full cast of resentful rivals – might surmise that adaptation simply provided Inchbald with an inexhaustible supply of ready-made plots. But to what extent might the activity of translation have given a writer such as Inchbald a peculiar form of moral and political freedom?

Elizabeth Inchbald's political sympathies were well known, as were her friendships with leading radicals such as Thomas Holcroft and William Godwin. In 1793, *The True Briton*, a leading conservative periodical, had denounced as Jacobin *Every One Has His Fault* (1793), Inchbald's new play then running at the Haymarket theatre.[10] Interestingly, Inchbald's controversial representation of poverty in this play extended in certain ways the depiction of necessity in her translation, *Next Door Neighbours* (1791), performed just two years earlier. Given the pervasive anxieties about radicalism in the theatre during the 1790s, and the persistent depiction of Kotzebue's drama as both morally and politically subversive, Inchbald's stage adaptations of *Lovers' Vows* (1798) and *The Wise Man* might be regarded as a likely focus for accusations of disloyalty and subversion. From another point of view, however, the split authorial identity entailed by the act of translation also provided a Napoleonic dramatist such as Elizabeth Inchbald with a strategic form of theatrical disguise, for how could the politics of the translator be distinguished from those of the translation?

With the exception of her preface to *Lovers' Vows*, Inchbald tells us very little about her translation practice. Some clues about the theatrical mediation of translation, however, can be found amongst the prologues and epilogues, composed by friends or hack-writers, for Inchbald's adaptations, notably those written for the production of *Next Door Neighbours* (Haymarket 1791), adapted from Philippe Néricault Destouches' play, *Le Dissipateur, ou, L'Honnête Friponne* and Mercier's *L'Indigent.* The Prologue to *Next Door Neighbours*, composed by Thomas Vaughan, explicitly refers to the play's status as a feminine translation: "A Female Scribbler is an harmless Wit; / And who so harmless as our present Bard, / Claiming no greater or distinct reward, / Than what from free Translation is her due."[11] Here, Vaughan seems to present the limited nature of the playwright's commercial gain as proof of the play's political innocence; the Prologue's tone appears uncertain and, even within the timorous genre of Prologues, peculiarly defensive. Moreover, Vaughan's Epilogue modestly defends the province of translation, presenting the playwright's role as "improving what was writ before, / Tho' Genius may be less, our Judgment's more." The Prologue-writer frames Inchbald's translation as if to capitalize on the notion of a female counter-revolution whereby patriotic women lead the reformation of contemporary manners or, as in this case, the expurgation of foreign texts.[12] Who "begot" this story – and the nature of begetting is an issue to which I shall return – is a matter of no importance, the Epilogue declares, dismissing questions of authorship in favor of the martial celebration of cultural patriotism and chauvinistic emendation – the attribution of "true BRITISH SPIRIT" to "Gallic Froth."

Through these theatrical paratexts, Inchbald is able to capitalize on a nationalistic concept of translation as patriotic liberation and martial warfare in which the "tinsels" of French dramatists (who will "ne'er complain of English Liberty") are transformed into a dramaturgy of solid English bullion, and "glory to behold their Tinsel shine, / Through the rich Bullion of the English Line" (Prologue, *Next Door Neighbours*). Though Vaughan's representation of *Next Door Neighbours* seems to assimilate Inchbald's translation into a masculine world of physical warfare, Inchbald's Preface to *Lovers' Vows* self-consciously invokes the translator's femininity as a guarantee of the moral probity and purity of the expurgated text.[13]

At Drury Lane, the performances of Sarah Siddons would become the theatrical symbol of feminine moral reform. Through Sarah Siddons, the controversial character of Adelaide Haller (the guilty, repentant wife of Kotzebue's *The Stranger*[14]) became amiable and delicate. "Do men of honour in real life take back faithless wives in their arms?" the *Anti-Jacobin*'s reviewer railed in fury. According to this critic, *The Stranger* confirmed Kotzebue's culpability in holding up "to esteem and respect, women who have deviated from the paths of virtue," not to mention the viciousness falsely attributed to characters of rank.[15] Yet, through what reviewers praised as "her unlimited controul over the passions," Siddons's performance – a self-conscious, deliberate theatrical translation in its own right – seemed to mediate, and thereby to mitigate, Adelaide's crime.[16] By expressing in her characterization both sympathy for and moral repugnance toward Adelaide Haller's actions, Sarah Siddons carefully framed her performance, rather as Inchbald presents the Preface to *Lovers' Vows*, as an act of feminine censorship.

The role of Elvira in *Pizarro*, performed at Drury Lane in 1799, represents another unacknowledged collaboration between Sheridan and Siddons through which one of Kotzebue's most immoral characters was transformed into a role of dignified grandeur and moral resolution. "Humbled in penitence, I will endeavour to atone the guilty errors, which . . . have long consum'd my secret heart" declared Elvira when she appeared as a ghostly visage at the end of Sheridan's celebrated adaptation. How different, as we shall now see, is the "unconquered" mind and moral contrariness of Anne Plumptre's Elvira.[17]

II

The day rainy; played five games at billiards before dinner. Went in the evening to see "Lovers' Vows" played for the first time at Covent Garden. Translated from the German by some retainer at court, as Mrs. Inchbald told Mr. Robinson, but corrected and altered by her. My legs so swelled that I could only stay the first four acts; which at times made me laugh, and cry heartily. Saw the Parrys at the theatre. James, as usual, fastidious and dissatisfied.[18]

Rain, billiards, and swollen legs dominate Thomas Holcroft's curiously detached recollection of the first night of *Lovers' Vows* in 1798. As well as having enjoyed an intimate and tempestuous relationship with Inchbald, Holcroft had a professional interest in the practice of theatrical translation. In 1784, he and a friend had gone to Paris to acquire a copy of Beaumarchais' controversial play, *Le Mariage de Figaro*. Having failed to obtain a manuscript, the two men attended performances of the play for more than a week, transcribing what they had seen and heard each night until they had produced a complete text for the London stage. Later, Holcroft's translation of Johannes Brandes's play, *The German Hotel*, would become one of the first adaptations from the contemporary German repertoire to reach the English stage; after the success of Inchbald's *Lovers' Vows*, Holcroft also seems to have embarked on the translation of a Kotzebue play.[19]

Watching Inchbald's play at Covent Garden that night was another professional playwright, albeit one who never saw her plays performed under her own name. Indeed, that playwright had just finished translating the Kotzebue drama which Inchbald had rendered as *Lovers' Vows*. Unlike Inchbald, who knew no German, this playwright had been able to work directly from Kotzebue's original play.[20]

"Satisfied, therefore, that the Work was in much more able hands," the playwright wrote, recalling her discovery that *Lovers' Vows* was soon to be staged at Covent Garden, she "totally relinquished her design" and abandoned any hope of stage performance. The account appears to have the status of a delicate compliment to Elizabeth Inchbald, but what follows has the character of an implicit rebuke, with a distant hint of authorial rivalry. For, at the first performance of *Lovers' Vows*, Anne Plumptre remembers being "much surprised at the extent of the Alterations and Omissions which had been made" to Kotzebue's play by Elizabeth Inchbald. Whilst recognizing "that these Alterations might have been necessary to accommodate the Play to the taste of an English Audience," the experience of watching *Lovers' Vows* "irresistibly" prompted Plumptre "to present her favourite Author to the Public, in the Form he had chosen for himself" (vii).

Though Plumptre offers some charitable explanations for Inchbald's alterations – the existence of a defective translation as Inchbald's model, and the demands of stage representation as opposed to those of "the closet" (ix) – the introduction to *The Natural Son*, her own translation, nevertheless lays down a bold challenge to the supremacy of Elizabeth Inchbald's *Lovers' Vows*. Here, Plumptre disputes in particular Inchbald's characterization of Amelia: in Inchbald's play, she alleges, the "artless innocent child of Nature, drawn by Kotzebue" is transformed into a "forward country hoyden." Through such challenges, *The Natural Son* seems to present itself as a dramatic and moral corrective to Inchbald's play, and indeed as a defense of Kotzebue's original drama. When *Lovers' Vows* later reappears in literary history as the play suppressed by Sir Thomas Bertram in Jane Austen's *Mansfield Park* (1814), it is worth remembering that the debate over Amelia's character which takes place in that novel is one whose moral positions had already been delineated in 1798 in the form of a dialogue between two women translators.

In the late 1790s, translating German dramatists, and especially the plays of Kotzebue, became the quintessential activity of educated

literary women, including Elizabeth Inchbald, Anne Plumptre, and
Maria Geisweiler. Several of these women, notably Inchbald and
Plumptre, were also sympathetic to and deeply interested in the
cause of Napoleon.[21] Maria Geisweiler, whose husband Constantin
had a shop in Pall Mall selling German, French, and Italian books,
published several Kotzebue plays in translation,[22] while in 1798 the
Margravine of Anspach adapted Schiller's *The Robbers* for private
performances at Brandenburgh House.

After her controversial second marriage to the Margrave of
Anspach, the Margravine (formerly Elizabeth Craven) had built a
theatre, designed in Gothic revival style, in the grounds of
Brandenburgh House on the banks of the Thames at Hammersmith.
There, though ostracized by much of London society, she produced
a wide range of English and French plays, and hired scene painters,
musical directors, and even actors from London theatres for her
lavish private performances. In her adaptation of *The Robbers* ("This
famed exotic, prun'd with British care," as she describes the play in
her Prologue), the Margravine shrewdly tried to anticipate moral
and political objections to the representation of Schiller's controversial play. She meticulously expunged, for example, the Moor's
"Jacobin" speeches (notably his confession in ii.ii that he has
assassinated a Count of the empire and taken jewels from the
corrupt ministers who have built their fortunes on the misery of their
fellow creatures), excised Schiller's oaths, and, in the most obvious
departure, made Amelia (whose part the Margravine herself played
at Brandenburgh House) flee to a convent.

At a time of political tumult and radical disaffection, Schiller's
play represented an extremely bold, even foolhardy, theatrical
choice. Though the first English translations of *Die Räuber* had
appeared in 1792, the play would not be staged publicly in London
until Joseph Holman's expurgated adaptation, *The Red-Cross Knights*,
was performed at the Haymarket in August 1799. Small wonder,
then, that critics were quick to denounce the Margravine's *Robbers*
as a Jacobin play.[23] Indeed, in her preface to the printed edition,
the Margravine declared that she was publishing *The Robbers* in
order that the public might make their own judgment about "the
ungenerous and false aspersions of Newspaper Writers, who have,
by various paragraphs, insinuated that it was played there with all
the Jacobinical Speeches that abound in the Original."[24] Chas-
tened, no doubt, by still more vituperative publicity, *The Robbers*

became the first and also the last of the Margravine's forays into
political drama.

Anne Plumptre (1760–1818), by contrast, became the foremost
British translator of Kotzebue's plays. An accomplished linguist (her
father Robert Plumptre, who was the President of Queens's College,
Cambridge, had ensured that she and her sister, Annabella, were
well educated), Anne Plumptre also published several novels, translated works of travel describing journeys through South Africa and
Brazil and wrote two travel books in her own right.[25] She numbered
amongst her acquaintances a handful of metropolitan radicals and
women writers, including the democrat Helen Maria Williams, and
Amelia Opie, another aspiring playwright (and friend of Elizabeth
Inchbald), with whom she saw at least one play at Drury Lane
theatre.

In 1810, Plumptre published her most explicitly polemical work, a
three-volume *Narrative of a Three Years' Residence in France* (1810) based
on her journey through France between 1802 and 1805. The third
volume contains an extended and sophisticated critique of British
prejudices about Napoleon and, by extension, of British foreign
policy. We have indulged our delusive views of Napoleon as a
domestic tyrant, argues Plumptre, because "we wished to reduce
France to insignificance as a power, and annihilate any hope she
might entertain of one day becoming our rival in commerce and
manufactures" (318). Such prejudices, she continues, not only
"degrade" Britain as a nation and as individuals, but prevent
Britons from contemplating "things as they really are, not as our
deluders wish them to be" (318). Rejecting Napoleon's status as the
tyrannical bogeyman of British culture, Plumptre draws her readers'
attention to Napoleon's humanitarian successes ("In all the governments where Buonaparte has any influence, he has uniformly been
the means of procuring relief to the people from some of the most
grievous of their oppressions," 384), his reputation for policies of
religious toleration, and his improvements in agriculture and political economy. Setting aside for a moment the sheer political
audacity of Plumptre's views, what is striking about the *Narrative* is
the sense of a rigorous and discriminating intellect at work, steadily
and methodically questioning her readers' assumptions about Napoleon and arguing her case with impassioned conviction.

Between 1789 and 1798, Plumptre published seven translations of
Kotzebue's plays. Several of these were highly successful and rapidly

passed through several editions: *The Count of Burgundy* (3 editions); *The Natural Son* (4 editions); *The Virgin of the Sun* (5 editions), *The Spaniards in Peru; or, The Death of Rolla* (6 editions).[26] Moreover, as her preface to *The Natural Son* makes clear, Plumptre certainly nursed ambitions for the performance of her translations.[27] She lacked, however, the intimate knowledge of London managers and theatrical practices garnered over many years by successful female actor-dramatists such as Elizabeth Inchbald.[28] To command a theatre audience, too, a sympathetic manager might have needed to temper the rhetorical floridity of Plumptre's prose. In any case, whatever the reasons, Plumptre's translations were never performed. Nevertheless, Plumptre's revisionist authorship played an important, vicarious role in the dramatic production of Drury Lane's *Pizarro* (May 1799) starring John Philip Kemble as Rolla, the Peruvian hero, and Sarah Siddons as Elvira, the mistress of Pizarro, the Spanish invader.

Anne Plumptre was not the only British translator of Kotzebue who never saw one of her translations performed in her own name. Almost overnight, a miniature cultural industry had sprung up among literary men and women, including Thomas Dutton, 'Monk' Lewis, Maria Geisweiler and Benjamin Thompson, to produce Kotzebue translations for an eager, almost insatiable readership. In turn, actors, managers, and other playwrights, including Elizabeth Inchbald and R. B. Sheridan, swiftly appropriated these texts as the raw narrative material for their theatrical adaptations.[29] Producing Kotzebue, both for the closet and the stage, was a fast-moving and highly competitive cultural business in late eighteenth-century London.

Plumptre was quick to recognize that a substantial market existed for English translations of Kotzebue's dramas. For the most part, her translations are exact and faithful, and for this fidelity she was warmly praised by contemporary reviewers.[30] In his study of Sheridan and Kotzebue published in 1799, for example, John Britton described Plumptre as "a young lady of distinguished merit in the literary world"; even the grudging, carping theatre critic and rival translator, Thomas Dutton, conceded that Plumptre's translations "will ever place her in the rank of a respectable writer."[31] Indeed, Plumptre's linguistic fidelity almost becomes a badge of her (virtually unquestioned) moral purpose. With the exception of the *Anti-Jacobin*'s reviewer who insinuated that both Plumptre and Sheridan were "industrious disciples" of the German "illuminati," no one ever stopped to inquire whether Plumptre's interest in Kotzebue might extend beyond the neutral concerns of a loyally dutiful female translator.[32] Under the guise of fidelity, however, translation provided Plumptre with a unique form of textual and ideological autonomy.

Pizarro's extraordinary success is usually credited to the theatrical opportunism and political acuity of R. B. Sheridan, who adapted Kotzebue's play for the Drury Lane stage.[33] Sheridan's drama was certainly remarkable for its visual spectacle and sensory magnificence (Pizarro's pavilion and the spectacular Temple of the Sun attracted special praise), for evocative and operatic music, and for the consummate performances of John Philip Kemble and Sarah Siddons in the two leading roles. Moreover, as theatre critics have been quick to point out, Sheridan craftily transformed Kotzebue's play into an eloquent piece of loyalist propaganda. In particular, Rolla's speech to the Peruvians ("THEY follow an adventurer whom they fear . . . WE serve a Monarch whom we love – a God whom we adore", II. ii. 669), came to symbolize Sheridan's adroit matching of barbarous imperial conquest to contemporary Napoleonic aggression. According to John Britton, Sheridan "has perhaps done more for the minister and government by the loyal sentiments in this play than all the pamphlets, newspapers, and Antijacobins, during the present war."[34]

Critical attitudes to Sheridan's adaptation of *Pizarro* can justly be distilled from the oft-repeated comment made by a contemporary reviewer: "The *body* may be Kotzebue's, but the SOUL is Sheridan's."[35] Above all, reviewers praised Sheridan for conferring dignity and virtue on the morally dubious figure of Elvira, Pizarro's Spanish mistress and "soldier's trull."[36] According to John Britton, for example, Sheridan "has produced a contrition in this magnanimous female, which cannot fail of pleasing the *candid Christian* (124).[37] But Sheridan's political opportunism and his genteel expurgation of Elvira, should not be allowed to obscure the role played by Anne Plumptre as the textual mediator of Kotzebue's play.

For the writing of *Pizarro*, Sheridan relied on translations of Kotzebue's play by Constantin Geisweiler (bought by Sheridan for £100), 'Monk' Lewis, and Anne Plumptre.[38] Plumptre's translation, however, was acquired by somewhat underhand means. Hearing that she had already sold the manuscript of her translation, *The*

Spaniards in Peru, to Richard Phillips, a leading radical publisher, Sheridan successfully persuaded Plumptre to delay publication for several weeks until after *Pizarro*'s opening at Drury Lane. But after this time had elapsed, Sheridan's play was still not ready, and Plumptre sent off her manuscript to the publisher. Only a few days before publication, however, Sheridan even appeared in person at Plumptre's house in order to request a further delay. At this stage, it would seem, he paid Richard Philipps a sum of money to hold back Plumptre's text (thus slyly maximizing the novelty of his production) and also extracted from the publisher a copy of Plumptre's translation.

Sheridan's acquisition of Plumptre's play serves to remind us of the absence of protection for dramatic property in late Georgian England.[39] At one level, given the substantial differences of language and dramatic organization between *The Spaniards of Peru* and *Pizarro*, this appropriation might seem to represent no more than a textual footnote in the play's evolution. But *The Spaniards of Peru* deserves recognition both as a distinctive and surprising text in its own right, and also (though this will not form a major part of my argument here) as the textual and ideological lens through which Sheridan reads and transforms Kotzebue's drama.

What we can trace in Plumptre's text, I think, is a remarkable engagement with the challenge posed by Elvira's character. In Elvira, Plumptre faced the problem of reconciling a woman Romantically infatuated with the Spanish leader (and, in other ways, a sexual opportunist, as in her overtures to Alonzo), who nonetheless becomes a living, moral protest against Pizarro's savage barbarity towards the Peruvians. In Sheridan's hands, Elvira is converted into a moral heroine: penitent, humbled, remorseful and, when she reappears in the play's final scene instructing the Spaniards that they have mistaken "the road to glory, or to power" (702), almost majestic.[40] Plumptre, by contrast, retains rather than excises the confusions and contradictions inherent in Elvira's character: her worship of heroes, her ironic, sometimes cynical perspective on the world, her injured, bitter, vengeful fury. Indeed, what seems to interest Plumptre about Elvira is the idea of a woman not "cast in a common mould" whose love, in one of the memorable phrases Plumptre bestows on Elvira, is "not of that tame and sequestered kind" (IV.iv.67). Elvira's language, too, subtly evokes the emerging, inchoate identity of a woman striving to articulate some form of public place in the world: "'Tis the province of our sex alone, to form heroes," she declares (i.ii.12). Moreover, at several moments in the drama, Plumptre's translation seeks to define what kind of role in political life might be envisaged for a woman. As Elvira boldly suggests, "Who can venture to defy tyrants with equal boldness, as woman?" (iv.iv.66).

Though in many ways acted upon rather than acting in her own drama, what is striking about Plumptre's Elvira is her skill in rationally articulating arguments and feelings. Elvira's language is eloquent, balanced, and antithetical, notably in iii.vii, when she embarks on a finely honed argument with Pizarro about why he should pardon rather than torture Alonzo.[41] Just as in Kotzebue's play, though not in Sheridan's production,[42] Elvira would have been seen by the audience, or imagined by the reader, as a woman dressed "in man's apparel," so Plumptre replicates this appearance of a doubled gender by endowing Elvira with the traditionally masculine skills of rhetoric and argument. At the same time, Elvira's fluency and linguistic verve seem to arise from another insight given to her by Plumptre in which she disdains the mechanical expression of feelings "according to scholastic rule." On the contrary, Elvira declares, her soul "is not formed to endure a tedious interval between the resolution and the action" (iv.iv.67): feeling and action become in her character one sinuous movement of emotion and response. In Plumptre's translation, Elvira's language seems to represent a world divided between the need to appropriate masculine habits of rhetoric in order to persuade men of the moral justice of her own arguments, and the desire, on the other hand, to create a passionate, feminine language which transcends scholastic rule.

The condescending and sometimes downright spiteful Thomas Dutton acknowledged Plumptre to be a "veteran" translator, more faithful to Kotzebue than Lewis, though urgently in need of a few hours' "exercise" each day, "under the auspices of a writer of taste," to prepare her for a career as a translator.[43] Apart from several alleged "perversions" of Kotzebue's meaning, Dutton's major complaint about Plumptre's translation concerned her propensity for rhetorical amplification. "Miss Plumtre (*sic*) has communicated a large portion of *adventitious eloquence* to this speech," Dutton remarked disdainfully of Elvira's final words in iv.xii, "which in the original chiefly recommends itself by its beautiful, yet energetic, conciseness."[44] In the eyes of Thomas Dutton, this florid elegance was

dangerous precisely because it implicitly licensed the interpretation
of Elvira as articulate heroine rather than merely as wronged,
immoral woman.

For the *Anti-Jacobin*'s critic, Elvira represented "one of the most
reprehensible characters . . . ever suffered to disgrace the stage."
Elvira, declared the writer, "is nothing more than a Godwinite
heroine, start-staring Mary all over; for, she loves not Pizarro from
principle."[45] Only Dutton, however, actually insinuated that Anne
Plumptre's translation might have been designed so as to enhance
our sympathy for Elvira. In certain ways, Sheridan's adaptation
completes the process inaugurated by Kotzebue, and developed by
Plumptre, of transforming Elvira into a character who might "excite
both compassion and admiration."[46] At the same time, however,
Sheridan seems to have identifed and rejected the rational, skeptical
Elvira created in Plumptre's translation in favor of a less various and
less contradictory character.

III

Anne Plumptre's theatrical authorship disappeared, unobserved and
unacknowledged, into plays such as Sheridan's *Pizarro*. Though
reviewers praised her linguistic fidelity to Kotzebue's texts,
Plumptre's subtle and also polemical amplification of Elvira represents a series of evocative variations on the original. Writing as if in
the margins of her source, Plumptre conducts a quiet but persuasive
vindication of Kotzebue's most notorious female character. In
Inchbald's dramatic writing, by contrast, the questions raised by
translation about ownership, subjectivity, and identity seem to be
articulated within the plays' very discursive structures. Fears about
plunder and thoughts about self-abnegation appear to provide
corporeal analogies for the thefts and self-slaughters entailed by
female translation.

Translation for Inchbald, I want to argue, entailed a set of
ideological dichotomies – between constraint and freedom; imprisonment and liberation, ownership and borrowed property – which
are then reimagined in the iconography and in the language of her
own plays. In *Next Door Neighbours* and *The Wise Man* in particular,
Inchbald's metamorphosis of her source texts incorporates what
seems to be a parallel theatrical and ideological discourse about
plunder and robbery, especially robbery of the self, and about

forgetting as an act of self-evaporation which, at its most intense, takes the form of suicide. Inchbald's characters wrestle with issues which lie at the heart of translation: Where does the authority of the original end, and self begin? What is myself? How do we belong to one another? For Inchbald, however, such questions are not limited to the puzzling shared ownership that translation confers. Rather, these questions help to map a set of preoccupations about the nature of human identity, especially feminine identity. For in her dramaturgical negotiations with her source texts, as in her plays as a whole, Inchbald returns again and again to the ways in which human beings are subjected, whether in biological relations (to parents), in legal ones (as wives to husbands) and, on a broader canvas, within political states.

That the equivocation of authorship entailed by translation interested and perplexed Inchbald would tend to be confirmed by what would seem to be her publication methods. In 1787, for example, *The Distressed Family*, an anonymous literal translation of Mercier's play, *L'Indigent*, appeared.[47] An editorial note indicates that the translator is female,[48] and the play's diction is strongly reminiscent of Inchbald's playwriting; four years later, of course, Mercier's drama would become one of the source plays for Inchbald's dark comedy, *Next Door Neighbours*. Then, in 1799, apparently at the same time that Inchbald published *The Wise Man of the East*, Robinson brought out an anonymous literal translation of *Das Schreibepult*, entitled *The Writing Desk; or, Youth in Danger*. In this case, however, circumstantial evidence would suggest that the translation had been made by Thomas Holcroft.[49]

The existence of at least one anonymous translation possibly undertaken by Inchbald suggests that the playwright may have been closeting her own authorship. Was Inchbald experimenting with the process of translation as a rehearsal for her own theatrical adaptations, as a test of her own dramatic agency? What are the limits of the theatrical self as translator? she might have been wondering. To what extent might the activity of disguising oneself within another's authorship – borrowing an alien set of theatrical clothes – actually permit a form of dramatic liberty?

What are the limits of translation? Where does the self of the female adapter become mere passive obedience to the male original, or self disappear into self-slaughter? What is so arresting about both *Next Door Neighbours* and *The Wise Man* is the way in which Inchbald endangers rather than expurgates her source texts. Suicide is one extreme form of jeopardy – absent from Inchbald's source texts – which lurks in the corners of both these plays, a haunting desire for death shared by Ellen, by Henry, and even by the now remorseful Claransforth. Indeed, suicide seems to have been built into the fabric of Inchbald's translations.

In *Next Door Neighbours*, Henry's thoughts of suicide arise as the terrible, logical conclusion of necessity. Interestingly, the major variations between the licensing manuscript and the printed text of the play concern Bluntly's allusions to necessity, and the plunder, initiated by the rich and allegedly colluded in by juries, of female virtue.[50] Sitting up late in their cold apartment, which (as the stage direction reads) "denotes the Poverty of the Inhabitants," Henry and Eleanor are too sorrowful to sleep and uncomfortably distracted, too, by the noise of pleasure and bustle at Sir George Splendorville's house next door. The scene echoes plangently with Harry's oblique references to his own despair. "When I am urged through impatience, to take away my own life," he tells Eleanor, "your lingering death . . . shall check the horrid suggestion, and I will live for you" (1.ii.13). Later, this fear seems to return in Henry's conversation with Eleanor about his feelings for her and for her father: "do not fear that I shall forget either him or you, though I might possibly forget myself" (1.ii.14). Similarly, in the scene where Eleanor draws a gun on Sir George Splendorville in her own self-defense, Inchbald offers her audience another glimpse, though swiftly swept away, of a character's potentially irrevocable self-abandonment. "No, it's not *myself* I'll kill – 'Tis you" (11.i.36).

The language of suicide is represented by Inchbald as a form of forgetting, a frightening disintegration of subjectivity. By contrast, in *Such Things Are* (Covent Garden, 1787), Inchbald represented forgetting as a form of political complicity. In the state of Sumatra, the selective amnesia of characters such as Lord Flint makes possible the survival of an arbitrary and unjust state where prisoners languish without trial and where summary executions can be carried out without opposition. Within the dramaturgy of *Next Door Neighbours*, a submerged discourse of robbery and abduction keeps rising to the play's textual surface. "Are you afraid of being stolen yourself?," Blackman asks Eleanor in the scene where he comes to demand the rent from her (1.ii.15). The plundering not of goods, but of other people's identity and subjectivity, pervades the play.

Though at some level commensurate with the conventional attributes of a sentimental heroine, Ellen's attempted suicide in *The Wise Man* is one of Inchbald's most audacious acts of theatrical jeopardy. Ellen's suicide imagines, albeit to redeem, a tragic ending beyond the boundaries of sentimental comedy, beyond the theatrical redemption of an all-consuming benevolence, and beyond, in particular, any last-minute moral conversion on the part of the sentimental hero. Ellen's gestural responses to the Wise Man, through which she signals (but does not explicitly voice) her willingness to marry Claransforth, apparently underline the plot's final conformity to a sentimental model. Yet Inchbald conspicuously denies her audience the knowledge or certainty of Ellen's forgiveness. That the Wise Man is also Claransforth's father[51] (a man whose parting letter to his son expressed the desire that Claransforth would take Ellen as his wife) seems only to deepen Ellen's isolation, to enhance the complicity of father and son in their stage-managing of a Romantic ending which sweeps away Claransforth's guilt and suppresses rather than acknowledges the pain implied by Ellen's desperate act of self-abnegation. As so often in Inchbald, the conventions of sentimental comedy acquire an uncomfortable, threatening edge.

In the prefaces she published to her own plays within *The British Theatre* (1806–08), Inchbald criticizes her own ironic and satirical treatment of sentimental plots and conventions. As editor, therefore, Inchbald portrays as improbable the systemic political repression depicted in her own play, *Such Things Are* (1788), representing the play's "hazardous" subject-matter as the work of a mere theatrical ingénue, "just admitted to the honours of an authoress" and lacking experience to "behold her own danger."[52] Her verdict on *Wives as they Were* (1797) seems still more deeply ironic:

The writer of this drama seems to have had a tolerable good notion of that which a play ought to be; but has here failed in the execution of a proper design.

Here are both fable and characters to constitute a good comedy; but incidents, the very essence of a dramatic work, are at times wanting, at other times ineffectual.

The first act promises a genuine comedy; and the authoress appears to have yielded up her own hopes with reluctance. In the dearth of true comic invention, she has had recourse at the end of her second act, to farce; though she certainly knew, that the natural, and the extravagant, always unite so ill, that in the combination, the one is sure to become insipid, or the other revolting.

Aware of this consequence, and wanting humour to proceed in the beaten track of burlesque, she then essays successively, the serious, the pathetic, and the refined comic; failing by turns in them all, though by turns producing chance effect; but without accomplishing evident intentions, or gratifying certain expectations indiscreetly raised.[53]

The authorial voice here seems to veer precariously between critical detachment and private self-interest, between prosecution and defense. It is almost as if, in these prefaces, the playwright transforms herself into the translator of her own dramatic work. In this respect, Inchbald's prefaces constitute a definitive act of self-censorship, a retrospective campaign to suppress her theatrical experiments and to deny her own radical dramaturgy.

The anonymous Prologue to *The Wise Man* requests the audience's blessing for this "German offspring" / "And begs to answer only for it's dressing." We should not be deluded by these tropes – or smoke-screens – of feminine authorial modesty. Through translation, Inchbald acquires plots and moral outcomes which she can simultaneously possess and disavow, reform and transgress, expurgate and jeopardize. Translation seems to have made possible for Inchbald a special kind of cultural identity – an identity conferred by passing through the body and text of the original play, of working self-consciously with materials not belonging to her.

The ideological slipperiness which translation makes possible for Inchbald did not pass entirely unnoticed. On the contrary, Dutton's poetical satire repeatedly calls attention to feminine "dressing" as strategic, artful (and, by implication, radical) disguise: "Think'st thou beneath this flimsy, thin disguise / To veil thy sophistry from searching eyes?" (*Apparition* 71). As we glimpsed in his earlier criticism of Plumptre, Dutton suspects in female translation a quintessential form of feminine deceit, a protean form of agency and political purpose which cannot be definitively identified. Hence the imagery underpinning *The Apparition of Zoroaster*, in which Inchbald is repeatedly characterized as the "obstetric dame."[54] Anti-Jacobin fulminations against German drama had already given ideological currency to a rhetoric of bastardy and miscegenation. By deploying the language of obstetrics against Inchbald, Dutton draws attention to the peculiar monstrosity of feminine translation, the guile within the "grand alexipharmic and magic filtering-stone" of Inchbald's mind.[55]

What Dutton half identifies in *The Apparition* is the political capaciousness of translation whereby Inchbald, like Plumptre, dissolves her own authorship into that of Kotzebue. As I have suggested, Inchbald imports into her translations a recurring preoccupation with the manipulation, coercion, and subordination of women by men. Yet the ideological impasse which translating *The Wise Man* produced, not to mention the play's turbulent life in the theatre, brought to a close Inchbald's career as a translator. Nevertheless, in her two subsequent plays, *A Case of Conscience* ([1833] not performed or published during the playwright's lifetime) and *To Marry or not to Marry* (Covent Garden, 1805), that theme of persecution which had lurked in the shadows of her adaptations escaped into open theatrical view.

"How, Mr. Bronzely, did you suppose she and I were two?" So asks Lord Priory, the patriarchal husband in Inchbald's disturbing comedy, *Wives as they Were*. The hapless Lady Priory has promised the rake Bronzely to reveal to no one the conversation he proposes to have with her (a conversation whose projected end, Bronzely calculates, will be Lady Priory's seduction):

BRONZELY: I charged you to keep what I had to tell you a profound secret.
LADY P: Yes; but I thought you understood I could have no secrets from my husband.
BRONZELY: You promised no one should know it but yourself.
LADY P: He is myself.
LORD P: How, Mr. Bronzely, did you suppose she and I were two?

The frivolous, irresponsible Miss Dorrillon in *Wives as they Were*[56] (whose character closely resembles that of Miss Milner in Inchbald's novel, *A Simple Story*) exemplifies the dangers of an improper education. Lady Priory, however, a woman deprived by her husband of sleep, company, and entertainment, a woman who seems entirely complicit in, and even at ease with, her husband's tyranny, provides a bizarre and disconcerting twist to this familiar contemporary subject of female education. Whilst Miss Dorrillon has to be rescued from a debtors' prison, Lady Priory not only survives abduction with her virtue intact, but also remains so calmly resolute that she actually strikes fear and shame into her seducer (v.i). Yet Lady Priory's calmness, as Inchbald underlines, arises from a rational, almost cynical, calculation. As she timidly explains to Bronzely, "your sex, in respect of us, are all tyrants. I was born to be the slave of one of you – I make the choice to obey my husband" (IV.ii. 51).

What is so disturbing about Lady Priory is her pragmatic decision to cooperate in her own slavery. During the final scene, however, for a single moment, Inchbald seems to hold out to her audience the possibility that Lord Priory's slave-driving will actually disintegrate. When Lord Priory demands to know whether his wife returns to him "with the self-same affection and respect, and the self-same contempt for this man – [To Bronzely] – you ever had," a short pause ensues:

LADY RAFFLE: She makes no answer.
LORD PRIORY: Hush! hush! She is going to speak. – [Another Pause.] – Why, why don't you speak?
LADY PRIORY: Because I am at a loss what to say.
LADY RAFFLE: Hear, hear, hear – do you all hear? (v.iv.76)

As in *The Wise Man*, a crisis in Inchbald's dramaturgy is hidden within a woman's silence; Thomas Dutton's shocked antipathy to the teasing scene in *The Spaniards of Peru* (omitted from Sheridan's production), in which Elvira refuses to leave Pizarro's council, declaring that she will remain occupied in silent thought, offers a telling parallel of the implicit threat posed by feminine silence.[57] Lord Priory (who has permitted his wife's abduction in order to prove her obedience) demands an answer from his wife commensurate with his absolute control over this "little domestic state," whilst Lady Mary Raffle, Miss Dorrillon's equally irresponsible and dilatory friend, clearly hopes for the downfall of Lord Priory's "management." Inchbald cleverly manipulates the scene to prolong first Lady Priory's silence, and then her equivocations, until finally she acknowledges that the only emotion she feels toward Bronzely is gratitude that he should so quickly have restored her to her husband.

For Lord Priory, of course, the episode serves only to prove his own system of wifely management; with one notable exception, spectators and reviewers concurred, perceiving the Priorys's theatrical marriage as a lost ideal, a celebration of the proper sphere of women.[58] Yet what is important about this concluding scene, surely, is the way in which the audience is invited, albeit momentarily, to imagine the collapse of patriarchal tyranny, immediately followed by the hollow, ironic triumph of Lord Priory's marital slave state.

Lady Priory's unexpected definition of "myself" as a self that includes two persons encodes a recurring problem of defining feminine identity, in marriage as well as in dramatic authorship, which Inchbald uses translation, and the equivocal identity that the process confers, to explore. Those questions of ownership, property, and subjectivity entailed by the activity of translation seem to pass here into the political unconscious of Inchbald's playwriting. Whereas Plumptre's experiments in translation are limited to the definition and justification of female character, Inchbald uses translation as a medium through which to conduct radical experiments into the limits of sentimental comedy. Whereas Plumptre's translations represent a series of polemical variations on the original text, Inchbald's plays seem to jeopardize, and even to disavow, their origins. In both cases, the practice of dramatic translation becomes inextricable from the dramatization of female identity.[59]

NOTES

Acknowledgements: An earlier version of this chapter was given at the symposium, Women in the Theater 1700–1850, hosted by the UCLA Center for 17th- and 18th-Century Studies at the Clark Library in May 1998. I should like to thank Professors Anne Mellor, Kathryn Norberg, and William Weber for their kind invitation to participate in this symposium, and also to acknowledge the great pleasure of sharing a workshop with Julie Carlson and Catherine Burroughs.

1 Rowe's play is derived from Thomas Southerne's *The Fatal Marriage: or The Innocent Adultery*, first performed in 1694 and itself based on Aphra Behn's novel, *The History of the Nun; or, The Perjur'd Beauty* (1688).
2 *The Wise Man of the East*, Larpent MS 1271, Act IV scene iv. The pages of the manuscript are unnumbered; subsequent references are given by scene within the text.
3 *The Wise Man of the East* from *The Plays of Elizabeth Inchbald*, ed. Paula R. Backscheider, 2 vols., in *Eighteenth Century English Drama*, general editor Paula Backscheider (New York: Garland, 1980).
4 Roger Manvell, *Elizabeth Inchbald* (Lanham, MD: University Press of America, 1987), p. 41, note 31.
5 *Morning Chronicle*, 2 December 1799.
6 See the Preface to Thomas Dutton, *The Wise Man of the East, or, The Apparition of Zoroaster, the Son of Oromases, to the Theatrical Midwife of Leicester Fields* (London: H. D. Symonds, 1800). Subsequent references will be given within the text.
7 James Boaden, *Memoirs of Mrs Inchbald*, 2 vols. (London: Richard Bentley, 1833), II, 27.
8 See *Morning Chronicle* review of the revised play, 3 December 1799, and, for continuing doubts, the paper's review for 4 December 1799.

9 Compare the scene in Kotzebue's play, *Das Opfertod*, in which the father of a starving family tries to commit suicide but is rescued. Inchbald would have known this drama through Henry Neuman's translation, *Family Distress; or Self Immolation* (London: R. Phillips, 1799). Neuman's play was performed four times at the Haymarket in June 1799 before being abandoned.

10 *True Briton*, 30 January 1793.

11 *Next Door Neighbours* in Backscheider, ed., *The Plays of Elizabeth Inchbald*, Prologue.

12 One of the most famous of these would be the playwright Hannah More whose *Strictures on the Modern System of Female Education*, first published 1799, 2 vols. (London: Cadell, 1826) became a definitive text of feminine moral reform. For More's animadversions on German drama, see 1, 39–45. On the reform of manners, and the history of moral censorship, see further M. J. D. Roberts, "The Society for the Suppression of Vice and its Early Critics, 1802–1812," *Historical Journal* 26, no. 1 (1983), 159–76; Donald Thomas, *A Long Time Burning: The History of Literary Censorship in England* (London: Routledge, 1969), chapter 8; and especially Joanna Innes, "Politics and Morals: The Reformation of Manners Movement in Late Eighteenth-Century England" in *The Transformation of Political Culture: England and Germany in the Late Eighteenth Century*, ed. Eckhart Hellmuth (London: German Historical Institute and Oxford University Press, 1990), pp. 57–118.

13 See Inchbald's reference to herself as a "female writer," and the uneasy diffidence of her first-person account ("I could trouble my reader . . . I could explain . . . I could inform . . . why I was compelled") in *The British Theatre . . . with Biographical and Critical Remarks, by Mrs Inchbald*, 25 vols. (London: Longman, Hurst, Rees, 1808), vol. XXIII. Catherine Burroughs makes an important argument about Inchbald's distinction between stage and closet in *Closet Stages: Joanna Baillie and the Theater Theory of British Romantic Women Writers* (Philadelphia, University of Pennsylvania Press, 1997), especially pp. 7–8.

14 *Meschenhass und Reue*, trans. Benjamin Thompson and adapted by R. B. Sheridan. See *The German Theatre*, 6 vols. (London, 1801), vol. I.

15 *Anti-Jacobin* 4 (September 1799), 105; 3 (August 1799), 439.

16 See *Morning Chronicle*, 26 March 1798. In his *Life of Mrs Siddons*, 2 vols. (London: Effingham Wilson, 1834), II, 224–25, Thomas Campbell describes Siddons's performance as "the most delicate and judicious that can be imagined." For the moral strictures of other critics, see Roger Manvell, *Sarah Siddons: Portrait of an Actress* (London: Heinemann, 1970), p. 204. Siddons also played Adelaide in *Adelaide of Wulfingen*, Thompson's adaptation of Kotzebue's play, *Adelaide of Wulfingen*, later collected in *The German Theatre*, vol. IV.

17 Richard B. Sheridan, *Pizarro* in *The Dramatic Works of Richard Brinsley Sheridan*, ed. Cecil Price 2 vols. (Oxford: Clarendon, 1973), vol. II, Act V,

scene iii, 702; Anne Plumptre, *The Spaniards in Peru; or, The Death of Rolla* (Dublin: J. Moore, 1799), Act IV, scene xii, 83. Subsequent references will be given within the text.

18 Holcroft's diary entry for 11 October 1798. See William Hazlitt, *Memoirs of the late Thomas Holcroft* in *The Complete Works of William Hazlitt*, ed. P. P. Howe, 21 vols. (London: J. M. Dent, 1930–34), III, 196.

19 See *Memoirs of the Late Thomas Holcroft*, 196. This unidentified play may be the anonymous translation of *Das Schreibepult*, discussed above. Other adaptations by Holcroft include his comedy, *The School for Arrogance* (Covent Garden, 1791), based on Destouches' play, *Le Glorieux*.

20 Inchbald's *Lovers' Vows* is based on a play given to her by Henry Harris. This play may have been the work of an unknown French translator (see Anne Plumptre's preface to *The Natural Son*) or even the literal translation made by S[tephen] P[orter], *Lovers's Vows; or, The Child of Love*, published in 1798.

21 E. Tangye Lean's study, *The Napoleonists: A Study in Political Disaffection, 1760–1960* (Oxford University Press, 1970), includes a chapter on Elizabeth Inchbald. On the Napoleonic sympathies of Anne Plumptre, see *Diary, Reminiscences and Correspondence of Henry Crabb Robinson*, ed. Thomas Sadler (London: Macmillan, 1869), 3 vols., I, 298–308, and Plumptre's *Narrative of a Three Years' Residence in France*, 3 vols. (London: J. Mawman, 1810), discussed below.

22 Maria Geisweiler, *The Noble Lie* (London: C. Geisweiler, 1799); *Poverty and Nobleness of Mind* (London: C. Geisweiler, 1799).

23 *The Morning Chronicle*'s critic declared, 31 May 1798, "The Democratic points of this heavy play were mostly cut out, but the tendency remains." See further C. A. Willoughby, "English Translations and Adaptations of Schiller's *Robbers*," *Modern Language Review* 16 (1921), 297–315. Sybil Rosenfeld discusses the performances at Brandenburgh House in *Temples of Thespis: Some Private Theatres and Theatricals in England and Wales, 1700–1820* (London: Society for Theatre Research, 1978), chapter 4.

24 *The Robbers* (London: H. Wigstead & M. Hooper, 1799).

25 Plumptre translated J. C. A Musaeus's *Physiognomical Travels* (1800) and F. C. Pouqueville's *Travels in the Morea* (1813). Her novels include *The Rector's Son* (1798) and *The History of Myself and a Friend* (1817).

26 See also *The Force of Calumny* (1799), *La-Peyrouse* (1799) and *The Widow and the Riding Horse* (1799).

27 *The Natural Son* being the original of *Lovers' Vows* (Dublin: H. Fitzpatrick, 1798). The Preface "Explaining the Alterations in the Representation" is dated 15 October 1798, vi.

28 Ellen Donkin's groundbreaking study, *Getting into the Act: Women Playwrights in London 1776–1829* (London: Routledge, 1995) discusses these questions in detail and devotes a chapter to Elizabeth Inchbald.

29 The first London production of a Kotzebue play was Sheridan's
adaptation of *The Stranger*, based on Thompson's translation and
performed at Drury Lane in April 1798. Sheridan's text is not extant.
The actor Alexander Pope made an adaptation of *The Count of Burgundy*
(Covent Garden, April 1799) which was based on Anne Plumptre's
translation. John Fawcett's pantomime, *Pérouse; or, The Desolate Island*
(Covent Garden, 1801) must have been based either on Thompson's
version or Plumptre's, both of which were published in 1799, though
here the relationship between translation and adaptation is much more
tenuous. In 1801, the Examiner of Plays seems to have banned the
performance of a drama based on Plumptre's *La-Peyrouse*. Perouse's two
wives, the Examiner may have concluded, could be seen as a theatrical
allusion to what many considered the Prince of Wales's bigamous
second marriage to Princess Caroline of Brunswick. The Prince had
secretly married Maria Fitzherbert in 1785, but since the marriage of
royalty under twenty-five years of age was illegal, the Prince was
technically free to marry again in 1795. See further, Leonard Conolly,
The Censorship of English Drama 1737–1824 (San Marino, CA: The
Huntington Library, 1976), pp. 127–28.
30 See letter to editor of the *Monthly Magazine* (February 1799), 105–07,
signed "T.S.N," which praises the fidelity of Plumptre and Shinck's
translations whilst criticizing Inchbald's adaptation of *Lovers' Vows* (with
its "very vain and pert preface") and Sheridan's "harlot embellish-
ments" to *The Stranger*. Cf. the subsequent letter, published in the
Monthly Magazine in July 1799, pp. 427–28, from "A.D." of the Inner
Temple, which similarly rebukes Sheridan's "reprehensible liberties" in
his adaptation of *Pizarro* and praises Neuman's "faithful" translation,
Family Distress.
31 [John Britton], *Sheridan and Kotzebue* (London: J. Fairburn, 1799), p. 69;
Dutton, *Pizarro in Peru, or the Death of Rolla* (London: W. West, [1799]),
[17].
32 See Britton, *Sheridan*, 127. The most plausible explanation for this
selective blindness can be found in the self-congratulatory discourse of
English character through which critics persistently interpreted the
translation of Kotzebue. See, for example, the comments of a *Times*
reviewer (6 February 1815) on the character of Adelaide Haller in *The
Stranger*: "The German boldly took the plunge, and made her an
adulteress; the translator, consulting that surviving rectitude of the
English character, which puts such a criminal beyond pity or hope,
diminished her culpability into a simple flight, issuing in an immediate
return."
33 On the politics of Sheridan's adaptation, see Julie Carlson's deftly
woven argument, "Trying Sheridan's *Pizarro*," *Texas Studies in Literature
and Language* 38 no. 3 & 4 (1996), 359–78.
34 Britton, *Sheridan*, 142. Compare *The Political Proteus*, chapter 4, in which

William Cobbett attacked Sheridan's political volte-face in *Pizarro* (and the "impudent" puffs published by the manager to encourage patriotic enthusiasm at Drury Lane theatre) and mocked Rolla's speech as "decked off with all the airs of typographical harlotry," 80.

35 Bisset's review, *Historical Magazine* (June 1799), cited Britton, *Sheridan*, 31. Cecil Price's introduction to *Pizarro* in *The Dramatic Works of Richard Brinsley Sheridan*, 2 vols (Oxford: Clarendon, 1973), II, 640–50, provides a detailed and comprehensive account of the textual questions surrounding the play as well as an invaluable collection of contemporary reviews.

36 *The Life and Times of Frederic Reynolds*, cited Price, *Pizarro*, 640.

37 See also Britton, *Sheridan*, 133; Dutton, *Pizarro in Peru*, 9. Most contemporary reviews either proceeded on the mistaken assumption that Sheridan had been working directly from Kotzebue (see *Monthly Mirror* review, cited Price, 626), or emphasized rather the originality of Sheridan's adaptation in language and characterization. See the reviews collected in Price, *Pizarro*, notably *Bell's Weekly Messenger* and the *Morning Herald*, 11 May 1799. Compare, however, Thomas Moore's account ("Mr. Sheridan's responsibility for the defects of *Pizarro* is not very much greater than his claim to a share in its merits"), cited Price, *Pizarro*, 638.

38 See report in the *New Monthly Magazine* (1816), cited Price, *Pizarro*, 641. On "Monk" Lewis's unhappiness about Sheridan's failure to acknowledge his own translation as a source, see *Medwin's Conversations of Lord Byron*, ed. E. J. Lovell, Jr. (Princeton University Press, 1966), 191.

39 The Drury Lane records state that Plumptre received two sums of £25 for the play in May 1799. It seems likely that this money was in fact paid to Phillips rather than to Plumptre. See BM Add. MS 297109, fol. 139, cited Price, *Pizarro*, 646. Madeleine Bingham discusses the episode in *Sheridan: The Track of a Comet* (London: George Allen & Unwin, 1972), 306–07.

40 Sheridan's alterations include this unprecedented appearance of Elvira, habited as a nun, and the suppression of Elvira's love for Alonzo.

41 See the language of hypothesis ("If it be farther related") and exposition ("[l]et us now take another view of the subject") in this scene, and Elvira's use of comparison and rhetorical question.

42 See Dutton, *Pizarro in Peru*, 9.

43 *Ibid.*, 31.

44 *Ibid.*, 96.

45 For the *Anti-Jacobin*'s criticism and Britton's ripostes, see Britton, *Sheridan*, chapter 7.

46 See Kotzebue's preface, included in Plumptre's translation, v.

47 Anon., *The Distressed Family*, translated from M. le Mercier (London: C. Elliott, T. Kay & Co., 1787).

48 See note 29, referring to Charlotte's speech praising Howard's poem,

"The Triumph of Benevolence" as the only alteration "she" (i.e. the translator) has made to Mercier's text.

49 Inchbald's Advertisement for *The Wise Man* alludes conspicuously to the simultaneous publication of a literal translation. See Anon., *The Writing Desk; or, Youth in Danger. A Play in Four Acts. Literally Translated from the German of Kotzebue* (London: G. G. & J. Robinson, 1799).

50 The licensing manuscript, Larpent 912, omits several of Bluntly's speeches, and it is impossible to know whether this text represents either an earlier version of the printed text, or a text from which potentially dangerous passages, notably those evoking the radical discourse of necessity, have been deliberately omitted. Bluntly's speech, II.i.38, on the currency of female virtue, and men's plunder of that virtue "without remorse," appears only in the printed text, whilst the licensing manuscript, fol. 44, includes some lines spoken by Bluntly which do not appear in the printed version ("But you and Innocence such as her's, I was afraid were Enticements that might tempt you to play the Thief – and then I was afraid, even a jury of your Countrymen, might acquit you, and the poor Girl obtain no redress"). Bluntly's dark speech on the subject of necessity ("I have heard necessity has no law – but if it has no conscience, it is a much worse thing than I took it for," III.i.54) appears only in the printed text.

51 The hidden observation of the son by the father is a favorite sentimental trope, familiar to audiences from stock plays like Richard Cumberland's *The West Indian* (Drury Lane, 1771), whose rake figure may well have influenced Inchbald, and, more recently, Sheridan's *The School for Scandal* (1777).

52 Inchbald, Remarks, *The British Theatre*.

53 *Ibid.*

54 Dutton, *Apparition*, preface. Obstetric images pervade Dutton's satire, e.g. pp. 40, 42.

55 *Apparition*, note, 35.

56 See Inchbald, Remarks, *The British Theatre*.

57 *The Spaniards in Peru*, I.iii.16. Dutton, *Pizarro in Peru*, 20, describes the passage, which is taken directly from the German, as "this wretched attempt at wit and humour."

58 For favorable reviews, see *Analytical Review* 25 (1797), 602, and especially *True Briton* (6 March 1797), which remarks that the wife, "by a proper submission to her husband, and a due observance of domestic duties, is respectable and easy; while the modest fair, though in the bloom of life, is reduced, by extravagance, to poverty and a prison." For one reviewer's anxiety about "the doctrine of passive obedience," see *Morning Chronicle*, 5 March 1797.

59 On the history of women as translators, see Mirella Agorni's essay, "The Voice of the 'Translatress': From Aphra Behn to Elizabeth Carter," *Yearbook of English Studies* 28 (1998), 181–195.

Remaking love: remorse in the theatre of Baillie and Inchbald

Julie A. Carlson

This chapter welcomes female playwrights into the Romantic theatre of remorse. It analyzes plays on remorse written by Joanna Baillie (*Henriquez* [1836]) and Elizabeth Inchbald (*A Case of Conscience* [composed 1800; published 1833]) and their efforts to display more rational forms of love and female beauty on stage. In so doing, it means to revise the gender one-sidedness of the authors considered in my *In the Theatre of Romanticism* (1994) and to pursue questions regarding how theatre achieves radical cultural reform in their day and ours.[1] The book emphasizes the centrality of theatre to English reactions to the revolution in France and of remorse to the theatrical projects of the canonical poets by characterizing their plays as efforts to display Godwinian reason as damaging to national and mental health. Plays distance themselves from the impending anarchy of the independent intellect and the mechanization of mind that comprises its necessity, and thus its heartlessness, as they work to reform social conditions by restaging mind. Especially, they stage the potential of the mind's modes of potentiality (imagination, illusion, dream) to disrupt, divert, or invalidate rational action. To a significant extent, this project of reforming mind accounts for familiar claims regarding the period's hostility to theatre and the correlative view that Romantic plays were written for the closet, not the stage.[2] The book argues instead that these poets invest in theatre to promote a vision of the spectacular insufficiency of action to powers of mind.

Coleridge's *Remorse* (1813), the book goes on to argue, exemplifies these paradoxical efforts to reform mind through the embrace of the illusion of theatre. As a play whose espoused morality and privileged interiority turn on sensational display (conjuring scenes, disguises, props of identity), *Remorse* displays the performative and transformative powers of remorse. Its trial run, *Osorio*, and brotherly rival, Wordsworth's *The Borderers* (both of 1797), have long been read as engagements with Godwin that express these poets' growing reservations over reason's capacity to achieve positive change. Its success on stage as the minimally revised *Remorse* confirms the possibilities of making a spectacle of remorse. To his delight, Coleridge discovers that the display of remorseful feelings turns him into an overnight sensation at the same time as it amends the record of his radical youth.[3] This revisionary strategy proves attractive to a generation of young men whose reflections on prior Jacobin activity are anguished, conflicted. It also voices paradoxical feelings about feeling: about one's insufficient feelings for feeling during the heyday of allegiance to reason; over one's juvenile bliss at approaching human nature from its golden side. More fundamentally, it destabilizes sources of feeling by complicating the interiority of the site and sight of remorse. Offered as the moral antidote to revenge, remorse in *Remorse* is a more blood-thirsty, self-satisfied, and self-aggrandizing form of revenge. In the case of one's foes, remorse leaves the vengeance to others and thus demonstrates the moral exemplarity of the protagonist's wise passivity. Arising within oneself, it keeps one in touch with prior radical energies while staging the *integrity* of one's mind.

The salience of remorse in the canonical poets' plays on mind and plays for sympathy had strikingly negative consequences for their treatments of women in and as theatre. The book claims that whether as characters in plays or as analogues of theatre in their alleged immanence, hyperactivity, commodified sexuality, or assault on possessive individualism, the same feature of "woman" is foregrounded: mindlessness. Within the plays, women themselves take action rather than persuading or goading their menfolk into action. But either they act without thinking (Maria, Theresa, Matilda, Thekla, Alhadra) or lose their minds as a consequence of acting (Beatrice Cenci). Virtuous female characters often do not act at all, but they are unconscious of the grounds of their virtue. Unlike their male counterparts, their nature is unconflicted but consequently unavailable to poetry. Even these virtuous heroines, however, accentuate the limits to the mind's comfort with theatre's mode of representation. As objects of vision, especially if they body forth passivity, female characters arouse mobile and aggressive fantasies from which spectators ultimately seek relief in comforts of the closet. "Woman" in and as theatre, then, assumes the weight of poets' attempts to dramatize remorse over revolutionary activity. By displacing action on to female characters or rendering female virtue intuitive and inarticulate, Romantic theatre accords space and sympathy only to male conflicts of mind.

Romantic drama's success at attaining sympathy for mental conflict plays an important role in theatricalizing self-division before psychoanalysis develops a language for analyzing it, but it plays a misogynist hand in its attempts to exclude female character from complexity and sympathy. Such is the basic tenet of *In the Theatre of Romanticism*, which this chapter's focus on the theatrical careers of Baillie and Inchbald both supports and challenges. For the book's exclusive engagement with the dramas of men gives rise to two regrettable consequences that in effect perpetuate the "Romanticism" that its analysis of remorse was intended to undo. It ignores the best and most prolific playwright of the age, Joanna Baillie, and implies that women writers underwent less passionate or protracted reflections on the radical activity of their youth. Clear differences in the range and scenes of action for men and women of the time do not translate into differences of intensity. Often quite the contrary, for reasons overdetermined by woman's conventional fixation on youth.

This chapter, then, situates Baillie and Inchbald in the theatre of remorse by exploring radical women's contributions to the revolution in female manners. These contributions aim to extend the sphere of radical activity beyond the issue of sexual infidelity and involve creating options for women outside of marriage and re-making love so that it accords better with reason and theatre. Such projects give rise to remorse but also differentiate female from male remorse on the score of timing. Even as they join their male compatriots of the 1790s in lamenting a fall from bliss, radical women's remorse is non-nostalgic and future-directed. For radical women encounter the two major objections to revolutionary activity voiced by Burke's *Reflections on the Revolution in France* as not simply challenging but inherently contradictory. Efforts to launch a revolution by reforming love meet their match twice, in reason and chivalry. The need to wage battle on both fronts, I hope to show, occasions the exhaustion as well as disillusionment audible in their remorse. It also highlights a crucial distinction in the reception of Godwin by radical writers, even Godwin himself, on reason's alleged antipathy to illusion and love.

Writers of the 1790s such as Inchbald, Mary Hays, Amelia

Alderson (Opie), and (until her death) Wollstonecraft stay sympathetic to both Godwin and reason longer than his male compatriots who, by 1797, have joined the general public outcry
against Godwin that dismisses both him and reason as too heart-
less and cold.[4] As writers *and* lovers – it is striking that all are
considered as potential lovers by Godwin – these women have
nothing to gain from the general cultural effort to place Godwin in
early retirement by discrediting the New Philosophy. Rather than
sanction the ensuing re-polarization of head and heart, reason and
passion that animates so many texts of the period, their writings
consistently champion female reason as one of the primary traits
of and reasons to love. Wollstonecraft's novels characterize as
"voluptuous" intellectual exchanges between men and women, and
her *The Wrongs of Woman, or Maria* (1798) vindicates the right of
women to pursue textual as sexual intercourse. Hays's *Memoirs of
Emma Courtney* (1796) makes even bolder rationalist claims for
women's future in contending that love *will* reward the demonstration of one's desirability, if the heroine makes her case
consistently and persistently enough.

There is no denying the melancholy and blockage that characterize these projects or their authors and that occasion the problematic influence of Wollstonecraft on feminist daughters.[5] Nor should
one deny the insufficiencies of their rationalist project by continuing
to make love in this spirit. Still, analysis of their accounts of
melancholy's deadening effects uncovers some promising directions
for considering time in its relation to change. Besides highlighting
the indispensability of timing, melancholy asks about the meantime
– in this case, how to live when one is living before one's time. Here
Wollstonecraft's second thoughts on the education of daughters
apply necessary pressure on the value of hope. Writing at once to
her baby daughter Fanny's father (Gilbert Imlay) and the men and
women of England, she voices the dilemma for a generation of
radical women living and loving before the emancipation of love has
arrived:

You know that as a female I am particularly attached to [my daughter] – I
feel more than a mother's fondness and anxiety, when I reflect on the
dependent and oppressed state of her sex. I dread lest she should be forced
to sacrifice her heart to her principles, or principles to her heart. With
trembling hand, I shall cultivate sensibility, and cherish delicacy of
sentiment, lest, whilst I lend fresh blushes to the rose, I sharpen the thorns

that will wound the breast I would fain guard – I dread to unfold her mind, lest it should render her unfit for the world she is to inhabit – Hapless woman! what a fate is thine![6]

Women sharpen the thorns of remorse for themselves and their female progeny in wishing to unfold female minds before the world considers intellectual women desirable. To make love more reasonable and thus more attractive for women is to forfeit one's loveability for a period of time.

This difference in the time that is mourned by male and female remorse – past or future – is reinforced by disputes over the historical period associated with illusion and love. For the project to remake love necessitates challenging not only the heartlessness of reason but its antipathy to the "pleasing illusions" of life deemed "gone" in the progress from "the age of chivalry" to enlightenment.[7] This opposition between reason and illusion is initially upheld by both sides of the revolutionary debate, as radicals of every sort meet Burke's challenge by mounting a frontal assault on illusion in the name of reason. Complicated border skirmishes ensue over revolution's status as theatre and radical attacks on the privileged sociological categories of theatre – aristocracy and women, whose alleged inauthenticity, oblivion to reality, and overinvestment in appearance make them major impediments to rational society. Initial responses to the *Reflections* voice their hostility to illusion through variously combined attacks on theatricality, aristocracy, and femininity. For example, *The Enquiry Concerning Political Justice* (1793) characterizes illusion, semblance, show as the enemy of reason and friend of aristocracy, and it rejects theatre as a form that undermines autonomy through its sanctioned repetition of prior words and states. *A Vindication of the Rights of Woman* (1792) advances the cause of women by promoting working-class over middle- and upper-class women on grounds that the former disarticulates show, illusion, beauty from standard conceptions of woman. Equally instructive about these initial oppositions is how quickly they are qualified, outgrown, amended, and yet how little the qualifications, rather than the opposition, are taken up in subsequent accounts of these writers' positions – a fact that has had long-term debilitating consequences on radical culture's recognition of illusion as a primary component of rational exchange. Subsequent texts by Godwin and Wollstonecraft, especially revised editions of the *Enquiry*, temper initial pronouncements regarding reason without thereby retracting their beliefs in perfectibility or forfeiting all claims to reason in the operations of illusion, theatre, or love. But where texts by Godwin and Wollstonecraft differ in their increasing engagement with illusion specifies a second difference in the time and timing of radical remorse. In parting company on the historical dating of illusion, they chart different paths for the sexes toward enlightened futures.

Godwin's increasing sympathy for illusion is generally ascribed to his growing receptivity to poetry, imagination, and love during the period of his intimacy with Wollstonecraft (1796–97) and Coleridge (1799).[8] It is only a slight exaggeration to characterize all the texts written between 1797 and 1805 (as well as revised editions of the *Enquiry*) as involved in proving that the New Philosopher has feelings, especially for domestic affection. This proof takes many curious forms, the most surprising of which is Godwin's increasing involvement and gradual reconciliation with chivalry. Announced in the preface and manifested in the context and content of *St. Leon* (1799), it culminates in his four-volume *Life of Chaucer* (1803) and his retraction of the grounds for his former attack on marriage. "I think, quite contrary to the vulgar maxim on the subject, that love is never love in its best spirit, but among unequals. An excellent invention of modern times, that, while woman by the nature of things must look up to man, teaches us in our turn to regard woman, not merely as a convenience to be made use of, but as a being to be treated with courtship and consideration and fealty."[9]

In contrast, Wollstonecraft's views on love from *Mary, A Fiction* (1788) on are indissociable from illusion, literature, fancy, but even after her rationalist attack on love in the *Vindication* remain inseparable from the belief that illusion forms part of the reason to love. Increasingly skeptical of the happiness or permanence to be found in love, Wollstonecraft does not recant on the reasonableness of attaining more rational bases for love, including other options besides marriage for women. In fact, considering illusion as a constituent of love is, to her, a first step toward understanding the formation as well as inevitable deformations of love. But even her extreme disheartenment in and about love never entails laments for the passing of chivalry. To retreat from enlightenment in the field of love is to lose all grounds for living. Her desire is to maintain reason within illusionary practices, including love, and to identify love with the age of reason in persons and history.

In this latter effort, she is joined by Baillie and Inchbald similarly working to reform love through illusion's most tangible form, theatre. Even granting its reputation as a debased aesthetic form, the London stage of this period offers some clear advantages for a professional reshaping of "woman." It stars women and pays women to write for it without subjecting them to the paternalizing mentorship of former managers like Garrick. It allows them to turn a quicker and larger profit than does novel-writing, and it houses and caters to more democratic audiences than other cultural-aesthetic forms.[10] The most famous actress of the period, Sarah Siddons, is celebrated for her strength of intellect, dignity, force, and the nature of her beauty is characterized as both feminine and sublime. At the same time, theatre approaches reform through its least rationalist side, being contrary to the methods and values of autonomy on virtually every score. It is a collaborative commercial enterprise, without a discernible author, originator, or director in this period, the success of whose transports necessitates suspension of judgment, the being beside oneself. These are questionable means, surely, for effecting any kind of revolution whose success depends on co-ordinating persons, means, and ends. And such means appear antipathetic to the desired revolution in female manners when that revolution entails re-forming the perception and reception of female beauty. For on this score the special timing associated with theatre reinforces precisely the feature of beauty that these writers are aiming to revise: convictions regarding its fleeting nature. Working against them from the start is the ephemerality that ostensibly constitutes the shared charm of theatre, passion, and female beauty. Part of the foresight of Baillie's and Inchbald's theatrical projects is their sustained assaults on the alleged unsustainability of female beauty *and* autonomy, in or apart from marriage, over time. That they place such novel visions of beauty on stage is a measure of their courage in conceiving both beauty and vision as receptive to change. As we will see, they characterize beauty as neither fleeting nor medieval but enlightened and associated with women's middle age. This challenge to the conventional time of beauty, in turn, challenges theatrical timing and the alleged suddenness of change. In this regard, Baillie's and Inchbald's efforts on behalf of mature beauty say some enlightening and disheartening things about performative models of change.

REASON TO LOVE

The theatrical careers of Baillie and Inchbald manifest crucial distinctions in their approaches to politics, female beauty, the stage, and effective modes of reform in metropolitan theatres. As Wordsworth's "model of an English Gentlewoman," Baillie hardly appears radical (though she is hardly "English" either).[11] Nor is she noted for beauty, delight in it, or the pleasures of sensuality more generally. Inchbald's radical credentials are more firmly established, as is her reputation as beauty, flirt, narcissist, and manipulator of men.[12] Important differences, too, characterize their engagement with theatre, the most obvious being degrees of success at having their plays staged. Only Inchbald has a working knowledge of theatre from early experiences as an actress and her ongoing attendance in the green rooms and auditoriums of several theatres. Baillie, though an active partisan of theatre, takes a more retiring approach toward the stage.[13] Her poetic style of composition as well as relative lack of success in representing her plays render her experiences closer to those of the canonical poets than to Inchbald's.

Such major differences only accentuate these writers' congruence in the theatre of remorse and the anomalous status that Baillie's *Henriquez* and Inchbald's *A Case of Conscience* assume in their respective playwriting careers. Even the nature of the anomalies instructs us about the theatre of remorse. The first implies that there is a necessary connection between remorse and tragedy, for Baillie alters her normal pattern of writing a comedy and a tragedy for each passion by composing only a tragedy for remorse, and Inchbald deviates from her preference for comedy and farce in writing a "drama" on the topic. The other underscores the special status of staging that pertains to remorse, *The Case of Conscience* being only one of two out of the twenty-one plays that Inchbald writes that never was performed and *Henriquez* being one of only four of Baillie's to make it to the London stage.[14] Inversion applies as well to the writers' political positions when treating remorse, where, in their characterizations of desirable heroines, Baillie is far more radical and rationalist than Inchbald. Yet both plays make a case for the sustainability of beauty and love within marriage and link remorse to tragic instabilities in men's capacity to distinguish illusion from delusion. And both writers censure dramatic tradition for restricting female expressions of remorse: in the first place by reducing the radical nature of female activity to illicit sexual activity and then by placing beyond sympathy not the fallen woman but the woman who refuses to depend. Both charges protest culture's investment in seeing beauty run out of time(s). If chivalry promotes regression in needing a woman to rescue, enlightened aesthetics reviles the beauty that claims autonomy for herself.

Baillie's special contribution to this question is in setting the stage for remorse more explicitly and theatrically than any other playwright of the period. Introductory discourses to her *Series of Plays on the Passions* specify *as* the moral interest of tragedy its attention to the theatricality of psychological states, training in which provides an early warning system in the detection of passion and thus the ability to curb passion before it usurps the mind. They also connect theatricality to remorse by stating that "[o]f all our passions, Remorse and Jealousy appear to me to be the best fitted for representation."[15] This stage-setting eventuates in *Henriquez*, the tragedy on remorse that culminates the series on passion in more than one sense. *Henriquez* ends the series, asserts the identity of theatre and remorse by making jealousy a component part of remorse, and stages remorse as productive of spectacle. In these ways, *Henriquez* can be said to culminate the entire Romantic theatre of remorse by leveling the strongest critique against male investments in remorse and remorse's perpetuation of chivalry. In its non-idealizing and non-degrading treatment of female beauty, I hope to show, *Henriquez* also ventures beyond the "inevitable" tragedy of remorse.

The plot of *Henriquez* is conventional, for the tragedy turns on a husband's (Henriquez) false suspicions of his wife (Leonora). Circumstantial evidence – letters, lockets, disguises – as well as Leonora's prideful and enigmatic behavior cause Henriquez to murder his best friend whom he suspects of seducing his wife but who is secretly courting his wife's exemplary younger sister, who is above reproach even on the score of pride. Henriquez discovers his error, falls into an agony of remorse from which nothing can free him except public sentence of death from the king. Predictable in plot, Baillie's treatment departs from standard prototypes in ways that accentuate the connection between spectacle and remorse. For Henriquez is remorseful by the start of the second act and spends the rest of the play literally orchestrating his remorse. An obvious counter to the last-minute reforms of villain-heroes that Coleridge indicts as espousing Jacobin morality, Baillie's treatment also revises the timing accentuated in Coleridge's *Remorse*, which focuses on the arousal, not the consequences, of remorse.[16] In contrast to Alvar's play-long efforts to "rouse remorse" in the soul of his brother, Henriquez focuses on the display of his remorse and *Henriquez* in the display that is remorse.

Henriquez clings to remorse when everyone in the play – the king, the man falsely accused, the dead man's loyal servant, his wronged wife – offers forgiveness. *Henriquez* suggests why: pageantry and honor grace the display of guilt. Henriquez's execution receives a public sentencing, an elaborate procession to the scaffold, and a sensational spectacle of death. Indeed, establishing the congruence between the shows of remorse and *Henriquez* seems to explain the insertion of prefatory remarks concerning theatre lighting into descriptions of the scene of execution.[17] The narrated effect of that scene on its spectators highlights the sensational honor in remorse and the sensations of honor sustained by it. "Never rose his form so nobly on the mind" as when Henriquez "stood arraign'd" at the bar, "Proving his secret guilt, against himself." And "when the fatal sentence was pronounced," he "seemed like some fallen seraph that again / Had won his way to bliss." "Old men did clasp their hands, and young men wept; / And those who on his victories bestowed / A cold and niggard praise, now, with full hearts, / Gave boundless tribute to his lofty virtue." Henceforth, the "very implements of execution" will be woven into the banners of "his proud house," commemorating the spectacle of honorable guilt."[18] Clearly, theatricality is essential to morality when heroism entails exposing one's secret guilt. The conventions and periods associated with honor also undergo revision when guilt appears at the head of the list.

That no woman, young or old, is shown as responding to Henriquez's display of guilt seems an intentional comment on the gender inequities that sustain remorse and a critique of Baillie's male playwriting contemporaries. In making this point, *Henriquez* qualifies the leveling tendencies that Baillie usually claims for her focus on passion, the human susceptibility to which links all manner of persons. Instead, Henriquez's expressions of remorse aim to silence Leonora, when they do not remove women altogether from the scene. Woman's forgiveness impedes male "ecstasy" by re-domesticating husbands. "To taste the slightest feeling of thy love / Were base – were monstrous now. / Follow me not. The ecstasy of misery spurns all pity" (370). Such revulsion toward Leonora persists even after Henriquez's confession otherwise restores his amiability. The night before his execution is spent entertaining everyone but his wife, whose appearance at his execution is deemed an affront. "My Leonora, wherefore art thou come? . . . thou wast my torment and my bliss, but O far more my bliss. So be content" (384). Through *this* display, Baillie highlights the modes of honor at stake in male remorse. Like medieval honor, remorse requires theatricality and spectacle, but the honor in both is a pride reserved for men.

Baillie sets many of her plays in the medieval period in order to highlight women's double-binding by enlightened forms of chivalry. Prefatory remarks to *Orra* (1812) make clear that by superimposing medieval and enlightened concerns, Baillie is interested in what contemporary audiences falsely think they have surmounted by living in a less credulous, and superstitious, age.[19] In that play, the eponymous heroine exemplifies the tragic fate for women who attempt to fashion characters that are neither idealizable nor dependent and who wish to make life choices that involve civic, not marital, service. The multiplication of suitors (two bad, one good) suggests "medieval" patriarchy's investment in marriage for women, while the scheme to force Orra into marriage by imprisoning her in a house haunted by murderous ancestors links superstition to coercion and presents both as the last resorts of men who have run out of reasons why beautiful women should marry them. Orra does not relent under this pressure, but she loses her mind. Baillie's darkest play on the reasons for marriage and the possibilities of achieving reasonable alternatives to marriage for women, *Orra* joins Baillie's less dire tragedies in specifying the trait in female character that suspends sympathy: not a capacity to fall but a refusal to depend. For women, there is no honor, whether medieval or enlightened, in pride.

The female characters that Inchbald both embodies on stage and composes for her plays are frequently fallen women or otherwise loyal and long-suffering wives. Even then, however, and certainly in written depictions of her own life, Inchbald's female characters work to align marriage with independence, and beauty and love with women's middle age. This is the case with the protagonist, Adriana, in *A Case of Conscience*, who is far more idealized than Leonora, but who embodies a similar case. A "secret subject of illegal love" is charged against Adriana by the man (Duke Cordunna) to whom

Adriana was betrothed as a girl and who has waited seventeen years
to wreak his revenge by disguising himself as a hermit in order to
offer proof to her husband, the Marquis of Romono, that their son,
Oviedo, is not his, but Cordunna's. Once again, irrefutable evidence
– letters, portraits – convinces the Duke that he has been duped,
causing him to estrange himself from his wife, oppose his son
Oviedo's engagement to Eudora, and surrender Oviedo to the
Inquisition. In contrast to *Henriquez*, tragedy is averted at the last
minute, forcing the Marquis to surrender his suspicions and his
remorse. But these differences in the outcome, though not the cause,
of remorse still point at a similar concern: how to view female
autonomy as compatible with love, beauty, and illusion and how to
sustain that view once fears arise that susceptibility to the latter traits
indicates that one has been deluded.

Such efforts to link female autonomy to love separate Baillie and
Inchbald from enlightened endorsements of chivalry but also from
pronouncements by Wollstonecraft regarding the ephemerality, and
thus illusory nature, of beauty and love. Both of Baillie's and
Inchbald's protagonists are mature beauties who have been married
happily for years and thus whose drama turns not on the arousal but
sustainability of love. Achieving this portrayal entails acknowledging
the crucial role of illusion in beauty and as the sustainer of both
beauty and love. Leonora appears in the play primarily to educate
her auditors about the true value of appearance. To advice that she
show that she knows her place by making herself small, Leonora
asserts the priority of illusion in self-formation and in others'
apprehension of self. "Away with such benumbing diffidence! / Let
buoyant fancy first bear up [one's] merit / And fortune and the
world's applause will soon / Support the freight."[20] To her, concern
with appearance is less the sign of aristocratic indifference than the
means of vivifying marital love. Delight in the trappings of honor are
the plumage *and* stuff of fidelity. "These pageantries / Give to the
even bliss of wedded love / A varied vivifying power, which else /
Might die of very sloth." Creating festival within the quotidian keeps
desire ardent, mobile, and eager for one's partner. "And for myself /
My love for him, returning from the wars, / Blazon'd with honours,
as he now returns, / Is livelier, happier, and, methinks, more ardent,
/ Than when we first were married" (365). Nor are such perceptions
visible only to female characters, whose investments in beauty's
sustainability and desire's immobility are proportional to their

unequal options. *A Case of Conscience* voices a husband's contentment in marriage over the long haul. "[F]or seventeen years after our marriage, I bore myself as a man well governing all his appetites – a happy, a *contented* man." It also ascribes the means of male contentment not to "calm lessons of philosophy" or will but to satisfactions in and from beauty.[21]

Tragedy threatens to ensue when this belief is no longer sustained because belief in the sustainability of female beauty, illusion, and love in marriage is threatened. What undermines this belief is usually some form of visual evidence that destroys the illusion; its alleged irrefutability entails the penetrating apprehension that the appearance of female fidelity cannot sustain itself once appearances are against it.[22] Judgment then intervenes to distinguish false from true seeming. Though neither play makes a case for love's constituent misrecognition, they both criticize this conflation of dramatic and amatory illusion. Judgment is not the enemy of illusion or love; to view it as such makes tragedy inevitable and sanctions the violence that attends men's perception of being duped. In its averting of tragedy, *A Case of Conscience* modifies the misogynist effects of remorse and presents reason as capable of restoring a couple's love. It also sees reason as generating love. In violating a promise, not a vow, of marriage, and one made without her consent, Adriana shows herself to be an enlightened lover and thereby absolved from guilt over her betrayal of Cordunna: "it was Virtue, not Vice, to break every promise extorted by your parents, before your judgment and experience were matured, so as to comprehend the nature of the vow you gave" (352).

Such passages are embarrassing in their heavy-handedness and, in their address to one's "better" judgment, threaten to ruin the show. Yet, even as they appeal to the reason in love, these plays are not blind to love's incommensurability with reason or to female resistance to reason in love. At the same time that they characterize delusion as the giving ground on the sustainability of illusion, they delight in the against-all-reason nature of love. Not only does erotic love seek oblivion and self-dissolution but newly emancipated women view such dissolutions as freedom. Moreover, both plays admit the rational paradoxes of choosing a partner to love. *Henriquez* names names: the man "wrongly" suspected of seducing Leonora and whom Henriquez considers his "second self" is Don Juan. *A Case of Conscience* presents as evidence for the autonomy of one's

choice a love that "seized on my heart by force" (308). Two
consequences of this recognition differentiate these authors' views on
love from those of the author of *Remorse*, though all three make love,
like successful theatre, a taking the house by storm. Baillie and
Inchbald share the fantasy but do not see the possibility of the reality
for women of what, according to Coleridge, comprises the irresist-
ibility of Don Juan: "to be so loved for one's self," that "even if I
were a criminal," another "would still die to save me."[23] Or, more
precisely, Baillie and Inchbald conceive the not-yet-possible fantasy
of women arousing love without conditions of having to marry or
fall. If being married is less of a categorical imperative for enlightened ages, falling is more of one, precisely as it retreats from
enlightenment. Suffering femininity keeps the age of chivalry alive
by giving enlightened noble men something to do. In this regard,
fallen women are not the real problem, even for a culture obsessed
with female chastity and marital fidelity in women. Women who are
uninterested in falling, especially for men, are. Either seduced by
men or by the necessity of displaying weakness in order to secure
sympathy, fallen women are forward in their sexual activity but at
home in a prior age.

   Accounts of Inchbald's life expose the difficulties of being forward
and putting oneself forward in other than sexual arenas. While most
accounts of actresses' lives of the period emphasize the troubles that
attend the sexualization of their art and work, memoirs of Inchbald
are striking in transcribing both the detail with which she reckons
her economic and amatory accounts and the incomprehension and
hostility expressed by commentators toward the independence that
both ledgers protect.[24] A similar degree of hostility greets her
practice as drama critic, in large part because of its pretensions
toward system. Inchbald's status as system-builder in relation to
theatre links her to Baillie and distinguishes them from other women
writing and/or working in Georgian theatre. Baillie's system involves
her series of plays and critical pronouncements on the passions,
while Inchbald's involves the composition of critical remarks on the
125 plays that comprise *The British Theatre* (1806–08). Both systems
criticize theatre's literary and historical mistreatment of women, and
both are the grounds for the presumption charged against each
writer. The first volume of Baillie's *Plays on the Passions* is hailed as a
landmark of critical and creative writing on theatre until the author
is discovered to be a woman (which happens on the second night of

the London performance of *De Monfort*), at which point the play falls
off in popularity and the "Introductory Discourse" provokes public
discussion of what a woman can know about tragedy. Inchbald is
celebrated as playwright (and tolerated as actress) until she becomes
a critic, at which point she is attacked for her pride in presuming to
judge the writings of men. Only over *this* aspect of her theatrical
career, moreover, does Inchbald ever express remorse – despite the
fact that her career as actress was constrained by a childhood stutter
– and in the language suited to female expressions of remorse: "In
one of those unfortunate moments, which leave us years of repentance, I accepted an overture . . ."[25] Criticizing plays indicates a
level of pride that is intolerable in women, especially when these
remarks challenge tenets of chivalry: for they assert female independence in and outside of marriage, associate female beauty with
women over thirty, avoid over-idealizing or denigrating women, and
censure plays in which male characters fall in love with foolish
women.[26] The published exchange between Colman the Younger
and Inchbald indicates the wounding of male honor at stake in her
remarks. Colman takes offense at Inchbald's suggestion as to the
unequal share Garrick and his father had in composing *The Clandes-
tine Marriage* and its manifestation of her insufficient gratitude for,
and deference to, male patronage. To which Inchbald responds by
establishing the "obligations" she owes Colman Senior as "no more
than those usual attentions which every manager of a theatre is
supposed to confer, when he first selects a novice in dramatic
writing, as worthy of being introduced, on his stage, to the public."[27]

Inchbald holds her own in this exchange, trading his "Mrs.
Dacier" for her "Homer" all the while "willingly subscrib[ing]
[her]self an unlettered woman," but the consequences of it prove
deadly. From then on Inchbald refuses all offers to write criticism on
theatrical matters and thus foregoes further critical opportunities to
change theatre's treatment of autonomous women.[28] Remarks to *The
British Theatre* indicate her dissatisfactions with the limited array of
roles for women and complement Baillie's assessment of the tragedy
for sociality of drama's characteristic depictions of women in love.
They object to the traditional focus on falling in love rather than the
sustaining of love and the correlative emphasis on young heroines
who idealize romance and are idealized for their innocence, youthful
beauty, and absence of thought.[29] On one level, Inchbald argues,
such representations aid in justifying the stage as a moral institution

for, far from fueling the passions by presenting love in its "most
glowing and bewitching colours," theatre actually "might cure the
most Romantic youth and damsel of the ardour of their mutual
attachment" by displaying the "insipidity of lovers, in almost every
play."[30] On another level, they degrade the world of the stage by
narrowing options for female character and opportunities for
transport.

Many Romantic writers second Inchbald's view of the insipidity of
love on stage but use it to reject theatre or the so-called "improvers"
of Shakespeare whose insertions of love scenes grant more playing
time to women. Inchbald and Baillie instead work to redesign stages
for women that do not pit illusion against reason or beauty against
time. In general, this means requesting smaller theatres, less harsh-
ness of lighting, and providing commentary within their plays on
how beauty appears: as illusion, part of whose value is its vivification
of the quotidian reality of love, but also as manifestable in a larger
array of forms. Offering this array challenges the idealization of
youthful beauty without denying the importance of beauty's physical
appeal. Even when portrayals emphasize the qualities of "inner"
beauty, they take in some body parts, as when the servant Beatrix
remarks of Adriana that "She is as fair as ever – or, if the rose be
faded on her cheek, good sense, compassion, and all the Christian
virtues, have rendered doubly bright her sparkling eye."[31] On the
beauty of Orra, the worthy suitor Theobald states, "O fair indeed as
woman need be form'd / To please and be belov'd! Though, to
speak honestly, / I've fairer seen."[32] The strains of such description
clearly capture a fantasy still in the making, both regarding the
erotic appeal of a variety of physical types and the ability of reason
to form and reform desire. Equally telling, however, is how these
phrases actually suit the beauty of those times, composed as they are
for and about the most famous actress of the day, Siddons.

Siddons's status, stature, and appearance are essential to the
sensation she embodies, one that inspires many new roles for mature
beauties on stage and some new roles for those who are off.[33] At
least as theatre spectators, aristocratic women come to see the
appeal "of a certain age." They guess the gender of the author of the
first volume of *Plays on the Passions* on the grounds that "no man
could or would draw such noble and dignified representations of the
female mind as Countess Albini and Jane de Monfort. They often
make us clever, captivating, heroic, but never rationally superior."[34]

Such receptivity to change is generative of new scripts and new fashions that display a new "nobility" in the rational beauty of age. "Make me some more Jane de Monforts," Siddons is reputed to say to Baillie.[35] Baillie complies with several mature heroines, and Inchbald composes Adriana in 1800 expressly for Siddons. Inchbald's remarks to *The British Theatre* find in Siddons's career "proof" that the indispensability of youthful beauty has had its day. "Mrs. Siddons performed on the London stage, in the prime of youth and bloom of beauty, yet was totally neglected: She came a few years after, with judgment for her aid, and was enthusiastically worshipped." "Who will allege, that mental powers have no charm in the female sex?"[36] But the keenness of Inchbald's understanding of theatrical time keeps her from believing that such conclusions are final.

IN THE MEANTIME

The project of redesigning female beauty so as to accommodate women's desires for autonomy in a medium whose special effects are seen as contradicting both sustainability and autonomy offers an excellent opportunity to interrogate confidence in theatre as a means of cultural change. Such confidence underlies contemporary theories of performance that claim that performance subverts the essential reality of identity and offers less mediated, more irreverent, and sensational means of change than does standard print media.[37] Elsewhere I have suggested what is short-sighted about a politics of visibility that fails to acknowledge how theatre specializes in training viewers what not to see in its modes of representation.[38] Whether we follow Coleridge in seeking "similitude in dissimilitude" or Lacan in acknowledging the scene of the Other, the point is to reckon from *necessarily* limited points of view.[39] The stage insists on these limitations in its physical structure, modes of embodiment, textual tradition, or business practices. The ways that it emphasizes restrictions on seeing, being seen, or getting heard are what make theatre/performance an "ideal" forum for cultural analysis. The loosening of rules, performance sites, and stage conventions that differentiates contemporary performance from late-Georgian "legitimate" theatre bolsters current confidence in the freedom attending the means and ends of performance.[40] My view is less progressive. Late-Georgian restrictions render more visible what change entails and from where it issues: the being bound by constraints – of vision, fashion, machinery, money, tradition – before, during, and after any movement toward freedom. Efforts to reform love heighten this lesson.

The particular restrictions of late-Georgian legitimate theatres emphasize the importance of historicizing illusion in ways that complement Baillie's and Inchbald's treatments of female beauty and love. While Baillie and Inchbald challenge the association of illusion with the age of chivalry in order to extend the time of beauty to women's middle age, the theatre of their day is considered in a transitional age in relation to illusion. Two sites of illusion illustrate the contradictory features of this transition and the capacity of theatre spectators to view contradictions as natural. Set designs are beginning to value historical accuracy, while costumes generally still reflect and affect current fashions.[41] Within each site, moreover, conflicting categories coexist. Hand-in-hand with the new priority on historical accuracy comes demand for exoticism, "spectacular fairylands," other-worldly locales.[42] Working-class actresses wear cast-off clothes of the aristocracy and foster the popularity of upper-class designs. These general stage realities affect the fashioning of beauty and of Baillie's and Inchbald's remorse – and not simply the remorse that expresses exhaustion over having to use recalcitrant means for the liberatory ends of extending the time of female beauty. Precisely the innovations of set design resituate illusion (and, in the case of Inchbald, love) in the Middle Ages. The person generally credited with initiating accuracy in set designs is John Philip Kemble, famous for his passion for medieval scenery and amatory "betrayal" of Inchbald. In hiring William Capon as principal designer at Drury Lane, Kemble satisfies both men's "passion for faithful recreation of the Middle Ages."[43] In refusing to propose marriage to Inchbald, he suits a self that legend claims "could never have borne with the independent turn of her mind" though she "would have jumped to have him."[44]

The general advantage in analyzing how illusion changes over time is to recall it as a historical phenomenon. Illusion did not always look this way nor does it stand in any predictable relation to reality. Trappings of fantasy change in unpredictable accord with materializations of reality. This historicized illusion in turn accentuates ephemerality as a cultural fantasy. Delight in the suddenness of change is part of the fantasy structure that maintains theatre as a subversive site. As critic and actress, Inchbald provides two ways of illuminating this fantasy structure without dismissing it. That is, some of her critical remarks on theatre question the impediment to rationality that the no-time-to-reason of illusion, beauty, and love ostensibly poses. For Inchbald endorses the party line regarding the suddenness and ephemerality associated with theatre in stating that plays "must please at first sight, or never be seen more."[45] Yet the consequence she draws from this fact hints at ways to alter rather than to endorse this maxim's customary justification of prejudice. Because "there is no reconsideration of *his* case," she writes, the playwright "must direct his force against the weakness, as well as the strength of his jury. He must address their habits, passions, and prejudices, as the only means to gain this sudden conquest of their minds and hearts."[46] Such realism regarding resistances, not simply impediments, to change is a first step toward making one's visionary projects less utopian. The point is neither to stop resistance nor to stop at resistances but to acknowledge their limiting effects. Among other things, this means perceiving the illusions in reason, the comfort of banalities, the uneven pace of change.

Stage conventions regarding beauty are particularly revealing of culture's investments in ephemerality as a means of circumventing the gradual and sedimented workings of time. In general, acting makes its presence known by screening laborious behind-the-scene preparations. And beauty's success depends on not perceiving the conventions and conventionality that sustain it. In Inchbald's day, these conventions highlight the natural as beauty's "newest" desirable feature.[47] Inchbald's major claim to stage-fame as beauty is in naturalizing her dress and hair. This beauty is perceived as a rejection of aristocracy and tradition even as descriptions highlight the partial and collaborative nature of such change.

Our fair readers will like to be told, that Mrs. Inchbald, with equal economy, taste, and purity, was among the first to try the effect of her natural hair upon the stage. On the second of August [1783] she absolutely appeared without powder; still, however, the natural shape of the human head was only to be guessed at, as at present, winged out by certain side boxes of curls, and the head thus describing an equilateral triangle, of which the base was uppermost. Still to be rid of the *larded meal* was something.[48]

Other accounts credit Siddons as the first to simplify hair and dress, though her naturalized features are usually seen as Grecian or "classical" – even as the stage character (Jane de Monfort), who best

represents Siddons in the simplicity of her mien and dress, is
medieval.[49] Pointing to the history of illusions of nature does not
mean that nothing changes when "new" bodies, skin tones, and
values become suddenly visible as beauty.[50] But it does mean that
the moments or persons credited with such change say less about the
nature of progress than of theatrical billing.

A final lesson gained from Baillie's and Inchbald's work on behalf
of mature beauty concerns revising cultural attitudes toward change,
toward both the time and layerings of historical times that change
requires and the living-in-the-meanwhile that it entails. If lived
experience makes optimism about change unrealistic and nostalgia
counterproductive, in relation to what time does one work or dream?
Especially when hope fuels despair as much as progress, especially
when living for the future ruins one's time and one's children's
prospects – not to mention the prospect of having either children or
prospects? Without the former, neither Baillie nor Inchbald fears that
she is sharpening the thorns of remorse for her daughters by unfolding
their minds (though Inchbald bequeaths to her niece, Ann Jarrett, an
inheritance "to be possessed by her free entirely from any control of
her husband").[51] And Inchbald advocates less remorse than apathy as
the proper attitude toward the time that puts beauty behind her:
"[Apathy] permits me to look in the glass without screaming with
horror – and to live upon moderate terms of charity with all young
people (without much hatred or malice), although I can never be
young again."[52] Still, this struggle with the meanwhile, its deferral of
success or loveability, suggests what in chivalry remains an active
challenge for forward subjects: finding the meaning of sacrifice, the
value in self-sacrifice. Legitimate skepticism toward the values of
violence associated with sacrifice, coupled with women's traditional
exclusion from them, has proved useful in demystifying and detrage-
fying heroism, patriotism, the going-it-alone.[53] But it has not proposed compelling alternate incentives to continue to enter the fray.
Usually such skepticism only intensifies the outrage, pain, and frustration experienced when efforts go unperceived or unrewarded. And it
intensifies one's sense of entitlement to these feelings and to a "self"
that such feelings sanction even after current forms of reason have
dismantled such notions of self. Radical culture has serious work to do
here because it has so much work to do generally. The ongoing
challenge of remorse is to live in a meantime without needing to make
either the meantime or the living a tragedy.

NOTES

1 Julie A. Carlson, *In the Theatre of Romanticism: Coleridge, Nationalism, Women* (Cambridge University Press, 1994). An early version of this chapter was presented at the conference, "Women and Theatre, 1700–1850," at the Clark Library (May 1998). I thank Anne Mellor for inviting me and conference participants for helpful responses. I also thank Zelda Bronstein and Laurie Carlson for spirited exchanges on these matters during the chapter's revision.

2 These assumptions have been discredited by many books written in the past decade, most recently by Catherine Burroughs, *Closet Stages: Joanna Baillie and the Theater Theory of British Romantic Women Writers* (Philadelphia: University of Pennsylvania Press, 1997), William Jewett, *Fatal Autonomy: Romantic Drama and the Rhetoric of Agency* (Ithaca: Cornell University Press, 1997), and Michael Simpson, *Closet Performances: Political Exhibition and Prohibition in the Dramas of Byron and Shelley* (Stanford University Press, 1998).

3 See Coleridge's descriptions of the "treble chear of Claps" that greeted him in the theatre and the "endless Rat a Tat Tat at our black & blue bruised Door" during the run of *Remorse* (*Collected Letters of Samuel Taylor Coleridge*, ed. E. Leslie Griggs, 6 vols. [Oxford: Clarendon Press, 1959], III: 431, 432).

4 For accounts of this reaction see B. Allen Sprague, "The Reaction against William Godwin," *Modern Philology* 16, 5 (1918): 57–75, Mark Philp, *Godwin's Political Justice* (Ithaca: Cornell University Press, 1986), and A. E. Rodway, ed., *Godwin and the Age of Transition* (London: Harrap, 1952). Here I follow Rodway's division of Godwin's career into three periods: Fame (1793–97), Attack (1797–1805), Oblivion (1805 on) (Rodway, *ibid.*, p. 39).

5 Concerns with this melancholic transmission are especially visible in recent criticism of Mary Shelley, especially Mary Jacobus, "Incest, Trauma and Literary Transmission: Mary Shelley's Unreadability," forthcoming in *The Scene of Reading* (Oxford University Press), and "In Love with a Cold Climate," *First Things: The Maternal Imaginary in Literature, Art, and Psychoanalysis* (New York and London: Routledge, 1995), pp. 63–83, and Tillotama Rajan, "Mary Shelley's *Mathilda*: Melancholy and the Political Economy of Romanticism," *Studies in the Novel* 26, 2 (1994): 43–68.

6. Mary Wollstonecraft, *A Short Residence in Sweden, Norway and Denmark*, ed. Richard Holmes (Harmondsworth: Penguin, 1987), p. 97.

7 Edmund Burke, *Reflections on the Revolution in France* and Thomas Paine, *The Rights of Man* (Garden City, NY: Anchor Books/Doubleday, 1973), pp. 90, 89. On the "relocation of chivalry" in male Romantic writing, see Tim Fulford, *Romanticism and Masculinity: Gender, Politics and Poetics in the Writings of Burke, Coleridge, Cobbett,*

Wordsworth, De Quincey and Hazlitt (Houndmills and London: Mac-Millan Press, 1999).

8 For example, William St. Clair dates Godwin's "discovery of poetry" to 1799 and claims that Coleridge has primary responsibility for this (*The Godwins and the Shelleys* [Baltimore: Johns Hopkins University Press, 1989], pp. 222, 225).

9 Godwin ascribes this wisdom to the age of chivalry in "Letters of Advice to a Young American: On the Course of Studies It Might be Most Advantageous for Him to Pursue," in *Uncollected Writings by William Godwin*, ed. Jack W. Marken and Burton R. Pollin (Gainesville: Scholars' Facsimiles & Reprints, 1968), p. 435.

10 See especially Ellen Donkin, *Getting into the Act: Women Playwrights in London 1776–1829* (London and New York: Routledge, 1996).

11 Margaret Carhart, *The Life and Work of Joanna Baillie* (New Haven: Yale University Press, 1923), p. 3. "The Life of Joanna Baillie" affixed to *The Dramatic and Poetical Works of Joanna Baillie* (London: Longman, Brown, Green, and Longmans, 1851) emphasizes the "consummate integrity," "moral courage," "simplicity," "deep feeling of devotion," and serenity of Baillie's character (pp. xvi, xix).

12 James Boaden's *Memoirs of Mrs. Inchbald* (London: Richard Bentley, 1833, 2 vols.) stresses the latter traits over the former, indeed works hard to minimize her allegiances to radical politics, as Cecelia Macheski (among others) points out (see her introduction to *Remarks for The British Theatre 1806–09* [Delmar, NY: Scholars' Facsimiles & Reprints, 1990], p. 8). More explicit accounts include Bruce Robertson Park, *Thomas Holcroft and Elizabeth Inchbald: Studies in the Eighteenth-Century Drama of Ideas* (New York: Columbia University Press, 1952) and Gary Kelly, *The English Jacobin Novel, 1780–1805* (Oxford: Clarendon Press, 1976).

13 Inchbald publicizes this opinion in her Remarks to *De Monfort*: "This drama . . . plainly denotes that the authoress has studied theatrical productions as a reader more than a spectator" (*Remarks for the British Theatre* [there is no consecutive pagination in this text]).

14 The other unstaged play of Inchbald's is *The Massacre* (1793), a tragedy. *Henriquez* joins *De Monfort, The Family Legend*, and *The Separation*. (Only two, then, of Baillie's *Plays on the Passions* were staged in London.)

15 "Preface to the Third Volume of *Plays on the Passions*," *The Dramatic and Poetical Works of Joanna Baillie* (London: Longman, Brown, Green, and Longmans, 1851), p. 231.

16 See Coleridge's "Critique of *Bertram*" in *Biographia Literaria*, 2 vols., ed. James Engell and Walter Jackson Bate. Volume VII of *The Collected Works of Samuel Taylor Coleridge* (Princeton University Press, 1983) and Carlson, *In the Theatre of Romanticism*, pp. 48–49, 60–61.

17 Baillie lists as one of the negative effects of large theatres an inability to produce variety of light and shadow, which "occasions the more solemn scenes of Tragedy to be represented in a full, staring, uniform light that

ought to be dimly seen in twilight uncertainty; or to have the objects shown by partial gleams only, while the deepened shade around gives a sombre indistinctness to the other parts of the stage, particularly favourable to solemn or terrific impressions. And it would be more difficult, I imagine, to throw down light upon the objects on such a stage . . . though it might surely be done in one of moderate dimensions with admirable effect" (234). Compare this with Balthazar's otherwise irrelevant commentary. "*Bal.* As I approach'd th' appointed place, I saw / Round the fenced spot, already gather'd, groups / Of men and women, young and old, whose faces / Did seem, from darkness, as from nothing sprung, / Touch'd with the torches' glaring light, which downward / Stream'd from the lofty scaffold, whereon forms / Of busy artists at their fatal work . . . Appear'd like blacken'd fiends" (*Henriquez*, in *The Dramatic and Poetical Works of Joanna Baillie*, p. 382).

18 *Henriquez*, p. 381.
19 She compares "a brave and wise man of the nineteenth century" with "a brave and wise man of the fourteenth century" on the similar intensity of their "emotions of Fear" even when their belief in ghosts is so different. I deal with this play at more length in "Baillie's *Orra*: Shrinking in Fear" (forthcoming in *Joanna Baillie, Romantic Dramatist: Critical Essays*, ed. Thomas Crochunis and Janice Patten [The Netherlands: Gordon and Breach]).
20 *Henriquez*, 365.
21 *A Case of Conscience* in *The Plays of Elizabeth Inchbald*, 2 vols., ed. Paula Backscheider (New York and London: Garland, 1980), II: 311, original emphasis.
22 In Remarks to George Farquhar's *The Constant Couple, Remarks for "The British Theatre,"* Inchbald treats another implication of different kinds of visual evidence. She remarks on the curiosity by which a lover, in search of his beloved after a period of separation, can sometimes spend days with her without recognizing "the shape, the air, the every feature of the dear beloved," but, once shown "a ring, a bracelet, a mole, a scar . . . remembrance instantly occupies its place."
23 Samuel Taylor Coleridge, *Biographia Literaria*, II: 220.
24 On actresses' *Lives* in this period, see Catherine Burroughs, *Closet Stages*, 36–51. Inchbald's accountings are some of the most oft-cited features of Boaden's *Memoirs*, especially what Boaden calls the "inventory of her perfections," which she allegedly calls a "Description of Me" (in which she describes her appearance item by item) and what Paul Zall, in "The Cool World of Samuel Taylor Coleridge: The Question of Joanna Baille," *Wordsworth Circle* 13 (1982), 17–20, calls her "happiness barometer," otherwise known as "Her Septembers" (a short reckoning of every September from 1772 until 1808, which lists her earnings, publications, age, and one-word emotional state). Interesting for our purposes is the later linkage of emotional state with

effect of age, as, for example, "1798, London (rehearsing *Lovers' Vows)*, Happy, but for suspicion amounting almost to certainty of a rapid appearance of age in my face," or "1802 . . . Very happy, but for ill health, ill looks, etc."

25 Inchbald, Remarks to George Colman's *The Heir at Law* in *Remarks for The British Theatre*.

26 Inchbald offers Nicholas Rowe's *The Fair Penitent* as a clear sign that the times have changed in terms of dramatic attraction: "Whatever reasons may be urged against the more elevated instruction of the sex at present, than in former days, one good consequence at least accrues from it – they are better qualified than heretofore to choose their lovers and husbands. It was in the age of female ignorance that the Lotharios, and the viler Lovelaces, flourished." On the desirability of mature marriages, see remarks to Mrs. Cowley's *The Belle's Stratagem*, William Congreve's *The Mourning Bride*, and Thomas Otway's *Venice Preserv'd*.

27 Remarks to George Colman's *The Heir at Law* in *Remarks for The British Theatre*.

28 Hoppner and Murray invite Inchbald to write for the inaugural issue of the *Quarterly Review* as a regular contributor, and John Bell offers "to make her a conductress of" *La Belle Assemblée*, but she refuses both offers (Boaden, *Memoirs of Mrs. Inchbald*, II: 115–30).

29 See especially Remarks to *Romeo and Juliet*: "The ardour of the youthful pair, like the fervency of children, gives high amusement . . . [T]he passion of love, in the young, is seldom constant, as poets describe it, but fickle as violent."

30 Remarks to Dr. Goldsmith's *The Goodnatured Man*.

31 *A Case of Conscience*, 298.

32 *Orra*, 237.

33 Charles Beecher Hogan, ed., comments that "nearly every season [Siddons] was seen in a new tragedy in which the part of the heroine was carefully tailored to suit her style of expressing, as nobody else on the stage was at all able to equal, such passions as pride, determination, scorn" (*The London Stage 1660–1800 in 5 Parts*. Part 5 (in 3 vols.): *1776–1800* [Carbondale: Southern Illinois University Press, 1968], I: clxxiv). Virtually everyone sees in the description of Jane de Monfort a "striking resemblance of both the person and mien" of Siddons (Inchbald's Remarks to *De Monfort*). Jeffrey Cox, ed., reads *De Monfort* as "an investigation of Siddons-mania" (*Seven Gothic Dramas, 1785–1825* [Athens: Ohio University Press, 1992], p. 53).

34 Margaret Carhart cites this statement by Mary Berry, as well as Hester Piozzi's reasons for ascribing the *Plays on the Passions* to a woman – "both the heroines are Dames Passées, and a man has no notion of mentioning a female after she is five and twenty" – in *The Life and Work of Joanna Baillie*, p. 15.

35 "Life of Joanna Baillie," *The Dramatic and Poetical Works of Joanna Baillie*, p. xi.

36 Inchbald, Remarks to Thomas Southerne's *Isabella; or, The Fatal Marriage*.

37 These claims have been associated most frequently (though sometimes unfairly) with Judith Butler, *Gender Trouble: Feminism and the Subversion of Identity* (New York: Routledge, 1990). See also Sue-Ellen Case, *Performing Feminisms: Feminist Critical Theory and Theatre* (Johns Hopkins University Press, 1990). W. B. Worthen recently has criticized the view of drama constructed by performance studies, claiming that the latter is so "'honored with dismantling textual authority, illusionism, and the canonical actor' that it is questionable whether any frontier remains between dramatic studies and performance studies." His essay thus aims to reinvigorate drama as a mode of performance theory ("Drama, Performativity, and Performance," *PMLA* 113, 5 [October 1998]: 1093–107).

38 See Carlson, "Forever Young: Master Betty and the Queer Stage of Youth in English Romanticism," *SAQ* 95, 3 (Summer 1996): 575–602.

39 The former phrase characterizes Coleridge's definition of aesthetic imitation (*Biographia Literaria* II: 72), the latter what Lacanian psychoanalysis brings to an analysis of theatre. On the latter question, see André Green, *The Tragic Effect: The Oedipus Complex in Tragedy*, trans. Alan Sheridan (Cambridge University Press, 1979) and Timothy Murray, *Drama Traumas: Spectres of Race and Sexuality in Performance, Video, and Art* (New York and London: Routledge, 1997).

40 A good recent account of those restrictions is Jane Moody, "'Fine Word, Legitimate!': Toward a Theatrical History of Romanticism," *Texas Studies in Literature and Language* 38, 3/4 (Fall/Winter, 1996): 223–44.

41 The wearing of Roman togas is an exception, but the general rule holds. At this period, the managers serve also as costume designer, though actors are generally responsible for procuring their own wardrobe. See Alicia Finkel, *Romantic Stages: Set and Costume Design in Victorian England* (Jefferson, NC and London: McFarland & Co., Inc., 1996).

42 *Ibid.*, p. 3; see 3–60.

43 *Ibid.*, p. 8.

44 Boaden, *Memoirs of Mrs. Inchbald*, I: 107. Capon's "crowning achievement" was "a set representing a fourteenth-century cathedral, with nave, choir, and side aisles, for Joanna Baillie's play *De Monfort*. The massive, superbly decorated interior, 56 feet wide, 52 feet deep, and 37 feet high, received universal acclaim" (Finkel, *Romantic Stages*, p. 9).

45 Inchbald, Remarks to George Bull's *John Bull; or, The Englishman's Fireside*.

46 *Ibid.*

47 On costume conventions in this period, see Nancy Bradfield, *Costume in*

Detail 1730–1930 (Boston: Plays Inc., 1968); Tracy C. Davis, *Actresses as Working Women: Their Social Identity in Victorian Culture* (New York: Routledge, 1991), 108–10; James Robinson Planché, *A Cyclopedia of Costume or Dictionary of Dress* (London: Chatto and Windus, 1876–79) and *History of British Costume* (London: C. Knight; New York: Jackson, 1834); and Aileen Ribeiro, *The Art of Dress: Fashion in England and France 1750 to 1820* (New Haven: Yale University Press, 1995).

48 Boaden, *Memoirs of Mrs. Inchbald*, I: 173; see also I: 82 and S. R. Littlewood, *Elizabeth Inchbald and her Circle: The Story of a Charming Woman* (London: Daniel O'Connor, 1921), p. 55.

49 See Burroughs on the congruence between diegetic descriptions of Jane de Monfort and Siddons's characteristic dress (*Closet Stages*, 122–29).

50 Gilles Lipovetsky dates the fashion system and its accelerated temporality with the Enlightenment era and argues that fashion "attests to human capacity to change" rather than "aristocratic" or "conceited unreasonableness." On this basis he views fashion as a system "that is inseparable from individualism" and the ends of democracy (*The Empire of Fashion: Dressing Modern Democracy*, trans. Catherine Porter [Princeton University Press, 1994], pp. 24, 32).

51 Boaden, *Memoirs of Mrs. Inchbald*, II: 287. Inchbald has two stepsons from her marriage to Joseph.

52 *Ibid.*, II: 126. Also, "It is only in the promises of the Gospel that I can ever hope to be *young and beautiful again*" (II: 292–3).

53 See the essays in *Domestic/Tragedy*, ed. Julie Carlson, *SAQ* 98: 3 (summer 1999) for various articulations of this problem. The best revision of an ethics of sacrifice and its associations with medievalism is Louise O. Fradenburg, *Sacrifice Your Love: Psychoanalysis, Historicism, Chaucer* (forthcoming, University of Minnesota Press).

Bibliography

All works that have contemporary reviews are listed under their titles, prefaced by "Rev."

"Account of Mrs. Inchbald's new Comedy [*Wives as They Were*]." *The Lady's Magazine* 28 (1797): 119–23.

Agorni, Mirella. "The Voice of the 'Translatress': From Aphra Behn to Elizabeth Carter." *Yearbook of English Studies* 28 (1998): 181–195.

Agulhon, Maurice. *Marianne into Battle: Republican Imagery and Symbolism in France, 1789–1880.* Trans. Janet Lloyd. Cambridge University Press, 1981.

Ahmed, Siraj. "'Where Rape and Murders are Tolerated Acts': British India in the Enlightenment." Unpublished Ph.D. dissertation, Columbia University, 1999.

Aikin, Lucy. *Memoirs, Miscellanies, and Letters of the Late Lucy Aikin.* Philip Le Breton, ed. London: Longman, Green, 1864.

Allison, Alexander W., Arthur J. Carr, and Arthur M. Eastman, ed. *Masterpieces of the Drama.* Sixth edition. New York: Macmillan Publishing Co., 1991.

"Analytical Essays on the Modern English Drama." *Blackwood's Edinburgh Magazine* 18 (July, 1825): 119–30.

Anderson, Bonnie S., and Judith P. Zinsser. *A History of Their Own: Women in Europe from Prehistory to the Present.* Vol. ii. New York: Harper & Row, 1988. 2 vols.

Anonymous. *The Distressed Family.* Translated from M. le Mercier. London: C. Elliott, T. Kay & Co., 1787.

"The Life of Joanna Baillie" in *The Dramatic and Poetical Works of Joanna Baillie.* London: Longman, Brown, Green, and Longmans, 1851.

The Writing Desk; or, Youth in Danger. A Play in Four Acts. Literally Translated from the German of Kotzebue. London: G. G. & J. Robinson, 1799.

Archer, William. "Introduction." In William Archer and Robert W. Lowe, ed., *Dramatic Essays by Leigh Hunt.* London: Walter Scott, 1894.

Armstrong, Nancy. *Desire and Domestic Fiction.* Oxford University Press, 1987.

Austin, J. L. *How to Do Things with Words.* Cambridge University Press, 1962.

Backscheider, Paula. *Spectacular Politics: Theatrical Power and Mass Culture in Early Modern England.* Baltimore: Johns Hopkins University Press, 1993.

Baer, Marc. *Theatre and Disorder in Late Georgian London.* Oxford: Clarendon Press, 1992.

Bailey, J. O. *British Plays of the Nineteenth Century: An Anthology to Illustrate the Evolution of the Drama.* New York: Odyssey Press, 1966.

Baillie, Joanna. *Constantine Paleologus* in *Miscellaneous Plays.* 1803. New York: Garland, 1977, pp. 279–438.

   The Dramatic and Poetical Works of Joanna Baillie. London: Longman, Brown, Green and Longmans, 1851.

   The Dramatic and Poetical Works of Joanna Baillie. Hildesheim and New York: Georg Olms Verlag, 1976.

   "Introductory Discourse." Vol. 1 (of 3 vols.) of *A Series of Plays* (1798). In *The Dramatic and Poetical Works of Joanna Baillie.* London: Longman, Brown, Green, and Longmans, 1851, pp. 1–18.

   "Introductory Discourse." In *A Series of Plays: In Which It Is Attempted to Delineate the Stronger Passions of the Mind.* Vol. 1. London: T. Cadell, 1802, pp. 1–71.

   "Introductory Discourse." In *A Series of Plays: In Which It Is Attempted to Delineate The Stronger Passions of the Mind: Each Passion Being the Subject of A Tragedy and A Comedy.* 1798. D.H. Reiman, ed. New York: Garland, 1977, pp. 1–72.

   "Preface." *Miscellaneous Plays.* London: Longman, 1804, pp. iii–xix.

   "To the Reader" of the Third Volume of *Plays on the Passions* in *The Dramatic and Poetical Works of Joanna Baillie.* London: Longman, Brown, Green, and Longmans, 1851, pp. 228–35.

   "To the Reader." *A Series of Plays: In Which It Is Attempted to Delineate the Stronger Passions of the Mind.* vol. II. London: T. Cadell, 1802, pp. vii–xi. 3 vols.

   "To the Reader." Originally published in vol. II (of 3 vols.) of *A Series of Plays* (1802) in *The Dramatic and Poetical Works of Joanna Baillie.* London: Longman, Brown, Green, and Longmans, 1851, pp. 228–35.

   The Tryal. A Series of Plays: In Which It Is Attempted to Delineate The Stronger Passions of the Mind: Each Passion Being the Subject of A Tragedy and A Comedy. 1798. D. H. Reiman, ed. New York: Garland, 1977, 194–299.

"Baillie's Series of Plays." *The Annual Review; and History of Literature* 1 (1802): 680–85.

Banaji, D. R. *Slavery in British India.* Bombay: D. B. Taraporevala Sons & Co., 1933.

Rev. of *The Battle of Waterloo, a Tragedy,* by Mary Hornby. *The British Stage, and Literary Cabinet* 3 (May, 1819), 131–33.

Beddoes, Thomas Lovell. In Edmund Gosse, ed., *The Letters of Thomas Lovell Beddoes.* New York: Macmillan, 1894.

Ben-Israel, Hedva. *English Historians of the French Revolution.* Cambridge University Press, 1968.

Bennett, Susan. "Genre Trouble: Joanna Baillie, Elizabeth Polack – Tragic Subjects, Melodramatic Subjects" in *Women and Playwriting in Nineteenth-Century Britain*, ed. Tracy C. Davis and Ellen Donkin. Cambridge University Press, 1999, pp. 215–32.

Theatre Audiences: A Theory of Production and Reception. 2nd edition. London: Routledge, 1997.

Bhabha, Homi K. "Introduction: Narrating the Nation." In Homi K. Bhabha, ed. *Nation and Narration*. London & New York: Routledge, 1990, pp. 1–7.

Bingham, Madeleine. *Sheridan: The Track of a Comet*. London: George Allen & Unwin, 1972.

Blackstone, William. *Commentaries on the Laws of England*. vol. 1. 1765. 15th edn. London, 1809. 4 vols.

Boaden, James. *Memoirs of Mrs. Inchbald*. 2 vols. London: Richard Bentley, 1833.

Memoirs of Mrs. Siddons Interspersed with anecdotes of authors and actors. London: Henry Colburn, 1827.

Boal, Augusto. *Theatre of the Oppressed*. Trans. Charles A. and Maria-Odilia Leal McBride. London: Pluto Press, 1979.

Bolton, Betsy. "Romancing the Stone: 'Perdita' Robinson in Wordsworth's London." *ELH*. 64 (1997): 727–59.

Booth, Michael R., Richard Southern, R. Davies, and F. and L. L. Marker, ed., *The Revels History of Drama in English, Vol. VI, 1750–1880*. London: Methuen, 1975.

Bradfield, Nancy. *Costume in Detail 1730–1930*. Boston: Plays Inc., 1968.

Bratton, Jacky. "Jane Scott the Writer-Manager." In *Women and Playwriting in Nineteenth-Century Britain*, ed. Tracy C. Davis and Ellen Donkin. Cambridge University Press, 1999, 77–98.

"Miss Scott and Miss Macauley: 'Genius Comes in All Disguises'." *Theatre Survey* 37 (1996): 59–73.

Bratton, Jacky and Gilli Bush Bailey, ed. "Appendix: *Camilla the Amazon* by Jane Scott." *Nineteenth Century Theatre* 27.2 (1999).

The British Theatre . . . with Biographical and Critical Remarks, by Mrs Inchbald, 25 vols. London: Longman, Hurst, Rees, 1808.

"British Women Playwrights around 1800," ed. Thomas C. Crochunis and Michael Eberle-Sinatra. <http://www-sul.stanford.edu/mirrors/romnet/ wp1800>, Website.

Britton, John. *Sheridan and Kotzebue*. London: J. Fairburn, 1799.

Brooks, Peter. *The Melodramatic Imagination*. New Haven: Yale University Press, 1976.

Bugajski, Ken A. "Joanna Baillie: An Annotated Bibliography." *Romanticism on the Net* 12 (November 1998). <http://www-sul.stanford.edu/mirrors/romnet.wp1800/>.

Bulwer-Lytton, Edward. In *England and the English*, ed. Standish Meacham. Chicago: University of Chicago Press, 1970.

Bunn, Alfred. *The Stage: Both Before and Behind the Curtain.* London: Richard Bentley, 1840.

Burke, Edmund. *Reflections on the Revolution in France.* Garden City, NY: Anchor Books/Doubleday, 1973.

Works and Correspondence of the Right Honourable Edmund Burke. London: Francis & John Rivington, 1852, IV: 212, 209.

The Writings and Speeches of Edmund Burke. Gen. ed. Paul Langford. Oxford: Clarendon, 1991, 9 vols.

Burney, Frances. *Complete Plays:Vol 1, Tragedies.* Peter Sabor, ed. London: William Pickering, 1995.

Burroughs, Catherine B. *Closet Stages: Joanna Baillie and the Theater Theory of British Romantic Women Writers.* Philadelphia: University of Pennsylvania Press, 1997.

"English Romantic Women Writers and Theatre Theory: Joanna Baillie's Prefaces to the *Plays on the Passions.*" In Carol Shiner Wilson and Joel Haefner, ed., *Re-Visioning Romanticism: British Women Writers 1776–1837.* Philadelphia: University of Pennsylvania Press, 1994, pp. 274–96.

"'Out of the Pale of Social Kindred Cast': Conflicted Performance Styles in Joanna Baillie's *De Monfort.*" in Paula R. Feldman and Theresa M. Kelley, ed., *Romantic Women Writers: Voices and Countervoices.* Hanover: University Press of New England, 1995, pp. 223–35.

"'A Reasonable Woman's Desire': The Private Theatrical and Joanna Baillie's *The Tryal.*" *Texas Studies in Literature and Language.* 38.3–4 (1996): 265–84.

"Teaching the Theory and Practice of Women's Dramaturgy." *Romanticism on the Net* 12 (November 1998). <http://www-sul.stanford.edu/mirrors/romnet/ wp1800>, Website.

Butler, Judith. *Bodies That Matter: On the Discursive Limits of "Sex."* New York: Routledge, 1993.

"Burning Acts – Injurious Speech." In Andrew Parker and Eve Kosofsky Sedgwick. ed., *Performativity and Performance.* New York: Routledge, 1995, pp. 197–227.

Excitable Speech: A Politics of the Performative. New York: Routledge, 1997.

Gender Trouble: Feminism and the Subversion of Identity. New York: Routledge, 1990.

The Psychic Life of Power: Theories in Subjection. Stanford: Stanford University Press, 1997.

Byron, Lord George Gordon. *Byron's Letters and Journals.* Leslie A. Marchand, ed. Cambridge, MA: Harvard University Press, 1973–81, 13 vols.

Campbell, Thomas. *Life of Mrs. Siddons.* Vol. II. London: Effingham Wilson, 1834, 2 vols.

Carhart, Margaret S. *The Life and Work of Joanna Baillie.* New Haven: Yale University Press, 1923; rpt. Archon, 1970.

Carlson, Julie. "Baillie's *Orra*: Shrinking in Fear." In *Joanna Baillie, Romantic Dramatist: Critical Essays*, ed. Thomas Crochunis and Janice Patten. The Netherlands: Gordon and Breach, forthcoming.

"Forever Young: Master Betty and the Queer Stage of Youth in English Romanticism," *SAQ* 95, 3 (Summer 1996): 575–602.

In the Theatre of Romanticism: Coleridge, Nationalism, Women. Cambridge University Press, 1994.

"Trying Sheridan's *Pizarro*." Special Issue: Romantic Performances. Ed. Theresa M. Kelley. *Texas Studies in Literature and Language.* 38.3–4 (1996): 359–78.

ed. *Domestic / Tragedy* in *SAQ* 98, 3 (1999).

Case, Sue-Ellen. *Feminism and Theatre.* New York: Methuen, 1988.

Ed. *Performing Feminisms: Feminist Critical Theory and Theatre.* Johns Hopkins University Press, 1990.

Cave, Richard Allen, ed. *The Romantic Theatre: An International Symposium.* Gerrards Cross, Bucks: Colin Smythe, 1986.

"Celebrated Female Writers. No. I. Joanna Baillie." *Blackwood's Edinburgh Magazine* 16 (August, 1824): 162–78.

Chandler, David. "'The Conflict': Hannah Brand and Theatre Politics in the 1790s." *Romanticism on the Net* 12 (November 1998).

Chisholm, Kate. *Fanny Burney: Her Life, 1752–1840.* London: Chatto & Windus, 1998.

Chorley, Henry. *Letters of Mary Russell Mitford.* 2 vols, second series. London: Richard Bentley & Son, 1872.

Cima, Gay Gibson. "'To Be Public as a Genius and Private as a Woman': The Critical Framing of Nineteenth-Century British Women Playwrights." in Tracy C. Davis and Ellen Donkin, ed., *Women and Playwriting in Nineteenth-Century Britain.* Cambridge University Press, 1999, 35–53.

Clarke, Norma. *Ambitious Heights. Writing, Friendship, Love – The Jewsbury Sisters, Felicia Hemans, and Jane Welsh Carlyle.* London & New York: Routledge, 1990.

Cobbett, William, *The Political Proteus.* London: Cox, Son, and Baylis, 1804.

Coleridge, Samuel Taylor. *Collected Letters of Samuel Taylor Coleridge*, ed. E. Leslie Griggs. Oxford: Clarendon Press, 1959, 6 vols.

"Critique of *Bertram*" in *Biographia Literaria*. Vol. VII of *The Collected Works of Samuel Taylor Coleridge*, ed. James Engell and Walter Jackson Bate. Princeton University Press, 1983.

Colley, Linda. *Britons: Forging the Nation, 1707–1837.* New Haven and London: Yale University Press, 1992.

Colombo, Claire Miller. "'This Pen of Mine Will Say Too Much': Public Performance in the Journals of Anna Larpent." *Texas Studies in Literature and Language* 38.3/4 (Fall/Winter 1996): 285–301.

Conolly, Leonard W. *The Censorship of English Drama 1737–1824.* San Marino: Huntington Library, 1976.

Cowley, Hannah. Preface. *A Day in Turkey; or The Russian Slaves.* London: G. J. and J. Robinson, 1792, pp. i–iii.

Preface. *A School for Greybeards; or, the Mourning Bride.* London: G. J. and J. Robinson, 1786, pp. iii–ix.

Preface. *The Town Before You, A Comedy.* London: Longman, 1795, pp. ix–xi.

"The Present State of the Stage, by Mrs. Cowley." *The Pocket Magazine; or, Elegant Repository of Useful and Polite Literature* 2 (1795): 108–09.

Cox, Jeffrey N. "Ideology and Genre in the British Antirevolutionary Drama in the 1790s," *ELH* 58 (1992): 579–610. (rpt. in *British Romantic Drama: Historical and Critical Essays*, ed. Terence Allan Hoagwood and Daniel P. Watkins [Teaneck, NJ: Fairleigh Dickinson University Press, 1998, pp. 88–114]).

In the Shadows of Romance: Romantic Tragic Drama in Germany, England, and France. Athens, OH: Ohio State University Press, 1987.

"Introduction" in vol. v of *Slavery*, Ed. Jeffrey N. Cox. Abolition, and Emancipation in the British Romantic Period. *The Drama.* 8 vols. Gen. ed. Debbie Lee and Peter Kitson. London: Chatto and Pickering, 1999. pp. vii–xxxiii.

ed. with an introduction. *Seven Gothic Dramas, 1789–1825.* Athens: Ohio University Press, 1992.

Craven, Elizabeth Berkeley. *The Robbers.* London: H. Wigstead & M. Hooper, 1799.

Crochunis, Thomas C. "British Women Playwrights around 1800: New Paradigms and Recoveries." Introduction to special issue of *Romanticism on the Net* 12 (November 1998).

"Dramatic Closets and Literary Studies." Unpublished essay.

"The Function of the Dramatic Closet at the Present Time." Special Issue: "British Women Playwrights Around 1800: New Paradigms and Recoveries." *Romanticism on the Net* 12 (November 1998) (http://www-sul.stanford.edu/mirrors/romnet/wp1800/ essays.html)

Crosby, Christina. *The Ends of History.* London & New York: Routledge, 1991.

Cross, Gilbert. *Next Week – East Lynne.* Lewisburg: Bucknell University Press, 1977.

Curran, Stuart. "Romantic Poetry: The 'I' Altered." In Anne K. Mellor, ed., *Romanticism and Feminism.* Bloomington: University of Indiana Press, 1988, pp. 185–207.

Shelley's 'The Cenci': Scorpions Ringed with Fire. Princeton University Press, 1970.

Darby, Barbara. *Frances Burney, Dramatist: Gender, Performance, and the Late Eighteenth Century.* Lexington: The University Press of Kentucky, 1997.

Davidoff, Lenore, and Catherine Hall. *Family Fortunes: Men and Women of the English Middle Class, 1780–1850.* Chicago: University of Chicago Press, 1987.

Davis, Gwenn and Beverly A. Joyce, ed. *Drama by Women to 1900: A*

Bibliography of American and British Writers. Toronto: University of Toronto Press, 1992.

Davis, Tracy C. *Actresses as Working Women: Their Social Identity in Victorian Culture.* London: Routledge, 1991.

"The Sociable Playwright and Representative Citizen." *Women and Playwriting in Nineteenth-Century Britain.* Ed. Tracy C. Davis and Ellen Donkin. Cambridge University Press, 1999. pp. 15–34.

"The Sociable Playwright and Representative Citizen." *Romanticism on the Net* 12 (November 1998).

Davis, Tracy C. and Ellen Donkin, "Introduction." *Women and Playwriting in Nineteenth-Century Britain.* Cambridge University Press, 1999, pp. 1–12.

Dawson, Anthony B. "Performance and Participation: Desdemona, Foucault, and the Actor's Body." In James C. Bulman, ed. & introd., *Shakespeare, Theory and Performance.* London: Routledge, 1996, pp. 29–45.

Rev. of *A Day in Turkey; or The Russian Slaves*, by Hannah Cowley. *The Critical Review* 4 (1792): 323–26.

Rev. of *A Day in Turkey; or The Russian Slaves*, by Hannah Cowley. *The European Magazine* 21 (1792): 443–46.

De Bruyn, Frans. *The Literary Genres of Edmund Burke.* Oxford: Clarendon Press, 1996.

Delamotte, Eugenia C. *Perils of the Night.* Oxford and New York: Oxford University Press, 1990.

"Dialogue on the Drama." *The Theatrical Inquisitor* (February, 1820): 74–76.

Dibdin, James C. *The Annals of the Edinburgh Stage.* Edinburgh: Richard Cameron, 1888.

Dolan, Jill. *The Feminist Spectator as Critic.* Ann Arbor: UMI Research Press, 1988.

Presence and Desire: Essays on Gender, Sexuality, Performance. Ann Arbor: University of Michigan Press, 1993.

Donkin, Ellen. *Getting into the Act: Women Playwrights in London 1776–1829.* London: Routledge, 1995.

"Mrs. Siddons Looks Back in Anger: Feminist Historiography for Eighteenth-Century British Theater." In Janelle G. Reinelt and Joseph R. Roach, ed., *Critical Theory and Performance.* Ann Arbor: University of Michigan Press, 1992, pp. 276–90.

Donohue, Joseph. *Dramatic Character in the English Romantic Age.* Princeton University Press, 1970.

Theatre in the Age of Kean. Totowa, NJ: Rowman and Littlefield, 1975.

Doody, Margaret Anne. *Frances Burney: The Life in the Works.* Cambridge University Press, 1989.

Dowd, Maureen A. "'By the Delicate Hand of a Female': Melo-dramatic Mania and Joanna Baillie's Spectacular Tragedies." *European Romantic Review* 9.4 (Fall 1998): 469–500.

Duff, David. *Romance and Revolution: Shelley and the Politics of a Genre.* Cambridge University Press, 1994.

Dutton, Thomas, *Pizarro in Peru, or the Death of Rolla*. London: W. West, 1799.
"Preface." *The Wise Man of the East, or, The Apparition of Zoroaster, the Son of Oromases, to the Theatrical Midwife of Leicester Fields*. London: H. D. Symonds, 1800.
The Wise Man of the East; or, The Apparition of Zoroaster, The Son of Oromanes, to the Theatrical Midwife of Leicester-Fields. London: H. D. Symonds, 1800.
Dyer, Richard. "Believing in Fairies: The Author and the Homosexual." in Diana Fuss, ed., *Inside/Out: Lesbian Theories, Gay Theories*. New York: Routledge, 1991, pp. 185–201.
Evans, Bertrand. *Gothic Drama from Walpole to Shelley*. Berkeley and Los Angeles: University of California Press, 1947.
Rev. of *Every One Has His Fault*, by Elizabeth Inchbald. *The European Magazine* 23 (1793): 148–49.
Ezell, Margaret J. M. "Revisioning Responding: A Second Look at Women Playwrights Around 1800." *Romanticism on the Net* 12 (November 1998). (http://www-sul.stanford.edu/mirrors/romnet/wp1800/ essays.html)
Writing Women's Literary History. Baltimore: Johns Hopkins University Press, 1993.
Rev. of *The Family Legend*, by Joanna Baillie. *The British Critic* 38 (July, 1811): 53–59.
Feldman, Paula, ed. *British Women Poets of the Romantic Era: An Anthology*. Baltimore: Johns Hopkins University Press, 1997.
Feldman, Paula R., and Theresa M. Kelley, ed. *Romantic Women Writers: Voices and Countervoices*. Hanover: University Press of New England, 1995.
Ferguson, William. *Scotland: 1689 to the Present*. Edinburgh: Oliver and Boyd, 1968.
Ferris, Lesley. *Acting Women: Images of Women in Theatre*. New York: New York University Press, 1989.
Finkel, Alicia. *Romantic Stages: Set and Costume Design in Victorian England*. Jefferson, NC and London: McFarland & Co., Inc., 1996.
Fitzball, Edward. *Thirty-Five Years of a Dramatic Author's Life*. London: T. C. Newby, 1859.
Flint, Christopher. *Family Fictions: Narrative and Domestic Relations in Britain, 1688–1798*. Stanford: Stanford University Press, 1998.
Folger Collective on Early Women Critics, The, ed., *Women Critics, 1660–1820*. Bloomington: Indiana University Press, 1995.
Foucault, Michel. "What is an Author?" Trans. Josué Harari, in Paul Rabinow, ed., *The Foucault Reader*. New York: Pantheon, 1984, pp. 101–20.
Fradenburg, Louise O. *Sacrifice Your Love: Psychoanalysis, Historicism, Chaucer*. Minneapolis: University of Minnesota Press, forthcoming.
Franceschina, John, ed. *Sisters of Gore: Seven Gothic Melodramas by British Women, 1790–1843*. New York and London: Garland Publishing Inc., 1997.
Friedman-Romell, Beth. "Staging the State: Joanna Baillie's *Constantine*

Paleologus." In *Women and Playwriting in Nineteenth-Century Britain*. Ed. Tracy C. Davis and Ellen Donkin. Cambridge University Press, 1999, pp. 151–73.

Fulford, Tim. *Romanticism and Masculinity: Gender, Politics and Poetics in the Writings of Burke, Coleridge, Cobbett, Wordsworth, De Quincey and Hazlitt*. Houndmills and London: Macmillan Press, 1999.

Gallagher, Catherine. *Nobody's Story: The Vanishing Acts of Women Writers in the Marketplace, 1670–1820*. Berkeley & Los Angeles: University of Caliornia Press, 1994.

Galperin, William. "The Theatre at Mansfield Park: From Classic to Romantic Once More." *Eighteenth-Century Life* 16 (1992): 247–71.

Gamer, Michael. "Authors in Effect: Lewis, Scott, and the Gothic Drama." *ELH* (Winter 1999).

"National Supernaturalism: Joanna Baillie, Germany, and the Gothic Drama." *Theatre Survey* 38.2 (1997): 49–88.

Ganzel, Dewey. "Patent Wrongs and Patent Theatres: Drama and Law in the Early Nineteenth Century." *PMLA*, 76.4 (1961), 384.

Garrick, David. Prologue. *Percy, A Tragedy*. By Hannah More. London: T. Cadell, 1778.

Geisweiler, Maria, *The Noble Lie*. London: C. Geisweiler, 1799.

Poverty and Nobleness of Mind. London: C. Geisweiler, 1799.

Gems, Pam. "Imagination and Gender." In Michelene Wandor, ed., *On Gender and Writing*. London: Pandora, 1983, pp. 148–51.

Genest, John. *Some Account of the English Stage, from the Restoration in 1660 to 1830*. [Spine title, *History of the English Stage*.] 10 vols. Bath: H. E. Carrington, 1832.

German Theatre, The, vols. I and IV of 6 vols. London, 1801.

Gilroy, Amanda. "From Here to Alterity: The Geography of Femininity in the Poetry of Joanna Baillie." in Douglas Gifford and Dorothy McMillan, ed., *A History of Scottish Women's Writing*. Edinburgh University Press, 1997.

Gilroy, Amanda and Keith Hanley, ed. *Joanna Baillie: A Selection of Poems and Plays*. London: Chatto and Pickering, 1997.

Godwin, William. "Letters of Advice to a Young American: On the Course of Studies It Might be Most Advantageous for Him to Pursue." In *Uncollected Writings by William Godwin*, ed. Jack W. Marken and Burton R. Pollin. Gainesville: Scholars' Facsimiles & Reprints, 1968.

Gray, Charles Harold. *Theatrical Criticism in London to 1795*. New York: Columbia University Press, 1931.

Green, André. *The Tragic Effect: The Oedipus Complex in Tragedy*. Trans. Alan Sheridan. Cambridge University Press, 1979.

Greg, W. W. *A Bibliography of the English Printed Drama to the Restoration*. Vol. IV. Oxford University Press, 1959, 4 vols.

Griggs, Leslie E., ed. *Collected Letters of Samuel Taylor Coleridge*. Oxford: Clarendon Press, 1959, 6 vols.

Hadley, Elaine. *Melodramatic Tactics: Theatricalized Dissent in the English Market-place 1800–1885.* Stanford University Press, 1995.

Hall, Catherine. *White, Male and Middle Class.* Oxford: Polity Press, 1992.

Hamilton, C. J. *Women Writers: Their Works and Ways.* First Series. London: Ward, Lock, & Bowden, 1892.

Hays, Mary. *Appeal to the Men of Great Britain in Behalf of Women.* London: J. Johnson, 1798; New York: Garland, 1974.

Hazlitt, William. *Complete Works,* vol. v. P. P. Howe, ed., London, Toronto: J. M. Dent and Sons, 1930–34, 21 vols.

"The Drama. No. I." *The London Magazine* 1 (Jan.–June, 1820): 64–70.

"The Drama. No. II." *The London Magazine* 1 (Jan.–June, 1820): 162–68.

Lectures on the English Poets. Catherine MacDonald MacLean, ed. London: Dent, 1967.

Memoirs of the late Thomas Holcroft. vol. iii. in P. P. Howe, ed., *The Complete Works of William Hazlitt.* 21 volumes. London: J. M. Dent, 1930–34.

A View of the English Stage; or A Series of Dramatic Criticisms. London: Robert Stoddart, 1818.

Heller, Janet Ruth. *Coleridge, Lamb, Hazlitt, and the Reader of Drama.* Columbia: University of Missouri Press, 1990.

Henderson, Andrea. "Passion and Fashion in Joanna Baillie's 'Introductory Discourse'." *PMLA* 112.2 (March 1997), 198–213.

Hewitt, David. "Scott's Art and Politics." In Alan Bold, ed., *Sir Walter Scott: The Long-Forgotten Melody.* Totowa, NJ: Barnes & Noble Books, 1983, pp. 44–52.

Hoagwood, Terence Allan. "Prologemenon for a Theory of Romantic Drama." *The Wordsworth Circle* 23: 2 (1992): 49–64.

"Romantic Drama and Historical Hermeneutics." *British Romantic Drama: Historical and Critical Essays,* ed. Terence A. Hoagwood and Daniel P. Watkins. Cranbury, NJ: Associated University Presses, 1998, pp. 22–55.

Hoeper, Jeffrey D., James H. Pickering, and Deborah K. Chappel, ed. *Drama.* New York: Macmillan Publishing Co., 1994.

Hofkosh, Sonia. *Sexual Politics and the Romantic Author.* Cambridge University Press, 1998.

Hogan, Charles Beecher. Critical Introduction and editorial notes. *The London Stage, 1660–1800 in 5 Parts.* Part Five: 1776–1800, ed. Charles Beecher Hogan, in 3 vols. Carbondale, IL: Southern Illinois University Press, 1968.

Holcroft, Thomas. Rev. of *To Marry, or Not to Marry,* by Elizabeth Inchbald. *The Theatrical Recorder* 1 (1805): 208–13.

Rev. of *Huniades, a Tragedy,* by Hannah Brand. *The European Magazine* 21 (1792): 66–67.

Hunt, James Henry Leigh. *Critical Essays on the Performers of the London Theatres.* London: John Hunt, 1807.

Hunt, Leigh. *Leigh Hunt's Dramatic Criticism*. Lawrence Hustorn Houtchens and Carolyn Washburn Houtchens, ed. New York: Columbia University Press, 1949.

"Mr. Young's Merits Considered," *Examiner*, 15 January 1809.

Hunt, Lynn. *The Family Romance of the French Revolution*. Berkeley: University of California Press, 1992.

"The Many Bodies of Marie Antoinette: Political Pornography and the Problem of the Feminine in the French Revolution," in Lynn Hunt, ed., *Eroticism and the Body Politic*. Baltimore: Johns Hopkins University Press, 1991, pp. 108–30.

Politics, Culture, and Class in the French Revolution. Berkeley: University of California Press, 1984.

Inchbald, Elizabeth, ed. *The British Theatre; or, A Collection of Plays, which are acted at the Theatres Royal, Drury-lane, Covent-garden, and Haymarket*. 25 vols, London: Longman, Hurst and Rees, 1808.

Next Door Neighbours. Larpent MS 971, Huntington Library, San Marino.

The Plays of Elizabeth Inchbald, 2 vols., ed. Paula Backscheider in *Eighteenth-Century English Drama*. New York and London: Garland, 1980.

Preface. *De Monfort; A Tragedy*. By Joanna Baillie. In Elizabeth Inchbald, ed., *The British Theatre*, vol. xxiv. London: Longman, 1808, pp. 3–6, 25 vols.

Preface to *The Dramatist; or Stop Him Who Can*. By Frederick Reynolds. In Elizabeth Inchbald, ed. *The British Theatre*, vol. xx. London: Longman, 1808, pp. 3–5, 25 vols.

Preface. *Every One Has His Fault*. By Elizabeth Inchbald. In Elizabeth Inchbald, ed., *The British Theatre*, vol. xxiii. London: Longman, 1808, 25 vols.

Preface. *The Heir at Law*. By George Colman, the Younger. In Elizabeth Inchbald, ed., *The British Theatre*, vol. xxi. London: Longman, 1808, pp. i–ix, 25 vols.

Preface. *Isabella; or The Fatal Marriage*. By Thomas Southerne. In Elizabeth Inchbald, ed., *The British Theatre*. vol. vii. London: Longman: 1808, pp. 3–5, 25 vols.

Preface. *The Rivals*. By Richard Brinsley Sheridan. In Elizabeth Inchbald, ed., *The British Theatre*. vol. xix. London: Longman, 1808, pp. 3–5, 25 vols.

Remarks for "The British Theatre" (1806–1809). By Elizabeth Inchbald. Cecilia Macheski, ed. Delmar, NY: Scholars' Facsimiles and Reprints, 1990.

Such Things Are, in Roger Manvell, ed. *Selected Comedies*. Lanham, MD: University Press of America, 1987.

"To the Artist," *The Artist* 1.14 (13 June 1807): 16.

The Wise Man of the East. Larpent MS 1271, Huntington Library, San Marino.

Innes, Joanna. "Politics and Morals: The Reformation of Manners Movement in Late Eighteenth-Century England." In Eckhart Hellmuth, ed., *The Transformation of Political Culture: England and Germany in the Late Eighteenth Century.* London: German Historical Institute and Oxford University Press, 1990.

Irigaray, Luce. *This Sex Which Is Not One,* 1977. Trans. Catherine Porter. Ithaca: Cornell University Press, 1985.

Jacobus, Lee A. ed., *The Bedford Introduction to Drama.* Second edition. New York: St. Martin's Press, 1993.

Jacobus, Mary. "Incest, Trauma and Literary Transmission: Mary Shelley's Unreadability" in *The Scene of Reading.* Oxford University Press, forthcoming.

"In Love with a Cold Climate." *First Things: The Maternal Imaginary in Literature, Art, and Psychoanalysis.* New York and London: Routledge, 1995, pp. 63–83.

Jeffrey, Francis. "Miss Baillie's *Miscellaneous Plays.*" *The Edinburgh Review* 5 (January, 1805): 405–21.

"Miss Baillie's *Plays on the Passions.*" *The Edinburgh Review* 2 (July, 1803): 269–86.

"Miss Baillie's *Plays on the Passions. Vol. III.*" *The Edinburgh Review* 19 (February, 1812): 261–90, 3 vols.

Jewett, William. *Fatal Autonomy: Romantic Drama and the Rhetoric of Agency.* Ithaca: Cornell University Press, 1997.

"Joanna Baillie's *Series of Plays.*" *The Critical Review* 1 (May, 1812): 449–62.

Johnston, John. *The Lord Chamberlain's Blue Pencil.* London: Hodder & Stoughton, 1990.

Johnston, Kenneth and Joseph Nicholes. "Transitory Actions, Men Betrayed: The French Revolution in the English Revolution in Romantic Drama." *Wordsworth Circle,* 23: 2 (Spring 1992): 76–96.

"Julian, a Tragedy, by Miss Mitford." *The Monthly Censor, or General Review of Domestic & Foreign Literature* 2 (April, 1823): 452–60.

Kelley, Theresa, ed. "Special Issue: Romantic Performances." *Texas Studies in Literature and Language,* 38.3–4 (1996).

Kelly, Gary. *The English Jacobin Novel 1780–1805.* Oxford University Press, 1976.

Women, Writing, and Revolution, 1790–1827. Oxford: Clarendon Press, 1993.

Klaus, Carl A., Miriam Gilbert, and Bradford S. Field, Jr., ed., *Stages of Drama.* Third edition. New York: St. Martin's Press, 1995.

Kowaleski-Wallace, Elizabeth. *Their Father's Daughters. Hannah More, Maria Edgeworth and Patriarchal Complicity.* Oxford University Press, 1991.

Kramnick, Isaac. *The Rage of Edmund Burke: Portrait of an Ambivalent Conservative.* New York: Basic Books, 1977.

Kritzer, Amelia Howe, ed. "Introduction." *Plays by Early American Women, 1775–1850.* Ann Arbor: University of Michigan Press, 1995, pp. 1–28.

Kucich, Greg. "'A Haunted Ruin': Romantic Drama, Renaissance Tradition, and the Critical Establishment." *The Wordsworth Circle* 23 (1992): 64–76.

"Staging History: Teaching Romantic Intersections of Drama, History, and Gender," *Approaches to Teaching British Women Poets of the Romantic Period*. Ed. Stephen C. Behrendt and Harriet Kramer Linkin. New York: MLA, 1997, pp. 89–96.

Lafler, Joanne. *The Celebrated Mrs. Oldfield: The Life and Art of an Augustan Actress*. Carbondale: Southern Illinois University Press, 1989.

Landes, Joan B. *Women and the Public Sphere in the Age of the French Revolution*. Ithaca: Cornell University Press, 1988.

Larpent, Anna Margaretta. "The Diary of Anna Margaretta Larpent," 16 vols. Huntington Library, San Marino, California, HM 31201.

Lawson, Philip. *The East India Company: A History*. London: Longman, 1993.

Lean, Tangye E. *The Napoleonists: A Study in Political Disaffection, 1760–1960*. London: Oxford University Press, 1970.

L'Estrange, A. G., ed. *The Life of Mary Russell Mitford, Related in a Selection from Her Letters to Her Friends*. 3 vols. London: Richard Bentley, 1870.

Lewis, 'Monk'. Preface. *Alfonso, King of Castile*. London: J. Bell, 1801, pp. iv–vii.

Lipovetsky, Gilles. *The Empire of Fashion: Dressing Modern Democracy*. Trans. Catherine Porter. Princeton University Press, 1994.

"List of Plays Licensed by John Larpent, 1801–1824 in 2 vols" (HM 19926).

Littlewood, S. R. *Elizabeth Inchbald and her Circle: The Story of a Charming Woman*. London: Daniel O'Connor, 1921.

Lott, Anna. "Sexual Politics in Elizabeth Inchbald." *Studies in English Literature*. 34.3 (1994): 635–48.

Lovell, E. J. Jr, ed., *Medwin's Conversations of Lord Byron*. Princeton University Press, 1966.

Macarthy, Eugene. *A Letter to the King, on the Question Now at Issue between the "Major", and "Minor" Theatres*. London: Effingham Wilson, 1832.

McGann, Jerome. *The Poetics of Sensibility: A Revolution in Literary Style*. New York: Oxford University Press, 1996.

Macheski, Cecelia. "Introduction" to *Remarks for "The British Theatre" 1806–1809, By Elizabeth Inchbald*, Delmar, NY: Scholars' Facsimiles & Reprints, 1990, pp. 7–12.

"Madame Vestris." *The British Stage, and Literary Cabinet* 5 (1821): 1–3.

Mann, David D. "Checklist of Female Dramatists, 1660–1823," *Restoration and Eighteenth-Century Theatre Research* 5 (1990): 30–62.

Mann, David D., Susan Garland Mann, with Camille Garnier. *Women Playwrights in England, Ireland and Scotland, 1660–1823*. Bloomington: Indiana University Press, 1996.

Mansfield Judgment, The (1772). In Anne K. Mellor and Richard E. Matlak, ed., *British Literature 1780–1830*. New York: Harcourt Brace College Publishers, 1996, pp. 56–57.

Manvell, Roger. *Elizabeth Inchbald: England's Principal Woman Dramatist and Independent Woman of Letters in 18th Century London. A Biographical Study*. Lanham, MD: University Press of America, 1987.

Sarah Siddons: Portrait of an Actress. London: Heinemann, 1970.

Marshall, Peter J. Editorial notes. *The Writings and Speeches of Edmund Burke.* Vol. VI (*India: The Launching of the Hastings Impeachment, 1786–1788*). Oxford: Clarendon, 1991, 9 vols.

Mayhew, Edward. *Stage Effect: or, The Principles which Command Dramatic Success in the Theatre.* London: C. Mitchell, 1840.

Maza, Sarah. "The Diamond Necklace Affair Revisited (1785–1786): The Case of the Missing Queen." In Lynn Hunt, ed., *Eroticism and the Body Politic.* Baltimore: Johns Hopkins University Press, 1991, pp. 63–89.

Mellor, Anne K. "A Criticism of Their Own: Romantic Women Literary Critics." In John Beer, ed., *Questioning Romanticism.* Baltimore: Johns Hopkins University Press, 1995, pp.29–48.

"Joanna Baillie and the Counter-Public Sphere." *Studies in Romanticism* 33 (Winter 1994): 559–67.

Mothers of the Nation: Women's Political Writing in England, 1780–1830. Bloomington: Indiana University Press. Forthcoming.

Romanticism and Gender. London: Routledge, 1993.

Mellor, Anne K., ed. *Romanticism and Feminism.* Bloomington: Indiana University Press, 1988.

"Memoir of Miss O'Neill." *The Theatrical Inquisitor* 8 (May, 1816): 326–32.

"Memoir of Mrs. Horn." *The Theatrical Inquisitor* 8 (May, 1816): 323–26.

Miles, Robert. *Gothic Writing 1570–1820: A Genealogy.* London: Routledge, 1993.

"Miss Baillie's *Miscellaneous Plays.*" *The Monthly Review* 49 (March, 1806): 303–10.

"Miss Baillie's Plays." *The Eclectic Review* 10 (1813): 21–32, 167–86.

"Miss Baillie's Plays." *The Literary Journal, or Universal Review of Literature Domestic and Foreign* 5 (1805): 49–64.

"Miss Baillie's *Series of Plays.*" *The Critical Review* 37 (February, 1803): 200–21.

"Miss Brand's *Plays and Poems.*" *The Monthly Review* 32 (August, 1800): 377–81.

"Miss Edgeworth's Comic Drama." *The Quarterly Review* 17 (April, 1817): 96–107.

"Miss Edgeworth's Comic Dramas." *The British Critic* 7 (May, 1817): 506–14.

"Miss Foote." *The British Stage, and Literary Cabinet* 3 (1819): 1.

"Miss J. Baillie's Miscellaneous Plays." *The British Critic* 27 (January, 1806): 22–28.

"Miss J. Baillie's Series of Plays. Vol. II." *The British Critic* 20 (1802): 184–94.

Mitford, Mary Russell. *Charles the First, An Historical Tragedy in Five Acts.* London: John Duncombe, 1834.

Dramatic Scenes. London: George B. Whittaker, 1827.

Letters from Mary Russell Mitford to Sir Thomas Noon Talfourd. Eng. Mss, 665. John Rylands Library, University of Manchester.

Recollections of a Literary Life. New York: Harper, 1852.

Recollections of a Literary Life. London: Richard Bentley, 1853.

Moers, Ellen. *Literary Women*. Oxford University Press, 1985.

Moody, Jane. "'Fine Word, Legitimate!': Toward a Theatrical History of Romanticism." *Texas Studies in Literature and Language* 38.3/4 (1996): 223–44.

    Illegitimate Theatre in London, 1787–1843. Cambridge University Press, forthcoming.

    "Illusions of Authorship." In Tracy C. Davis and Ellen Donkin, ed., *Women and Playwriting in Nineteenth-Century Britain*, Cambridge University Press, 1999, pp. 99–124.

More, Hannah. *Percy*. In *The Works of Miss Hannah More in Prose and Verse*, 2 vols., Cork: Thomas White, 1778, pp. 249–309.

    Strictures on the Modern System of Female Education. 2 vols. London: Cadell, 1799.

    The Works of Hannah More, vol. ii, London: T. Cadell, 1830, 5 vols.

Moskal, Jeanne. "Cervantes and the Politics of Mary Shelley's *History of a Six Weeks' Tour*." In Stuart Curran and Betty T. Bennett, ed., *Mary Wollstonecraft Shelley in her Times*. Baltimore: Johns Hopkins University Press, forthcoming.

    "Introduction to Mariana Starke's *The Sword of Peace*." In Thomas C. Crochunis and Michael Eberle-Sinatra, ed., *British Women Playwrights Around 1800*. January 2000 (http://www-sul.stanford.edu/mirrors/romnet/wp1800).

    "Napoleon, Nationalism, and the Politics of Religion in Mariana Starke's *Letters from Italy*." In Kari Lokke and Adriana Craciun, ed. *Women Writers and the French Revolution*. Albany: State University of New York Press, forthcoming.

    "Politics and the Occupation of a Nurse in Mariana Starke's *Letters from Italy*." In Amanda Gilroy, ed., *Romantic Geographies: The Discourse of Travel in the Romantic Period*. Manchester University Press, 2000.

"Mrs. Cowley's *Works*." *The Anti-Jacobin Review* (February, 1814): 134–38.

"Mrs. Cowley's *Works*." *The European Magazine* 66 (August–September, 1814): 128–30; 232–34.

"Mrs. Gibbs." *The British Stage and Literary Cabinet* 2 (1818): 217–18.

"Mrs. Hemans's *Vespers of Palermo*." *The Monthly Review, or Literary Journal* 102 (December, 1823): 164–69.

"Mrs. Robinson's *Sicilian Lover; a Tragedy*." *The Analytical Review* 23 (April, 1796): 394–97.

"Mrs. W. S. Chatterley." *The British Stage, and Literary Cabinet* 4 (1820): 238.

"Mrs. West's *Poems and Plays*." *The Critical Review* 27 (October, 1799): 131–36.

"Mrs. West's *Poems and Plays*." *The Monthly Review* 30 (November, 1799): 262–64.

Murray, Timothy. *Drama Traumas: Spectres of Race and Sexuality in Performance, Video, and Art*. New York and London: Routledge, 1997.

Musselwhite, David. "The Trial of Warren Hastings." In Francis Barker, Peter Hulme, Margaret Iversen, and Diana Loxley ed., *Literature,*

Politics, and Theory: Papers from the Essex Conference, 1976–84. London: Methuen, 1986, pp. 77–103.

Rev. of *The Mysterious Marriage, or the Hermit of Roselva*, by Harriet Lee. *The Monthly Mirror* 5 (March, 1798): 166–69.

Nachumi, Nora. "Acting Like a 'Lady': British Women Novelists and the Eighteenth-Century Stage." *Romanticism on the Net* 12 (November 1998).

"'Those Simple Signs': The Performance of Emotion in Elizabeth Inchbald's *A Simple Story.*" *Eighteenth-Century Fiction* 11.3 (April, 1999): 317–38.

Nangle, Benjamin. *The Monthly Review, Second Series 1790–1815.* Oxford: Clarendon Press, 1955.

Nelson, Alfred L. and Gilbert B. Cross, ed. *The Adelphi Theatre Calendar, part 1, The London Stage 1880–1900: A Documentary Record and Calendar of Performances.* New York: Greenwood Press, 1990.

Neuman, Henry, *Family Distress; or Self Immolation.* London: R. Phillips, 1799.

Newman, Gerald. *The Rise of English Nationalism: A Cultural History 1740–1830.* New York: St. Martin's Press, 1987.

Nicholson, Watson. *The Struggle for a Free Stage.* 1906. New York: Benjamin Blom, 1966.

Nicoll, Allardyce. *A History of English Drama 1660–1900.* 3rd edition. Cambridge University Press, 1952–59, 6 vols.

"The Theatre." In *A History of English Drama, 1660–1900, vol. 4, Early Nineteenth Century Theatre,* 1930. Cambridge University Press, 1955, pp. 1–57.

A History of Late Eighteenth-Century Drama, 1750–1800, Cambridge University Press, 1927.

"On the Present State of the Drama." *The Universal Magazine of Knowledge and Pleasure* 92 (May, 1793): 357–60.

O'Quinn, Daniel. "Elizabeth Inchbald's *The Massacre*: Tragedy, Violence and the Networks of Political Fantasy." In Thomas C. Crochunis and Michael Eberle-Sinatra, ed., *British Women Playwrights around 1800.* Website. http//www-sul.stanford.edu/mirrors/romnet/wp1800/massacreintro.html

"Inchbald's Indies: Domestic and Dramatic Re-Orientations," *European Romantic Review* 9.2, 1998, 217–230.

"The Marriage Plot in *The Sword of Peace.*" In Thomas C. Crochunis and Michael Eberle-Sinatra, ed., *British Women Playwrights Around 1800.* August 1999.

"Scissors and Needles: Inchbald's *Wives as They Were, Maids as They Are* and the Governance of Sexual Exchange," *Theatre Journal* 51 (1999): 105–25.

Otten, Terry. *The Deserted Stage: The Search for Dramatic Form in Nineteenth-Century England.* Athens: Ohio University Press, 1972.

Paine, Thomas. *The Rights of Man.* (orig. 1791) Garden City, NY: Anchor Books/Doubleday, 1973.

Park, Bruce Robertson. *Thomas Holcroft and Elizabeth Inchbald: Studies in the Eighteenth-Century Drama of Ideas*, New York: Columbia University Press, 1952.

Parker, Andrew and Eve Kosofsky Sedgwick. "Introduction." In Andrew Parker and Eve Kosofsky Sedgwick, ed., *Performativity and Performance*. New York: Routledge, 1995, pp. 1–18.

Pascoe, Judith. *Romantic Theatricality: Gender, Poetry and Spectatorship*. Ithaca, NY: Cornell University Press, 1997.

Paulson, Ronald. *Representations of Revolution (1789–1820)*. London and New Haven: Yale University Press, 1983.

Pavis, Patrice. "From Page to Stage: A Difficult Birth." Trans. Jilly Daugherty. *Theatre at the Crossroads of Culture*. London: Routledge, 1992, pp. 24–47.

Philp, Mark. *Godwin's Political Justice*. Ithaca: Cornell University Press, 1986.

Pitt, William, Lord Lennox. *Plays, Players, and Playhouses at Home and Abroad, with Anecdotes of the Drama and the Stage*. vol. 1. London: Hurst and Blackett, 1881, 2 vols.

Place, Francis. *A Brief Examination of the Dramatic Patents*. London: Baylis and Leighton, 1834.

Planché, James Robinson. *A Cyclopedia of Costume or Dictionary of Dress*. London: Chatto and Windus, 1876–79.

   History of British Costume. London: C. Knight; New York: Jackson, 1834.

"Plays and Poems, by Miss H. Brand." *The British Critic* 11 (May, 1798): 525–28.

"Plays, by Joanna Baillie." *The Imperial Review; or London and Dublin Literary Journal* 1 (1804): 335–44; 2 (1804): 89–97.

Plumb, J. H. *England in the Eighteenth Century*. Pelican History of England, no. 7. Baltimore: Penguin Books, 1950.

Plumptre, Anne. *"La-Peyrouse." A Drama in 2 Acts by Kotzebue translated by Anne Plumptre*. Dublin: H. Colbert, 1799.

   A Narrative of a Three Years' Residence in France, 3 vols. London: J. Mawman, 1810.

   "The Natural Son" being the original of "Lovers' Vows," now performing at Covent Garden. Dublin: H. Fitzpatrick, 1798.

   The Spaniards in Peru; or, The Death of Rolla. Dublin: J. Moore, 1799.

Rev. of *Poems and Plays, Vols I–II*. By Jane West. *The Monthly Review* 30 (November, 1799): 262–65.

Rev. of *Poems and Plays, Vols. III–IV*. By Jane West. *The Annual Review and History of Literature* 4 (1805): 602–04.

Pointon, Marcia. *Strategies for Showing: Women, Possession, and Representation in English Visual Culture 1665–1800*. Oxford University Press, 1997.

Polwhele, Richard. *The Unsex'd Females*. In Anne K. Mellor and Richard E. Matlak, ed., *British Literature 1780–1830*. New York: Harcourt, 1996, pp. 42–44.

Poovey, Mary. *The Proper Lady and the Woman Writer: The Ideology of Style in*

Mary Wollstonecraft, Jane Austen, and Mary Shelley. University of Chicago Press, 1984.

"Postscript." *Helvetic Liberty, An Opera in Three Acts by a Kentish Bowman.* London: Wayland, 1792, p. vi.

Powell, Kerry. *Women and the Victorian Theatre.* Cambridge University Press, 1997.

Power, Frank and Frank Palmer. *Censorship in England.* 1913, rpt. New York: Burt Franklin, 1970, pp. 155–64.

Price, Cecil. "Introduction to *Pizarro.*" Vol. II of *The Dramatic Works of Richard Brinsley Sheridan,* 2 vols. Oxford: Clarendon, 1973, pp. 640–50.

Probyn, Elspeth. *Sexing the Self: Gendered Positions in Cultural Studies.* New York: Routledge, 1993.

Purinton, Marjean D. "Pedagogy and Passions: Teaching Joanna Baillie's Dramas." In *Nineteenth-Century Contexts.* Forthcoming.

"Revising Romanticism by Inscripting Women Playwrights." Special Issue: British Women Playwrights Around 1800: New Paradigms and Recoveries." Ed. Thomas C. Crochunis. *Romanticism on the Net* 12 (November 1998) Online. Internet.

Romantic Ideology Unmasked: The Mentally Constructed Tyrannies in Dramas of William Wordsworth, Lord Byron, Percy Shelley, and Joanna Baillie. Newark: University of Delaware Press, 1994.

"The Sexual Politics of *The Election*: French Feminism and the Scottish Playwright Joanna Baillie." *Intertexts* 2.2 (1998): 119–30.

Rajan, Tillotama. "Mary Shelley's *Mathilda*: Melancholy and the Political Economy of Romanticism." *Studies in the Novel* 26.2 (1994): 43–68.

Ralli, Augustus. *A History of Shakespearian Criticism.* Vol. I. New York: The Humanities Press, 1965, 2 vols.

Ranger, Paul. *'Terror and pity reign in every breast': Gothic Drama in the London Patent Theatres, 1750–1820.* London: The Society for Theatre Research, 1991.

Reid, Christopher. "Burke's Tragic Muse: Sarah Siddons and the 'Feminization' of the *Reflections.*" In Steven Blakemore, ed., *Burke and the French Revolution: Bicentennial Essays.* Athens, GA: University of Georgia Press, 1992, pp. 1–27.

Report from the Select Committee Appointed to inquire into the laws Affecting Dramatic Literature (1832), Irish University Press Series of British Parliamentary Papers, Stage and Theatre, vol. I. Shannon: Irish University Press, 1968, 3 vols.

Ribeiro, Aileen. *The Art of Dress: Fashion in England and France 1750 to 1820.* New Haven: Yale University Press, 1995.

Richards, Eric. *A History of the Highland Clearances: Agrarian Transformation and the Evictions 1746–1886.* London: Croom Helm, 1982.

Richards, Sandra. *The Rise of the English Actress.* New York: St. Martin's, 1993.

Richardson, Alan. *A Mental Theater: Poetic Drama and Consciousness in the*

Romantic Age. University Park, PA: Pennsylvania State University Press, 1988.

[Rivers, David]. *Literary Memoirs of living authors of Great Britain.* 1798. Rpt. 2 vols. New York: Garland Publishers, 1970.

Roberts, M. J. D. "The Society for the Suppression of Vice and its Early Critics, 1802–1812." *Historical Journal,* 26.1 (1983).

Roberts, William. *Memoirs of the Life and Correspondence of Mrs. Hannah More,* vol. 1. London: R. B. Seeley & W. Burnside, 1835, 4 vols.

Robinson, Henry Crabb. *Diary, Reminiscences and Correspondence of Henry Crabb Robinson.* Thomas Sadler, ed. 2 vols. London: Fields, Osgood, 1869.

Rodway, A. E., ed. *Godwin and the Age of Transition.* London: Harrap, 1952.

Rogers, Katharine. "Britain's First Woman Drama Critic: Elizabeth Inchbald." In Mary Anne Schofield and Cecilia Macheski, ed., *Curtain Calls: British and American Women and the Theater, 1660–1820.* Athens, OH: Ohio University Press, 1991, pp. 277–90.

Feminism in Eighteenth-Century England. Urbana: University of Illinois Press, 1982.

Roper, Derek. *Reviewing Before the Edinburgh, 1788–1802.* London: Methuen, 1978.

Rosenfeld, Sybil. *Temples of Thespis: Some Private Theatres and Theatricals in England and Wales, 1700–1820.* London: Society for Theatre Research, 1978.

Ross, Marlon B. *The Contours of Masculine Desire: Romanticism and the Rise of Women's Poetry.* Oxford University Press, 1989.

Rowson, Susanna. *Slaves in Algiers* in *Plays by Early American Women, 1775–1850,* ed. Amelia Howe Kritzer, pp. x–xx.

Rubik, Margarete. *Early Women Dramatists, 1550–1800.* Basingstoke: Macmillan, and New York: St. Martin's Press, 1998. <http://www-sul.stanford.edu/mirrors/romnet/wp1800>. Website.

Russell, Gillian. *The Theatres of War: Performance, Politics, and Society 1793–1815.* Oxford: Clarendon Press, 1995.

Ruwe, Donelle. "Response to Daniel O'Quinn," in Thomas C. Crochunis and Michael Eberle-Sinatra, ed., "British Women Playwrights Around 1800." August 1999.

Sabor, Peter and Geoffrey Sill, ed. *The Witlings and The Woman Hater by Frances Burney.* London: Chatto and Pickering, 1997.

St. Clair, William. *The Godwins and the Shelleys.* Baltimore: Johns Hopkins University Press, 1989.

Sareen, T. R. "Slavery in India under British Rule 1772–1843," *Indian Historical Review* 15.1–2 (1989): 257–68.

Schneider, Elisabeth, Irwin Griggs, and John D. Kearn. "Early Edinburgh Reviewers: A New List," *Modern Philology* 43 (1946): 192–210.

Schofield, Mary Anne and Cecilia Macheski, ed. *Curtain Calls: British and*

American Women and the Theater, 1660–1820. Athens, Ohio University Press, 1991.

Scott, Jane. "Address to the Audience, 27 December 1814." *The Adelphi Scrapbook.* Compiled by James Winston. Theatre Museum, London, Adelphi File.

(Broad Grins; or) Whackham and Windham; or, the Wrangling Lawyers (1814), Larpent no. 1798.

(Broad Grins; or) Whackham and Windham; or, the Wrangling Lawyers (1814), transcribed and introduced by Jacky Bratton in "British Women Playwrights around 1800," ed. Thomas C. Crochunis and Michael Eberle-Sinatra (http://www-sul.stanford.edu/mirrors/romnet/wp1800).

Camilla the Amazon; or, the Mountain Robber. Larpent Collection, Huntington Library, San Marino, CA, 1954.

The Old Oak Chest (1816). In John Franceschina, ed., *Sisters of Gore: Seven Gothic Melodramas by British Women, 1790–1843.* New York and London: Garland, 1997, pp. 121–72.

Scott, Sir Walter. *Essay on the Drama. Essays on Chivalry, Romance, and the Drama.* London: Frederick, Warne, nd.

The Letters of Sir Walter Scott, vol. 2. H. J. C. Grierson, ed. London: Constable & Co., 1932–36. 12 vols.

Scullion, Adrienne, ed. *Female Playwrights of the Nineteenth Century.* London: J. M. Dent, 1996.

"Some Women of the Nineteenth-Century Scottish Theatre: Joanna Baillie, Frances Wright, and Helen MacGregor." In *A History of Scottish Women's Writing,* ed. Gifford and McMillan, pp. 161–65.

Shaffer, Julie. "Romance, Finance, and the Marketable Woman: The Economics of Femininity in Late Eighteenth- and Early Nineteenth-Century English Novels." In Deborah S. Wilson and Christine Moneera Laennec, ed., *Bodily Discursions: Genders, Representations, Technologies.* Albany: State University of New York Press, 1997, pp. 39–56.

Shattock, Joanne. *Politics and Reviewers: The Edinburgh and the Quarterly in the Early Victorian Age.* Leicester University Press, 1987.

Sheridan, Richard B. *Pizarro* in Cecil Price, ed., vol. ii of *The Dramatic Works of Richard Brinsley Sheridan.* 2 vols. Oxford: Clarendon, 1973.

Simpson, Michael. *Closet Performances: Political Exhibition and Prohibition in the Dramas of Byron and Shelley.* Stanford University Press, 1998.

Singh, Jyotsna G. *Colonial Narratives/Cultural Dialogues: "Discoveries" of India in the Language of Colonialism.* London: Routledge, 1996.

Slagle, Judith Bailey. "Evolution of a Writer: Joanna Baillie's Life in Letters." In Janice Patten and Thomas C. Crochunis, ed., *Joanna Baillie, Romantic Dramatist: Critical Essays.* The Netherlands: Gordon and Breach, forthcoming.

The Collected Letters of Joanna Baillie. Cranbury, NJ: Associated University Presses, Inc., 1999, vol. i, 2 vols.

Snodgrass, Charles. "Narrating Nations, Negotiating Borders: The Scottish Romantic Novel in Blackwood's Circle." Unpublished Ph.D. Dissertation. Texas A&M University, Spring, 1999.

Somerville, Martha. *Personal Recollections from Early Life to Old Age of Mary Somerville.* Boston: Roberts Brothers, 1874.

Spear, Percival. *The Nabobs: A Study of the Social Life of the English in Eighteenth-Century India.* Second enlarged edition. London: Curzon, 1963.

Sprague, B. Allen. "The Reaction Against William Godwin." *Modern Philology* 16, 5 (1918): 57–75.

Stanton, Judith Philips. "'This New Found Path Attempting': Women Dramatists in England, 1660–1800." In Mary Anne Schofield and Cecilia Macheski, ed., *Curtain Calls: British and American Women and the Theater.* Athens, OH: Ohio University Press, 1991, pp. 325–54.

Starke, Mariana. *The Beauties of Carlo Maria Maggi, paraphrased; to which are added Sonnets: by Mariana Starke.* Exeter: privately printed, 1811.

   Letter to *The Morning Chronicle.* Rpt. in David Erskine Baker, Isaac Reed, and Stephen Jones, ed., *Biographia Dramatica; or, a companion to the playhouse: containing historical and critical memoirs . . .* 3 vols (vol. III in 2 parts separately paginated). London: Longman, Hurst, Rees, Orme, and Brown, 1812, vol. III, part 2, p. 313.

   The Sword of Peace; or, A Voyage of Love: A Comedy in Five Acts (1788). London: J. Debrett, 1789.

   The Sword of Peace; or, A Voyage of Love: A Comedy in Five Acts (1788) in Thomas C. Crochunis and Michael Eberle-Sinatra, ed., "British Women Playwrights Around 1800," January 2000. <http://www-sul.stanford.edu/mirrors/romnet/wp1800>. Website.

   The Sword of Peace; or, A Voyage of Love: A Comedy in Five Acts (1788). In vol. V of *Slavery, Abolition, and Emancipation in the British Romantic Period. The Drama,* Jeffrey N. Cox, ed. London: Pickering and Chatto, 1999.

   Travels in Italy between the years 1792 and 1798 . . . 2 vols. Second edition. London: R. Phillips, 1802.

   The Widow of Malabar: A Tragedy in three Acts. As it is performed at the Theatre-Royal Covent Garden. Third edition. London: William Lane, 1791.

Stephens, John Russell. *The Profession of the Playwright. British Theatre 1800–1900.* Cambridge University Press, 1992.

Stone, Lawrence. *The Family, Sex and Marriage in England 1500–1800.* New York: Harper & Row, 1977.

Straub, Kristina. *Sexual Suspects: Eighteenth-Century Players and Sexual Ideology.* Princeton University Press, 1992.

Straznicky, Marta. "Recent Studies in Closet Drama." *English Literary Renaissance* 28.1 (1998): 142–60.

Sulloway, Alison. *Jane Austen and the Province of Womanhood.* Philadelphia: University of Pennsylvania Press, 1989.

Thackeray, T. J. *On Theatrical Emancipation and the Rights of Dramatic Authors.* London: C. Chapple, 1832.

Rev. of *Theodora, or the Spanish Daughter; a Tragedy,* by Lady Sophia Burrell. *The British Critic* 16 (December, 1800): 682.

Thomas, Donald. *A Long Time Burning: The History of Literary Censorship in England.* London: Routledge, 1969.

Thompson, Ann and Sasha Roberts, ed. *Women Reading Shakespeare, 1660–1900.* Manchester University Press, 1997.

Rev. of *The Three Strangers,* by Harriet Lee. *The Monthly Review* (January, 1826): 138–47.

Rev. of *To Marry or Not to Marry,* by Elizabeth Inchbald. *The Anti-Jacobin Review* 21 (1805): 208.

Rev. of *To Marry or Not to Marry,* by Elizabeth Inchbald. *The Annual Review and History of Literature* 4 (1805): 640.

Tomlins, Frederick G. *The Past and Present State of Dramatic Art.* London: C. Mitchell, 1839.

A Brief View of the English Drama. London: C. Mitchell, 1840.

The Nature and State of the English Drama. London: C. Mitchell, 1841.

Trumpener, Katie. *Bardic Nationalism: The Romantic Novel and the British Empire.* Princeton University Press, 1997.

Turley, David. *The Culture of English Antislavery, 1780–1860.* New York: Routledge, 1991.

Tytler, Sarah and J. L. Watson. *Songstresses of Scotland,* vol. II. London: Strahan, 1871, 2 vols.

Uphaus, Robert W. and Gretchen M. Foster, ed. *The "Other" Eighteenth Century: English Women of Letters 1660–1800.* East Lansing: Colleagues Press, 1991.

Vickery, Amanda. *The Gentleman's Daughter: Women's Lives in Georgian England.* New Haven: Yale University Press, 1998.

"Golden Age to Separate Spheres? A Review of the Categories and Chronology of English Women's History." *The Historical Journal.* 36: 2 (1993): 383–414.

Wahrman, Dror. *Imagining the Middle Class: The Political Representation of Class in Britain, 1780–1840.* Cambridge University Press, 1995.

"The New Political History: a Review Essay." *Social History.* 21: 3 (1996): 343–54.

Waldie, John. "Journals and Letters of John Waldie of Hendersyde Park, Kelso, Scotland." Special Collections, University of California at Los Angeles, vol. IV, 169/8.

Waldron, Mary. *Lactilla, Milkwoman of Clifton.* Athens, GA: University of Georgia Press, 1996.

Ward, S. Candace. "'Active Sensibility and Positive Virtue': Wollstonecraft's 'Grand Principle of Action.'" *European Romantic Review.* 8.4 (Fall 1997): 409–31.

Ward, William, ed. *Literary Reviews in British Periodicals. 1789–1797.* New York: Garland, 1979.

ed. *Literary Reviews in British Periodicals. 1798–1820.* New York: Garland, 1972.

ed. *Literary Reviews in British Periodicals. 1821–1826.* New York: Garland 1977.

Watkins, Daniel P. *A Materialist Critique of English Romantic Drama.* Gainesville: University Press of Florida, 1993.

Watson, Ernest Bradlee. *Sheridan to Robertson: A Study of the Nineteenth-Century London Stage.* New York: Benjamin Blom, 1926; 1963.

Watson, Frederick. *The Story of the Highland Regiments, 1725–1925.* London: A. & C. Black, 1925.

Webb, Timothy. "The Romantic Poet and the Stage: A Short, Sad History." In Richard Allen Cave, ed. *The Romantic Theatre: An International Symposium.* Totowa, NJ: Barnes and Noble Books, 1986, pp. 9–46.

West, Jane. "Preface to the Plays." *Poems and Plays.* Vol. IV. London: Longman, 1799, pp. iii–xv, 4 vols.

Rev. of *What is She?*, by Charlotte Smith. *The Anti-Jacobin Review* 3 (June, 1799): 150–55.

Willoughby, C. A. "English Translations and Adaptations of Schiller's *Robbers.*" *Modern Language Review* 16 (1921): 297–315.

Rev. of *Wives as they were, and Maids as they are*, by Elizabeth Inchbald. *The British Critic* 10 (August, 1797): 133–36.

Wollstonecraft, Mary. *The Wrongs of Woman; or Maria.* 1798. New York: Norton, 1994.

A Short Residence in Sweden, Norway and Denmark, Richard Holmes, ed. Harmondsworth: Penguin, 1987.

A Vindication of the Rights of Woman, 1792. In D. L. Macdonald and Kathleen Scherf, ed., *The Vindications: The Rights of Men, The Rights of Woman.* Peterborough, Ontario: Broadview Press, 1997, pp. 99–343.

Worthen, W. B. ed., *The Harcourt Brace Anthology of Drama.* Second edition. New York: Harcourt Brace and Co., 1996.

Shakespeare and the Authority of Performance. Cambridge University Press, 1997.

"Drama, Performativity, and Performance." *PMLA* 113 (5 October 1998): 1093–107.

Yearsley, Ann. *Earl Goodwin, an Historical Play.* London: G. G. J. and J. Robinson, 1791.

Young, John Roach. "Highland Regiments." In Gerald Newman *et al.*, ed., *Britain in the Hanoverian Age 1714–1837.* New York: Garland, 1997.

Young, Mary Julia. *Memoirs of Mrs. Crouch, including a retrospect of the stage during the years she performed.* 2 vols. London: James Asperne, 1806.

Yudin, Mary F. "Joanna Baillie's 'Introductory Discourse' as a Precursor to Wordsworth's 'Preface to *Lyrical Ballads*'." *Compar(a)ison* 1 (1994): 101–11.

"Z." "Cockney School of Poetry. No. IV." *Blackwood's Edinburgh Magazine* 3 (August, 1818): 519–24.

Zall, Paul M. "The Cool World of Samuel Taylor Coleridge: The Question of Joanna Baillie." *Wordsworth Circle* 13 (1982): 17–20.

Index